Hermann Carl George Brandt

A Grammar of the German Language for High Schools

and Colleges, Designed for Beginners and Advanced Students. Sixth Edition

Hermann Carl George Brandt

A Grammar of the German Language for High Schools
and Colleges, Designed for Beginners and Advanced Students. Sixth Edition

ISBN/EAN: 9783744774932

Printed in Europe, USA, Canada, Australia, Japan

Cover: Foto ©Paul-Georg Meister /pixelio.de

More available books at **www.hansebooks.com**

A

GRAMMAR

OF THE

GERMAN LANGUAGE

FOR

HIGH SCHOOLS AND COLLEGES

DESIGNED FOR BEGINNERS AND ADVANCED STUDENTS

BY

H. C. G. BRANDT

HAMILTON COLLEGE, CLINTON, N. Y.

SIXTH EDITION

WITH AN APPENDIX CONTAINING FULL INFLECTIONS, AND A LIST OF STRONG
AND IRREGULAR VERBS

𝕭𝖔𝖘𝖙𝖔𝖓
ALLYN AND BACON
1894

PREFACE TO THE FOURTH EDITION.

THIS is the first thoroughly revised edition. Of the criticisms of this work, I have been able to accept and embody especially those of Professor A. L. Ripley, of Yale College, and of Professor Geo. O. Curme, of Cornell College (Iowa), to both of whom I express my sincere thanks. The strictures made upon my classification of nouns and upon the standard of pronunciation I do not think well founded. The classification of nouns is historical and scientific. If the best standard should finally settle upon *kh*, *jh* (§ 375) for g and not upon *k* (surd stop), nothing would please me better. "Hard" g except after n is a bitter pill for a North German. To the objection that the work is too concise, let me say that I have tried to make it concise. The Accidence and Part II. were once as large again as they are now. The first contained too much syntax, until, following the excellent method of the French grammarians, I resolved to separate entirely inflection and syntax. I have in this edition transferred several paragraphs from Part I. to Part II. Part II. is a historical foundation broad enough for Part I. to rest upon. It is not intended to be a minute historical reference-grammar for teachers and specialists only.

The word-index has been very much enlarged. With the demand for the traditional list of irregular verbs, "which no grammar should be without," I have complied so far as to include all the irregular verbs in the word-index (see introductory remarks on p. 271). I wanted to make the G.-Eng. vocabulary cover all the sentences and words, but found that it would swell the book too much. It is complete only for Part I. (see p. 271).

The list of reference-books has been omitted at the suggestion of Prof. Ripley.

It may not be out of place to enumerate the distinguishing features of the grammar: (1) the complete separation of inflection and syntax; (2) the historical treatment of the latter, that should make it a welcome aid in the reading of 16th, 17th, and 18th century Literature; (3) the attempt to treat German grammar with regard to the present stage of Germanic philology; (4) the scientific analysis of German sounds and accent.

THE AUTHOR.

PREFACE TO THE SIXTH EDITION.

I HAVE finally complied fully with the demand for a separate List of Strong and Irregular Verbs, and have also added more extensive inflections of substantives, adjectives, and verbs, to be used in connection with the first section of the grammar.

H. C. G. B.

CLINTON, N. Y.,
April, 1893.

TABLE OF CONTENTS.

PART I. SECTION 1.

	PAGE
ACCIDENCE.	1–47
Pronunciation with Alphabets	1–5
The Articles	6–7
Declension of Nouns	7–17
Declension and Comparison of the Adjective	17–21
Numerals	21–23
Pronouns	23–30
Conjugation	30–47
Weak Verbs	35–37
Strong Verbs	37–43
Anomalous Verbs	44–47

SECTION 2.

SYNTAX.

SPECIAL SYNTAX	51–130
Articles	51–55
Nouns	56–74
Gender	56–62
Singular and Plural	62–64
Cases	64–74
Adjectives	74–80
Numerals	80–82
Pronouns	82–96
Personal Pronouns	82–85
Reflexive and Reciprocal Pronouns	86

	PAGE
Possessive Pronouns	86–88
Demonstrative Pronouns	88–91
Interrogative Pronouns	91–93
Relative Pronouns	93–95
Indefinite Pronouns	95–96
VERBS	97–118
Classification of Verbs	97
Auxiliary Verbs	97–99
Modal Auxiliaries	99–102
Voice	102–104
Tenses	104–110
Moods	110–112
Infinitive	113–116
Participles	116–118
Gerundive	118
ADVERB	119
PREPOSITION	119–130
CONJUNCTION	130
GENERAL SYNTAX	131–152
THE SIMPLE SENTENCE	131–135
THE COMPOUND SENTENCE	135–147
Coordinate Sentences	135–137
Subordinate Sentences	137–147
Substantive Clauses	137–138
Adjective Clauses	139
Adverbial Clauses	140–147
WORD-ORDER	147–154

PART II. ADVANCED GRAMMAR.

A. PHONOLOGY	157–193
Historical Notes on the Orthography	157–160
Analysis and Description of German Sounds	160–176
Ablaut, Umlaut	176–182
Grimm's Law, Verner's Law	182–189
Accent	189–193

	PAGE
B. HISTORICAL COMMENTARY UPON THE ACCIDENCE........	194–216
Noun-Declension...................................	194–198
Adjective-Declension	198–199
Pronouns..	200–203
Conjugation.......................................	203–216
C. HISTORY OF THE LANGUAGE.........................	217–230
Characteristics of the Germanic Languages...........	217
Classification of the Germanic Languages............	218
Classification of the German Dialects................	219–221
History of "German".............................	221–228
The German Word-stock...........................	228–230
D. WORDFORMATION	231–264
Derivation and Composition of Substantives..........	232–245
Derivation and Composition of Adjectives and Numerals..	245–251
Derivation and Composition of Verbs................	252–261
Derivation of Adverbs, Conjunctions, and Interjections..	261–264
LIST OF ABBREVIATIONS AND SYMBOLS THAT REQUIRE EXPLANATIONS.......	265
SUBJECT-INDEX...	266–270
WORD-INDEX AND GERMAN-ENGLISH VOCABULARY.......	271–286
APPENDIX: Fuller Inflections of Substantives, Adjectives, and Verbs; and a List of Strong and Irregular Verbs...	287–314

FIRST PART.

FIRST SECTION.

ACCIDENCE.

THE GERMAN ALPHABET.

1—2.

German type.	German script.	Name.	German type.	German script.	Name.
U a		ah	N n		en
B b		bay	O o		oh
C c		tsay	P p		pay
D d		day	Q q		koo
E e		(b)ay	R r		air
F f		ef	S ſ s ß		es
G g		gay	T t		tay
H h		hah	U u		(t)oo
I i		e	V v		fou(l)
J j		yot	W w		vay
K k		kah	X x		ix
L l		el	Y y		ipsilon
M m		em	Z z		tset

Ae ä Ä		ah-umlaut (h)ai(r)		tsay-hah
Oe ö Ö		oh-umlaut		tsay-kah
Ue ü Ü		oo-umlaut		es-tsay-hah (= sh)
Äu		au-umlaut (= oi)		

PRONUNCIATION.

The German sounds are here only very inaccurately represented by English words and letters. A full analysis is found in the second part, p. 160. The following description, with a few key-words, will suffice for the beginner; but it is meant to be only a popular description. As soon as the student begins to read, he ought to study Part II., p. 160–174.

3. ā as in Eng. *father:* Vater, Aal, Zahl. ă, not in Eng., but similar to Scotch *a* as in Sc. *hand, land:* Mann, Land, Hand.

4. b = Eng. *b,* but surd (= *p*) at the end of words: Bube, Haube, Dieb, Laub.

5. c, d = Eng. *k:* Carl, Backe, Bäcker.

6. ch, not in Eng., but in Scotch as in *loch.* A single guttural sound. Two kinds: 1. Palatal (forward) after palatal vowels, viz.: e, i, ö, ü, ä, ei, eu, and in the suffix =chen, *e. g.,* ich, Wächter, Blech, möchte, euch, Gerücht, weich, Mädchen, Mamachen. 2. Back-guttural after the other vowels, a, o, u, au, *e. g.,* ach, Dach, Loch, Buch, Bauch (betrog in N. G.). In Charfrei′tag and in foreign words = *k:* Chara′kter, Chor; also like sch in foreign words: Champa′gner, changie′ren, Chance.

7. d = Eng. *d,* but surd (= *t*) finally: du, doch, Bad, lud.

8. e, long, similar to Eng. *a, ay,* as in *pay, pate, rate;* short, like Eng. ĕ, as in *met,* ē: gehn, Beet, wert; ĕ: recht, Wette.

9. f = Eng. *f:* hoffen, Hafen, führen, Flagge.

10. g = Eng. *g,* but surd (= *k*) finally: glauben, plagen, graben; but Tag, Zug, fragte, trug, Balg.

11. h = Eng. *h* if it stands initially: Hund, Hose, Hase. After a vowel and after a t it is silent: stehn, seh(e)n, sah, thun, That, Thal. See the dropping of h, p. 159.

12. ĭ similar to Eng. *i:* bin, finde, bringe.

ī or ie = Eng. *ee* in *feet:* vier, siegen, mir, dir, Igel, Biber.

13. j similar to Eng. *y*: jung, jagen, Jagd.

14. k, ck = Eng. *k*: Katze, Zacke, Haken.

15. l similar to Eng. *l*: Lage, lachen, wohl, Saal, bald.

16. m = Eng. *m*: Molch, Saum, schwimmen.

17. n = Eng. *n*. 1. Initially, finally, and before a dental: Nagel, nun, fein, senden, Fant, Fund. 2. In the stem-syllable before k, and combined with g like Eng. *ng* in *sing, singer*: Anfang, Sänger, Finger, Bank, senken, blinken; but an=ge=kommen, un=geheuer.

18. ō = Eng. *o, oa*, in *hold, foal*: Bote, Boot, tot, rot, Loos, los, Thon (clay). ŏ not in Eng., but short Sc. *o*; *e. g.*: Woche, Loch, Stock, Rock (not at all like Eng. *stock, rock*, but see p. 164).

19. p = like Eng. *p*: plagen, Kappe, Trapper, Galo'pp.

pf = p + f: Pfund, Napf, Sumpf, tapfer. In Eng. only in accidental juxtaposition, *e. g.*, "a cap for him," "stop for me."

ph in foreign words only = f: Philologie', Telegra'ph.

20. q always followed by u, similar to Eng. *qu*: quer, Quast, Quart, bequem.

21. r unlike Eng. *r*. 1. Trilled: Regen, Rache, fern, Furt, treu. This is the standard *r*. 2. Uvular or guttural in N. G., very much like the guttural ch, but sonant.

22. ſ, ſſ, s, ß = Eng. surd *s*: Haus, Mäuſe, Waſſer, Fluß, Muße, ſein; but initially and after a vowel it begins surd and ends sonant, as in N. and M. G. Standard unsettled. But see p. 175.

23. ſch = Eng. *sh* (surd): ſchicken, ſchenken, haſchen, Schlange.

24. ſt, ſp = ſcht, ſchp initially in the standard pronunciation and in S. and M. G. But in the middle and at the end of words, in N. G. also at the beginning of words = Eng. *st, sp*; ſcht, ſchp: Stein, Straße, Stuhl, Spaß, ſprießen; *st, sp*: haſt, wüſte, berſten, Wurſt, Weſpe, haſpeln. N. G.: Spieß, Stock.

25. t, th = Eng. *t*: hat, hatte, That, Naht.

26. u = Eng. *oo* in *too*: Hut, Wut, Blume, Buch, Buhle. ŭ = Eng. *u* in *put*: Butter, stutzen, Gulden.

27. v = Eng. *f* in German words: Vater, Frevel, viel. v = German w in foreign words: Vika'r, vindizie'ren, Vaka'nz.

28. w like Eng. *v* dento-labial: Wetter, Wasser, warnen. After sch labio-labial like u after q, but not quite like Eng. *w*: Schwester, Schweiß, Schwelle. But see p. 170.

29. x in foreign words and chs, chs = Eng. *x*: Alexander, Wachs, Fuchs, Füchsin, sechs.

y = ü, which see.

30. z, tz = Eng. *ts*, as in *cats, rats*: Zunge, Zeug, Warze, Mütze, Pfütze.

c in foreign words before e, i, y, ä = *ts*: cerebral, Cäsu'r, Cika'de, Cyklo'p; but the spelling is unsettled: Ziga'rre, Zentner, Zensu'r.

31. **Modified Vowels (Umlauts).**

ä long = Eng. *ai* in *fair*: Väter, Räder, stählern.

ä short = Eng. and Ger. ĕ: Hände, Wände, fällen.

ö not in Eng. It has the lip-position of o, the tongue-position of e: long in böse, lösen, Herzöge; short in Böller, Zölle, Geröll.

ü not in Eng. It has the lip-position of u, the tongue-position of i: long in Mühle, Bücher, Küchlein; short in Müller, Sünde, Büttel.

y = ü, as in Cya'n, Cypre'sse, only in foreign words.

32. **Diphthongs.**

ai (rare) and ei = Eng. *i* in *find*: Kaiser, Mai, leise, weiß, bleiben. au = Eng. *ou* in *house*: blau, Haus, Maus.

äu and eu similar to Eng. *oi* in *exploit*: Mäuse, läuten, Beute, heute.

Quantity of Vowels.

33. Vowels are long in an open syllable, *e. g.*, Ta=ges, zo=gen. Bü=cher. They are also indicated: 1. By doubling, but only in the case of a, e, o: Saal, Seele, Moos. 2. By h after the vowel and after t: Hahn, Ohm, ihn, Thran, Thor. 3. By e after i: lieb, Tier, viel. 4. a and e are generally long before r, rt, rd: war, rar, der, wert, werden, zart, Pferd. Short in fertig (< Fahrt), Warte, Scharte, Herz, Schmerz.

34. The vowels are short before more than one consonant: handeln, bergen, Nacht, Gelübde, hassen.

35. ß counts as a single consonant; it becomes ſſ medially (see "Rules," § 12), *e. g.*, Fluß — Flusses, Flüsse; fließen — floß, geflossen. The vowel remains long before inflectional endings, *e. g.*, loben, lobst, gelobt (but gehabt, gemocht); also in a closed syllable, when the stem-vowel stands in an open syllable under inflection, *e. g.*, Tag, Ta=ges; Zug, Zu=ges. But see p. 175.

Since ch cannot be doubled, there is no telling the quantity of the preceding vowel from the mere looks of the word: *e. g.*, long in Buch — Buches; Tuch — Tuches; brach — brachen; but short in Bach — Baches; lachen, wachen. As a rule, shortness may be expected.

36. The division into syllables differs somewhat from the English custom. The "Rules" § 26 show how words are divided at the end of a line. The following examples will illustrate sufficiently: ha-ben, such-te, be-ehren, Bee-re, ver-irren, ge-irrt, Was-ser, Stra-ße, lö-schen, ro-ter, Fin-ger (but see 17), He-xe, Wei-zen, Hit-ze, Kar-pfen, be-ob-achten, nach-sa-gen, be-glau-bi-gen.

37. German orthography is now regulated by the government, and the student who is to write German should provide himself with the official, Regeln und Wörterverzeichnis für die deutsche Rechtschreibung in den preußischen Schulen. Berlin. It is a small convenient guide of 46 pages, with a quite full word-list. See 361, 2.

THE ARTICLES.

38. The definite article is der, die, das + *the*; the indefinite, ein, eine, ein + *one, an, a.*

The definite article declines:

	masc.	fem.	neuter.	common gender.
Sing. N.	der	die	das	*Plu.* die
G.	des	der	des	der
D.	dem	der	dem	den
A.	den	die	das	die

The indefinite article declines:

Sing. N. ein	eine	ein	
G. eines	einer	eines	
D. einem	einer	einem	
A. einen	eine	ein	

39. The articles are unaccented.

The definite article is the weakened demonstrative pronoun, which has chief stress. It retains the short original forms of the same. The indefinite article is the weakened numeral ein, which also has chief stress. To mark the demonstrative pronoun and the numeral, they are sometimes printed spaced or with a capital letter: Nur Einen Schritt, so bist du frei, F. 4563; but Es war einmal ein König, F. 2212. Der Mohr kann gehn (Sch.). Es thut mir lang' schon weh, daß ich dich in d e r Gesellschaft seh', F. 3470-1.

40. Owing to their lack of accent both articles suffer aphæresis and apocope, and contraction with the preceding word, most frequently with a preposition: dem and das are, according to good usage, combined with the following prepositions: an, auf, bei, durch, für, hinter, in, über, um, unter, von, vor, and zu; *e. g.*, am, ans, aufs, ins, ums, vom, etc. In general, contractions with dissyllabic prepositions are rarer in the classics, common in the spoken language, which allows the contraction of den whether dative plural or accusative singular masculine with the above and also with other prepositions. Some such are even in the classics: in = in'n, F. 2429, „in Sessel,„ Lessing's Nathan, „in Sack,„ „in Kopf,„ „an Tag.„ In, um contain long (see **389, 5**) consonants and the article is not absent, as is generally explained. In conversation is heard: um Arm, von Bäumen, auf'n Feldern, mit'n Händen, durch'n Wald. The apostrophe in auf'ê, über'ê, etc., is not at all indispensable. Der, dative singular feminine, combines properly only with zu into zur.

41. Attractions of the definite article, especially of the neuter, to preceding words other than prepositions are common in the spoken language, *e. g.*, „ich will's Buch holen," „er hat sich's Bein gebrochen." „Bind't's Pferd hauß an" (G.). „Und haft's Küssen verlernt" (F. 4485).

1. The aphæresis of „ein" common in the spoken language is also found in the written, *e. g.*, „Warf auf 'nen Stuhl die Handschuh'"(Uh.). Bold abbreviations are these in Chamisso's, „'s war mal 'ne Katzenkönigin." The dropping of ein before mal is not unusual: „Es war mal ein Kaiser;" „Auch war mal ein Abt" (Bü.). Notice so'ne for so eine. The early N. H. G. (16th century) eim for einem (comp. M. H. G. *eime* for *eineme*), einn or ein for einen occur still in some South German dialects. In M. H. G. the aphæresis of "*ein*" is unheard of, while the definite article is much more pliant than in the present classical language. Apocope of the same is still allowable in certain S. G. dialects.

DECLENSION OF NOUNS.

42. *There are three systems of Declension, the Strong (Vowel, Old), the Weak (Consonant, n-Declension or New), and the Mixed.*

The strong declension (see **43**, 1) *has* (e)s *in the genitive singular; the weak has* (e)n *in all cases, singular and plural, except in the nominative singular; the mixed has* (e)s *in the genitive singular,* (e)n *in the whole plural.*

General Rules.

43. 1. Feminine nouns never vary in the singular.

2. The only case-endings are (e)s for the genitive singular and (e)n for the dative plural.

3. e in the case-suffix ought to stand in nouns ending in f, ß, sch, z, d, t, st.

e is always dropped after el, en, em, er, chen, lein. In other cases it is optional. If the genitive singular has es, then the dative singular has e as a rule: Hauses, zu Hause.

a. Distribution of nouns among these declensions according to gender:

1. The bulk of feminine nouns belong to the n-declension. No neuters at all.
2. To the strong declension belong mainly masculine and neuter nouns, and a few feminines.
3. The mixed declension includes a few masculine and neuter nouns.

Strong Declension.

44. We distinguish for practical reasons four classes, according to the formation of the plural:

1. No sign unless it be umlaut: das Wunder, die Wunder; der Vater, die Väter.
2. -e without umlaut: der Tag, die Tage; das Los, die Lose.
3. -e with umlaut: der Sohn, die Söhne; die Kraft, die Kräfte.
4. -er always with umlaut: das Bad, die Bäder; das Haus, die Häuser.

45. First Class.—*a.* No sign:

Sing. N. der Spaten	das Gewerbe	der Engel
G. des Spatens	des Gewerbes	des Engels
Plu. D. den Spaten	den Gewerben	den Engeln

All other cases singular and plural like nominative singular.

b. With umlaut:

Sing. N., D., A. der Faden	der Bruder
G. des Fadens	des Bruders
Plu. N., G., A. die Fäden	die Brüder
D. den Fäden	den Brüdern

DECLENSION OF NOUNS.

46. To this class, which never take e in the G. and D. sing., belong:

1. Masculine and neuter nouns in –el, –er, –en, –chen, –lein, –sel, e. g., der Hebel, der Ritter, der Boden, der Hopfen, das Hündchen, das Kindlein, das Räthsel.

2. Neuters of the form Ge–e, e. g., das Getreide, Geschmeide.

3. The names of kindred in –er: Vater, Bruder, Tochter, Mutter, Schwager, all with umlaut. Also der Käse.

4. Certain nouns, if they take –n in the nominative singular, as they may according to usage: der Felsen, der Brunnen, der Tropfen, der Schrecken (these so generally). The following not so frequently in the written language: der Funke(n), Balke(n), Friede(n), Gedanke(n), Gefalle(n), Glaube(n), Haufe(n), Name(n), Same(n), Schade(n).

47. 1. Atem (Odem), Brodem, Eidam, Brosam stand isolated. The plural, if it occurs, is the –e of the next class. Brosamen, f., is more common than Brosame. See 501.

2. All nouns sub 4, except Friede, Gefalle, and Gedanke, were weak in M. H. G., and are not yet fully established in the strong declension. Since usage is unsettled, they might all be put under the mixed or weak declension.

48. 1. The nouns of this class that take umlaut, besides the names of kindred in –er, are : der Apfel + apple, Acker + acre, Boden + bottom, soil; Faden, thread (die Faden + fathoms), Garten + garden, Hafen, harbor, + haven; Hammer + hammer, Laden (?), shutter, shop (store); Mangel, want, Nagel + nail, Ofen + oven, stove; Sattel + saddle, Schaden, harm (but es ist Schade, it is too bad); Schnabel beak, Schwager brother-in-law, Vogel, bird, + fowl. Two neuters take umlaut: Kloster + cloister < L. *claustrum*, and Lager (?), camp.

2. In none of these is there any cause that could produce umlaut as in *i* and *jo* stems or before –*ir*. Umlaut has arisen from analogy with these. Väter, Mütter, Brüder, Töchter had umlaut already in M. H. G. This way of forming the plural is on the increase, because it is so convenient and some way of indicating the plural seems necessary. Wägen, Läger, etc., still sound objectionable, but have no worse and no better claim to correctness than the above.

49. Second Class.—Plural -e, no umlaut.

Sing. N., A.	Hund	die Drangsal	das Jahr
G.	des Hundes	der Drangsal	des Jahres
D.	dem Hunde	der Drangsal	dem Jahre
Plu. N., G., A.	Hunde	Drangsale	Jahre
D.	Hunden	Drangsalen	Jahren

50. To this class belong:

1. A small number of feminines in –nis and -sal, *e. g.*, die Drangsal, Trübsal; die Finsternis, Betrübnis, pl. –nisse.

2. Many masculines; some capable of umlaut, but without it. These may be considered exceptions to the third class: der Aal + eel, Aar eagle, Arm + arm, Besuch visit, Amboß + anvil, Dachs badger, Docht, wick, Grad + degree, Halm, blade, + haulm, Huf + hoof, Hund dog, + hound; Lachs salmon, Laut sound, Luchs + lynx, Pfad + path, Punkt + point, Schuh + shoe, Tag + day, Stoff material, + stuff; Thron + throne, Versuch, attempt, and a very few others.

3. Masculines in –ig, –(i)ch, –ing, –ling, –(e)nd, –at, –is, –icht, *e. g.*, der Freund + friend, Gänserich + gander, Habicht + hawk, Hering + herring, Iltis (pl. Iltisse) pole-cat, Jüngling + youth, König + king, Molch salamander, Monat + month.

4. Many neuters, among which monosyllabics; those with the prefix Ge–; in –nis, –sal: das Jahr + year, Geschenk present, Gefängnis (pl. –sse) prison, Schicksal fate.

51. The group sub 2 is on the decrease, because we cannot tell on the surface whether a noun has umlaut or not. To avoid the difficulty, several nouns form very anomalous plurals: der Bau, die Bauten instead of Baue. Of Mord, pl. Morde is rare, rather Mordthaten; of Schmuck, pl. Schmucke is rare, rather Schmucksachen; Schluck, pl. Schlucke is seldom used, since it stands in the singular after a number, *e. g.*, drei Schluck Branntwein. See **173**.

52. Third Class.—Plural -e, with umlaut.

Sing. N., A. der Stamm	die Kuh	die Braut
G. des Stammes	der Kuh	der Braut
D. dem Stamme	der Kuh	der Braut
Plu. N.. A., G. Stämme	Kühe	Bräute
D. Stämmen	Kühen	Bräuten

53. To this class belong:

1. The majority of strong masculine nouns, mostly monosyllabics: der Gesang + song, Gebrauch use, Ball + ball, Gast + guest, Sohn + son, etc.

2. A number of feminine nouns: die Angst + anxiety, Art + axe, Bank + bench + bank, Brunst, heat, lust; Brust + breast, Faust + fist, Frucht + fruit, Gans + goose, Gruft vault, Hand + hand, Haut + hide, Kluft + cleft, =kunft in compounds as in Einkunft + income; Laus + louse, Luft air, Lust desire, Macht + might, Magd + maid, servant; Maus + mouse, Nacht + night, Naht seam, Nuß + nut, Sau + sow Schnur string, Stadt city, Wand wall (of a room), Wurst sausage, Zunft guild; Ausflucht evasion, Armbrust cross-bow, Geschwulst + swelling.

54. Only two modern neuter nouns belong here, the last of which is of doubtful gender, viz.: Das Floß raft (**429**, 1); der or das Chor + choir, chorus.

55. No neuters belong here really except O. H. G. *meri*, das Meer, die Meere, now according to 2d Class. Der and das Chor, borrowed from church-Latin "chorus," has joined the group sub 2. Das Boot, die Böte because it was also der Boot, a modern borrowed word < D. Die Boote is more elegant. Das Rohr, die Röhre is not good. Besides there is die Röhre, feminine singular, the pipe, tube.

DECLENSION OF NOUNS.

56. Fourth Class.—Plural -er, always with umlaut:

Sing. N., A.	das Rad	Irrtum
G.	des Rades	des Irrtums
D.	dem Rade	dem Irrtume
Plu. N., G., A.	Räder	Irrtümer
D.	den Rädern	den Irrtümern

57. To this class belong:

1. About sixty neuter monosyllabics: das Aas (Äser), Blatt, Dach, Fach, etc.

2. All in -tum, whether masculine or neuter: das Herzogtum, der Reichtum.

3. Some masculines, viz.: der Bösewicht*, Dorn*, Geist, Gott, Leib, Mann, Ort*, Rand, Strauch*, Vormund, Wald, Wurm.

4. A few neuters, with the prefix Ge-: das Gemach, Gemüt, Geschlecht*, Gesicht*, Gespenst, Gewand*.

58. Only neuters had this plural -er at first. Of the sixty sub 1, some twenty form a different plural, and usage is unsettled; so do those sub 3 and 4 marked with a *. In the following a distinction is made in meaning between the different forms of the plural:

Sub 1, 2, 4,—

das Band,	Bande, ties,	Bänder, ribbons.
Denkmal,	-male, monuments,	-mäler, figurative sense.
Ding,	Dinge, things,	Dinger, coll., e. g., girls.
Gesicht,	Gesichte, visions,	Gesichter, faces.
Gewand,	Gewande (poetic),	Gewänder (commonly).
Land,	Lande (poetic),	Länder (commonly).
Licht,	Lichte, candles (only),	Lichter, lights.
Schild,	masc. Schilde, shields,	Schilder (sign-board).
Stift,	masc. Stifte, pencils,	Stifter, institutions.
Tuch,	Tuche, kinds of cloth,	Tücher, cloths, shawls.
Wort,	Worte, words (their meaning),	Wörter, parts of speech

Sub 3, —

der Mann, Mannen, retinue, Männer, men.
Ort, Orten, D. and G. pl. only, Örter, places, towns.

59. Trümmer occurs in the plural only. But a weak plural Trümmern occurs in the classics. Singular Trumm + thrum. „Häupten," as dative plural, is isolated in „zu den Häupten." Mann was originally a *cons*-stem, *mann*- (see Kluge's Dict.). The form Mann in fünfzig Mann is the real nominative plural of the *cons*-stem. Mensch was originally neuter, being an adjective O. H. G. *mennisco*. Das Mensch, die Menscher, now implies a slur, speaking of woman = strumpet (see Kluge's Dict.). Wicht in Böse-wicht was also once a neuter, + wight. See **431**.

60. In early N. H. G. many of the neuters still occur without -er. Kindes Kind werden deine Werk preisen (B.). Kinder und Kindes Kind (erzählen) von dem Volk noch und seinen Scharen (Sch.).

The plural in -s is not elegant. Säbels, Jungens, Frauens, Fräuleins are more than colloquial, though found in the classics. This -s is strictly Low German, and identical with English *s*. The parts of speech are used with s: die Achs, die Abers, die Wenns.

Weak or n-Declension.

61. Characteristics: (e)n in the plural and also in the singular of masculine, except the nominative.

	Masc.		Fem.
Sing. N.	der Bote	Whole *sing.*	Zunge
G.	des Boten		
All through *sing.* and *plu.*		Whole *plu.*	Zungen

Only feminine and masculine nouns belong to this declension.

Like Zunge decline all feminines, except: 1. Mutter and Tochter. 2. The few in -nis and -sal (see **50.** 1). 3. The strong of the 3d class (see **53**, 2).

62. Of the masculines belong here:

1. All of two or more syllables ending in e, except Käse and the doubtful strong ones sub 4, 1st class (see **46**).

2. The following which generally do not show the e, which belongs to them: der Bär, Bauer, Bursch, Fürst, Fink, Geck, Gesell(e), Graf, Hagestolz, Held, Herr, Hirte, Insasse, Mensch, Mohr, Narr, Ochse, Prinz, Pfau, Spatz, Sproß, Steinmetz, Thor (fool), Vorfahr.

3. Many nouns of foreign origin, which are difficult to tell from strong nouns, many of them names of persons and animals. They generally end in -t, -nt, -st, with the suffix -graph, -arch, -trat, -log(e), -nom, *e. g.*, Poe't, Bandi't, Israeli't, Patrio't, Archite'tt, Kome't, Plane't, Konsona'nt, Stude'nt, Phanta'st, Telegra'ph, Geogra'ph, Patria'rch, Mona'rch, Autokra't, Demokra't, Astrolo'g(e), Philolo'ge, Astrono'm, Ökono'm (polite for "farmer"); also Tyra'nn.

4. Some names of nationalities in -ar, and -er, *e. g.*, der U'ngar, Bulga'r(e), Tata'r, Baier, Pommer, Kaffer.

5. The adjective used as a noun when preceded by the article (see **220**).

REMARK.—An isolated form is now „auf Erben." Erbe was either weak or strong. But „in Ehren," „mit Freuden" are old datives plural (see **434, 1**). Notice the spelling Königin, pl. Königinnen.

Mixed Declension.

63. Characteristics: G. sing. (e)s, the whole pl. (e)n.

Only masculine and neuter nouns belong to this declension, and very few have not double forms for genitive singular and for the plural. The following generally belong here:

1. Auge, Bett, Ende, Gevatter, Hemd, Lorbeer, Mast, Muskel, Ohr, Panto'ffel, Schmerz, See, Stachel, Staat. Nachbar, Untertban, Vetter sometimes retain in genitive singular the (e)n of their former declension. Bauer, peasant sub **62**, 2 is sometimes classed here.

Das Herz inflects G. des Herzens, D. dem Herzen, A. das Herz; allowing for its being a neuter, which always has nominative and accusative singular alike, it really comes under 1st Class, strong, sub 4 (see **46**). Schmerz rarely has Schmerzens. Der Sporn, des Spornes, has taken an –n in the singular, but the old weak plural Sporen is still the rule, though Spornen occurs. Thronen, borrowed in M. H. G. < Gr.-L. *thronos*, is very rare. The plural of Dorn is either Dorne (old) or generally Dornen; also Dörner.

The mixed declension is quite modern, and does not exist in M. H. G.

2. Foreign nouns in –or (o long and accented in the plural, short and unaccented in the singular), *e. g.*, der Do'ktor, die Dokto'ren, der Profe'ssor, die Professo'ren. Also Insekt, Interesse, Juwe'l, Statu't, and others.

Colloquially one hears sometimes –n after nouns in –el and –er: die Hummern, lobsters; Stiefeln, boots; but they are not to be imitated.

Declension of Foreign Nouns.

64. Those which are fully naturalized come under the declensions already treated of. It remains to speak of those not at all or partly naturalized, and their inflection is very irregular and complicated.

1. Those that retain their foreign inflection, *e. g.*, Jesus Christus, Jesu Christi; Maria, Mariae; Modus, pl. Modi; Cajus, pl. Caju; Cherub, pl. Cherubim; Conto, pl. Conti; Sackulum, pl. Sackula; Lord, pl. Lords; Tempus, pl. Tempora. Their number is decreasing.

2. Those which take a German plural ending, –en for instance, and do not inflect in the singular, *e. g.*: das Drama, pl. Dramen; Thema, pl. Themen; Individuum, pl. Individuen. Globus, Rythmus. But these are also found with –s in genitive singular, and then come under the mixed declension.

3. Nouns whose foreign plural ended in *–ia* take *–ien:* Studium, pl. Studien; Gymnasium, pl. Gymnasien. The ending of the singular may have been lost, and they have –s in genitive singular, as Adve'rb, Partici'p, Semina'r, Minera'l, Fossi'l, pl.

Adverbien, Fossilien, etc. Notice Pri'mas, Prima'ten; A'tlas, Atla'n=
ten; Krisis, Krisen. On the whole, there is a great deal of ir-
regularity, and therefore freedom, in the inflection of foreign
words.

Declension of Proper Nouns.

65. 1. The names of nations and peoples are inflected both
in the singular and plural. Those in –er (except Baier and
Pommer, where –er is not suffix, denoting origin) go according
to 1st Class (strong). All the others go according to the
n-declension: der Hamburger, des Hamburgers, etc., D. pl. den
Hamburgern. But der Sachse, des Sachsen; der Preuße, des Preußen,
etc.

2. Certain geographical names (see **147**), which always
have the definite article, are treated like any common noun,
e. g., der Rhein, des Rheins, das Fichtelgebirge des –es; das Elsaß, des
Elsasses; die Schweiz, der Schweiz, etc.

3. Names of persons are uninflected if preceded by the article (an adjective or title between article and name makes no
difference), e. g., des Karl, des Kaisers Karl, dem großen Friedrich.
If the title follows the name, or if the name in the genitive,
modified by an adjective, stands before the noun upon which
it depends, then the name takes –s, e. g., das Reich Ludwigs des
Frommen, des großen Friedrichs Generäle.

4. Names of persons, places, and countries without an article take a genitive in –es: Goethe, Goethes; England, Englands;
Anna, Annas. But names of males ending in a sibilant, if
inflected at all and an apostrophe is not preferred, and feminine names in –e, form a genitive in –ens, e. g., Marens, Franzens,
Mariens, Sophiens. Surnames in a sibilant certainly prefer an
apostrophe, e. g., Musäus' Volksmärchen, Opitz' Werke, Gauß' Tod.
Names of places in a sibilant are constructed with von: die
Reichsfreiheit von Ko'nstanz, die Befestigungen von Pari's.

66. A dative and an accusative in –en of names of persons are hardly in use now, as *e. g.*, Schillern, Goethen, Klopstocken. Christian feminine names retain them more easily than masculine, *e. g.*, Hast du Marien gesprochen? See **68**, 3. Such genitives as Mutters Tod, Tantens Geburtstag are hardly proper.

67. Plurals of names of persons are formed in various ways. The general rule is: –e for masculine and –e(n) for feminine names, *e. g.*, Heinriche, Marien; but also Brunhilde, Elisabete. –s forms the plural of masculines ending in a vowel and of feminines in –a: Annas, Hugos.

68. 1. Here also belongs the plural of surnames denoting the members of the family, formed by –s if ending in a consonant not a sibilant; by –(e)n if ending in a vowel or a sibilant (occurs only in familiar language however), *e. g.*, Steinbrüggen, the Steinbrügges; Suhlings, the Suhling family; Klüts. Other endings for the plural, generally of foreign names however, are –ne, –nen: Cato, Catone; Scipionen, Ottone, and Ottonen; but the first n belongs to the stem of course. Compare L. *Scipio, Scipionis*. This s was perhaps originally a G. sing.

2. Biblical names retain foreign inflection: Evangelium Matthaei, in Jesu Christo, Mariae Heimsuchung.

3. It should be borne in mind that the rule in the classical writers before Goethe's death is not the rule now. Lessing wrote des Luthers, des Melanchthons; Goethe, Leiden des jungen Werthers. The dative and accusative in –en are the rule in them, the exception now, Haben Sie Karlen geschrieben, Wilhelmen gesucht?

DECLENSION OF THE ADJECTIVE.

69. *The adjective is inflected according to two systems of declension, the Strong and the Weak. It is inflected strong when there is no limiting word before it; weak, when there is an article or demonstrative pronoun. It is uninflected in the predicate.*

1. Strong:

	masc.	fem.	neuter.		common gender.
Sing. N.	guter	gute	gutes	Plu. N.	gute
G.	gutes	guter	gutes	G.	guter
D.	gutem	guter	gutem	D.	guten
A.	guten	gute	gutes	A.	gute

2. Weak:

	masc.	fem.	neuter.
Sing. N.	der gute	die gute	das gute
A.	den guten	die gute	das gute

All other cases, *sing.* and *plu.*, guten.

Notice that the nominative and accusative singular of the feminine and neuter forms are alike.

70. After ein, fein, and the possessive pronouns the adjective is strong in the nominative singular of all genders and in the accusative singular of feminine and neuter, since it is like the nominative. The whole pl. is weak.

Sg. N. ein großer Dichter, eine rote Kirsche, ein herrliches Gedicht.
G. eines großen Dichters, einer roten Kirsche, eines herrlichen Gedichtes
D. einem großen Dichter, einer roten Kirsche, einem herrlichen Gedichte
A. einen großen Dichter, eine rote Kirsche, ein herrliches Gedicht.

71. Adjectives ending in -el, -er, -en as a rule drop the e of these suffixes when inflected, sometimes however the e of the case-ending -en, *e.g.*, edel, edler, edle, edles; mager, magrer, magre, magres; eigen, eigner, eigne, eignes; but heitern and heitren, eblen and ebeln. Those in -er like to retain both e's: heiterer, heitere, heiteres. Note therefore: Ein magrer Ochse, eines magern or magren Ochsen, etc.; der heitere or heitre Himmel, des heiteren, heitren, or heitern Himmels, etc.; mein eignes Haus, meines eigenen or eignen Hauses, etc. For hoch, hoher, hohe, hohes see **490**, 3, b.

72. The genitive singular masculine and neuter, -es, is now so regularly replaced by -en, that this should perhaps appear in the paradigm. Though strictly according to rule, -es has become the exception; -en has prevailed since the 17th century. Voss, Klopstock, and Grimm opposed it. Goethe favors it. Ein, fein, the possessive and the demonstrative pronouns never allow -en for -es; never seines Mannes, diesen Buches.

COMPARISON OF THE ADJECTIVE

73. Adjectives are compared by means of the inflectional suffixes –er and –(e)ſt, e. g.:

positive.	comparative.	superlative.
jung	jünger	jüngſt
ſchön	ſchöner	ſchönſt
reich	reicher	reichſt

Those in –el, –en, –er lose this e before the comparative –er; but retain it and lose the e of –eſt in the superlative, e. g., mager, magrer, magerſt; dunkel, dunkler, dunkelſt. e in –eſt is as a rule retained after d, t, ß, ſe, z, rch, ß, and ſt, but not necessarily, e. g., lauteſte, gewiſſeſte, ſüßeſte. Größte alone is classical, but in the spoken language ſüßte, heißte, kürzte, etc., are heard. „Hoch" retains the former h in the comparative höher, and h in nahe becomes ch: nächſt. See **490, 3,** *b.*

74. The umlaut generally takes place, but it is very difficult to tell when it does not. A not small number are doubtful, e. g., blaß, geſund, fromm, etc. No umlaut in: 1. Those with the stem-vowel au, e. g., lau, blau, etc. 2. Foreign ones: brav, nobel, etc. 3. Participles: beſucht, gewandt, etc. 4. Derivatives: ſtrafbar, ſchalthaft, langſam, unglaublich, etc. 5. Bunt, blank, dumpf, falſch, flach, froh, hohl, hold, kahl, klar, lahm, laß, los, matt, morſch, platt, plump, raſch, roh, rund, ſanft, ſatt, ſchlaff, ſchlank, ſchroff, ſtarr, ſtolz, ſtraff, toll, voll, wahr, zahm, zart.

75. The comparative and superlative forms are declined just like the positive. Examples:

Größerer Spaß, größeres or größeren Spaßes, etc.; der größere Spaß, des größeren Spaßes, etc.; ein größerer Spaß

Klarſtes Waſſer, das klarſte Waſſer, ein klarſtes Waſſer.

Edlerer Mann, der edlere Mann, ein edlerer Mann; eitelſter Burſch, der eitelſte Burſch, ein eitelſter Burſch.

Heiſrer Sänger, der heiſrere Sänger, ein heiſrerer Sänger, G. eines heiſreren Sängers, etc.; der heiſerſte Sänger.

76. 1. Irregular Comparison.
By the use of different stems:

Positive.	Comparative.	Superlative.
gut + good	beſſer, adv. baß + better	beſt + best
viel	mehr + more	meiſt + most
	mehrer	mehrſt
(gering or wenig)	minder	mindeſt

Gut and viel are never compared regularly. Mehrer and mehrſt are due to double comparison. „Mehrſt," though occurring in Goethe and Schiller, is not classical. Mehr and minder are really not adjectives, but are used adverbially and substantively. „Baß„ (mehr, very, much) is now archaic. „Doch baß hetzt ihn der linke Mann" (Bü.). Fürbaß (onward); „baß" also means ſehr, ſtark: „Das macht, er thät ſich baß hervor" (Sch.). „Und ward nicht mehr geſehn" (G.). Morgen ein mehreres = to-morrow (I will write) more.

2. Defective and Redundant Comparison.

a. There is a class of adjectives derived from adverbs and prepositions:

Adv. or prep.	Comparative.	Superlative.
(außer)	äußer	äußerſt
(hinter)	hinter	hinterſt
(inner)	inner	innerſt
(nieder)	nieder (rare)	niederſt
(ob[er])	ober	oberſt
(unter)	unter	unterſt
(vor, fort)	vorder	vorderſt

For the derivation of these adverbs, see **551**, 3. The superlative suffix -ſt is added to the comparative. This is due to their former full comparison, as for instance, O. H. G. pos. *hintaro*, comp. *hintaróro*, superl. *hintaróst*. The present comparatives hintere, obere are not even now felt as real comparatives; äußer has a spurious umlaut; „öberste" and „förberste" are colloquial; „vorder" comes from „fort," O. H. G. *fordar;* compare Eng. *further,* which has nothing to do with *far.*

	Positive.	Comparative.	Superlative.
b.	(mittel) + middle	mittler	mittelst
	(ehe, conj.)	(eher, adv.) + ere	erst + erst
	(laß + late)		letzt + last
	(für)	(fürder, adv.)	Fürst (subst.) + first

The first compares regularly like an adjective in -el. The positive occurs only in compounds now, and the comparative has the force of the positive.

NUMERALS.

77. Cardinals.

eins, + one
zwei, + two
drei, + three
vier, + four
fünf, + five
sechs, + six
sieben, + seven
acht, + eight
neun, + nine
zehn, + ten
elf, eilf, ölf, + eleven
zwelf, zwölf, + twelve
dreizehn, + thirteen
vierzehn, + fourteen
fünfzehn, + fifteen
sech(s)zehn, + sixteen
zwanzig, + twenty
ein und zwanzig, + twenty-one
zwei und zwanzig, + twenty-two
drei und zwanzig, + twenty-three
dreißig, + thirty
ein und dreißig, + thirty-one
vierzig, + forty
fünfzig, funfzig, + fifty
sechszig, sechzig, + sixty
sieb(en)zig, + seventy
achtzig, + eighty
neunzig, + ninety
hundert (das Hundert), + a hundred
(ein) hundert und ein(s), + a hundred and one
(ein) hundert und zwei, + a hundred and two
(ein) hundert (und) zehn, + a hundred and ten

(ein) hundert und zwanzig, + a hundred and twenty
(ein) hundert ein und zwanzig, + a hundred and twenty-one
(ein) hundert acht und achtzig, + a hundred and eighty-eight
zweihundert, + two hundred
dreihundert sechs und siebzig, + three hundred and seventy-six
tausend (das Tausend), + a thousand
(ein) tausend und ein(s), + a thousand and one
(ein) tausend drei und vierzig, + a thousand and forty-three
(ein) tausend einhundert or elfhundert, + a thousand and one hundred
ein tausend achthundert drei und achtzig or achtzehn hundert drei und achtzig, + one thousand eight hundred and eighty-three
drei(mal) hundert tausend, + three hundred thousand
eine Millio'n, + a million
eine Millia'rde, a thousand millions
eine Billio'n, + a billion

78. Inflection.

Fully inflected are only eins, zwei, drei, as follows:

	Masc.	Fem.	Neuter.
N.	einer	eine	ein(e)s
G.	eines	einer	eines, when used substantively.
N.	ein	eine	ein, like the indefinite article when used attributively.

„'s war einer dem's zu Herzen ging" (Ch.) ; „eins von beiden," one of two things.

| N. zwei | G. zweier | D. zweien | A. zwei |
| N. drei | G. dreier | D. dreien | A. drei |

79. Older inflections were masc. zween, fem. zwo. Zwei, the neuter, has crowded out the masculine and feminine forms, which may still be found in the older modern classics, and still in use in the S. G. dialects. Was zweien recht ist, ist dreien zu enge. Durch zweier Zeugen Mund wird allerwärts die Wahrheit kund (F., I. 3013). Zween, die mit mir überfuhren

. . . . (Uh.). Zwo Hosen eines Tuchs, cut from the same cloth. „Zwo Jungfern in den besten Jahren" (Gellert). The plurals zweie and dreie are in analogy with the strong noun and adjective declensions From 4–12 the e in the plural represents O. H. G. *i* when they were *i*-stems, fünfe < *fimfi*. The only other case in which these numbers are inflected is the dative plural (in –en): auf allen Vieren kriechen, alle Viere von sich strecken; mit Sechsen fahren; zu Dreien. Zweier, zweien are according to the adjective inflection.

80. Ordinals.

The ordinals are formed from the cardinals by adding –te to the numbers from 2–19, and –ste from 20 on.

  (der) erste, + first   sechste, + sixth
  zweite, + second   sechzehnte, + sixteenth
  dritte, + third   zwanzigste, + twentieth
  vierte, + fourth   hundertste, + hundredth
  fünfte, + fifth   tausendste, + thousandth

Their inflection is that of adjectives; zweiter, der zweite, ein zweiter; G. eines zweiten. See **438**, 1.

PRONOUNS.

81. Personal Pronouns.

		Common gender.		Special forms for gender in the singular.		
	I.	II.	III. Reflexive.	III. Masc.	Fem.	Neuter.
Sing. N.	ich	du		er	sie	es
G.	meiner	deiner	seiner	seiner	ihrer	seiner
	(mein)	(dein)	(sein)	(sein)		(sein, es)
D.	mir	dir	sich	ihm	ihr	ihm
A.	mich	dich	sich	ihn	sie	es
Plu. N.	wir	ihr	—	sie		
G.	unser	euer	—	ihrer		
	(unsrer)	(eurer)				
D.	uns	euch	sich	ihnen		
A.	uns	euch	sich	sie		

The first and second persons and the plural of the third person are of common gender. The singular of the third person has a form for each gender.

82. In the genitive singular the longer forms in -er are common; the others are now archaic and poetic, *e. g.*, „Vergißmeinnicht" (the flower). „Ich denke Dein," etc. (G.). The lengthened forms eurer, unsrer are not yet sanctioned, though common in the spoken language, and, especially eurer, not very rare in the classics, *e. g.*, „(Wie er) bei Tafel Eurer selbst nicht achtet" (Sch.). „Dann bedarf es unserer nicht„ (Sch.). The genitive singular neuter „es" occurs still in certain constructions, generally called an accusative: „Er hat es keinen Hehl daß . . . ." (Sch.). Ich bin es müde. Es nimmt mich Wunder. (See **183, 199,** 2.)

83. Reflexive Pronouns.

For the first and second persons the personal pronouns serve as such, *e. g.*, ich fürchte mich, wir freuen uns, ihr scheut euch. For the third person the forms are made up of the personal and the old reflexive pronouns:

Masc. and neuter.	Fem.	Common gender.
Sing. G. seiner	(ihrer, pers. pron.)	*Plu.* (ihrer, pers. pron.)
D., A. sich	sich	sich

84. The reciprocal pronoun has no special form; as such are used uns, euch, sich, einander, meaning "each other," "one another." Ex.: Ihr schlagt euch. Wir schelten einander nicht.

The Possessive Pronouns.

85. The possessive pronouns are: mein + my; dein + thy; sein, his, its; ihr, her; unser + our; euer + your; ihr, their; Ihr, your; der meine + mine; der deine + thine, etc.; der meinige + mine; der deinige + thine, etc.

They are inflected like adjectives (see **69**); but mein, dein, sein, unser, euer, ihr, like the indefinite article (see **38**), in which the nominative singular masculine and the nominative and accusative singular neuter are uninflected, *e. g.*:

	Neuter.	Feminine.
Sing. N., A.	mein Tuch	deine Nichte
G.	meines Tuches	deiner Nichte
D.	meinem Tuche	deiner Nichte
Plu. N., A.	meine Tücher	deine Nichten
G.	meiner Tücher	deiner Nichten
D.	meinen Tüchern	deinen Nichten

For the declension of der meine, der meinige, see the weak adjective, **69**, 2. The rest stand uninflected used predicatively and when they follow the noun (now archaic), *e. g.*, Was mein ist, das ist dein und was dein ist, das ist mein (B.). Du hast das Herze mein so ganz genommen ein (Song).

86. Euer, Eure, Seiner, Seine are often abbreviated into Ew., Er., Se.: Se. Majestät, Ew. Wohlgeboren. Ihro is archaic, *e. g.*, Ihro Gnaden. It is an imitation of the old G. hero (see **89**). It does not occur before the seventeenth century. It stands for masculine and feminine sing. and pl. in titles: Ihro Gnaden, Eminenz, Durchlaucht.

87. The possessive pronouns form certain compounds with wegen, halben, willen, and gleichen. Ex.: meinetwegen, ihretwegen, meinethalben, ihresgleichen, euresgleichen. The compounds with wegen and halben are really D. plu. meinen wegen, deinen halben. After n sprang up the excrescent t = meinentwegen, deinenthalben, current in the sixteenth century. These became the now classical meinetwegen, deinethalben, though the longest forms are still heard; also meinthalben, even meintshalben, occur, but they are not good. Meinetwillen < meinentwillen < meinenwillen are original accusatives, *e. g.*, um meinen willen = for my sake.

The origin of ihresgleichen, etc., is not so clear. Gleichen is without doubt the adjective used as a noun and governing a preceding genitive. which was at first the genitive of the personal pronoun and became later the possessive pronoun agreeing with gleichen (M. H. G. *sîne gelîchen*). But whence s? Is it the genitive sign -es in compound nouns, Liebesbrief, Mittagsstunde, which was looked upon as a mere connective? (See **518**, 2.) In M. H. G. was a Gen. *mines, dines,* which with *mîner*, stood for mìn, almost exclusively before *selbes*. But beinesgleichen is not old enough to connect with M. H. G. *dines selbes*.

Other compounds with the possessive, like meinesteils, meinerseits (see 552), are clearly genitives.

Demonstrative Pronouns.

88. These are : 1. der, die, das + the, that ; 2. dieser, diese, dieses + this ; jener, jene, jenes, that, + yon. The first, when used with the noun, differs only in accent and not in declension from the article (see **39**). When used substantively (without the noun) it declines :

		Masc.	Fem.	Neuter.		Common gender.
Sing.	N.	der	die	das	*Plu.*	die
	G.	dessen	deren	dessen		deren
		des	der	des		derer (der)
	D.	dem	der	dem		denen
	A.	den	die	das		die

89. The spelling of „deß" for „des" is unwarranted. It implies that it is an abbreviation of „dessen," which it is not.

„Dero" is the O. H. G. form retained in certain phrases, as in dero Gnaden. Derentwegen, -halben, etc., are forms like meinetwegen, etc., but rarely lose the n before t. For their explanation see **87**.

	Masc.	Fem.	Neuter.
90.	dieser	diese	dieses and dies + this
	jener	jene	jenes + yon, that

These are declined like strong adjectives, and stand adjectively and substantively: diese Feder, dieses Tintenfaß, jener Baum. Jenes dort ist mein Buch.

91. Another group of demonstrative pronouns, sometimes called " determinative," consists of :

Masc.	Fem.	Neuter.
derjenige	diejenige	dasjenige, the, that
derselbe	dieselbe	dasselbe, the same
derselbige	dieselbige	dasselbige, the same
selber, selbst (uninflected), selbiger	selbige	selbiges, the same
solch(er)	solch(e)	solch(es), + such

1. The inflection of the first three is that of „ber" and a weak adjective, e. g., berjenige, besjenigen, bemjenigen, etc. Their composition is apparent. -ig is the usual adjective suffix (see 525, 1).

In the 16th century ber is still separated from felb-, jen-, and earlier the latter were even declined strong. ber jener, bem felbem, but they soon followed the n-declension. „Der jene," from which „berjenige" developed, becomes obsolete in the 17th century. „Derfelbige" < „berfelbe.". Accent: be'rjenige, but berfe'lbe.

2. Selber is a stereotyped form like voller, and felbft is a genitive singular of felb, M. H. G. *selbes*. The excrescent t appears first in the 13th century.

3. Solch is inflected like any adjective, even with -en in the genitive singular, e. g., folchenfalls, folchen Glaubens. It may be uninflected, always if followed by ein and generally if followed by another adjective. An apostrophe after folch is uncalled for. Solch ein Mann, folch schöne Blumen. Eine solche Beleidigung kann ich nicht vergeffen. Als er solches sah . . . . (B.).

92. Interrogative Pronouns.

Wer + who; was + what; welcher + which; was für ein, what sort of.

1. Wer declines:

Masc. and fem.	Neuter.
N. wer	was
G. weffen, wes	weffen, wes
D. wem	—
A. wen	was

Weß or wefs: wes as beffen: bes. See 89. The genitive lengthened by -en like bes > beffen was not yet established in the 16th century. Wes is now archaic, except in compounds, e. g., weshalb, weswegen. For weffenthalben, see beffent-, berenthalben, 87, 89.

2. Welch + which, what, declines strong. Before „ein" it is

always, and before an adjective it is often left uninflected, also in poetry when used adjectively: Welch Getümmel Straßen auf! (Sch.). Welch ein Gefühl (F. 1011). Welcher Mann war es?

3. Was für, was für ein, what, what kind of. „Ein" alone is inflected like the indefinite article if used adjectively; like a strong adjective if used substantively: „Was für Berge, was für Wüsten . . . . trennen uns denn noch?" (Le.). Was für ein Baum ist das? Was für Dinte ist dies?

93. Relative Pronouns.

1. Der, die, das, which, + that, who, declines like the demonstrative, but the genitive plural is never derer : Keiner siegte noch der nicht gestritten hat (Bo.).

2. Welcher, welche, welches, + which, who, that, always declines strong: Das Buch, welches ich gelesen habe.

3. Wer, + who, whoever. The inflection is the same as that of the interrogative: Wer es (auch) sei, whoever it be.

4. Was, + what, whatsoever. The inflection is the same as that of the interrogative : Was er (auch) sagen mag, no matter what he says.

Indefinite Pronouns and Indefinite Numerals.

94. Anderer, andere, anderes, + other, different : der andere, die andere, das andere, die anderen. Declined like any adjective, used substantively and adjectively.

95. Einer, eine, eines, + one, the numeral with its derivatives kein, none, and einige, generally only plural " some."

Ein– is always strongly inflected and stands only substantively. Standing adjectively it is declined like the indefinite article (see 39). With def. art.: der eine, die einen.

Kein is inflected like the indefinite article, but standing substantively is declined keiner, keine, kein(e)s : Keiner wird als Meister geboren (Prov.).

PRONOUNS.

96. Etlich–, some; etwas, anything; wer, anybody; was, anything, something; welch–, some, any; einig–, some.

Etlich– and welch– are always inflected strong. The singular of etlich is rare, having the force of "tolerable," "some": mit etlichem Erfolge, with some success.

97. Compounds with je: jeder, every, each; jeglich, jedweder (= jeder) stand adjectively and substantively; jedermann, everybody; jemand, anybody; niemand, nobody.

Jeder, jeglich–, jedweder, each, every, are declined like strong adjectives. Jeglich and jedweder are not common now; they have the same meaning. Jedermann has only a genitive singular in –s. Jemand and niemand decline: N. jemand, G. jemand(e)s, D. jemandem, –den, A. jemanden.

If jeder, jeglich, jedweder are preceded by the indef. art., they are declined like any adjective preceded by ein, e. g. ein jeder, eines jeden, einem jeden, einen jeden.

The accusative and dative are N. H. G., taken from the adjective inflection. Though the classics are full of these cases, the best usage for the spoken language favors no case-ending for accusative and dative.

98. Man, one, any one. It is only nominative. The other cases are made up from ein– or wir. Man is old spelling for Mann, from which in M. H. G. it was not distinguished. Its corresponding possessive is sein: Man glaubt ihm nicht. Man kann seinen eigenen Kopf nicht essen (Prov.).

99. Nichts, nothing, allows of no further inflection. It is itself the genitive of M. H. G. niht = ni-wiht and nio-wiht. Compare Eng. naught = na-wiht. Nichts, the genitive, stands for the emphatic combination nihtes niht, "not a thing" = gar nichts.

Zu nichte, mit nichten, "not at all," show still that nicht was once a noun fully inflected: Besser etwas denn nichts (Prov.).

100. As indefinite numerals it is customary to classify all + all; beibe + both; beibes + each or either; ganz, whole; lauter, "nothing but;" manch + many; mehr + more; mehrere, several; bie meiften + most, the majority; bie mehrften (= bie meiften); ein paar, a few, lit. "a pair;" fämtliche, all, altogether; das übrige, bie übrigen, the rest; viel, much, many; wenig, little, few; ein wenig, a little; genug + enough.

Of these, all, ganz, manch, viel, wenig may stand uninflected. Otherwise they are inflected like adjectives: Viel Steine gab's und wenig Brot (Uh.). Ganz Deutschland lag in Schmach und Schmerz (Mosen). Das ganze Deutschland soll es sein (Arndt).

Lauter, mehr, ein paar, ein wenig, genug are indeclinable.

CONJUGATION.

101. The verb varies for person and number; for tense (present and preterit) and mood (indicative and subjunctive). From the present stem are formed the imperative and the noun-forms of the verb, viz., the infinitive, present participle with the gerundive, and the past participle in -(e)t. According to the formation of the preterit we distinguish two great systems of conjugations, the "*strong*" and the "*weak.*" The strong verbs form the preterit by substituting a different stem-vowel from that of the present, *e. g.*, geben — gab, tragen — trug; the weak, by adding -(e)te to the stem, *e. g.*, loben — lobte, glauben — glaubte.

102. The infinitive, the preterit, and the past participle are generally given as the "principal parts" of a verb. The infinitive represents the forms with the present stem. Knowing the preterit or the past participle, one can tell whether a verb is weak or strong. If the preterit ends in -(e)te the past participle ends in -(e)t; if the preterit is strong, the past participle ends in -en, *e. g.*, sagen, sagte, gesagt; saugen, sog, gesogen.

The infinitive and the past participle help form the compound tenses.

103. The following paradigms show the various inflections:

	WEAK.			STRONG.		
PRESENT.		PRETERIT.	PRESENT.		PRETERIT.	
Ind.	*Subj.*	*Ind. and subj.*	*Ind.*	*Subj.*	*Ind.*	*Subj.*
ich lobe	lobe	lobte	ſinge	ſinge	ſang	ſänge
du lobſt	lobeſt	lobteſt	ſingſt	ſingeſt	ſangſt	ſängeſt
er lobt	lobe	lobte	ſingt	ſinge	ſang	ſänge
wir loben	loben	lobten	ſingen	ſingen	ſangen	ſängen
ihr lobt	lobet	lobtet	ſingt	ſinget	ſangt	ſänget
ſie loben	loben	lobten	ſingen	ſingen	ſangen	ſängen

	Imp.	*Inf.*		*Imp.*	*Inf.*
2. sg.	lobe (du)	loben	2. sg.	ſing(e) (du)	ſingen.
1. pl.	loben wir	*Pres. part., Gerundive.*	1. pl.	ſingen wir	*Pres. part., Gerundive.*
2. pl.	{ lob(e)t (ihr) / loben Sie	lobend	2. pl.	{ ſing(e)t (ihr) / ſingen Sie	ſingend
		Past part. gelobt			*Past part.* geſungen

104. The personal suffixes are:

Sg. 1. p. –e, except for strong preterit.
    2. p. –(e)ſt for both tenses and moods.
    3. p. –(e)t for the present indicative. In the pres. subj. and in the pret. ind. and subj. the 3. p. is like the first.

Pl. 1. p. –(e)n for both tenses and moods.
    2. p. –(e)t for both tenses and moods; also for the imperative.
    3. p. –(e)n for both tenses and moods.

The retention or rejection of the thematic or connecting vowel –e– is treated later. See 118.

105. Imperative. The 2. p. sg. ends in –e in all verbs excepting those strong ones that have the interchange of e—i or e—ie in the 2. and 3. p. sg. pres. ind., *e. g.*, traue, ſchaue, bete, bitte, grabe, hebe, but ſprich, friß, nimm.

106. Infinitive. It always ends in -en except in those weak verbs in which it is preceded by -el, -er: wandeln, wandern; also in ſein, thun, which are non-thematic verbs. See **449**, 2.

107. Participles. The present part. and the gerundive always end in -end: hoffend, helfend, ein Liebender, ein zu beweiſender Satz, a proposition to be demonstrated. They are declined like adjectives.

The past participle is formed by the prefix ge-, and the suffix -(e)t for weak verbs, the suffix -en for strong ones: lieben — geliebt, blättern — geblättert, tragen — getragen, ſingen — geſungen.

108. Ge- does not stand:

1. Before heißen, laſſen, ſehen, helfen, lernen (?), lehren (?), hören, when an infinitive depends upon them in a compound tense: Ich habe ihn gehen heißen, kommen laſſen, ſagen hören. For lernen and lehren, gelernt and gelehrt are better usage.

2. In the preterit-present verbs (= modal auxiliaries, see **134**) which form similar past participles, viz., können, dürfen, mögen, müſſen, ſollen, wollen. Man hat das wilde Tier nicht fangen können. See **113**.

3. In the past participles of verbs having inseparable prefixes, *e. g.*, verlaſſen, entſagt, bedeckt, gedacht, except freſſen < ver + eſſen and verbs in which b and g are no longer felt to be the prefixes be and ge (see **543**), *e. g.*, gefreſſen, geblieben < bleiben, geglaubt; geglichen < gleichen. See gegeſſen, **128**.

4. In verbs with the foreign ending -i'eren, *e. g.*, marſchieren — marſchiert; probieren — probiert. Even when these are compounded with separable Germanic prefixes, they take no ge-: ausmarſchiert, einſtudiert.

5. Worden < werden never takes ge-, when it is an auxiliary in the passive voice, *e. g.*, Er iſt gelobt worden.

Compound Tenses.

109. These are formed by means of the auxiliary verbs haben, sein, werden; the last in the future active and the whole passive; haben and sein in the active voice. As a matter of convenience the simple tenses of these auxiliaries are given here.

110.

PRESENT.		PRETERIT.		PRESENT.		PRETERIT.	
Ind.	*Subj.*	*Ind.*	*Subj.*	*Ind.*	*Subj.*	*Ind.*	*Subj.*
ich habe	habe	hatte	hätte	bin	sei	war	wäre
du hast	habest	hattest	hättest	bist	seiest	warst	wärest
er hat	habe	hatte	hätte	ist	sei	war	wäre
wir haben	haben	hatten	hätten	sind	seien	waren	wären
ihr habt	habet	hattet	hättet	seid	seiet	waret	wäret
sie haben	haben	hatten	hätten	sind	seien	waren	wären

	Imperative.	*Inf.*		*Imperative.*	*Inf.*
2. *sg.*	habe (du)	haben	2. *sg.*	sei (du)	sein
1. *pl.*	haben wir	*Pres. part.,*	1. *pl.*	seien wir	*Pres. part.*
2. *pl.*	{ habet (ihr)	*gerund.*	2. *pl.*	{ seid (ihr)	seiend
	{ haben Sie	habend		{ seien Sie	*Past part.*
		Past part.			gewesen
		gehabt			

PRESENT.		PRETERIT.			*Imperative.*	
Ind.	*Subj.*	*Ind.*	*Subj.*	2. *sg.*	werde (du)	
ich werde	werde	ward, wurde	würde	1. *pl.*	werden wir	
du wirst	werdest	wardst, wurdest	würdest	2. *pl.*	{ werdet (ihr)	
er wird	werde	ward, wurde	würde		{ werden Sie	
wir werden	werden	wurden	würden	*Inf.* werden		
ihr werdet	werdet	wurdet	würdet	*Pres. part.* } werdend
sie werden	werden	wurden	würden	*Gerund.* }
				Past part. worden		

111. 1. Haben has contracted forms for the 2. and 3. pers. sing.: hast < *häst* < *habest*; hat < *hât* < *habet*. The pret. has undergone the same contractions: hatte < *hâte* < *habete*, etc. The pret. subj. has umlaut due to the influence of strong and pret.-pres. verbs. In dialect the old contracted forms with *â*, prevailing through the whole present, are still heard. In M. H. G. *haben* as auxiliary has the contracted forms; as an independent verb, the uncontracted.

2. Werben is a regular strong verb of the 3. class. It is the only verb that has retained the two pret. vowels, generally the vowel of the sing. prevailing over that of the plural. Warb is more common as independent verb; wurbe, as auxiliary. In elevated style warb is preferable.

112. The **Perfect** is formed with the present of haben or sein and the past participle, *e. g.*, ich habe getragen, I have borne; ich bin gefahren, subj. ich sei gefahren, I have ridden. Perfect Infinitive: getragen haben, gefahren sein, to have carried, ridden.

The **Pluperfect** is formed with the preterit of haben or sein: ich hatte getragen, subj. ich hätte getragen, I had borne; ich war gefahren, subj. ich wäre gefahren, I had ridden.

113. The past participles without ge- accompanied by an infinitive (see **108**, 1, 2), the modal auxiliaries and weak verbs which followed their analogy, form such tenses as these: Ich habe ihn gehen heißen, I have ordered him to leave. Sie haben einen Rock machen lassen, you have had a coat made or ordered a coat to be made. Der Knabe hat die Lektion nicht lernen können, the boy has not been able to learn the lesson. Er hat es nur sagen hören, he has only heard it said. Der Nachbar hat den Bettler arretieren lassen wollen (or wollen arretieren lassen), my neighbor wanted to have the beggar arrested.

114. The **Future** ind. and subj. is formed with the present of werden and the infinitive, *e. g.*, ich werde tragen, ich werde fahren, I shall carry, ride.

The **Future Perfect** is formed with the present of werden and the perfect infinitive, *e. g.*, ich werde getragen haben, ich werde gefahren sein, I shall have carried, ridden.

115. The first **Conditional** is formed with the preterit subj. of werden and the infinitive, *e. g.*, ich würde tragen or fahren, I should carry or ride.

The second or perfect **Conditional** is formed with the preterit subj. of werden and the perfect infinitive: ich würde getragen haben or gefahren sein, I should have carried or ridden.

Passive Voice.

116. The passive voice is formed by werben except in the imper. The tense of the auxiliary with the past participle of the verb forms the corresponding passive tense. Werben forms its compound tenses with sein and werben.

PRESENT : ich werde gelobt, I am praised, am being praised.
PRETERIT : ich ward or wurde gelobt, I was praised.
PERFECT : ich bin gelobt worden, I have been praised.
PLUPERFECT : ich war gelobt worden, I had been praised.
FUTURE : ich werde gelobt werden, I shall be praised.
FUTURE PERFECT : ich werde gelobt worden sein, I shall have been praised.
1. CONDITIONAL : ich würde gelobt werden, I should be praised.
2. or CONDITIONAL PERFECT : ich würde gelobt worden sein, 1 should have been praised.
IMPERATIVE : sei (du) gelobt, be (thou) praised.
seid (ihr) gelobt }
seien Sie gelobt } be (you) praised.
INFINITIVE : gelobt werden, to be praised.
gelobt worden sein, to have been praised.

Weak Conjugation.

117. The weak conjugation forms the principal parts by suffixing –te or –ete in the preterit: loben, lobte, retten, rettete; by prefixing ge– and suffixing –t or –et in the past participle: gelobt, gerettet. For the simple tenses see **103**, for the compound, **112-115**.

_{1. Verbs of this conjugation are with few exceptions derivative verbs, and most of them can be recognized as such by certain marks of derivation, such as suffixes (-eln, -ern, -igen, -leren, -sen, -schen) or umlaut. (But there are a few strong verbs with umlaut: lügen, trügen, gebären, etc.).}

118. 1. The connecting vowel always stands before t, whether personal suffix (3. p. sg. and 2. p. pl.) or in the participle and preterit, if the stem ends in b or t (th); if the stem ends in m and n, preceded by another consonant which is not m or n, *e. g.*, er rebet, ihr melbet, wir walteten, getröstet, er atmete, ich zeichnete.

Those in m and n have lost an e before these consonants. Compare them with their nouns: Atem, Zeichen. Those in n are often treated like those in el, er, to which they really belong (see sub 3): zeichente, regente. But these forms are not elegant.

2. The connecting vowel stands in the 2. p. sg. present ind. also after stems in ſ, ſch. ß, ſſ, z, tz, besides the stem-endings sub 1, *e. g.*, du rebeſt, walteſt, ſchmachteſt, rechneſt, reiſeſt, fiſcheſt, ſpaßeſt, faſſeſt, widmeſt, beizeſt, ſtutzeſt.

3. Verbs in -eln and -ern rarely show the connecting vowel *e, c. g.*, ich handelte, er handelt, gelächelt, wir wanderten. In the 1. p. sg. present ind. and subj., in the imperative 2. p. sg. they generally lose their own *e, e. g.*, ich wandle, wandre, ſchmeichle (du).

4. In solemn diction and in poetry any verb may retain the connecting vowel. On the other hand, the poet and the people take many liberties in the omission of it (sub 1 and 2). For instance, Das neue Haus iſt aufgerichtʼt (Uh.). Seid mir gegrüßt, befreundʼte Scharen! (Sch.). Neb'ſt du von einem der da lebet? (id.). Gegrüßet ſeid mir, eble Herrn! Gegrüßt ihr, ſchöne Damen (G.). See F. 3216, 3557. In fact though such full forms as du fiſcheſt, raſeſt, faſſeſt, putzeſt, etc., are written, one generally hears du fiſcht, raſt, faßt, putzt, etc. This applies also to strong verbs, *e. g.*, du wäſcht, ſtößt, reißt.

5. The present subj. nearly always shows full forms, but the preterit ind. and subj. have coincided: daß du liebeſt, ihr liebet; daß ich liebte, rebete.

Irregular Weak Verbs.

119. There are two groups of these verbs. One has a difference of vowel which looks like ablaut, the other has besides different vowels also a change in consonants.

1. The stems show nn or nd:

Inf.	Pret. ind.	Subj.	Past participle.
brennen	brannte	brennte	gebrannt
ſenden	ſandte	ſendete	geſandt

Here belong brennen, + burn; kennen, to be acquainted with, + ken; nennen, + name; rennen, + run; ſenden, + send; wenden, to turn, + wend, went. The last two have also a preterit ind. ſendete, wendete.

2. The stems show nf, ng. Here belong:

Inf.	Pret. ind.	Subj.	Past participle.
denken	dachte	dächte	gedacht
dünken	deuchte (däuchte)	deuchte	gedeucht
	dünkte	dünkte	gedünkt
bringen	brachte	brächte	gebracht

Strong Conjugation.

120. Strong verbs must have different stem-vowels in the preterit and present, since in this way difference of tense is expressed. But the vowel of the past participle may coincide with that of the present, as in geben, gab, gegeben v, fahren, fuhr, gefahren vi, halten, hielt, gehalten vii; or with that of the preterit, as in beißen, biß, gebissen i, biegen, bog, gebogen ii, glimmen, glomm, geglommen viii. The past participle ends in -en, and has the prefix ge-, *e. g.*, gestohlen, gerufen. For simple tenses see **103**.

121. The personal suffixes are the same as in weak verbs. Compare liebte, liebtest, liebte, etc.; sah, sahst, sah, etc. The imperative 2. p. sg. has no ending when the present ind. has interchange of e-i, ie, *e. g.*, ich berge, du birgst, er birgt; imp. birg; brechen—brich; essen—iß. This interchange of e-i, ie occurs in iii 3, iv, v; in verbs which do not have it there is no difference of stem-vowel in the imperative and the present, *e. g.*, halten—halt ; schwimmen—schwimm. But often e is added in analogy with weak verbs, always when the verb is either strong or weak, *e. g.*, rufen—rufe vii ; schlagen—schlage vi ; always webe, bewege, erwäge viii. In the last group there is of course no interchange of e-i, *e. g.*, du bewegst, er bewegt. When the stem ends in t, -tet in the 3. p. sg. is contracted to single t, if the stem-vowel changes. M. H. G. *giltet* > *gilt't* > *gilt*. *E. g.*, gelten — er gilt; fechten — er ficht; raten, rät; but reitet, schneidet. Special mention is made of these peculiarities under each class and verb. The preterit subj. always has umlaut and the 1. and 3. p. sg. end in e, *e. g.*, id) fab, bu fabft, er fab, etc.; but id) fäbe, bu fäbeft, er fäbe.

The verbs are best classified according to the ablaut-series. (See **393**.)

122. I. Class. Ablaut : ei   i, ie   i, ie.

1. Division : ei   i   i.

The stem ends in ß (ff), f, ch, t, d–t.

Examples: beißen, biß, gebiffen; fchleifen, fchliff, gefchliffen; fchreiten, fchritt, gefchritten; weichen, wich, gewichen; leiden, litt, gelitten.

The following verbs belong here : beißen, + bite ; bleichen (intrans.), + bleach, but also weak, always when trans.; fich befleißen, to apply one's self; gleichen, to be + like, strong since the 17th century, in the sense of + liken it is still weak, a N. H. G. distinction, M. H. G. only weak; gleißen, + glitter, nothing to do with the rare gleifen < gelihsen, to deceive, or entgleifen, to run off the track < Geleife, track ; gleiten, + glide ; greifen, to seize, + gripe ; greinen, + grin, rare and generally weak, grinfen, its derivative, has taken its place ; keifen, to quarrel, is strong or weak, < L. G. ; kneifen, to pinch, L. G. > N. H. G. ; kreifchen and kreißen, to scream, are related, both weak and strong, not H. G.; leiben, to suffer, + loathe ; pfeifen, to whistle, + pipe < L. pipare ; reißen, to tear, + write, draw ; reiten, + ride on horseback ; fchleichen, to sneak (+ slick and sleek) ; fchleifen, to grind, + slip, weak in the sense of " to drag, raze "; fchleißen, + slit, split ; fchmeißen, + smite, throw ; fchneiben, to cut ; fchreiten, to stride ; fpleißen, + split, L. and M. G. ; ftreichen, to wipe, cross, +strike, etc., with very varying meanings ; ftreiten, to strive ; weichen, to yield ; compare weich, + weak, wicker ; weak, it means to soak, soften.

2. Division : ei   ie   ie.

Examples : gebeihen, gebieh, gebiehen; reiben, rieb, gerieben.

Here belong: bleiben, to remain (+ leave); gebeihen, to thrive, the part. has a doublet, gebiehen, thriven, gebiegen, solid, pure ; leihen, to borrow, + lend ; meiben, to avoid ; preifen, + to praise, strong only since the 15th century, < Preis < M. H. G. *prīs* < O. Fr. *pris* < L. *prĕtium*, analogous to Fr. *priser ;* reiben, to rub (+ rive) ; fcheiben, to separate ; fcheinen, + shine ; fchreiben, to write (+ shrive) ; fchreien, to scream (?) ; fchweigen, to be silent, weak in the sense of " to still a child"; fpeien, to spit, + spew ; fteigen, to climb ; treiben, + to drive ; weifen, to point out, in the 16th century still weak ; zeihen, to accuse (+ indict).

123. Notice the interchange of b–t in the first division, e. g., ſchneiben, ſchnitt, geſchnitten ; but not in the second, viz., melben, mieb, gemieben ; ſcheiben, ſchieb, geſchieben. (See 416.) When the stem ends in ß or ſ, the 2. p. sg. present ind. is heard merely as ending in ſt, whether spelt so or not. The full form -eſt stands only in elevated diction, e. g., bu ſchmeißt, beißt, befleißt bich ; bu welfeſt and weiſt, bu preiſeſt and preiſt. (See 118, 4.) Notice also the doubling of t and ſ in ſchreiten, ſchritt ; ſtreiten, ſtritt ; ſchleifen, ſchliff, etc.

124. II. Class. Ablaut : ie (ü, au)   ŏ, ō   ŏ, ō.

1. Division : ie (au)   ŏ   ‾ ŏ.

The stem ends in ß (ſſ), ch, f, b–t.

Examples : fließen, floß, gefloſſen ; triefen, troff, getroffen.

Here belong : verdrießen, to disgust, vex ; fließen, + flow (+ fleet) ; gießen, to pour ; kriechen, + to crouch, creep (?) ; genießen, to enjoy ; riechen, to smell, + reek ; ſchießen, + to shoot ; ſchliefen, to slip, rare, supplanted by its derivative ſchlüpfen ; ſchließen, to close, lock ; ſprießen, + to sprout ; triefen, + to drip ; ſaufen, to drink (of animals) ; ſieben, see index.

2. Division : ie, ü, au   ō   ō.

Examples : fliegen, flog, geflogen ; trügen, trog, getrogen ; ſaugen, ſog, geſogen.

Here belong : 1. In ie : biegen, to bend ; bieten, to offer, + to bid ; fliegen, + to fly ; fliehen, + to flee ; frieren, + to freeze ; klieben, + to cleave, split ; ſchieben, + to shove ; ſtieben, to scatter ; verlieren, + to lose ; ziehen (zog, gezogen)), to draw.

2. In ü : küren (kieſen), + to choose ; lügen, + lie ; trügen, to deceive.

3. In au : ſaugen, + to suck ; ſchnauben (ſchnieben), to snort, L. and M. G. ; ſchrauben, to screw (+ ?), L. G. > late M. H. G.

2., 3. pers. sg. pres. show archaic forms sometimes in eu : fleußt, treucht, fleugt. (See 406.) Of those in au only ſaufen has umlaut, viz., ſäufſt, ſäuft. The stem ending in ß, the 2. p. sg. may be bu ſchießt, genießt. Notice the interchange of h–g in ziehen, zog, gezogen, but h is silent. (See 416.) Notice also the doubling of ſ : ſaufen, ſoff, etc.

125. III. Class. Ablaut : ĕ, i   ă   ŭ, ŏ.

1. Division : i   ă   ŭ.

The stem ends in n + cons. (d, g, k).

Examples : binden, band, gebunden ; ſpringen, ſprang, geſprungen.

Here belong : binben, + to bind ; bingen, to hire, originally and still at times weak, the isolated weak past part. bebingt is a regular adjective ; bringen, to penetrate ; finben, + to find ; gelingen, to be successful ; klingen, to be heard, resound ; ringen, to struggle, + wring ; schinben, + to skin, pret. schunb; schlingen, to twine, + sling, it also has the force of the now lost schlinben, to swallow ; schwinben, to disappear ; schwingen, + to swing ; singen, + to sing ; sinken, + to sink ; springen, + to spring ; stinken, + to stink ; trinken, + to drink ; winben, + to wind ; zwingen, to force.

2. Division : ĭ ă ŏ.
The stem ends in mm and nn.

Examples : spinnen, spann, subj. spänne and spönne, gesponnen; schwimmen, schwamm, schwämme and schwömme, geschwommen.

Here belong : beginnen, + to begin ; rinnen, to flow, + run ; sinnen, to think ; schwimmen, + to swim ; spinnen, + to spin ; gewinnen, + to win.

3. Division : e–i ă ŏ.
The stem ends in l, r + cons. except breschen.

Examples : helfen (hilft), half (hülfe, hälfe), geholfen ; werfen (wirst), warf (würfe), geworfen.

Here belong : bergen, to hide, + bury, burrow ; bersten, + to burst ; breschen, + to thrash ; gelten, to be worth, pass for ; helfen, + to help ; schelten, + to scold ; sterben, to die (+ starve) ; verberben, to spoil (intrans.) ; verberben (weak), to corrupt ; werben, to enlist, woo ; werben, to become, + worth (see 110) ; werfen, to throw (+ warp).

126. Notice the double preterits subj. (See 464, 3.) Sub 2, rinnen never has „ränne." The 3. division has generally and better ü, because you cannot tell „hälfe" from „helfe" by ear. Dreschen and bersten, once belonging to the next class, have brösche — brüsche, bärste — börste.

The 2. and 3. p. sg. present ind. have i instead of e. (See 403.) As to the suffix, bersten has bu birst, birstest, er birst; gelten, bu giltst (pronounced gilst), er gilt; werben, bu wirst, er wirb; schelten like gelten.

127. IV. Class. Ablaut : ă,ĕ,ĕ̄ — ĭ, ie ā ō, ŏ.
The stem contains l, r, m after or before the root-vowel.

Examples : brechen (brichst), brach (bräche), gebrochen ; stehlen (stiehlst), stahl (stähle, stöhle), gestohlen.

Here belong: brechen, + to break; gebären, + to bear, bring forth; befehlen, to command; empfehlen, to recommend; erschrecken (erschrak), to be frightened; nehmen, to take, + nim; sprechen, to speak; stechen, + to stick, stab; stehlen, + to steal; treffen (traf), to hit; kommen, kam, gekommen, + to come. (See 489, 1.)

Befehlen and empfehlen belonged to the III. Class, and have double subjunctives, beföhle — befähle, etc. So has stehlen, stöhle — stähle. The umlaut in gebären is only graphic for ē < ĕ. Those in -hl and gebären have ie in 2. and 3. p. sg. present ind.: empfiehlt, gebiert. The rest have i: trifft, spricht; du kömmst, er kömmt are quite common, but not elegant.

128. V. Class. Ablaut: i, ĕ, ē — i, ie   ā   ĕ, ē.

The stem ends in any sound but a liquid.

1. Division: e, ē — i, ie   ā   ĕ, ē.

Example: geben (giebst, gibst), gab (gäbe), gegeben.

Here belong: essen, + eat; fressen, + eat (said of animals); geben, + give; genesen, to recover; geschehen, to happen; lesen, to read; messen, + to measure, + mete; sehen, + to see; treten, + to tread; vergessen, + to forget; (wesen) war, gewesen, to be, + was.

2. Division: i, ie   ā   ĕ, ē.

Here belong: bitten, bat, gebeten, to ask, + bid; liegen, lag, gelegen, + to lie; sitzen, saß, gesessen, + to sit.

The form of the 2. and 3. persons sg. of the present ind. of verbs ending in ſſ is -ſt; of those in ſ is ſt for both persons: du, er iſt, vergißt, frißt; du, er lieſt. But geneſen, du, er geneſt, has no ie, probably because genieſt would have coincided with genießt < genießen, genoß, u.; du ſitzeſt may be contracted > ſitzſt, pronounced merely „ſitzt." The participle of eſſen, viz., gegeſſen, has ge- twice, because geeſſen was contracted into geſſen very early. This is now colloquial. (See F. 2838, 4415.) Notice du trittſt, er tritt; du bitteſt, er bittet.

129. VI. Class. Ablaut: ă, ā-ä   u   ă, ā.

The stem-vowel is short before more than one consonant.

Example: backen, (bäckst), buk (büke), gebacken.

Here belong: backen, + to bake, in N. G. generally weak; fahren, to ride, + fare; graben, to dig; laben, to invite, and laben, + load; laben (strong),

+ to load, and laben (weak), to invite, have been confounded since early N. H. G.; they are of different origin; ſchaffen (ſchuf), to create (weak, "to work"); ſchlagen, to strike, + slay; tragen, to carry; wachſen, to grow, + wax; waſchen, + to wash; (ſtehen), ſtund, ſtand (ſtünde, ſtände), geſtanden, + to stand, ſtund is still common in S. G.

Here belonged also formerly: heben (hebſt), hub, gehoben, to raise, + heave; ſchwören (ſchwörſt), ſchwur—ſchwor, geſchworen, + to swear. Fragen (frägſt), frug (but never gefragen), "to ask," are frequently heard; also jagen (jägſt), jug, "to chase." The forms are still frowned upon by grammarians because they are "wrong," but the people use them just the same.

In the 2. and 3. p. present ind. ă is the rule excepting ſchaffen, ſchaffſt, which is under the influence of the weak verb. Notice du and er wächſt, du wäſchſt (pronounced wäſcht). Isolated participles: gemahlen, ground; mahlen is now weak, mahlte, gemahlt, to grind; erhaben, lofty, < erheben, erhoben.

130. VII. Class. Characteristic is ie in the preterit, which is no ablaut, while the past participle always has the vowel of the infinitive.

For convenience we make two groups.

1. Division. The seeming ablaut is : ă, ā   ie   ă, ā.

ă before more than one consonant, ie = short i before -ng.

Examples: fangen (fängſt), fieng, gefangen; braten (brätſt, brät), briet, gebraten.

Here belong: blaſen, + blow, + blare (?); braten, to roast, fry; fallen (fiel), + to fall; fangen (rarer fahen), to catch; (gehen), gieng, gegangen, + go, went, gone; halten, + to hold; hangen, + to hang; laſſen, + to let, cause; raten, to advise; ſchlafen, + to sleep.

Umlaut is the rule in the 2. and 3. p. present ind. Notice du rätſt, er rät; du, er bläſt; du hältſt (pronounced „hälſt"), er hält; du läſſeſt or du, er läßt. The umlaut in this whole class is late; in later M. H. G. they have it rarely. The "Rules" prefer the spelling i to ie, viz., hing, fing, ging.

131. 2. Division: au, ei, ō, ū   ie   au, ei, ō, ū.

Here belong: hauen, hieb (b < w), gehauen, + to hew; laufen, lief, gelaufen, to run, + leap; heißen, hieß, geheißen, to call, command, + hight; ſtoßen (ſtieß), to kick, thrust; rufen (rief), to call.

Only ſtoßen and generally laufen take the umlaut: bu, er ſtößt; bu läufſt.

Scheiden, once of this class, has gone into I; „geheßen," according to I, is sometimes heard, but must still be rejected as incorrect. Of this class there are a great many isolated participles of verbs that have changed conjugation, *e. g.*, beſcheiden, modest (but beſchieben, "ordered"); geſchroten, rough-ground; geſalzen, + salt; geſpalten, "split"; gewalzen, rolled, etc. Ruſen, ruſte, geruſt is not correct.

132. VIII. Class. Characteristic is o in the preterit and past participle, long or short according to the following consonants.

The verbs belonging here are stragglers from all the other ablaut-series. There must be therefore a number that are still afloat; that is, according to the usage of the period in which they are taken, they belong to their regular class or to this. Present usage in the spoken language always favors o — o, *e. g.*, ſchwören, ſchwor, geſchworen, VI; dreſchen, broſch, gebroſchen, III; heben, hob, gehoben, VI, which have been assigned by us, however, to their proper classes. Lügen, II, and trügen, II, have sprung from liegen and triegen under the influence of the nouns Lüge, Trug. They might be classed here; as also füren, II, for fieſen; compare the noun Kur(-fürſt), elector.

**133. The vowels of the present may be e, i, a, ä, ö.
The ablaut is most frequently   e   o   o.**

We count here: bellen (bellt, billt), to bark, III; fechten (fichtſt, ficht), + to fight, IV, III; flechten (flichtſt, pronounced flichſt, flicht), to braid, IV, III; pflegen, to carry on, undertake, V, IV, in the sense of "to be accustomed," "to care for," always weak; melken (melkt and milkt), + to milk III; quellen (quillt), to swell, gush, III; ſchellen (ſchillt archaic), generally ſchallen the weak verb, "to resound," weak = to cause to resound, ring, III; ſchmelzen (ſchmilzſt, ſchmilzt), + to melt, III; ſchwellen (ſchwillt), + to swell, III; weben (webſt), strong and weak, + to weave, V; bewegen (bewegſt), to induce, weak = to move, V; glimmen, to glow, III, 2; klimmen, + to climb, III, 2; gären (gärt), to ferment, also weak, IV; erwägen (erwägſt), to consider; wägen or wiegen (if ie, II), wägſt, wiegſt, + to weigh (-wägen, wiegen, -wegen are in M. H. G. the same word, V); rächen (rächt), + to wreak, sometimes has roch, gerochen, but is generally weak, IV; erlöſchen, intrans., to die out (of a flame), (erliſcheſt, erliſcht), but trans. löſchen, to extinguish, III; verwirren, to confuse, III, is generally weak, but has an isolated participle, verworren = intricate, complicated; ſcheren (ſchierſt, ſchiert) + shear, IV, is sometimes weak.

ANOMALOUS VERBS.

I. The Preterit-Present Verbs.

134. To this group belong the modal auxiliaries and wiſſen. They are originally strong verbs, whose preterits are used as presents. New preterits, past participles, and infinitives were formed weak. The infinitives, the present plural, and the new strong participle have the same vowel, sometimes with an irregular umlaut : können (inf.), wir können, können (past part.). The different vowels of the present in the sg. and pl. weiß, wiſſen; the subjunct., with umlaut, mag, möge; the lack of t in the 3. p. sg., er mag, are still traces of their strong conjugation. The weak preterit was formed without connecting vowel, and has umlaut in the subjunctive : mögen, mochte, möchte, gemocht. (See **119**, 2, and **454**, 3.) The strong participle in –en stands in the compound tenses, when an infinitive depends upon the auxiliary: ich habe ſchreiben müſſen, but ich habe gemußt. An imperative, the meaning permitting, is made up from the subjunctive, *e.g.*, wolle, möge.

135. 1. Wiſſen, ɪ, to know, + to wit (wot, he wist).

Inf.	Pret. ind.	Subj.	Participles.
wiſſen	wußte	wüßte	{ wiſſend { gewußt

The pres. ind. inflects: ich weiß, du weißt, er weiß, wir wiſſen, ihr wiſſ(e)t, ſie wiſſen. Subj.: ich wiſſe, wiſſeſt, wiſſe, etc. Imp.: wiſſe, wiſſet, wiſſen Sie.

2. Dürfen, ɪɪɪ, to be permitted.

Inf.	Pres. sg.	Pret. ind.	Subj.	Past part.
dürfen	darf	durfte	dürfte	{ gedurft { dürfen

Pres. ind.: darf, darfſt, darf, dürfen, dürſt, dürfen. Subj.: dürfe, dürfeſt, dürfe, etc.

ANOMALOUS VERBS.

3. Können, III, to be able, + can.

Inf.	Pres. sg.	Pret. ind.	Subj.	Past part.
können	kann	konnte	könnte	{ gekonnt { können

Pres. ind.: kann, kannst, kann, können, etc. Subj.: könne, könnest, könne, etc. Imp.: könne, könnt, können Sie.

4. Mögen, V, IV, to be able, + may.

Inf.	Pres. sg.	Pret. ind.	Subj.	Past part.
mögen	mag	mochte	möchte	{ gemocht { mögen

Just like können.

5. Sollen, IV, + shall.

Inf.	Pres. sg.	Pret. ind. and subj.	Past part.
sollen	soll	sollte	{ gesollt { sollen

Pres. ind.: soll, sollst, soll, sollen, etc.

This is almost entirely weak now. The vowel-difference in the pres. has been levelled away. Comp. Eng. shall, should.

6. Müssen, VI, + must.

Inf.	Pres. sg.	Pret. ind.	Subj.	Past part.
müssen	muß	mußte	müßte	{ gemußt { müssen

Pres. ind.: muß, mußt, muß. Subj.: müsse, etc.

This too is almost entirely weak.

7. Wollen, I, + will.

Inf.	Pres. sg.	Subj.	Ind. and subj. Pret.	Past part.
wollen	will	wolle	wollte	{ gewollt { wollen

Pres. ind.: will, willst, will, wollen, wollt, wollen. (See **472**, 2.)

II. The verbs g e h n, + to go, s t e h n, + to stand, t h u n, + to do.

136. 1. Geh(e)n.

Pres. ind.: ich gehe, du gehst, er geht, wir gehn, ihr geht, sie gehn.
Subj.: ich gehe, du gehest, er gehe, etc.
Imp. sg.: geh; pl., geht, gehen Sie. Part.: gehend.
Pret. ind.: ich gieng. Subj.: ich gienge.
Part.: gegangen. According to VII; from a stem "*gang.*"

2. Steh(e)n.

Pres. ind.: ich stehe, du stehst, er steht, wir stehn, ihr steht, sie stehn.
Subj.: ich stehe, du stehest, er stehe, etc.
Imp. sg.: steh; pl., steht, stehen Sie. Part.: stehend.
Pret. ind.: ich stand (stund). Subj.: stände (stünde).
Part.: gestanden. According to VI; from a stem "*stand.*"

3. Thun.

Pres. ind.: ich thue, du thust, er thut, wir thun, ihr thut, sie thun.
Subj.: ich thue, du thuest, er thue, wir thun, ihr thut, sie thuen.
Imp. sg.: thu; pl., thut, thun Sie. Part.: thuend.
Pret. ind.: ich that, du thatst, er that, wir thaten, ihr thatet, sie thaten. Subj.: ich thäte, du thätest, er thäte, etc.
Part.: gethan.

The full forms with e of these three verbs are not used in the indicative. The h is merely graphic, and is not pronounced, *e. g.*, ich geve is not ge-he, but ge or ge'e.

137. The **compound verbs** are not inflected differently from the simple verbs. Notice the position of the separable prefix, and ge- in separable compound verbs: ich schreibe an, schrieb an; imp. schreibe (du) an, ich habe angeschrieben, ich werde anschreiben. The separable prefix stands apart from the verb in the simple tenses (pres. and pret.), but only in main clauses; ge-, zu- stand between prefix and verb, angeschrieben, anzuschreiben. Ex.: Ich schreibe, schrieb den Brief ab, but während ich den Brief abschrieb (dependent clause). In inseparable compounds notice the participle has no ge : ich verstehe, verstand, habe verstanden, werde verstehn. (See **108**, 3.)

1. Notice a class of inseparable compounds derived from compound nouns. These have ge. They can be easily recognized by the chief stress falling on the first element: das Frü'hstück, verb frü'hstücken, frühstückte, gefrühstückt, to breakfast; der Ra'tschlag, verb ra'tschlagen, ratschlagte, geratschlagt, to take council.

138. Additional examples of verb inflections.

1. Strong presents with the second persons sing. and pl. of the imperative.

a. streiten, strive, I. ; ich streite, du streitest, er streitet, wir streiten, ihr streitet, sie streiten ; streite, streitet.

b. bitten, ask, V. ; ich bitte, du bittest, er bittet, wir bitten, ihr bittet, sie bitten ; bitte, bittet.

c. tragen, carry, VI. ; ich trage, du trägst, er trägt, wir tragen, ihr traget, sie tragen ; trage, traget.

d. raten, advise, VII. ; ich rate, du rätst, er rät, wir raten, ihr ratet, sie raten ; rate, ratet.

2. Reflexive verb : sich sehnen, to long.

a. Present : ich sehne mich, du sehnst dich, er sehnt sich, wir sehnen uns, ihr sehnt euch, sie sehnen sich.

b. Perfect : ich habe mich gesehnt, du hast dich gesehnt, er hat sich gesehnt, wir haben uns gesehnt, ihr habt euch gesehnt, sie haben sich gesehnt.

3. Separable compound and reflexive verb : sich anmelden, announce one's self.

a. Present : ich melde mich an, du meldest dich an, er meldet sich an, wir melden uns an, ihr meldet euch an, sie melden sich an.

b. Perfect : ich habe mich angemeldet, du hast dich angemeldet, er hat sich angemeldet, wir haben uns angemeldet, ihr habt euch angemeldet, sie haben sich angemeldet.

FIRST PART.

SECOND SECTION.

SYNTAX.

SYNTAX.

139. For practical reasons we divide the Syntax into **Special** and **General Syntax**.

The **Special** treats of the function of the word, inflected or uninflected, in a sentence.

The **General** treats of the combination of words into a sentence, of the word-order, and of the combination of clauses into a compound sentence.

It is of course difficult to keep these two divisions separate, as in fact all the different branches of grammar. Thus the separation of inflection and function, of phonology and inflection, of word-formation and syntax is a violent one. The division into special and general syntax is the custom of French grammarians, who have succeeded best in freeing their grammatical system from the strait-jacket of Latin and Greek grammars.

SPECIAL SYNTAX.

The parts of speech are treated here in the same order as they are in the Accidence.

Syntax of the Article.

140. The use of the demonstrative pronoun as definite article is much older than that of the numeral „ein" as indefinite article. „Ein" was used where the definite article could not stand; hence the plural of ein Mann is still Männer. In O. H. G. the article is still lacking; its use spread in M. H. G., so that now it is almost a necessity.

Some General Cases of Absence of the Article.

141. Proper names, names of materials always when preceded by nouns expressing quantity and measure, have no article. Ex.: Goethe erreichte ein hohes Alter. Schiller starb verhältnismäßig jung. Blei ist weicher als Gold. Ein Pfund Zucker.

142. No noun preceded by a genitive can take an article: Des Denkens Faden ist zerrissen (F. 1748). Der alten Götter bunt Gewimmel (G.).

143. There is no article before nouns (connected by und, weder, noch or unconnected) in certain set and adverbial phrases; in an enumeration of objects belonging to the same class or genus. Ex.: Geld und Gut. Haus und Hof. Mit Gott für König und Vaterland. In Saus und Braus. Sinn und Verstand verlier' ich schier (F. 2504). Nicht irdisch ist des Thoren Trank noch Speise (F. 301). Soll ich mit Griffel, Meißel, Feder schreiben? (F. 1732). Urahne, Großmutter, Mutter und Kind in dumpfer Stube beisammen sind (Schwab). Zu Tisch, zu Bette, Haus an Haus, Stein auf Stein, nach Osten, gen Süden, von Norden (but notice im Osten, im Süden, etc.

144. All pronouns exclude the article, except solch, manch, welch, was für, which allow an indefinite article after them, and all(e), which allows the definite article after it; e. g.: Was soll all der Schmerz und Lust (G.). Welch ein geschäftig Volk eilt ein und aus (id.). Was für ein Landsmann bist du, Jäger? (Sch.).

145. An abstract noun, and any noun denoting profession, rank, position have no article in the predicate after neuter verbs; e. g.: Philokte't, der ganz Natur ist, bringt auch den Neoptole'm zu seiner Natur wieder zurück (Le.). Heiße Magister; heiße Doctor gar (F. 360). (Ich) bin Soldat, komme niemals wieder (Sch.), Eng., I am *a* soldier.

146. 1. In technical phrases some nouns and adjectives used as such take no article: Schreiber dieses, the writer of this; Kläger, plaintiff; Besagter; Gedachter; Obiges; Folgendes, etc. In headings: Ueber Anmut und Würde (Sch.). Casuslehre, Flexionslehre.

2. In folk-lore and folk-songs: Rotkäppchen, Little Red Riding-hood; Schneewittchen. Knabe sprach: ich breche dich. Röslein sprach: ich steche dich (G.). Thürchen knarrt. Mäuslein pfeift.

Article with Proper Nouns.

147. The rule is: no article before proper nouns just as in English.

1. Names of persons may take an article when the bearer is

well known and his name has become a common noun; to express familiarity and intimacy, also contempt; to mark gender and case more clearly (this applies also to names of places and countries); when the author's or artist's name is used for his work; before names of planets, of ships, of the characters of a play, of titles of books taken from a person. Ex.: Ein Waſhington, der Welfe, die Ottonen. Schiller's Tell and Wallenstein, Goethe's Götz and Lessing's M. von Barnhelm are full of examples of the second use (familiarity, etc.). Die Büſte des Sokrates. Wär' ich dem Ferdinand geweſen, was Octavio mir war . . . (Sch.). Läßt ſich nennen den Wallenſtein (Sch.) (contempt). Devrient ſpielte den Nathan. Mein Freund hat den Corot verkauft (painting by Corot). Der Herkules iſt beſchädigt.

2. Names of countries and provinces which are not neuter take the definite article. Most of these are feminine and a few masculine, viz., compounds: der Breisgau, Rheingau, der Sundgau; also der Haag (+the Hague); der, das Elſaß. Feminines in -ei: die Türkei', Wallachei'; in -au: die Moldau, die Wetterau; in -mark: die Neumark, die Oſtmark; die Lauſitz, die Schweiz, die Krimm, die Levante, die Pfalz. Some neuters in -land: das Vogtland, das Wendtland, die Niederlande, pl.

3. Names of oceans, lakes, straits, rivers, mountains, and forests always have the definite article, *e. g.*, das Mittelmeer, die Oſtſee, der Bodenſee, der Belt, der Sund, der Rhein, die Donau, der Harz, der Speſſart, die Alpen, der Schwarzwald.

4. Names of the seasons, months, days of the week, of the streets of a city: „Der Winter iſt ein Ehrenmann" (Claudius). Im Januar, des Sonntags, auf or in der Kaiſerſtraße, im Frühling.

148. Appellatives have an article as in English: die Thräne quillt, die Erde hat mich wieder (F. 784). For exceptions see **141-146**.

149. Abstract nouns have no article when they denote a characteristic or state of mind: Mut zeiget auch der Mameluck;

Gehorsam ist des Christen Schmuck (Sch.). Freude war in Troja's Hallen (id.) Krieg ist ewig zwischen List und Argwohn (id.). But when they denote an act or motion they are treated as appellatives. They may also take the article that has generalizing force, e. g., Der Tod ist der Sünden Sold (B.). Die Wahl steht dir noch frei (Sch.). Die Kunst ist lang und kurz ist unser Leben (F. 558-9). Die Botschaft hör' ich wohl, allein mir fehlt der Glaube (F. 765). Das war ein Schuß! (Sch.).

150. Names of materials have the generalizing article, which denotes the whole kind or substance, or an article that singles out a certain kind or quantity, e. g., Der Wein erfreut des Menschen Herz (B.). Das Gold ist kostbar. Die Steinkohle ist schwarz oder braun. Without article: Silber und Gold habe ich nicht (B.). Blut ist geflossen (Sch.). Laß mir den besten Becher Weins in purem Golde reichen (G.).

151. Collective nouns take an article except when taken in a partitive sense: Was rennt das Volk? (Sch.). Weit dahinten war noch das Fußvolk (id.). Wir haben Fußvolk und Reiterei (id.).

152. All classes of nouns qualified by an adjective, by a genitive, by a relative clause, etc., take an article in the singular, excepting names of materials and nouns in the vocative, in the predicate or in certain adverbial phrases. The plural has the definite article or none. Ex.: Der kleine Gott der Welt bleibt stets von gleichem Schlag (F. 281). Der Gott, der Eisen wachsen ließ . . . (Arndt). Die Hauptstadt von Frankreich. But (Sie) sprachen laut voll hohen Sinns und Gefühles (G.). Nach alter Weise. Es gab schönre Zeiten als die unsern (Sch.). Der alte Barbarossa (Uh.).

153. The genitive preceding a noun always has the article except a proper name: In des Marmors kalte Wangen (Sch.). In des Waldes Mitte (id.). Schiller's „an Ufer's Rand" Goethe would have made a compound, „Ufersrand." Comp. „Bergeshöhle" and other compounds of Goethe.

154. The definite article stands for an Eng. possessive pronoun, when the possessor cannot be mistaken. There may or may not be a personal pronoun as object in the sentence. Ex.: Der Kopf thut mir so weh (Song). Habt ihr mir den Finger blos genommen? (Sch.). (Sie) rührt ihm leise die Schulter (H. and D. 4, 63). See **243**, 3.

155. 1. In S. G. the definite article is always applied to members of the family instead of the possessive pronouns. In N. G., as in Eng., no article is necessary: Grüß' den Vater und Vaters Brüder! (Sch.).

2. As with proper names so names of materials and abstract nouns often have the definite article in the genitive and dative merely to show the case: der Milch Wasser vorziehen.

156. The definite article is used in German for the indefinite in English in a distributive sense: Butter kostet anderthalb Mark das Pfund, a pound; dieses Tuch kostet 90 Pfennig(e) die Elle; fünfmal das Jahr or im Jahre. This "a" in Eng. represents the preposition "on," and is not the indefinite article.

157. Ein can stand in German before certain indefinite pronouns and neuter adj. where it does not stand in Eng.: ein jeder, ein jeglicher, ein solcher, ein mancher (better manch einer); ein festes, = a fixed sum; ein mehreres, = more; ein weniges, = little. Ich schreibe nächstens ein mehreres.

Repetition of the Article.

158. Before each of several nouns of different gender the article must be repeated if it stand at all: Der Vater, die Mutter die gingen vor des Hauptmanns Haus (Song). If two nouns, connected by und, denote different persons the article should be repeated: Der Onkel und Pathe des Kindes war bei der Taufe zugegen (one person). But der Onkel und der Pathe . . . (two persons).

Both rules are often offended against by Luther, Goethe, and Lessing, and frequently in the spoken language: Wenn man den Maler und Dichter mit einander vergleichen will . . . (Le.).

The article before an apposition is treated as in English.

SYNTAX OF THE GENDER.

159. The grammatical gender of nouns is threefold, masculine, feminine, neuter. As to living beings, the nouns denoting males are masculine, and those denoting females feminine. Ex.: der Fuchs, Löwe, der gute Mann, Neffe, Knecht, Ochs, Bock; die Kuh, Ziege, Base, schöne Magd, die Sau, Stute.

1. Exceptions: nouns denoting the young of animals, diminutives, and das Weib, das Mensch (see **59**), das Frauenzimmer are neuter. Ex.: das Ferkel, Füllen, Kalb, Mädchen, Fräulein.

2. Any grammatical gender is ascribed to the names of the species without regard to sex. Neuter: das Pferd, das Schwein, das Schaf, das Reh. Fem.: die Nachtigall, Ameise, Biene, Maus, Ratte. Masc.: der Fisch, Hase, Dachs, Luchs.

160. Where the grammatical gender does not coincide with the natural, the following rules may be of service, based on the meanings of nouns and on their derivation. See **159**, 1.

GENDER ACCORDING TO MEANING.

1. Masculine are:

The names of the points of compass, of the winds, seasons, months, days of the week; of mammals (a few small ones like die Maus, die Ratte excepted), most of the larger birds, most fish, and stones.

Ex.: der Nord or Norden; Sommer; Februar, August; Montag, Sonnabend; der Esel, Löwe, Elefant; der Strauß, Adler, Storch; der Hai, Aal, Karpfen (all compounds with –fisch, of course, as der Walfisch, Klippenfisch); der Kiesel, Diama'nt, Feldspat.

2. Feminine are:

The names of most rivers, trees, plants, and flowers (in –e), insects, small singing birds, and nearly all derivative abstract nouns.

Ex.: die Weſer, Oder, Elbe; die Eiche, Tanne, Buche; die Nelke, Roſe, Rübe, Neſſel, Kartoffel; die Ameiſe, Wanze, Biene; die Nachtigall, Schwalbe, Lerche; also die Krähe, Eule. Die Liebe, Tugend, Jugend, Demut, Freundlichkeit, etc.

3. Neuter are:

The names of places and countries except those always having the article (see **147**, 2), collective nouns (particularly those with Ge-); most names of materials including metals, of the letters of the alphabet; other parts of speech used as nouns, particularly adjectives not denoting persons (see **169**).

Ex.: „das ſchöne Spanien," „ein klein Paris," das Volk, Heer, Gebirge, Geſchütz; das Holz, Heu, Schmalz, Obſt; das Eiſen, Blei, Kupfer, Zinn; das W, Y; das Bummeln, „Das Wenn und das Aber," das Gute, das Wahre, das Schöne.

REMARK.—So many rivers are feminine because they are compounded with -aha (+ Lat. aqua): Weſer and Werra < Weserâ(h), Werraha; die Salza(ch). But notice der Rhein, Main. Die Schweiz, Türkei have the article really on account of their exceptional gender. American rivers are masculine: der Hudſon, der Mohawk.

161. GENDER ACCORDING TO DERIVATION AND ENDINGS.

1. Masculine are:

Most monosyllabics by ablaut, e. g., der Spruch, Sproß, Stich, Schirm; those in -er, -ler, -ner (denoting agents); in -el (denoting instrument); all in -ling; many in -en; dissyllabics in -e according to the n-declension (denoting living beings); in -ich.

Ex.: der Schreiber, Künſtler, Pförtner; der Deckel, Hebel, der Frembling, Günſtling, Säugling; der Segen, Degen; corresponding to Eng. -om, Buſen, Beſen; der Knabe, Löwe, Bote; Gänſerich, Wüterich, Fittich.

2. Feminine are:

Many dissyllabics (by ablaut, see **496**) in -e; abstract nouns in -e, mainly from adjectives; in -ie, mostly foreign; many in

–t; all in –ei, –in, –ung, –heit, –keit, –schaft: some in –nis and –sal; foreign ones in –age (see **163**, 5).

Ex.: die Größe, Höhe; die Sprache, Gabe; die Philosophie, Galanterie; die Haft, Macht, Kraft; die Jägerei, Juristerei, Melodei; die Freundin, Lehrerin; die Duldung, Widmung; die Freiheit, Frömmigkeit; Freundschaft; die Wildnis, Fäulnis; die Blamage, Courage.

3. Neuter are:

All in –chen, –lein; most in –sel, –sal, –nis, –tum; nearly all of the form Ge–e or Ge– without e; some in –el.

Ex.: das Hündchen, Knäblein; das Rätsel, Überbleibsel; das Schicksal, Labsal; das Gedächtnis, Vermächtnis; das Königtum, Christentum (only two masc., der Reichtum and Irrtum); das Gefilde, Gemälde; das Gebild, Geschick; das Bündel, Gesindel, and the S. G. diminutives das Rindel, Bübel, etc.

On the whole the gender of nouns has changed very little in the history of the language. Ex. of changes are: die Sitte < O. H. G. *der situ*, already M. H. G. sometimes *diu site*. Die Blume was O. H. G. both masc. and fem. Die Fahne was O. H. G. *der fano*.

162. The following groups of nouns have varying genders, though some are of the same origin and have the same meaning. They should be fully treated in the dictionary, to which the student is referred. Only a few examples are given in each group.

1st group. The same form and meaning, but double gender (m. and n.); der and das Meter, Thermome'ter, Barome'ter, Bereich, Schrecken, Zeug, etc.

2d group. Double gender (m. and f.) with varying forms, but the same meaning and origin: der Schurz — die Schürze; der Trupp — die Truppe; der Quell — die Quelle; der Spalt — die Spalte.

3d group. Double gender, the same form in sg. and pl. if the plural be formed of both genders, but of different meaning and sometimes of different origin (the latter with *).

GENDER OF FOREIGN WORDS.

All adjectives: ber Gute, + the good man; bie Gute, + the good woman; pl. bie Guten.

ber Heibe, heathen	bie Heibe, heath	pl. bie Heiben
*ber Bulle, bull	bie Bulle (document)	bie Bullen
ber Erbe, heir	bas Erbe, inheritance	bie Erben
ber Verbienft, earnings	bas Verbienft, desert, merit	bie Verbienfte
*ber Geifel, hostage	bie Geißel, scourge	bie Geißeln -feln
*ber Meffer, measurer	bas Meffer, knife	bie Meffer

There are perhaps forty in all.

4th group. Double gender, double plural, but different meaning and sometimes different origin (the latter marked *). Perhaps a dozen or more.

ber Banb, volume	pl. Bänbe	bas Banb, ribbon	pl. Bänber
*ber Marfch, march	Märfche	bie Marfch, marsh	Marfchen
ber Schilb, shield	Schilbe	bas Schilb, sign-board	Schilber
*ber Thor, fool	Thoren	bas Thor, gate	Thore

GENDER OF FOREIGN WORDS.

163. Foreign words retain generally the original gender: bie Pein < L. *pœna*, later *pēna;* bas Klofter < L. *claustrum;* ber Kerfer < L. *carcer(em)*.

Many have changed gender for various reasons. They were fully Germanized and followed German models according to ending or meaning, or they followed French (Romance) rules. Some changes are difficult to account for.

1. Examples of neuter nouns that became masculine, masculines that became neuter, and feminines that became neuter: ber Pala'ft, < *palatium;* ber Balfam, < *balsamum;* ber Mantel, < *mantellum;* ber Preis, < *prētium;* ber Punft, < *punctum.* Neuter nouns in –at: bas Konfula't, < *consulatus;* bas Forma't, *formatum* or –*us;* bas Ries, < V. L. *risma* (f.); bas Kreuz, < *cruc(em)* (f.).

2. Examples of nouns that have changed gender in analogy with German words similar in meaning and ending: ber Ziegel, < *tegula;* ber

Marmor, *marmor*, n., on account of der Stein (see **160**, 1); der Körper, < *corpus*, n.; der Kada'ver, < *cadaver*, n., on account of der Leib, der Leichnam, and the many masculines in -er; die Nummer, < *numerus*, since die Zahl. Europa, Sparta, Athen, Troja, now all neuter (see **160**, 3).

3. Nouns in *-arium, -orium, -erium, -are*, became all masculine in analogy with H. G. words in -er, < *œre* < *ari :* der Alta'r, < *altare;* der Keller, < *cellarium;* der Psalter, < *psalterium;* der Weiher, < O. H. G. *wiwâri* < *vivarium;* der Piaster, < It. *piastra*, f., < V. L. *plastrum*.

4. Neuter nouns, whose plural ended in *-a* in Gr. or L., became feminine in German from analogy with feminines in -e, < *â*, and also through Romance influence: die Bibel, < *biblion*, V. L. *biblia;* die Orgel, < *organum, -a;* die Pfründe, < V. L. *provenda* (pl.); die Stubie, < *studium;* die Prämie, < *præmium*.

5. Words in *-a'ge*, masculine and feminine in French, are all feminine in G., *e. g.*, die Baga'ge, die Blama'ge, die Coura'ge, etc. Die Schrift, < *scriptum*, die Pacht, < *pactum*, are due to analogy with G. nouns in -t, viz., die Fracht, Sicht, Schicht, Macht, etc.

GENDER OF COMPOUND NOUNS.

164. Compound nouns have the gender of the last noun: der Birnbaum, die Hausthür, das Schilderhaus, das Frauenzimmer (lady).

EXCEPTIONS: *a.* Many compounds with -mut: die Demut, die Wehmut, die Sanftmut; but der Hochmut, der Freimut, etc. They are, however, only seeming exceptions, -mut going back to compounds with O. H. G. and M. H. G. *-muot*, m., and *-muoti*, f. This has given rise to the double gender of the same noun: O. H. G. *hôhmuoti*, f. only, but M. H. G. *hochmüete, hochmuot,* f., and *hochmuot*, m.; die Demut, < M. H. G. *diemüete, diemuot*, always feminine: der Kleinmut, die Anmut, die Großmut; also der Großmut; always der Hochmut. For Armut, which is no compound with -mut, see **511**, 2, *a*.

b. Der Abscheu seems an exception, because die Scheu is old and more common than der Scheu.

c. Names of cities and places are neuter even if ending in nouns of different gender: das schöne Hamburg, Lüneburg, Annaberg, etc.; but die Wartburg, Herrenburg, because these are castles, = Burgen, f., and not towns.

d. Der Mittwoch (Woche, f.) appears by the side of the legitimate die Mittwoch, already in M. H. G. It has followed the other days of the week, which are all masculine. (See 160. 1.)

e. Die Antwort had double gender in O. H. G., but the neuter was more common. Luther has still die and das Antwort.

Concord of Genders.

165. This subject can be best treated under the head of concords as between noun and adjective, noun and pronoun, subject and predicate. The general rule that adjectives and pronouns take the grammatical gender of the noun to which they refer is only set aside when the grammatical gender does not coincide with the sex. In that case the pronoun or adjective can take the natural gender.

166. Mädchen, Mägblein, Weib, Fräulein admit of this construction according to the sense, most commonly; not so, Kind, Frauenzimmer, Männlein, Söhnlein, and the other diminutives: Und schnell war ihre Spur verloren, sobald das Mädchen Abschied nahm (Sch.). Jenes Mädchen ist's, das vertriebene, die du gewählt hast (H. and D., IV. 210). Du gebenedeiete unter den Weibern (B.). Sie unglücklicher, Sie unglückliche, you unhappy man, woman. The adjective therefore also agrees with the sex.

Fräulein and the diminutives of names of females have „die" sometimes in colloquial language: die Fräulein, die Sophie'chen, die Dortchen (Dorothy). But „Ihre Fräulein Tochter" is quite common and correct: Ihre Fräulein Tochter . . . war ausgelassen (unrestrained) (G.).

167. Names in the predicate, not capable of forming a feminine from a masculine, like Lehrerin < Lehrer, Vorsteherin < Vorsteher, of course retain the grammatical gender, no matter what the sex of the subject: Sie ward . . . gleich mit besonderer Achtung als Gast behandelt (G.). But even predicate nouns capable of forming a feminine by suffix if used in the abstract sense, and not the personal, form an exception, *e. g.*, Herr, Meister sein or werden, "to be or become master of." Denn ich bin euer König (Sch.). Sie war der Verbrecher (id.).

168. The neuter pronouns (es, jedes, das, alles, etc.) may refer to a masc. or fem. noun, even to the plural and to a masc. and fem. noun together: Sie kommen hervor ein Weib da, ein Mann . . . das recht nun, es will sich ergetzen sogleich, die Knöchel zur Runde, = they stretch their bones for the dance, eager to enjoy themselves (in Goethe's „Totentanz"). Alles rennet, rettet, flüchtet (Sch.). Da mag denn Schmerz und Genuß, Gelingen und Verdruß mit einander wechseln wie es kann (F. 1756-8). Stillschweigend hörten sie (three persons) zu, indem jedes in sich selbst zurückkehrte (G.).

169. When adjectives are used substantively, the masculine and feminine denote sex, the neuter an abstract noun or thing: der Gute, die Gute, the good man, woman; das Gute, the good (abstract). Komm' herab, o holde Schöne, und verlaß dein stolzes Schloß (Sch.). Du hast Herrliches vollbracht (id.). Das Böse, das ich nicht will, das thue ich (B.).

SYNTAX OF SINGULAR AND PLURAL.

170. Names of persons and materials can take a plural only when they denote several persons, species, or kinds, viz., die Heinriche, die Berthas, die Öle (the various kinds of oil), die Gräser, die Fette, die Salze.

171. Abstract nouns do not as a rule admit of a plural, but as in English the plurals of such nouns were once quite common, viz., Minne, Gnade, Wonne, Huld, Ehre. Some of these plurals are left in certain phrases: in Ehren, zu Ehren; von Gottes Gnaden; zu Schulden kommen lassen, to be guilty of; Ew. Gnaden; die Herrschaften. Compare Eng. thanks, loves (in Shakspere), favors, regards.

172. To the sg. -mann in composition corresponds often -leute, pl. only, which in sense really corresponds to Mensch, Menschen, without regard to sex. Examples: Edelmann — Edelleute, gentry; Landmann, peasant, — Landleute, country folk; Ehemann, married man, — Eheleute, married people; but the pl. Ehemänner means "married men"; Fuhrmann — Fuhrleute, drivers, carters; Kaufmann — Kaufleute, merchants, etc. But Biedermann, honest man; **Ehrenmann**, man of honor; **Staatsmann**, and a few more, form only the regular plural in -er.

173. For certain nouns which form no plural, plural compounds are used, some of which have also a singular.—*E. g.*:

das Feuer	die Feuersbrünste
der Tod	die Todesfälle
der Rat	die Ratschläge
der Dank	die Danksagungen

174. Nouns only used in the plural are:

a. Diseases: **Blattern, Masern, Röteln**.

b. Certain dates: **Ostern, Pfingsten, Weihnachten, Ferien, Fasten, in Wochen** = in childbed.

c. Names of relationship: **Eltern; Gebrüder,** brothers, as **Gebrüder Grimm,** the brothers Grimm, but generally only in the names of firms; **Geschwister,** brothers and sisters, rarely in the sg. = brother and sister; other nouns as **Gefilde, Zinsen, Briefschaften, Einkünfte,** etc.

175. Masc. and neuter nouns denoting quantity, weight, extent, preceded by numerals, stand in the singular, but fem. nouns (except **Mark**) in the plural as in Eng., *e. g.*, 6 **Glas Bier,** 10 **Faß Wein;** „an die dreimal hunderttausend Mann" (Song of Prince Eugene), 5 **Fuß tief,** 3 **Mark** 70 **Pfennig(e),** 70 × 7 = **siebenzig mal sieben mal** (B.). Feminines: 3 **Meilen breit,** 10 **Flaschen Portwein,** 12 **Stunden.** The coins, **das Jahr, der Monat, Schritt** generally stand in the plural, *e. g.*, 50 **Pfennige machen** 5 **Groschen,** 3 **Dukaten,** 20 **Schritte lang;** yet also sing., „90 **Jahr—gebückt zum Tode";** 7 **Monat(e) alt;** but **zehn Mark.**

176. In older German the plural was used in all genders just as in Eng. That the singular was ever used came from the analogy of masc. nouns and "*diu mare*" with the neuter nouns, in all of which sing. and pl. would not be distinguished. See **431,** 2. The fem. of the n-declension never followed this analogy. For **Mann** see **59.** Compare the Eng. "a ten-year-old boy," now colloquial. "Year" is an old plural just like **Jahr.** In the D. pl. the coins, etc., in **175** almost always have **en.**

177. Notice the use of the singular in German for English plural in such phrases as: unter dem vierten und fünften Grade nördlicher Breite (Hu.); der erste und der fünfte Vers wurde(n) gesungen; die drei Schüler müssen zur Strafe die Hand auf den Mund legen; viele haben das Leben verloren, many lives were lost or many lost their lives.

SYNTAX OF THE CASES.

NOMINATIVE.

178. The nominative is the case of the subject and of direct address: Mein Freund, die Zeiten der Vergangenheit sind uns ein Buch mit sieben Siegeln (F. 575-6). Mit euch, Herr Doctor, zu spazieren ist ehrenvoll und ist Gewinn (F. 941). Absolute N. **297**.

179. Neuter verbs and verbs in the passive voice which govern two accusatives in the active, are construed with a predicate nominative. See **270**.

Such are: 1. Sein, werden, bleiben, dünken, scheinen, heißen (to be called), gelten, wachsen, sterben, etc.: Des Himmels Fügungen sind immer die besten (Le.). Aller Tod wird neues Leben (He.). Er wird ein großer Prinz bis an sein Ende scheinen (Sch.). Das allein macht schon den Weisen, der sich jeder dünkt zu sein (Le.). These verbs denote a state or transition. Preceded by als the construction may be called an apposition: Allein er starb als Christ (F. 2953). Ich komme als Gesandter des Gerichts (Sch.). Er gilt als ein reicher Mann, = He passes for . . .

2. Verbs of calling, thinking, making, choosing, scolding, viz., genannt, gedacht, angesehen, gemacht, betrachtet, gewählt, gescholten werden, and others: Wilhelm von Oranien wird der Schweiger genannt, Wilhelm von der Normandie, der Eroberer. Er ward ein Dieb gescholten, als ein Taugenichts betrachtet. Ich darf mich nicht des Glückes Liebling schelten (Körner).

GENITIVE.

180. The genitive is used chiefly as the complement of nouns and adjectives, but also of the verb (object). The genitive with nouns expresses the most varied relations. The principal ones are briefly given and illustrated below. German does not differ from other languages.

1. *G. of origin*, cause, authorship, relationship : Das Wunder ist des Glaubens liebstes Kind (F. 766). Goethes Faust. Die Früchte des Baumes.

2. *Subjective G.*: Die Liebe Gottes, welche höher ist denn alle Vernunft (B.). Der Gesang der Vögel. Das ist der Kampf der Pferde und Fische (Hu.).

3. *Objective G.*: Der Anblick dieser Gegend (Hu.). Die Erfindung der Buchdruckerkunst.
The personal pronoun is rarely found in this construction. Instead of „die Liebe seiner" stands die Liebe zu ihm, gegen ihn.

4. *Possessive G.*: Des Fatums unsichtbare Hand (Sch.). Der Garten des Königs. Doch besser ist's, ihr fallt in Gottes Hand als in (die) der Menschen (Sch.). Sometimes the possessive pronoun is put after the G. in colloquial language. Lessing has it several times : Das schien der alten Artisten ihr Geschmack nicht zu sein (Le.). See **242, 2**.

5. *G. of quality* or *characteristic*: Der Jüngling edlen Gefühles (H. and D., IV. 66).
This G. and the preceding stand also in the predicate after neuter verbs : Selig sind, die reines Herzens sind (B.). Einer Meinung sein; des Todes sein. Ein solcher Wasserstand war also eines Alters mit den rohen Denkmälern menschlichen Kunstfleißes (Hu.).

6. *Appositive* or *specifying G.*: Der Fehler des Argwohns; das Laster der Trunksucht; die Sünde der Undankbarkeit. Karl erhielt den Beinamen des Großen.
This G. and that of characteristic are frequently supplanted by von + Dative : Eine Eiche von hohem Alter wurde vom Blitze getroffen. Dieb von (einem) Bedienten; Teufel von Weibe (Le.). See Prepositions, **303, 15**.

7. *Partitive G.*, dependent upon nouns of quantity, weight, measure ; with numerals, various pronouns; comparative and superlative. Ex. : Thut nichts (= no matter). Er (der Mantel) hat der Tropfen mehr (Le.). Nun der Bescheidenheit genug (id.). Dem reichte sie der Gaben beste, der Blumen allerschönste dar (Sch.). Fünf unsers Ordens waren schon . . . des kühnen Mutes Opfer worden (id.). Lasst mir den besten Becher Weins in purem Golde reichen (G.). Du schlugst dich durch mit hundert achtzig Mann durch ihrer Tausend (Sch.). Unser einer kann sich das nicht leisten, = "One like (of) us cannot afford that."

181. In the spoken language and also in the classics (excepting poetry) this partitive G. has passed into mere apposition ; especially after nouns of weight, measure ; after numerals ; after nichts, nicht, and the indefinite pronouns. Ex.: Ein Pfund Thee ; drei Scheffel Korn. Etwas Schönes, nichts Böses, viel Gutes are no longer felt as genitives. The adjective used as noun is governed independently of the pronoun or numeral. Ex.: Zeigt das verfälschte Blatt nicht, man wolle zu nichts Gutem uns verbinden? (Sch.). Das könnte zu etwas Schrecklichem führen (id.). From Luther to Lessing this G. is still quite frequent, and it still remains in certain phrases, e. g., Hier ist meines Bleibens nicht, "I cannot stay here." Viel Aufhebens machen, "to make much ado." Wenn ich mit Menschen- und mit Engelzungen redete und hätte der Liebe nicht . . . (B.), literally "and had nought of charity." It is supplanted by von, aus, unter + D. See Prepositions, 303. Wer von uns, unter uns?

Genitive Dependent upon Adjectives.

182. It stands after adjectives denoting possession and interest or lack and want; fulness or emptiness; knowledge or ignorance; desire or disgust; guilt or innocence; e. g., fähig, *habhaft, sicher, teilhaftig, unfähig; bar, *los; *voll, *satt, leer, quitt, verlustig; kundig, *gewahr, unkundig; *müde, begierig; schuldig, ledig, etc. Ex.: Des langen Haders müde (Bü.). Des Leibes bist du ledig (id.). Des Gerichts schuldig (B.). (Hengste) begierig des Stalles (H. and D., VI. 313). Sie sind voll süßen Weins (B.). Du bist es doch zufrieden, Ritter? (Le.).

183. The adjectives marked * and others not given admit also of the accusative. In the last illustration „es" was felt as A., and therefore „das" is much more common. See Pronouns, **199, 2.** E. g., Ich bin das satt, müde, "I have enough of it," "am tired of it."

The prepositions nach, von, etc., + D. frequently supplant the genitive, e. g., „begierig nach dem Stalle" would be commoner; voll, rein sein von etwas.

Genitive after Verbs.

184. It may stand as nearer object, as remoter object, and adverbially.

As direct object after verbs with meanings similar to the adjectives in **182**; also achten, warten, harren, spotten, lachen, schonen genießen, sterben, pflegen, denken, vergessen, lohnen, verfehlen, brauchen, and others.

Ex.: Das Vergißmeinnicht. Ich denke dein (G.). Hungers sterben. Das lohnt der Mühe nicht, = It is not worth the trouble. Es sind nicht alle frei die ihrer Ketten spotten (Le.). Gebraucht der Zeit, sie geht so schnell von hinnen (F. 1908).

185. After verbs governing an A. of the person the G. of the thing stands as remoter object, such as judicial verbs, those with privative meaning, verbs of emotion; after many reflexive verbs with meanings similar to the adjectives in **182**, *e.g.*, zeihen, verklagen, freisprechen, beschuldigen, berauben, entladen, entlassen, entbinden, überheben, versichern, belehren, mahnen, and others; sich freuen, bedienen, erinnern, schämen, befleißen, erfrechen, sich wehren.

Ex.: Entlaßt mich meiner Ahnenprobe, ich will euch eurer wiederum entlassen (Le.). Wer kann mich einer Sünde zeihen? (B.). Jemand des Landes verweisen; eines Verbrechens anklagen, überführen, etc. Entschlage dich aller schwarzen Gedanken (Le.). Du darfst dich deiner Wahl nicht schämen (Sch.). But many of these genitives are supplanted by auf, über + A., and by A. alone.

186. Certain impersonal verbs expressing feelings, which are construed with the A. of the person feeling and with the G. of the cause and object of the feeling.

Ex.: Es ekelt mich, es reut, erbarmt, jammert, verdrießt mich; es lohnt sich. Darob erbarmt den Hirten des alten hohen Herrn (Uh.). Und da er das Volk sahe, jammerte ihn desselbigen (B.). But the nominative supplants here the A. of the person, and the A. the G. in the spoken language as a rule; „es" was again felt as A. See **183**. Ex.: Das gereut mich, dauert mich. Der Gerechte erbarmt sich seines Viehes (B.).

Adverbial Genitive.

187. It expresses place, time, manner, and other adverbial relations.

Ex.: Place: linker Hand, rechter Hand, aller Orten, "everywhere." Ich möchte (it is not likely that . . .) dieses Weges sobald nicht wieder kommen (Le.).

Time: dieser Tage, des Abends, „des Morgens in der Frühe."

Manner: trocknen Fußes, dry-shod; stehenben Fußes, immediately; vernünftiger Weise, reasonably. Sie kamen unverrichteter Sache zurück, they returned without having accomplished their object.

A large number of these genitives have passed into adverbs, *e. g.*, flugs, rechts, morgens, abends, nachmittags.

For genitive after Prepositions, see 302.

Genitive in Exclamations.

188. Interjections are followed by a genitive only when it denotes the cause or occasion of the exclamation. Wohl and weh(e) have often a dative of the person and a genitive of cause or origin: O des Franzosen, der keinen Verstand, dieses zu überlegen, kein Herz dieses zu fühlen gehabt hat (Le.). O des Glücklichen, dem es vergönnt ist, e i n e Luft mit euch zu atmen (Sch.).

DATIVE.

189. It is the case of the indirect object, less remote than the genitive. The nearer object can also stand in the dative, but is more remote than the nearer object (the direct one) in the accusative.

190. The dative stands as nearer object after intransitive verbs denoting: 1, approach and removal, similarity and dissimilarity; 2, pleasure and displeasure; 3, advantage and disadvantage; 4, command and obedience; 5, yielding and resistance; 6, belonging to, agreement, trust, etc. A large number of these verbs are compounds, viz., those with ent-, ver-, ab-, an-, auf-, bei-, ein-, mis-, nach-, vor-, voran-, wider-, zu-, and those with noun, adjective, or adverb: leid thun, wohlwollen, sauer werden, zustatten kommen, weis machen, zu teil werden, das Wort reden, "to defend," etc. 1, nahen, nachgehen, begegnen, gleichen, ähneln, zusehen, entsprechen, fehlen, entgehen, nachstehen; 2, gefallen, danken, genügen, behagen, huldigen, mißfallen, schmeicheln, lassen (to look), drohen, grollen, fluchen; 3, helfen, nützen, dienen, beistehen, frommen, wehren, schaden; 4, gebieten, befehlen, hören, gehorchen, folgen; 5, weichen, willfahren, widerstehen, widerstreben, trotzen; 6, antworten, erwiedern, gehören, eignen, beistimmen, zureden, trauen, glauben, vertrauen.

Ex. : Des Lebens ungemischte Freude ward keinem Sterblichen zu teil (Sch.). Straflose Freiheit spricht den Sitten Hohn (id.). Du redest ihm das Wort, anstatt ihn anzuklagen (id.). Das Stehen wird ihm sauer, It is hard work for him to stand. 1. Du gleichst dem Geist, den du begreifst, nicht mir (F. 512). Das zwingst du ihr (der Natur) nicht ab mit Hebeln und mit Schrauben (F. 675). 2. Einem Wirte läßt nichts übler als Neugierde (Le.), Nothing looks worse in a host than curiosity. So fluch' ich allem, was die Seele mit Lock- und Gaukelwerk umspannt (F. 1587). Der Landvogt grollte dem Tell. 3. (Sie) wehret den Knaben, she restrains the boys (Sch.). Der Knappe folgt dem Ritter. Gott hilft denen, die sich selber helfen. 4. Soll ich gehorchen jenem Drang? (F. 631). Du folgst mir doch bald nach (Sch.). Gehörst du mir? (id.). 5. Und die Gebilde der Nacht weichen dem tagenden Licht (id.). Wohl weißt du, daß ich deinem Zorn nicht trotze (id.). 6. Traue, schaue wem. Wem eignet Gott (Le.), To whom does God belong, = Who possesses him exclusively? Compound verbs: Ich habe dir nicht nachgestellt (F. 1426). Sehr gern steht Karlos dem Mini'ster nach (Sch.). Die Königin sah dem Kampfe zu (id.).

191. After transitive verbs the indirect object stands in the dative and the direct in the accusative (see **198**): Verhülle mir das wogende Getränge (F. 61). Das Menschenrecht, das ihm Natur vergönnt (F. 136).

192. A dative still farther removed from the verb is the ethical dative, or dative of interest (on the part of the speaker or hearer). It is generally a personal pronoun.

Ex.: Geht mir, nichts weiter davon (Sch.), "Go, I tell you, no more of that." Mir zu Liebe, for love of me. Ihm zu Ehren. (Sie) sind dir gar lockere, leichte Gesellen (Sch.). Die Uhr schlägt keinem Glücklichen (id.).

193. After impersonal verbs: es ahnt, beliebt, ekelt, geht, fehlt, gebricht, es graut, grauset, gelingt, liegt (mir) an etwas, kommt (mir auf etwas) an, schaudert, schwindelt, träumt, ziemt, and many verbs in **190** can be counted here: Dem Vater grauset's (G.). Es liegt mir viel daran, I care much for it. Dem Kaiser ward's sauer in Hitz' und in Kälte (Bü.).

Dative after Adjectives.

194. These have meanings similar to the verbs in **190**, e. g., angenehm, ähnlich, eigen, feind, folgsam, dienstbar, gnädig, hold, nachteilig, verbunden, zuträglich. Ex.: Das sieht ihm ähnlich, = that's like him. Auch war der Anfang ihren Wünschen hold (Sch.). Die meisten sind mir zugethan (id.), "devoted."

195. Substitution of preposition + case, both after verbs and adjectives.

Für, auf, an, gegen, über + accusative, mit and von + dative may replace the dative : Ich zürne auf dich, ich glaube an dich, vertraue auf ihn; bin freundlich gegen die Armen. Der Anzug (suit) ist sehr passend für dich, etc.

196. Verbs with unsettled constructions.

With a number of verbs usage is either unsettled or the classics still show two cases, while the spoken language has settled upon one, *e. g.*, now only es däucht mir, but es dünkt mich, classics have D. or A. after either. Glauben with D. only, or an + A.; but F. 3438: Ich glaub' ihn (Gott) nicht. Es ekelt mir and mich. Man bezahlt den Knecht (person), das Brot (thing), dem Bäcker das Brot. Ich rufe dir, I call out to you ; ich rufe dich, I call you, etc.

197. The few reflexive verbs after which the reflexive pronoun stands in the dative are really transitive verbs, and the pronoun is the indirect object: Er bildet sich etwas ein, "he imagines something," "is conceited." Ich darf mir schmeicheln (Le.); but see **190**, sub 2: Ich denke mir die Sache so.

ACCUSATIVE.

198. The accusative is the case of the direct object after transitive verbs, including many inseparable compounds of intransitive verbs with be-, ent-, er-, ver-, zer-, durch-, hinter-, über-, unter-, um-, voll-, wieder-; such as befahren, befolgen, befeuchten, entkräften, entscheiden, erfahren, erfinden, verlachen, vertreiben, zerstreuen, durchse'geln, hinterge'hen, überse'tzen, umge'ben, vollbri'ngen, wiederho'len.

Ex.: Ihr seht einen Mann wie andere mehr (F. 1874). Verachte nur Vernunft und Wissenschaft (F. 1851). Die Rüben haben mich vertrieben (Folk-song). Cook hat die Welt umsegelt. B. Taylor hat den Faust übersetzt.

199. Two accusatives may stand, one of the person and one of the thing, after verbs meaning to ask for, to inquire, teach, to cause to do a thing or have a thing done, and similar ones, *e. g.*, fragen, lehren, laſſen, bitten. Ex.: Wer lehrte dich dieſe gewaltigen Worte? (Le.) Lehre mich thun nach deinem Wohlgefallen (B.) (thun = second acc.). Wollen Sie den Arzt nicht kommen laſſen?

1. After *fragen, bitten, überreden, bereden,* the two accusatives stand, as a rule, only when the accusative of the thing is a neuter pronoun, *e. g.*, ich bitte, frage dich etwas, nichts, viel. If the pronoun is lacking, then fragen nach + D., bitten um + A., überreden von or zu + D. or the G. without preposition is the prevailing construction: Haſt du nach ihm gefragt? Ich habe ihn darum gebeten.

Lügen ſtrafen, Wunder nehmen govern an A. of the person: Das nimmt mich Wunder, "I wonder at that."

2. But these pronouns, das, nichts, viel, stand for old genitives which were felt as accusatives. The construction was: Wunder nimmt mich des or deſſen, wonder seizes me on that account. (See 186.) Lügen is probably a G. of cause: Jemand wegen der Lügen ſtrafen. Lernen for lehren, though found in Goethe, is wrong.

200. Notice a choice of construction in certain cases, when the personal object is further defined by another case or preposition and case. The verbs that concern us here are such as ſchlagen, treffen, treten, ſtechen, and similar ones.

1. Dative of the person and accusative of the affected part: Ich waſche mir die Hände or meine Hände.

2. Dative of the person and preposition + A.: Ich trete ihm auf den Fuß, ſchlage ihm in's Geſicht.

3. Accusative of the person and preposition + A.: Wir ſchlagen den Feind auf's Haupt. Wir treten die Schlange auf den Kopf. The choice is between 2 and 3. But 2 is preferable after intransitive verbs; 3 after transitives.

201. These accusatives are both object-accusatives, but after verbs meaning to name, scold, regarding, and others of similar meaning, the second accusative is a predicate or factitive accusative, while the first is direct object, *e. g.*, after *nennen,* ſchelten, ſchimpfen, glauben, taufen, heißen (trans.).

Ex.: In tiefster Seele schmerzt mich der Spott der Fremdlinge, die uns den Bauernadel schelten, "who call us by the nickname of 'peasant nobility'" (Sch.). Die Treue . . . ist jedem Menschen wie der nächste Blutsfreund, als ihren Rächer fühlt er sich geboren (id.). Noch fühle ich mich denselben, der ich war (id.). Ich achte ihn als einen Ehrenmann.

202. 1. After lassen + sein and werden a predicate A. by attraction is found instead of the predicate nominative, but the latter is the preferable construction, *e. g.*, Laß das Büchlein deinen Freund sein (G.). Laß diese Halle selbst den Schauplatz werden (Sch.). Fiesco V. 12. Mich laßt den ersten sein.

2. For the passive construction, see **179, 2.** The verbs in **199, 1,** may retain the accusative (pronoun), also lehren. This would also admit an accusative predicate noun in the passive: Das Schlimmste, was uns widerfährt, das werden wir vom Tag gelehrt (G.). Ich werde den Tanz gelehrt. But it is best to avoid all these predicate accusatives. They sound pedantic. Better say: Ich habe Tanzunterricht, Tanzstunde. Ich werde immer wieder darnach gefragt, darum gebeten.

203. The inner or nearer object stands in the accusative called the "cognate." The noun has the same meaning as the verb. Its idea is generally included in the verb: Einen guten Kampf habe ich gekämpft (B.). Eine Schlacht schlagen, heiße Thränen weinen, etc.; Karten spielen, Schlittschuh laufen. Gar schöne Spiele spiel' ich mit dir (G.).

204. Notice that the noun is sometimes replaced by an indefinite pronoun, was, es, eins, etc. Compare Eng. "to lord it," the unclassical "to come it over somebody." Aber die Eifersucht über Spanien gewann es diesmal über diese politische Sympathie (Sch.). Die Götter halten es mit den Tapfersten (id.); sich was rechtes (zurechte) laufen, springen, tanzen, "to run, etc., a great deal." Lügen Sie mir eines auf eigene Rechnung vor (Le.). Ich schwatze eins mit (Le.). See also F. 3416.

205. After many impersonal verbs and some other verbs the logical subject stands in the accusative (see **186**). The verbs denote states of the body and mind: es dürstet, hungert, schläfert, wundert, kränkt, verdrießt mich.

Here belong also es gibt, es hat, es setzt, es gilt: Dergleichen Stimmen gibt's (Sch.), "There are such voices." Es hat Gefahr, wenn wir nicht gehen, "There is danger ... ". Es setzt Hiebe, Händel, Schläge, There is a fight, a quarrel going on, somebody is being whipped. Comp. French *il y a*. See **236,4**.

206. After reflexive verbs the pronoun generally stands in the accusative: Entschließe dich. Besinne dich wo du bist (Sch.). But see **185** and **197**.

Adverbial Accusative.

207. It denotes measure (amount), time, and place.

1. It denotes measure after verbs like wiegen, kosten, gelten; after adjectives like lang, breit, hoch, alt, wert, etc.

Ex.: Die Ruhe deines Freundes gilt es, "is at stake" (Sch.). Die Kiste wiegt drei Kilogramm, zwei Zentner, fünf Lot, etc. Die Brücke ist mehrere Tausend Fuß lang, hundert sechzig hoch und achtzig Fuß breit. Das Dorf liegt eine Stunde (an hour's walk) von der Stadt. Friedrich ist einen halben Kopf größer als Dietrich.

The usage as to the case of the person with „kosten" is unsettled: Der Scherz kostet mich or mir viel Geld. Grimm's Dictionary favors the A.

2. It stands with verbs of motion to express the distance and the way, the noun being often followed by an adverb.

Ex.: Weiche keinen Schritt zurück. Zwei Wanderer sieht er die Straße ziehn (Sch.). Es zieht ein Haufe das ob're Thal herab (Uh.). Der Fels rollte den Berg hinab. Mit leisen Schritten schlich er seinen bösen Weg (Sch.).

The A. of measure and distance supplanted the G. of an older period; that denoting the way is old. The G. still occurs frequently. See **181**.

208. The accusative of time denotes the duration and the moment of an action. The former is often followed by an adverb, lang, durch, über. Ex.: Der Bote kann den Augenblick hier sein (Sch.). Er schläft den ganzen Morgen. Du hast es Jahre lang bedacht.

1. Compare the G. of time (see **187**), which denotes a repetition of the action or a custom. The A. denotes a definite point of time or fixed period: (Der) ließ Betstund' halten des Morgens gleich (Sch.). Sonnabends Nachmittags haben wir keine Schule (= custom). Nächsten Mittwoch haben wir keine Schule. Noch diese Nacht muß er Madrid verlassen (Sch.). The G. denoting duration of time is rarer now: Ein Gift das neun ganzer Jahre dauert (Le.). This may be partitive G.

Absolute Accusative.

209. This is generally accompanied by an adverbial phrase, and denotes that with which the subject is provided. Ex.: Zu Dionys, dem Tyrannen, schlich Möros, den Dolch im Gewande (Sch.). Schon den Hals entblößt, kniet' ich auf meinem Mantel (Le.).

SYNTAX OF THE ADJECTIVE.

210. The adjective may be used attributively, predicatively, and substantively: der reiche Nachbar; der Nachbar ist reich; der Reiche.

Attributive Use of the Adjective.

211. Some adjectives are only or mostly used attributively, as: 1, the superlatives and ordinals; 2, certain adjectives derived from adverbs: hiesig, dortig, seitherig, bisherig, e. g., die hiesige Zeitung, but not die Zeitung ist hiesig; 3, many adjectives in –isch, –lich –en: nordisch, irdisch, täglich, anfänglich, endlich, golden, seiden, silbern, gläsern; 4, the comparatives and superlatives in 76, 2.

1. If they do stand in the predicate, they must be inflected, and the noun may be understood, e. g., die Lieferung ist eine stündliche, not stündlich.

For the adjectives in –en and –ern, von + noun is substituted, e. g., ein Becher von purem Golde. But in poetry the adjective is found: Der Stuhl ist elfenbeinern (R.).

212. The attributive adjective is inflected and agrees with its noun in gender, number, and case: Mit süßer Kost und frischem Schaum hat er mich wohl genähret (Uh.). It may stand uninflected, however: 1. Before a neuter noun in N. (and A.) (very rarely before a masc. or fem.): Meine Mutter hat manch gülden Gewand (G.). Es ist ein pudelnärrisch Tier (F. 1167). Frequently in certain phrases like „bar Geld", "cash"; „auf gut Glück". Rare: Groß Macht und viel List (Lu.). Das Alter ist ein höflich Mann (G.); „fremd und fremder Stoff" (F. 635.). 2. When it stands after the noun, mainly in poetry; commonly after coins, weights, and measures: Der Hauptmann führt im Schild ein

Röslein rot von Golde und einen Eber wild (Uh.). Ein Schwarm von Gästen groß und klein (Bü.). Zehn Fuß rheinisch, fünf Pfund flämisch. In prose also, when the adjective or participle has adjuncts: Dort ein gutartiges, gesittetes Handelsvolk, schwelgend von den üppigen Früchten eines gesegneten Fleißes, wachsam auf Gesetze, die seine Wohlthäter waren (Sch.). 3. Of two adjectives the first stands uninflected in certain set phrases; when the two express one idea; in poetry, very frequently in Schiller : Die großherzoglich badische Regierung; das königlich preußische Zollamt. Weh dem, der an den würdig alten Hausrat ihm rührt (Sch.). Den falsch verräterischen Rat (id.). „In die weit und breite Welt" (G.). Schiller has „traurig finstrer Argwohn"; „weltlich eitle Hoheit"; „O unglückselig jammervoller Tag"; „mit grausam teuselischer Lust," etc.

1. Lauter, and generally eitel, both in the sense of "pure," "nothing but," also the adj. in -er, **507**, 2, are undeclined: Das ist lauter Unsinn. Esset eitel ungesäuert Brot (B.). Der Kölner Dom.

213. The attributive adjective is inflected weak after certain limiting words, viz., after the definite article and pronouns declined like it; after ein, kein, and the possessives, excepting the N. sg. of all genders and the A. sg. neut. and fem. Ex.: der gute Apfelbaum (Uh.); zur glücklichen Stunde; zu jenem frohen Feste; eines schönen Tages; an einem langen Aste (Uh.); sein grünes Haus (id.); eine arme Bäuerin (N. and A. sg.); ein seidenes Kleid (N. and A. sg.).

214. The adjective is therefore declined strong, when not uninflected (see **218**) and when not preceded by any of the above limiting words, mentioned in **213**, e. g., Holde Sehnsucht, süßes Hoffen (Sch.). Stumme Hüter toter Schätze (Platen ?). Also after the uninflected pronouns welch, solch, viel, wenig, mehr, etwas, nichts, and after uninflected numerals. Ex.: Er gibt dem treuen Hirten manch blankes Stück (piece of money) davon (Uh.). Welch reicher Himmel (G.). Solch trefflicher Monarch (Sch.) (see **216**, 4; **221**).

215. The syntactical distinction between strong and weak inflection of the adjective, though very old, is by no means clearly drawn even now. The oldest inflection of the adjective is the so-called "uninflected," identical with the strong noun declension. When the pronominal endings spread over the adjective declension, forming the present strong adjective declension, the adjective probably was still declined strong even after a pronoun (ind. article). Of this there are traces from O. H. G. down to the 17th century. The n-declension of the adjective is a characteristic of the Germanic languages. Having less distinctive and fewer endings than the strong, it is natural that the adjective should be declined according to it, when preceded by a word which had the strong endings. This has given rise to the syntactical distinction and to the feeling that two strong forms should not stand side by side. When an adjective became a substansive or was used as such, it was always inflected weak, with or without article. This explains 221, 1. In Gothic the present participle and the comparatives were always inflected weak. In O. H. G. appear only a few strong comparatives and superlatives.

216. Unsettled usage as to strong and weak forms.

1. The strong genitive sg. m. and n. turned weak in the 17th century, and this is now the prevailing form: „Hohes Muts" (Bü.); blut'gen Ruhms (Uh.). „Worte süßen Hauchs" (Sch.). The pronouns always remain strong, except jener, jeder, of which a weak form is rare, e. g., jeben Volfs (Uh.); jenen Tags (Bü.). This weakening is due to the feeling, that two strong forms should not stand together. See **215, 217.**

2. After personal pronouns the rule is strictly the strong form, as the pronoun is not a limiting word. But as early as M. H. G. weak forms begin to appear. Usage now favors: after ich, du, er (in address), mich, dich *only* the strong form, e. g., „du starker Königssohn" (Uh.); ich armer Mann; after mir, dir mostly the strong form; after wir, ihr the weak (if fem. always), e. g., Wer nie sein Brot mit Thränen aß . . . der kennt euch nicht, ihr himmlischen Mächte! (G.). In „Gegrüßt ihr, schöne Damen! (G.), the comma makes a difference. After uns and euch (A.) strong and weak are equally frequent. After uns and euch (D.) strong and weak coincide of course: Man sollte euch schlechte Kerle beistecken (arrest) lassen. Euch faulen Burschen ist jetzt der Brotkorb höher gehängt.

3. In the vocative the rule now is strong form both in sg. and pl., e. g., Unverschämter! wenn dich jemand gehört hätte (G.). Du, armer Geist (Sh.). The plural is still found weak, but rarely, as: Lieben Freunde, es gab beff're Zeiten als die unfern (Sch.).

In O. H. G. the weak form was the rule; in M. H. G., the strong in the sg.

4. After certain pronouns, pronominal adjectives, and indefinite

numerals, such as solche, welche, einige, etliche, alle, manche, keine, and others, there stands in the N. and A. pl. very frequently the strong form against the rule, but rarely in the G. pl. This strong form is the older. Even after diese and jene strong adjectives may be found in the classics. Ex.: Der Blumenhändler hat keine schöne Rosen mehr. Wo hast du solche halb-verfaulte Birnen gekauft? After the G. pl. zweier and dreier the weak adjective is frequent, but in the spoken language these genitives are very rare: der Ankauf von zwei neuen Häusern or zwei neuer Häuser, and not zweier neuen (or -er) Häuser.

217. If two or more adjectives hold the same relation to the noun, they have the same inflection. If the second adjective, however, be more closely related to the noun, forming a joint idea, then it usually stands in weak form in G. and D., not in N. and A It can often be formed into a compound noun, and has less accent than the first adjective: Er traktierte uns mit schlechtem roten Weine (= Rotwein); die Folgen blutiger bürgerlichen Kriege (= Bürgerkriege).

1. After certain adjectives like folgender, obiger, erwähnter, gedachter, etc., the second adjective, as a rule, is inflected weak in all cases: Genanntes unumstößliche Prinzip, obiger anerkannte Satz.

The Adjective in the Predicate.

218. The predicate adjective is uninflected. If it stand inflected in the predicate, the noun is supplied and the adjective is looked upon as attributive: Die Kraft ist schwach, allein die Luft ist groß (F. 2203). Dein Geschäft ist ein schwieriges (supply "one"); „des Polizisten Los ist kein glückliches."

The adjective (or participle) is also uninflected when it is an appositional or factitive predicate: Wir kamen glücklich an. Nun, das sind ich dumm (F. 961). Der Glaube macht selig (B.).

219. Certain adjectives are only used predicatively. Some of these are really nouns, like feind, freund, heil, schade, not, nütze, schuld. Others, originally adjectives or past participles, have been restricted to this use, like habhaft, abhold, getrost, ansichtig, verlustig. All of them have not yet become full adjectives; and many, if with adjective form, are of late derivation: abspenstig, abhold, abwendig, ausfindig, handgemein. Ex.: Ottilie konnte dem Märchen nicht feind sein (G.). Ein schöner Mann, eine schöne Frau! ist der Direktor glücklich genug, ihrer habhaft zu werden, so ... (id.). Die Knechte wurden handgemein.

1. In O. H. G. the adjective in the predicate is still inflected, though not always. In M. H. G. it is rarely inflected. In N. H. G. voller and halber are stereotyped strong forms used for both numbers and all genders: Die Nacht ist halber hin (coll.); „des Nachts um halber Zwölf" (student song). Voller Schmerzen und Krankheit (B.).

Substantive Use of the Adjective.

220. The adjective when used as a noun is inflected according to the rules already given for the adjective proper: Mit Kleinem fängt man an, mit Großem hört man auf (Prov.). Zu Schwert an meiner Linken (Körner). Die Ersten werden die Letzten sein (B.). For gender see **160, 3**. No inflection is the rule in certain set phrases: Gleich und Gleich gesellt sich gern (Prov.). Jung und Alt, Groß und Klein, Reich und Arm, von Klein an, von Jung auf; also in the names of languages: Englisch, Französisch; mein geliebtes Deutsch (F. 1223). Wie heißt dies auf Italienisch? Er hat von Kind auf Norwegisch gekonnt. Also of colors: Grün, Blau.

221. Usage admits of many irregularities.

1. The weak form in the plural when no article precedes as Bedienten, Beamten, Schönen, Jungen, or rarely the strong form in the singular like any feminine noun, invariable in the sg.: der Schöne, instead of der Schönen (G. sg.). See **215**.

2. The strong or weak plural after alle, einige, etliche, etc.: alle Gelehrte, einige Gesandte.

3. After was, etwas, viel, etc., the weak form is rare. See **214**.

4. If an adjective precede an adjective-substantive and is inflected weak, the latter is of course weak; if the adjective is inflected strong, then the substantive may be either strong or weak. The latter form is perhaps more common for the neuter, the strong certainly for the masculine nouns: Nein, sie (das Weib) ist, o holde Schönen, zur Geselligkeit gemacht (G.). Die armen Verwandten sind gewöhnlich nicht willkommen. Hochgestellte Beamte sind entlassen. Der neue Bediente hat ein angenehmes Äußere. See F. II. 6842.

a. Do not confound das Recht, law—das Rechte, the right thing; das Gut, property — das Gute, the good (abstract); (das) Schwarz, black (the color) — das Schwarze (the bull's eye of a target), etc.

Syntax of Comparative and Superlative.

222. These may be used just like the positive, only that the superlative is never used predicatively, *i. e.*, uninflected, excepting allerliebst, *e. g.*, die Blume ist allerliebst. If it stands in the predicate, it is always weak, being preceded by the definite article: Dieser Baum ist der höchste or dieser Baum ist am höchsten. These two should not be used indiscriminately, however, as they too generally are in the spoken-language. The first is the strictly relative comparison; it can be strengthened by aller-, *e. g.*, der höchste von allen, der allerhöchste. The prepositional superlative should only be used when not so much the objects themselves or different objects are to be compared, but the same objects under different circumstances of time and place. This is generally the "absolute" superlative, expressed by an adverbial phrase: Der Starke ist am mächtigsten allein (Sch.), "The strong man is most powerful standing alone, unimpeded by the weak." Die Äpfel sind auf der sonnigen Seite des Gartens am reifsten. Als Booth Richelieu spielte, war das Theater am vollsten.

1. The "relative" superlative is generally preceded by the definite article, the "absolute" has, as a rule, ein or no article. Goethe is very fond of such an absolute superlative: Ein allerliebstes Kind, a most lovely child. Dies deutet auf ein spätestes Naturereignis (G.). Notice also: weil's die Wenigsten können (G.), because very few know how; der Fürst, die Eltern, die neueren Sprachen, and other examples. They show absolute comparison with the definite article. The absolute superlative is best expressed by an adverb + adjective in the positive. The more common adverbs used are: sehr, recht, höchst, äußerst, überaus, *e. g.*, eine höchst angenehme Überraschung, ein recht dummer Junge.

223. Any adjective can be compared by –er, –est, except those that are never used attributively (see **219**) and a few whose form seems awkward, like knechtisch, herrisch, but the latter are not absolutely excluded. Allein, weiß Gott, sie war mehr schuld als ich (F. 2960).

224. When two qualities belonging to the same object are compared, mehr, weniger, minder are now used, but the classics are still full of the comparatives in -er.

According to Lehmann (L. Sprache, p. 206) Lessing uses mehr only once: Diese Ausrufungen sind rhetorischer als grünblich (Lc.). Present usage: Der Geselle ist weniger heimtückisch als bumm. Der Soldat ist mehr tapfer als klug.

225. Logically the superlative cannot be used of two objects, but it is so used much more frequently in German than in English, *e. g.*, Zwei Söhne, wovon sie den ältesten . . . mit einem Pfeile erschoß (Lc.).

1. For the conjunctions benn, als, after the comparative, see **333**.

2. Notice the bold comparative in H. and D., IX. 311 : Nun, ist das Meine meiner als jemals. Such forms as der Deinigste, etc., at the end of letters are rare. Leiber is a comparative of leib (adj.), which became a noun very early. Öfterer occurs in Lessing.

SYNTAX OF THE NUMERALS.

226. The cardinals, used attributively, are indeclinable now, except ein, eine, ein. The G. and D. of zwei and drei now and then occur still: Zweier Zeugen Mund macht alle Wahrheit kund (Prov.). (Here „zweier" shows the case; zwei Zeugen Mund would not be clear.) Zähle von eins bis hundert.

1. To express the year the cardinal is merely added to „im Jahr(e)" or to „in," as im Jahre achtzehn hundert ein und achtzig, or shorter, in 1813. The cardinal shows the year, the ordinal the month: Göthe starb den 22ten März 1832. Hannover, den (1.) ersten August 1881. The ordinals used only attributively, see **211**.

2. The time is expressed in various ways. Answering to such questions as: Wieviel Uhr ist es, welche Zeit ist es or haben wir? wie ist es an der Zeit? we say: Es ist zwölf vorbei, aber noch nicht eins. Es ist ein Viertel drei or auf drei, or ein Viertel nach (über) zwei (all mean a quarter past two). Es ist drei Viertel drei or auf

drei or ein Viertel vor drei, = a quarter of three. Es ist halb zwölf, = half past eleven, on the same principle as viertehalb (see **229**). We can say: 20 Minuten nach zehn (past ten), zwanzig vor zehn (of ten). Der Zug fährt 3 Uhr 20 Minuten nachmittags ab. Wir wollen uns um fünf treffen.

227. Used substantively the cardinals are more frequently inflected, having a plural in -e (see **429**) and a dative in -en. (see **79**): Es waren ihrer fünf(e), zwölf(e).

1. Colloquially this -e is very commonly used as far as 19 incl., even when the figure itself be meant, which stands in the feminine singular: Diese Acht(e) ist nicht gut gemacht. Diese Neun(e) steht schief. Elf ist die Sünde. Elfe überschreitet die zehn Gebote (Sch.).

2. Die Million, die Billion, die Milliarde are regular nouns, and, unlike hundert and tausend, stand in the plural after the cardinals, e. g., drei Millionen, but fünf hundert, sechs tausend. Das Hundert, das Tausend are common nouns, pl.: Hunderte + hundreds, Tausende + thousands: e. g., zu Hunderten, a hundred at a time; bei Hunderttausenden die Menschen drücken (Le.).

228. „Beide" corresponds to Eng. "both" in form and use: Ist das Pferd an beiden Augen blind? It may have the definite article before it: die beiden Kühe, "both the cows."

1. The singular beid- means "either," "each" (of two). Beides läßt sich hören = either statement is reasonable; das Abendmahl unter beider Gestalt, the communion in either form; but the masc. and fem. are archaic. Denn zu einem großen Manne gehört beides: Kleinigkeiten als Kleinigkeiten und wichtige Dinge als wichtige Dinge zu behandeln (Le.). Beides has supplanted beide, *beidiu* (pl.), which are still common in the 16th and 17th centuries.

Notice beides — und = both — and. Beides, ein löblicher König und mächtiger Schwinger der Lanze (Bü.).

229. 1. Peculiar are the compounds of the ordinals with halb following them and selb preceding them: Viert(e)halb (3½), neunt(e)halb (8½), meaning das vierte nur halb or weniger ein halb, das neunte nur halb. Dreizehntehalb Faß = 12 Faß aber das 13te nur halb. Ags., Icelandic, Danish, and L. G. have the same forms, though in the two latter "half" precedes the ordinal. It does not go back to O. H. G. Selbander = er(selbst) der zweite, two of them; selbdreizehnt, himself the 13th, thirteen of them (G.); selbdritt, selbviert generally uninflected. Selbst zwanzigster (Le.). The cardinal is not common, but Lessing has „felb fünfziger." This composition is more common than halb- in the modern dialects.

2. Notice also the cardinals in -er, as in ben fünfziger Jahren—either "from 1850-60" or "from 50-60 years old." It is now classical. This -er occurs in the names of the unit, ten, etc.: ber Einer, ber Zehner, etc. See 507, 1. Zu zweit, britt also occur for zu zweien, breien.

SYNTAX OF THE PRONOUNS.

Syntax of the Personal Pronoun.

230. 1. Du, sg., ihr, pl., are used in familiar intercourse in the family and among intimate friends, in addressing God, in sermons, in solemn discourses and in poetry. Ex.: Kennst du das Land, wo die Citronen blühn? (G.). Blinder, alter Vater! du kannst den Tag der Freiheit nicht mehr schauen; du sollst ihn hören (Sch.). Erhab'ner Geist, du gabst mir, gabst mir alles, warum ich bat (F. 3218).

2. Sie, 3. p. pl., is used everywhere else, even among relatives in some families; also when grown children address the parents: Wo wohnen Sie, wenn ich fragen darf?

3. This peculiar use of Sie sprang up early in the 18th century. It is due, no doubt, to the use of the singular Er and Sie in address, which were the height of politeness in the 17th century. Er and Sie are due to the use of Herr and Frau in direct address. In Chamisso's „Peter Schlemihl" the gray-coat always addresses Peter with „der Herr," e. g., „Möge der Herr meine Zubringlichkeit entschuldigen . . . ich habe eine Bitte an ihn." Herr, Frau, Ihre Gnaden, Eure Excellenz, Seine Majestät were followed by the "plural of majesty" (see 311, 2): Herr Doktor wurden da katechisiert (F. 3524). Fürs erste wollen Seine Majestät, daß die Arme's ohn' Aufschub Böhmen räume (Sch.). Herr was roduced to mere „er" as early as M. H. G., e. g., er Sigfrid; in the 16th century, „Werter er Pfarrer." This form encouraged the use of the pronoun er in direct address.

4. Ihr, in addressing one person, was early very respectful and has maintained itself in the drama, except in comedy, to this day, and might be called the "stage-address," and is due to Eng. and Fr. influence. See Schiller's Maria Stuart.

231. The gradation as to politeness and etiquette now is about as follows: 1. For princes and all persons of high standing, Ihre Gnaden, Eure Excellenz, Eure Majestät, with the verb in the pl. 2. Sie, addressing one or more persons, verb always in the pl., e. g., dürfte ich Sie begleiten? 3. Ihr, pl. of du, and Ihr in the drama addressing one or more persons, *e. g.*, Spät kommt Ihr, doch Ihr kommt (Sch.). See F. 981, 988. 4. Er, Sie, addressing one person, now rare. 5. Du, ihr, as in **230**, 1.

232. The genitive of the pronouns of the 1. and 2. persons stands very rarely after nouns. Goethe has it once, „mein, des Geognosten," "of me the geognost," but it is common as the object of verbs, after adjectives and numerals : Ich bitt' euch, nehmt euch meiner an (F. 1875). The uninflected possessive mein, dein are by some interpreted as predicate genitives, *e. g.*, der Becher ist dein (Sch.). As it is much more probable that the possessive adjectives were used as genitives of the personal pronoun than *vice versa*, this interpretation is hardly correct. (See **441**, *a*.)

233. The personal pronouns always accompany the verb. In the imperative „Sie" always stands, but du and ihr only for emphasis: Liebet eure Feinde (B.). Bleiben Sie gefälligst. See F. 1908.

1. In poetry, colloquially, and in merchants' letters the pronoun is often omitted : Bin weder Fräulein, weder schön, kann ungeleitet nach Hause gehn (F. 2608). See F. 3429. Ihr Wertes (viz., Schreiben) vom 18ten dieses (viz., Monats), habe empfangen. Notice the set phrases bitte, I pray ; danke, thank you ; geschweige (conjunction, " say nothing of "), before which ich has to be supplied. Thut nichts, der Jude wird verbrannt (Le.), no matter, the Jew . . .

2. Colloquially the subject, if a noun, may be repeated in the shape of a pronoun, as in Eng.: der Kirchhof, er liegt wie am Tage (G.). See **244**, 3.

234. The pronouns of the third person have demonstrative and determinative force. (Compare the cognate Latin *is, ea, id*.) Hence if they refer to lifeless objects or abstract nouns, they rarely stand in the G. and D. cases, but they are supplanted by the regular demonstrative pronouns or, if governed by prepositions, by da(r), hin, her + the preposition. Ex.: Dem Liebchen keinen Gruß ! Ich will davon nichts hören (F. 2104). Habt euch vorher wohl präpariert (F. 1958). Allein ich glaub', du hältst nicht viel davon (viz., von der Religion) (F. 3418).

1. Also es (A.) is thus supplanted, when referring to an individual object: Wo liegt Paris ? . . . Den Finger drauf (not auf es) das nehmen wir (Arndt). Nenn's Glück! Herz! Liebe! Gott! ich habe keinen Namen dafür (F. 3455–6), Kennst du London? Besuche dasselbe jedenfalls.

Concord of Pronoun and Noun.

235. The pronoun of the third person agrees with the noun which it represents in gender and number. The concord of the pronoun with the natural and grammatical gender has been treated, see **165, 166**; also the neuter sg. es representing a plural and any gender, see **168**.

On the use of „es".

236. 1. Es is the *indefinite* subject of impersonal verbs denoting states of the weather and other natural phenomena, *e. g.*, es regnet, donnert, blitzt, schneit, hagelt, es hat geglä'tteist, es tagt, es wintert, es dunkelt, dämmert, taut, etc.

2. Es is made the *indefinite* subject of verbs, not really impersonal: Es schlägt elf; es brennt, es klopft, klingelt, es geht los, läutet; also in the passive and reflexive: es wird getanzt, gesungen, gespielt; compare man tanzt, man ruft. Es geht, spielt sich hier gut = it is good walking, playing here. Wohin soll es nun gehn (F. 2051).

a. Such an es is used by poets to give a vague, mysterious, ghostly impression. Schiller's „Taucher," Goethe's „Hochzeitlied" and „Totentanz" are full of them: Und als er im willigen Schlummer lag, bewegt es sich unter dem Bette (G.). The es (treated so far) except in the passive and reflexive verbforms cannot be omitted like, for instance, the expletive „es" sub 3, 5.

3. Es is made the *grammatical* subject of a verb, when the *logical* subject follows later: Es zogen drei Bursche wohl über den Rhein (Uh.). Es schritt ihm frisch zur Seite der blühende Genoß (Uh.). See F. 3490–1; 3674–77.

The logical subject cannot be another pronoun, *e g.*, es war ich, es waren Sie, as in Eng. "it was I," "it was you," which is a late construction.

a. In ballads and other folk-lore this es is not required and inversion is still possible, as was the rule in O. H. G., without es at the head of the sentence. For after all, es was here used not merely to denote an indefinite subject, but to account for an inversion which had no apparent cause. It is an "*expletive*" and superfluous as soon as any other part of the sentence stands at the head bringing about the inversion. It is oftenest translated by "there." German tales begin „Es war einmal . . .", "There was once ... ". Saß ein Knab' ein Röslein stehn (G.). Stellt' ein Knabe sich mir an die Seite (id.). The construction ich bin es, Ihr selb es, "you are it," as in Ags. and as English-speaking children still say, is already the rule in O. H. G. Nor can we say in German „ich bin er" and „Sie sind er," but ich bin es, das bin ich, der bin ich, ich bin derjenige, welcher ..., I am he who ...

4. Peculiar is the impersonal „es giebt," "there are" or "is," which is not a very old phrase, but rare in M. H. G., in which es with pl. verb was even possible.

„Es" is here the indefinite subject and has taken the place of the more definite „das" or a noun, which "gave," "furnished," "produced" a certain thing. Hence „es giebt" is always followed by the accusative: „es giebt Schläge," "Somebody is giving or will give somebody a whipping." Ei, da gab's westfäl'schen Schinken (Scheffel). „Es giebt" is not well followed by a noun in the sg. denoting one object or individual, e. g., Es giebt hier einen Hund, but by nouns in the pl., by abstract and material nouns: Es giebt keinen Zufall (Sch.). See F. 1118.

5. Es is used as the subject of impersonal verbs followed by an objective personal pronoun (D. or A.), denoting states of mind and body: Es dürstet mich, es hungert ihn, es reut mich, es ist ihm bange.

If the objective pronoun or any other part of speech precede the verb, es is not necessary, but it may be retained. Ex.: Ich schwöre euch zu, mir ist's als wie ein Traum (F. 2040). Dir wird gewiß einmal bei deiner Gottähnlichkeit bange (F. 2050). Mir ist schlecht zu mute, "I do not feel well."

6. Es stands further as indefinite predicate and as indefinite object. See **204**. In diesem Sinne kannst du's wagen (F. 1671). See further, F. 2012-14; 2080. Sie meint, du seist entflohn; und halb und halb bist du es schon (F. 3331-2).

In the last illustration and in similar ones es, if translated at all, may be rendered by "so": Sie sind wohl müde? O nein, aber ich bin es gewesen, = I was (so).

Syntax of the Reflexive Pronoun.

237. The reflexive pronoun always refers to the subject: Es ist der Lohn der Demut, die sich selbst bezwungen (Sch.). Die hat sich jegliches erlaubt (id.).

86   SYNTAX OF THE RECIPROCAL PRONOUN.   [238-

1. The dative was already lost in O. H. G. In M. H. G. the use of ſich as dative is very rare. Luther's Bible is still full of the dative of the personal pronoun for the reflexive, e. g, Die Heiden, da ſie das Geſetz nicht haben, ſind (ſie) ihnen ſelbſt ein Geſetz. Die Weisheit läſſet ihr ſagen, = wisdom will take advice. Gott ſchuf den Menſchen ihm zum Bilde. Lessing has: Wer ſich Knall und Fall ihm ſelbſt zu leben nicht entſchließen kann, der lebet anderer Sklav' auf immer. But this „ihm" stands also because there is already one ſich. It is very rare in the classics and does not occur in the spoken language.

2. Selbſt, ſelber strengthens the reflexive pronoun and prevents its confounding with the reciprocal. For examples see above. But ſelbſt (ſelber) is far from as common as the Eng. self (selves).

Syntax of the Reciprocal Pronoun.

238. As such are used uns, euch, ſich, both in the accusative and dative: Und (ſie) nickten ſich (D.) zu und grüßten ſich (A.) freundlich im Spiegel (H. and D., VII. 42). Wenn ſich die Fürſten befehden, müſſen die Diener ſich morden und töten (Sch.).

But if any ambiguity arises, as is frequently the case, the unvarying form einander or the inflected einer (der eine) den andern referring to masc. nouns, die eine die andere referring to fem. nouns, die einen die andern pl. of both, are used instead of them and even, though tautologically, in addition to them. Ex.: und lieben uns unter einander (B.). Sie ſpotten der eine des andern.

Syntax of the Possessive Pronouns.

239. The possessive pronoun used adjectively agrees with the noun like any other adjective. See **212.** The uninflected forms mein, dein, ſein stand in the predicate and can be subjects only when used as nouns with or without the article, e. g., Mein und Dein iſt alles Zankes Urſprung (Prov.).

1. Standing in the predicate, therefore, it is right to say: Das Buch iſt mein, meines, das meine, das meinige. As subjects referring to das Buch: Meines, das meine, das meinige iſt verloren, = mine is lost.

2. Care should be taken that the right possessive be used when persons are addressed with Sie, du, ihr (Ihr). Ihr refers to Sie, dein to du, euer (Euer) to ihr (Ihr), e. g., Sie haben Ihre Frau Mutter verloren? Wohin

wird dich deine Vermessenheit noch führen? Durch des Mannes Übermut, den Ihr durch Euer Brautgemach zum Throne geführt (Sch.).

240. Of der, die, das meine (der, die, das meinige), when used substantively, der, die Meine, pl. die Meinen (with capital letters), denote persons, viz., friends, relatives, etc.; das Meine or das Meinige denote my property, duty, share, deserts.

Ex.: Der Herr kennet die Seinen (B.). Sie hat das Ihrige erhalten (her dowry). Kardinal! Ich habe das Meinige gethan. Thun Sie das Ihre (Sch.). Diesen Morgen, als ich Sie im Kreise der Ihrigen fand . . . (id.). "Ganz der Ihrige," "die Deinige," "die Deine" are proper letter-endings.

241. The possessive pronoun must be repeated like the article with nouns of different gender: Sein hoher Gang, seine edle Gestalt, seines Mundes Lächeln, seiner Augen Gewalt . . . (F. 3395–8).

242. 1. As sein and ihr are both reflexive (referring to the subject of the sentence) and non-reflexive (referring to another noun) an ambiguity may arise, which should be avoided by using the demonstrative pronouns instead; either dessen, deren always preceding, or desselben, derselben either preceding or following the noun. Ex.: Roland ritt hinterm Vater her mit dessen Schild und Schwerte (Uh.). „Mit seinem Schild" would have meant Roland's shield. Compare the following lines of the same poem, in which ihm prevents ambiguity: R. ritt hinterm Vater her und trug ihm seinen starken Speer zusamt dem festen Schilde. Compare Frau N. N. ging mit der Haushälterin und ihrer Nichte nach dem Markte, i. e., Mrs. N. N.'s niece; but mit der Haushälterin und deren Nichte, i. e., the housekeeper's niece. Es eifre jeder seiner (the father's) unbestochenen, von Vorurteilen freien Liebe nach (Le.).

2. The possessive of the 3. person is in the people's language often repeated for emphasis after a genitive of possession and also after a dative: „Meinem Vetter sein Garten." Comp. "John his mark." This is not to be imitated though it occur now and then in the classics and quite frequently in the 18th century: Auf der Fortuna ihrem Schiff (Sch.); des Illo seinem Stuhl (id.). Ihr artet mehr nach eures Vaters Geist als nach der Mutter ihrem (id.). See **180, 4**.

3. The definite article cannot precede the attributive possessive pronoun. Jener, dieser and such adjectives as obgedachter, erwähnter seemingly do, but such constructions as dieser dein Sohn, obgedachter mein Schreiber are rather appositional.

243. 1. By a license the possessives lose inflectional endings in such set phrases as occur in Ich möchte brum mein Tag nicht lieben (F. 2920). Mein Lebtag benk' ich bran (Sch.). Hab' ich dich doch mein Tage nicht gesehen (F. 4440). These phrases are in the transition stage to adverbs and the apostrophe may stand or not.

2. Sein is in proverbs and in one phrase „seiner Zeit" = "in due time," "in — time," still used for the feminine ihr, a remnant of the earlier periods, when ihr could not be used as the reflexive possessive: Sein Thor kennt jede Kuh (Prov.). Untreue schlägt seinen eigenen Herrn (Prov.). „Seiner Zeit" is an adverbial genitive, in which seiner has become non-reflexive so that it apparently stands at times for ihrer, unseres, etc. Reflexive: „Alles Ding währt seine Zeit" (Hymn); but non-reflexive: Sie war seiner Zeit (once) eine große Sängerin.

Compare the relation of Eng. "his" and "its." The latter sprang up in Shakspere's time. "Its" is the genitive of "it." In Sh. "his" stands frequently where later "its" is used.

3. The use of the German definite article where in Eng. the possessive is used, is by no means as strict and as common in the spoken language as the grammarians would have us believe. Take for instance: Mein armer Kopf ist mir verrückt. Mein armer Sinn ist mir zerstückt (F., I. 3383–6). Solang ich mich noch frisch auf meinen Beinen fühle, genügt mir dieser Knotenstock (F. 3838–9). See **154**.

In the 17th century „sich" was used also for all persons. "Simplicissimus" is full of this misuse.

Syntax of the Demonstrative Pronoun.

244. Der, die, das, always accented, points out without reference to nearness in time or space. It is generally well translated by "that," also by "this," and by a personal pronoun.

Ex.: Dem Volke hier (this) wird jeder Tag ein Fest (F. 2162). Aber, wie ich mich sehne dich zu schauen, habe ich vor dem (that) Menschen (Mephistopheles) ein heimlich Grauen (F. 3480–1). O glücklich der (he), den ihr belehrt! F. 1981). Der (for her) hab' ich die Freude verbittert (Bo.). Wehe dem, der Voltair(en)s Schriften überhaupt nicht mit dem skeptischen Geist liest, in welchem er einen Teil derselben geschrieben (Le.).

1. The genitives des, dessen, deren sg. fem., derer and deren, pl., are used substantively as follows:

a. Des is archaic, but occurs in compounds like beshalb, beswegen, bergestalt, etc., *e. g.*, Des freut sich das entmenschte Paar (Sch.). Wir sind der keines wert, das wir bitten (Lu.), We are worthy of none of those (things), etc.

b. Dessen, deren G. sg. fem. and G. pl., are used when they have the force of possessives (see **242**).

c. The present usage favors derer, G. pl., referring to persons and deren, dessen referring to things. But the classics do not agree with this. Generally these forms are antecedents of relative pronouns. Ex.: Jetzo sag' mir das Ende derer, die von Troja kehrten (G.). Hat das Kind schon Zähne? Es hat deren vier. Dort sieht man die Güter derer (of the gentlemen, lords) von Webeloh.

2. The lengthened forms in –en and –er sprang up as early as the 15th century both in the article and in the pronoun. Luther has „denen," D. pl., but the short genitives „des" and „der." In the 18th century they lost –er and –en again, owing, no doubt, to the desire of distinguishing between article and demonstrative, and between the substantive and adjective uses of the latter. Goethe has still „und von denen Menschen die sie besonders schätzen." Present usage, however, requires the short forms of the pronoun, when used adjectively.

3. Notice the frequent emphatic force of the pronoun, *e. g.*, Vom Rechte, das mit uns geboren ist, von dem ist leider nie die Frage (F. 1978–9).

Dieser, jener.

245. Dieser points out what is near in time and space, jener what is remoter. Dieser is "the latter," jener, "the former." They are used substantively and adjectively: Dieses junge Frauenzimmer hat Gefühl und Stimme (Le.). Dieser will's trocken, was jener feucht begehrt. Dies Blatt hier — dieses willst du geltend machen? (Sch.).

1. Das, dies like es, but less frequently, can be the indefinite subjects of neuter verbs. See **236**. *E. g.*, Das ist die Magd des Nachbars. Das ist ein weiser Vater, der sein eigen Kind kennt (Sch.). Dies ist die Art mit Hexen umzugehn (F. 2518). The verb may be in the pl. See **313**.

2. Dies und das, dies und jenes have the force of „irgend ein," *e. g.*, Wir sind nicht mehr beim ersten Glas, drum denken wir gern an dies und das (Song). Und er streckte als Knabe die Hände nicht aus nach diesem und jenem (H. and D. V. 64).

3. Dieser is strengthened by hier; der, jener and das by da, *e. g.*, Mit dem da werden Sie nicht fertig (Sch.). Jener, in the sense of "the other" and

"to come," „in jener Zeit", in jenem Leben. Shakspere's Gespenst kömmt wirklich aus jener Welt (Le.).

246. When not referring to persons hier + preposition may take the place of dieser, and da + preposition the place of der and jener, *e. g.*, Wer sonst ist schuld daran als ihr in Wien? (Sch.). Davon schweigt des Sängers Höflichkeit (?). Hiernach (according to this) muß die Lesart eine ganz andere gewesen sein.

1. Notice the two strong forms in Lessing's Alles dieses, seine Erfindungen und die historischen Materialien, knetet er denn in einen fein langen, fein schwer zu fassenden Roman zusammen. For an das, was . . . , von dem, was . . . no daran was . . . , davon was . . . should be substituted, though this is done colloquially. „Wir dachten daran, was du jetzt anfangen würdest" is not elegant.

247. Der-, die-, dasjenige is generally used substantively followed by a relative clause or a genitive. Used adjectively it stands for der, die, das when a relative clause follows, *e. g.*, diejenigen Menschen, welche . . . The best usage accents der, die, das. Used adjectively it has only medium stress.

Ex.: Diejenigen der Knaben, welche ihre Aufgaben nicht gemacht hatten, mußten nachsitzen (stay after school). Liebet diejenigen, welche euch verfolgen (B.).

248. Der-, die-, dasselbe denotes identity. It refers to something known or mentioned. It is used equally well substantively or adjectively. It can be strengthened by „eben": Mit aller Treue verwend' ich eure Gaben; der Dürftige soll sich derselben erfreuen (H. and D. II., 74–5).

1. Der nämliche also denotes identity, but is not written as one word. „Derselbige" is rarer than derselbe. War das nicht der Dienstmann (porter), der die Auswanderer betrogen hat? Der nämliche.

2. Selbig without der is rare, *e. g.*, Selbiges weiß ich gewiß (Heyse).

249. Selb, selber, selbst distinguishes one object from another. It strengthens personal and reflexive pronouns. It is made emphatic by eben, also in the phrase ein(er) und derselbe. Selber and selbst do not differ in meaning, but in use. Selber is never made an adverb as ſelbſt is. Selber always follows the word it qualifies, though it need not stand necessarily directly after it: Ich ſelber or ſelbſt habe ihn geſehen. Wer zweifelt, Nathan, daß ihr nicht (see **309**, 2) die Ehrlichkeit, die Großmut ſelber ſeid? (Le.) Wer andern eine Grube gräbt, fällt ſelbſt hinein (Prov.).

1. Selbſt has become also an adverb with the force of „ſogar," and then stands best at the beginning of the sentence, unaccented: Selbſt ein ſo himmliſches Paar (viz., Psyche and Amor) fand nach der Verbindung ſich ungleich (G.).

2. Notice the compounds daſelbſt, hie(r)ſelbſt, in that or this very place; also the force of „von ſelbſt" in: Die Mühle geht nicht von ſelbſt (of its own accord).

For ſelb with ordinals see **229**. Alone it is very rare, *e. g.*, weil er in ſelbem (im Pala'ſte) alle um ſich verſammelt hatte (Le.).

250. Solch means + " such." It describes what is pointed out. It is used adjectively and substantively: Hilfreiche Mächte! einen ſolchen (Weg) zeigt mir an, den ich vermag zu gehen (Sch.). Wo war die Überlegung, als wir . . . ſolche Macht gelegt in ſolche Hand (id.).

1. The use of ſolch for the personal pronoun or der-, die-, daſſelbe is not good although found now and then in the classics, *e. g.*, Als ſie die Moos-hütte erreichten, fanden ſie ſolche auf das luſtigſte (see **300**, 2) ausgeſchmückt (G.).

2. For ſolch ein, ſo ein is a frequent equivalent. It is more common in the spoken language than ſolch ein. Lessing and Goethe are very fond of it, *e. g.*, So ein Dichter iſt Shakſpere und Shakſpere faſt ganz allein (Le.). Ich kann mich nicht, wie ſo ein Wortheld, ſo ein Tugendſchwätzer, an meinem Willen wärmen und Gedanken (Sch.).

„So ein" does not come from „ſolch ein," but from ein ſo before adjective and noun: „ein ſo hoher Turm" — „ſo ein hoher Turm," then „ſo ein Turm."

Syntax of the Interrogative Pronoun.

251. Wer, + " who," " which," and was, + " what," are used substantively only: Was kümmert es die Löwin, der man die Jungen raubt, in weſſen Walde ſie brüllt (Le.). Nun, wen lieben zwei von euch am meisten (id.). Was ist der langen Rede kurzer Sinn? (Sch.).

1. Once the genitive after wer and was was common. Wer is almost entirely supplanted by welcher, and was by was für ein. But was + genitive, which generally looks like an accusative, still remains in phrases like Was Wunder(s) (Le.). Was des Teufels, Was Henkers. Was ist Weißes dort am grünen Walde (G.). See 181, 188.

2. Wem only refers to persons. When it refers to things or whole sentences wo(r) + preposition is substituted. Wozu der Lärm? (F. 1322). Woran erkennst du den Dieb. Wor before a vowel, wo before a consonant.

3. In the spoken language „was" is preceded by a preposition that does not govern the accusative: zu was, mit was; but womit, wozu are preferable. The classics have it too. Even für was, um was, durch was are supplanted by wofür, worum, wodurch. Zu was die Posse? (G.) Mit was kann ich aufwarten?

4. Was in the sense of warum and wie is originally an absolute accusative, e. g., Was steht ihr und legt die Hände in (= in den) Schoß (Sch.). Was wird das Herz dir schwer (F. 2720).

5. Mark the interrogative adverbs: wo, + where; wann, + when; wie, + how; wo(r)- with preposition; warum, + wherefore, + why, only interrogative. For their etymology see 551.

252. Welch means + "which" and singles out the individual, though etymologically it inquires after the quality. It stands adjectively and substantively: Und welcher ist's, den du am meisten liebst? (Sch.). Welches Ungeheure sinnet ihr mir an? (id.).

In exclamatory sentences welch is originally interrogative, often followed by ein: Welch ein Jubeln, welch ein Singen wird in unserm Hause sein! (Song). See F. 742.

253. Was für, was für ein inquires after the nature and qualities of a person or thing. Was für always stands adjectively, was für ein adjectively and substantively. Was is separable from für ein. Lessing is particularly fond of this separation. Was für stands before the singular of a noun denoting material and before a collective noun; before the plural of any noun. Was für ein inquires also after an individual.

Ex.: Was für Wein ist dies? Was für Berge . . . trennen uns denn noch? (Le.). Was in Babylon ich dir für einen schönen Stoff gekauft (id.).

Syntax of the Relative Pronouns.

254. There being no original relative pronouns, the other pronouns were used as such or conjunctions like *so, dar, da, unde* (see below) connected coordinate sentences, one of which later became subordinate. The first pronoun used as a relative was ber, bie, bas, in O. H. G. Welcher, wer, was developed into relative pronouns gradually. First they were made indefinite pronouns by means of the particle *so*, O. H. G. *so hwelich(so), so hwer(so), so hwas(so)* > M. H. G. *swelich, swer, swas* = whosoever, whatsoever > N. H. G. welcher, wer, was, which can be strengthened by nur, auch, immer (= ever). To say therefore that the interrogative is used as the relative is hardly correct, though, no doubt, the indirect question had its influence in the coincidence of the forms of the interrogative and indefinite relative pronouns. The demonstrative ber, bie, bas introduced the coordinate clause, which afterwards became subordinate; and clause and pronoun were then called *relative*. Welcher is only of the 16th century.

255. Der and welcher are equivalent. After personal pronouns ber is preferable. Euphony should decide which is to be used. Ein Frauenzimmer, das denkt, ist eben so ekel als ein Mann, der sich schminkt (Le.). Welcher is preferable after berjenige. The following sentence is bad: Die, die die Mutter der Kinder war, ist gestorben.

1. Of the four relatives ber, welch-, wer, was only welch- can also be used adjectively, the other three only substantively. The genitive of ber, bie, bas is always bessen, beren, sg. and pl., never berer. Ex.: Wer kein Gesetz achtet, ist eben so mächtig als wer kein Gesetz hat (Le.) Am Montag, an welchem Tage wir abreisten . . . But this is not very elegant.

256. Der and welcher will take any antecedent soever. But wer, was, having sprung from indefinite and compounded pronouns, require none. Wer admits of no antecedent at all; was may have any other neuter pronoun, an adjective (preferably in the superlative), or a whole clause, *e. g.*, Für was drein geht und nicht drein (ins Gehirn) geht, ein prächtig Wort zu

dienſten ſteht (F. 1952–3). Alles was iſt, iſt vernünftig (Hegel). Was du ererbt von deinen Vätern haſt, erwirb es um es zu beſitzen (F. 682–3). Dem Herrlichſten, was auch der Geiſt empfangen, drängt immer fremd und fremder Stoff ſich an (F. 634–5).

1. Er, wer; der Mann wer; der, wer are impossible. But Goethe has (in the " Walpurgisnacht "), F. 3964: So Ehre dem, wem Ehre gebührt. The proverb says: „Ehre, dem Ehre gebührt," the Bible „Ehre, bem die Ehre gebührt."

2. Was referring to a substantive and welches referring to a whole clause are not present usage, though the classics use them so. Die Alten kannten das Ding nicht, was wir Höflichkeit nennen (Le.). Von früher Jugend an hatte mir und meiner Schweſter der Vater ſelbſt im Tanzen Unterricht gegeben, welches einen ſo ernſthaften Mann wunderlich genug hätte kleiden ſollen (G.).

3. If wer has a seeming antecedent the latter stands after the clause. The antecedent is nothing but the subject of the main clause repeated for emphasis in the shape of another pronoun. If, however, wer and its seeming antecedent do not stand in the same case, the latter is indispensable. Ex.: Wer Pech angreift beſudelt ſich (Prov.). Wer über gewiſſe Dinge den Verſtand nicht verliert, der hat keinen zu verlieren (Le.). Wer vieles bringt, wird manchem etwas bringen (F. 97). But Wer ein Mal lügt, dem glaubt man nicht und wenn er auch die Wahrheit ſpricht (Prov.). Wer da hat, dem wird gegeben (B.). The same is true of was: Was man nicht weiß, das eben brauchte man und was man weiß, kann man nicht brauchen (F. 1066–7). Früh übt ſich, was ein Meiſter werden will (Sch.). For the gender in this illustration see **168**.

4. The old short form wes is now archaic except in **weshalb, weswegen**: Wes Brot ich eſſe, des Lied ich ſinge (Prov.).

257. If the dative and accusative, governed by a preposition, do not refer to a person, **wo**, now rarely **da**, with that preposition, are generally substituted: Nichts iſt Zufall; am wenigſten das, wovon die Abſicht ſo klar in die Augen leuchtet (Le.).

1. So, the oldest relative conjunction, has now been crowded out from the spoken language, though it was very common in the 16th and 17th centuries: Die linke Hand, dazu das Haupt, ſo er ihm abgehauen (Uh.). Von allen, ſo da kamen (Bü.).

258. The relative adverbs **wo**, "where" and **da** (colloquially); da, wann, wenn, wo, "when"; wie, "as" take the place of a relative pronoun governed by a preposition when they refer to nouns denoting time, place, and manner.

Ex.: Kennſt du das Land wo die Citronen blühn? (G.). Es gibt im Menſchen-leben Augenblicke, wo er dem Weltgeiſt näher iſt als ſonſt (Sch.). In dieſem Augen-blicke, da wir reden, iſt kein Tyra'nn mehr in der Schweizer Lande (id.). „Die Art und Weiſe wie," "the manner in which." („Wie" is more forcible than „in welcher.") O ſchöner Tag, wenn endlich der Soldat ins Leben heimkehrt (Sch.).

1. This construction is old only with the demonstrative adverbs used as relatives, viz., *da, dâr, danne*. Allwo, allda, woſelbſt are archaic.

Syntax of the Indefinite Pronouns.

259. Ein and einige can precede a numeral generally followed by a noun. They mean "some," "or so," "odd": ein acht Tage, a week or so; einige vierzig Jahr, forty odd years. The order may also be: „ein Jahr fünfzehn."

1. Grimm thinks this phrase has lost „ober," as if it meant einen Tag oder zehn, ein Jahr oder fünfzehn. No doubt „einige vierzig Jahr" has lost „und" and stands for einige und vierzig Jahr, forty (and) odd years.

260. Ein, etwas, was, wer, jemand, welche, einige can be strengthened by irgend (compounded of *io + hwar* and *gin* = "ever," "where," "you please," *gin* corresponding to L. *-cun*). For the origin of was, wer, welch, see **254**. Ach, wenn ich etwas auf dich könnte! "if I could influence you at all (F. 3423). Was anders ſuche zu beginnen (F. 1383). Die Jagd iſt doch immer was und eine Art von Krieg (G.). Hier ſind Kirſchen zu ver-kaufen. Willſt du welche? Haſt du irgend was verloren?

1. They stand generally only in the nominative and accusative. Einig is rare in the singular, and for it irgend ein is better used.

261. All–. The following examples show the many various forms of all–: all das Geld, all des Geldes, alles das Geld, was ſoll das alles? Alle ſangen. Alle Menſchen müſſen ſterben.

1. Alle stood in M. H. G. only after prepositions as still now, *e. g.*, bei alle bem, "withal." Mir wird von alle bem so bumm (F. 1946). The form alle before the article and not preceded by a preposition, though very common in the classics and in the spoken language, is not so good as all or all with strong endings, *e. g.*, All ber Schmerz (G.). All or alle in such phrases as ber Wein ist all, "there is no more wine," has hardly been satisfactorily explained yet.

2. Notice the following meanings: Alle Stunben einen Theelöffel voll, "a teaspoon full every hour." The singular in the sense of "every" is rarer, auf allen Fall, in every case. Aller Anfang ist schwer (Prov.). Alles Ding währt seine Zeit, Gottes Lieb in Ewigkeit (Hymn). The singular in the sense of Eng. "all" is archaic, allen Winter (Logau, quoted in Grimm's Dict.), all winter. For all day, all night, we say best bie ganze Nacht, ben ganzen Tag. Notice also in aller Früh, "very early," in aller Stille, in alle Welt.

3. The plural of jeber, jebweber, jeglicher is rare. It is expressed by „alle." Even the singular of the last two is now archaic and rare.

262. Mancher does not differ from the Eng. "many" in use and force. Compare ein mancher, manch einer, mancher gute Mann, manch ein guter Mann, manche schöne Blume.

263. Viel and wenig, denoting the individual and used substantively denoting persons, must be inflected; if they denote an indefinite number, quantity, mass, they are generally uninflected. Denn viele sind berufen, aber wenige sind auserwählet (B.). Viel noch hast du von mir zu hören (Sch.). Zwar weiß ich viel, doch möchte ich alles wissen (F. 601). Es studieren viel Amerikaner in Deutschland.

1. Vieler, -e, -es denotes "various sorts," *e.g.*, vieler Wein; in composition vielerlei Wein, "many kinds of wine."

A fuller treatment of the large number of indefinite pronouns and numerals belongs rather to the Dictionary.

SYNTAX OF THE VERB.

CLASSIFICATION OF VERBS.

264. According to meaning and construction the verbs may be variously divided: 1, into independent verbs; 2, into the small class of *tense* auxiliaries and the *modal* auxiliaries. See **267**. Again: 1, into *personal* verbs, which can have any person, the 1., 2., or 3., as subject; 2, into *impersonal* verbs, which have the indefinite subject es, „es regnet." See **236**.

The personal verbs again divide: 1, into neuter or subjective verbs, as die Sonne scheint (see **179**); 2, transitive or objective verbs, the direct object of which stands in the accusative (transitive proper, see **198**) or in the genitive or dative (called also intrans., see **184, 190**).

As subdivisions of transitive verbs may be regarded: 1, the reflexive verbs; 2, the causative.

The reflexives again: 1, into reflexives proper, which occur only as reflexives, *e. g.*, sich grämen, to pine; sich erbarmen, to feel pity; 2, into both transitive and intransitive verbs used reflexively, *e. g.*, sich waschen, sich vereinen, sich tot lachen.

The pronoun is always in the accusative, but see **197**.

1. Transitive verbs have often intransitive or neuter force, but there can be no direct object then. Das Pferd zieht den Wagen, but Die Wolken ziehen am Himmel. Personal verbs can also be used without a logical subject: Das Wasser rauscht, but Es rauscht im Rohre. Also the modal auxiliaries occur still as independent verbs: Was soll das? but Wohin soll der Dieb geflüchtet sein? See **267**.

Syntax of the Auxiliaries.

I. Haben and sein.

265. Haben forms the compound tenses, active voice:

1. Of all transitive verbs: ich habe getragen, ich habe bedeckt, ich habe angeklagt.

2. Of the modal auxiliaries, of reflexive and impersonal verbs proper. Er hat es nicht gemocht, hat sich gewaschen, es hat geregnet, es hat mich gereut.

3. Of intransitive verbs which have no direct object, at most the object in the G. or D. Er hatte mein gespottet, er hat mir geschadet, er hatte gelacht, geweint, geschlafen.

4. Of (intransitive) verbs of motion when the mere action within a certain space, the effort, and its extent are to be emphasized, without reference to direction, point of departure or destination. A. von Humboldt hat viel gereist, = was a great traveler. Der Stallknecht hat eine Stunde hin und her geritten. Er hatte in Wien zehn Jahre gefahren (Le.). Das Lämmchen hat gehüpft, der Fisch hat geschwommen. Das Kleine (the little one) hat noch nie gegangen (has never walked). Sophie hat geklettert und sich die Schürze zerrissen. Der Schnellläufer hat schon längst gelaufen (finished running long ago). Good usage favors: Die Uhr hat einmal gegangen, aber jetzt steht sie still. Die Mühle, die Maschine, das Rad hat gegangen, but ist is frequently used.

5. Of sitzen, stehen, liegen, anfangen, beginnen, aufhören. But in S. G. sein is more common and it is also found in the classics. Wo habt ihr gesessen, gestanden? Wann hat die Schule angefangen?

266. Sein forms the compound tenses:

1. Of all verbs of motion, except some, which take haben, when action simply is denoted. See **265, 4.** These take sein when the direction, points of departure, destination and arrival are mentioned. These circumstances are often expressed by inseparable and separable prefixes in compound verbs. Ex.: „Der Mai ist gekommen." Er wird gefallen sein, = he probably fell. Wir sind schnell hinabgestiegen. Die Seefahrer sind auf der Insel Skye gelandet. Die Störche sind nach Süden gezogen. Der Stallknecht ist in einer Stunde hin und her geritten, = he rode to a certain place (there) and back. Die Feinde sind entflohen, entlaufen, eingetroffen. Wir sind schon mehrere Male umgezogen (moved).

2. Of certain verbs denoting a springing into being or passing away, a transition and development, growth and decay, often expressed by er-, ver-, zer-, and separable prefixes. Die Milch ist gefroren (< gefrieren, but es hat gefroren < frieren, there was a frost). Das Seil ist zerrissen. Der Schnee ist geschmolzen. „Der Bruder wäre nicht gestorben." Das Bäumchen ist gewachsen. Die reichen Leute sind im Kriege verarmt. Das Licht ist erloschen. Die Schale ist gesprungen (cracked). Der Lehrling war eingeschlafen (had fallen asleep). In the compound verbs it is just this prefix that called for sein. Compare trinken — ertrinken, scheinen — erscheinen, wachen — erwachen, hungern — verhungern, frieren — erfrieren.

3. Of sein, bleiben, begegnen, folgen, gelingen, geschehen, glücken, for which it is hard to account by meaning, but see **283**, 2. Ex.: Es ist ihm nicht gelungen, geglückt. Das ist schon alles dagewesen. Ein süßer Trost ist ihm geblieben (Sch.).

4. Haben has gained upon sein in German, but not so much as English "to have" upon "to be." Folgen and begegnen were once generally compounded with haben. Also the tendency to use intransitive verbs as transitives, so strong in Eng., has increased in German. While in Eng. one can "run" a locomotive, a sewing machine, a train, a ship, in German führen, leiten, in Gang bringen, gebrauchen, or the verb of motion + lassen or machen, will have to be used. Der Kutscher hat uns schnell gefahren. Der Postillion hat den Wagen vorgefahren. Man konnte die Feuerspritze nicht in Gang bringen.

5. The difficulty as to the use of haben and sein lies after all mainly in the way in which a verb is used, transitively or intransitively, and in the meaning. The student should attend particularly to these points and not be too timid, as in many cases usage is by no means settled.

As to the omission of haben and sein in dependent clauses, see **346**.

II. Special Uses of the Modal Auxiliaries.

This subject belongs really rather to the Dictionary, but the appreciation and translation of these verbs is so difficult that a brief treatment of them is given here.

267. 1. Können denotes ability: Der Fisch kann schwimmen. Hier steh' ich, ich kann nicht anders (Lu.). Possibility: Ihr könntet ihr Werkzeug sein, mich in das Garn zu ziehen (Sch.). Knowledge, "to know how," its oldest meaning: Kannst du Italie'nisch? Compare können, "to have learnt," then "to be able"; kennen (< *kanjan*, causative of kann—können), "to be acquainted with"; wissen, "to know."

2. Dürfen denotes: 1. Permission and authorization: Du darfst auch

ba nur frei erscheinen (F. 336). Ohne Jagdschein darf niemand auf die Jagd gehn. 2. "To have occasion to," "reason for," "need": Man darf den Schlüssel nur zwei Mal umdrehen und der Riegel springt zurück, "You need . . ." Du darfst hinausgehen, die Luft ist hier sehr schlecht, "You have good reason to go out . . ." This force is the oldest, but rather rare now. 3. "To trust one's self to": Wer darf ihn nennen und wer bekennen: Ich glaub ihn (Gott) (F. 3433–5). This force has sprung from 1 and 2 and from the verb tar — türren + dare, whose meaning was embodied in darf — dürfen. On the other hand, it has nearly given up the original force of "need," "want," still apparent in 2, to its compound bedürfen. In some editions of the Bible dürfen, "to want," and tar — türren, "to dare," are still the rule. In later editions bedürfen and dürfen have been substituted for them. 4. The preterit subjunctive (potential, see **284**, 3) dürfte is used for a mild assertion: Die Nachwelt dürfte Bedenken tragen, dieses Urteil zu unterschreiben (Sch.), "Posterity very likely will . . ." Das dürfte zu spät sein, "I fear very much, that is too late." Etiquette admits such redundant phrases as: Dürfte or darf ich mir erlauben, etc.

3. **Mögen** denotes: 1. In its oldest, but now rare sense except in dialect, "ability" and "power." This it has given up to „können." Compare its cognates "may" and "can" in Eng.: Ihr Anblick gibt den Engeln Stärke, wenn keiner sie ergründen mag (F. 247–8), "although no one is able . . ." 2. Concession, no interference on the part of the speaker: Der Bursche mag nach Hause gehn (It lies with him, I have no objection). Wer mir den Becher kann wieder zeigen, er mag ihn behalten (Sch.). 3. Possibility, the action does not concern or influence the speaker; können means a possibility that lies in the ability of another person or object. Was für Grünröck' mögen das sein (Sch.). Er mag das gesagt haben, er mag das thun, It is possible he said so, he may do it. Das Tier mag zehn Jahre alt sein. With this force it supplants the potential and concessive subjunctives; if it stands itself in the subjunctive of the present or preterit, it supplants also the optative subjunctive. Ich wünsche daß die ganze Welt uns hören mag, hören möge. Möchte auch doch die ganze Welt uns hören (Le.). 4. From 2 springs the force of "inclination," "liking," "wishing." Was sich verträgt mit meiner Pflicht, mag ich ihr gern gewähren (Sch.). Ich möchte, daß er es nicht wieder erführe. Ich esse was ich mag und leide was ich muß (Prov.).

4. **Müssen**, + must, denotes: 1. In its oldest sense, "to have occasion, room," "to be one's lot," "it is the case." A trace of this is left in the following uses: Mein Hund war ohne Maulkorb hinausgelaufen. Nun mußte auch gerade ein Polizi'st daher kommen (as luck would have it, a police-

man came along). Der Zufall mußte ihn grabe hin bringen. Zum zweiten Mal soll mir kein Klang erschallen, er müßte denn (unless it should) besondern Sinn begründen (G., quoted in Sanders' Dict.). 2. Necessity of various kinds: Alle Menschen müssen sterben. Der Senne muß scheiden (Sch.). Ein Oberhaupt muß sein (id.). Das muß ein schlechter Müller sein, dem niemals fiel das Wandern ein (Song). Er muß sehr krank gewesen sein; er ist noch so schwach. The force of dürfen: Ich muß nicht vergessen, "I must not forget."

Brauchen + negative generally takes the place of müssen + negative when it denotes moral necessity. Das brauchst du nicht zu thun, wenn du nicht willst. Wohl dem, der mit der neuen (Zeit) nicht mehr braucht zu leben (Sch.).

5. Sollen, + shall, denotes: 1. Duty and obligation. Du sollst Gott deinen Herrn lieben von ganzem Herzen, von ganzer Seele und von ganzem Gemüte (B.). Du hättest da sein sollen, You ought to have been there. 2. Necessity and destiny: Diese Furcht soll endigen! ihr Haupt soll fallen. Ich will Frieden haben (Sch.). Ich weiß nicht was soll es bedeuten (Heine). Was soll das? What (is that) for? Darin sollte er sich täuschen, In that he was bound to be deceived, disappointed. 3. It denotes the statement and claim of another, "is to," "is said to": Das Meter soll acht Thaler kosten. Der Schatz der Nibelungen soll im Rheine liegen. Sieben Sträflinge sollen entkommen sein. 4. Sollte approaches the force of the conditional, + "should." Sollte er noch kommen, sag' ihm, ich hätte nicht länger warten können. Sollte er auch wohl krank sein? Is it possible that he is sick?

6. Wollen, + will, denotes: 1. The will and purpose of the subject. Was wolltest du mit dem Dolche? sprich (Sch.). Ich will es wieder vergessen, weil Sie doch nicht wollen, daß ich es wissen soll (G.). Wolle nur was du kannst und du wirst können was du willst. 2. "To be about," "on the point of." Ein armer Bauer wollte sterben (Nicolai). Es will regnen. Frequent in stage-directions, „will gehen," „will abgehn." Will sich Hector ewig von mir wenden? (Sch.). 3. The claim and statement of another, who "says" or "claims to": Der Zeuge will den Angeklagten gesehen haben. Du willst ihn zu einem guten Zwecke betrogen haben. Notice the ambiguity of such a sentence as Der Herr will es gethan haben, "claims he did it," or according to 1, "wills or wishes that it be done."

Wollen is really the most difficult to understand and use. It occurs in a great many more idioms with ever varying shades of meaning. Notice, e. g., Es will verlauten, "It is spread abroad." Was will das sagen? = "What does that amount to?" "that is nothing." Ich will es nicht gesehen haben, I will act as if I had not seen it or "nobody shall see it," according to 1. Wenn der Schüler doch diese Regel lernen wollte, "If he only would . . . = conditional. Wollte Gott daß . . . , would to God that . . . Diese Feder will nicht, this pen does not write (well). But it is impossible to give all these meanings.

Still Eng. "will" is not far behind the German. Sollen and wollen should not be confounded with Eng. "shall" and "will" of the future, see 279, 3.

7. Laſſen, sometimes classed here, is really a causative auxiliary and never used as such without an inf., which stands as a further object. Keine Klage läßt ſie ſchallen (Sch.). Unverzüglich ließ er drei Batterien aufwerfen (id.). See 202, 1. A second force is "to allow," "not to hinder." Der Gefangenwärter ließ den Gefangenen entwiſchen. Laſſen Sie das bleiben (= to leave a thing undone. Laſſen, to look, is a neuter verb.

For laſſen + reflexive, see 272 ; in the imperative, see 287, 4.

REMARK.—Verbs of motion can be omitted, particularly when an adverb expresses the direction. Willſt du mit? Ich muß hin. Das Packet ſollte fort (ought to be sent). Der Hut muß in die Schachtel. But all except müſſen and dürfen can be used as independent verbs, i. e., no other verb need be supplied. There is no call for a verb in Was ſoll der Hut? (Sch.), "What is this hat (here) for? Notice that ſollen, mögen, and wollen are really the only ones that deserve the term modal auxiliaries, since they assist in expressing the mood. See 287.

THE PASSIVE VOICE.

268. The active voice needs no comment. Only transitive verbs form a complete passive. But transitives whose meaning admits only of an object of the thing, also intransitives and subjective verbs, form only the third person singular with the grammatical subject es or without it. Ihnen wird geholfen. Es wird gelacht und geſungen. Geſtern wurde geſpielt. Bei uns zu Hauſe (where I come from) wird viel Whiſt geſpielt.

269. In the transformation of the active into the passive voice, the direct object in the accusative becomes subject-nominative and the former subject is expressed by von + dative denoting the agent and by durch + accusative denoting means and instrument. Baumgarten erſchlug den Wolfenſchießen. W. wurde von B. erſchlagen. Der Brief wurde durch einen Dienſtmann beſorgt (through a porter). See prepositions, 304, 2.

270. When a verb governs two accusatives both accusatives become nominatives with the verbs of naming, calling, scolding. Er wurde ſein Freund genannt. See 179, 2.

1. With lehren and fragen the accusative of the thing may be retained, particularly if that accusative be a pronoun, e. g., Das Schlimmste, was uns widerfährt, das werden wir vom Tag gelehrt (G.). For etwas gelehrt werden it is better to use unterrichtet werden; for etwas gefragt werden, better nach etwas gefragt werden. The accusative of the noun now sounds pedantic, though lehren in M. H. G. always retained the accusative in the passive. See 202, 2.

271. With a verb governing an accusative, a genitive, or a dative, the accusative becomes nominative in the passive, but the genitive and dative are retained. H. wurde des Hochverrats angeklagt. Deiner wurde gedacht (no grammatical subject) or es wurde deiner gedacht. Mir wurde gefolgt, *I* was followed.

1. The verbs folgen, helfen, gehorchen, schmeicheln, widersprechen, danken often form a personal passive in the classics and in the spoken language, but it is very questionable whether this use should be imitated; certainly not by foreigners who are accustomed to this construction in their own language and are apt to make mistakes in the active and say „ich folge dich" if they hear or say „ich werde gefolgt, geschmeichelt." Those who defend the personal passive appeal to the older accusative after helfen and schmeicheln.

272. The reflexive, encouraged by French influence, and man, es + active often replace the passive. For Es wird gesungen, gepocht stands Man singt, pocht. Da öffnet sich das Thor, Then the gate is opened. Der Schlüssel wird sich finden, The key will be found. More frequent than the reflexive alone is sich . . . lassen, e. g., Er wird sich bestimmen lassen zu . . . , He will let himself be influenced to . . . , He can be induced to . . . Das läßt sich leicht machen, That is easily done. Das läßt sich hören, That is plausible. See **290, 3,** *b*. It is clear from this that the German passive is less frequent than the English. The grammars boast more of the full and long compound tenses than actual usage justifies.

273.   Origin of the Passive Voice.

1. In O. H. G. sein (*sin, wesan*), werden (*werdan*) were used to express the passive. Gothic alone shows traces of anything like a Latin passive, but even there the periphrastic form had to be resorted to. In M. H. G. the present is *ich wirde gelobet*; preterit, *ich wart gelobet*; perfect, *ich bin gelobet*; pluperfect, *ich was gelobet*. *Worden* was added to the perfect from the 13th century downward, but was not considered essential until the 17th century. The passive idea lies originally only in the past or passive participle and not in werden, which means only "I enter into the state of being „geliebt," „geschlagen," etc. Compare the future, ich werde lieben, "I enter into the state of loving." The M. H. G. *ich bin geliebet, ich was (war) geliebet* are by no means lost. Only they are not called tenses now. Ich bin geliebt, das Zimmer ist gefegt mean "I am

in the state of being loved," "the room is in a swept state," "has been cleaned," "is clean." The participles are felt as adjectives. Ich bin geliebt worden, das Zimmer ist gefegt worden mean ' I have passed into the state of being loved," "the room has passed into the state of being swept." The transition into this state, and not the present state, but the fact or action are emphasized, hence the idea of *tense* is prominent. The fitness of the name of perfect passive for this form and not also for ich bin geliebt is apparent because ich bin geliebt worden is composed of ich bin (ge)worden (the perfect) + geliebt. In O. H. G. fein still formed the present as "to be" now in Eng., but already in M. H. G. *werden* was the prevalent auxiliary (see above), while *sein* was prevalent in the perfect.

2. Perhaps the following examples will illustrate the force of the various forms:

Die Tochter ist verlobt, is engaged to be married. Vom Eise befreit sind Strom und Bäche (F. 903). Dieser Kessel ist von Bergen begrenzt (Hu.) These three are not passive tenses. But compare: Zu dem Lächerlichen wird ein Contra'st von Vollkommenheiten und Unvollkommenheiten erfordert (Le.) (present tense). Dieser Punkt ist viel bestritten worden (perf. pass.). The same difference between wurde + participle (= imperfect pass.) and war + participle (no tense), *e. g.*, Home'r war vor Alters unstreitig fleißiger gelesen als jetzt (Le.). Die Häuser waren festlich geschmückt (no tense). Der Räuberhauptmann war schon gefangen genommen worden, als seine Leute herbeikamen (pluperfect pass.). Der Spio'n wurde ohne weiteres an einen Ast geknüpft und erhängt (imperfect pass.).

Examples of the future and conditional perfects passive are very rare in the classics.

Syntax of the Tenses.

Simple Tenses.

274. The Present.

1. It denotes an action as now going on. Wie glänzt die Sonne, wie lacht die Flur (G.).

2. It is the tense used in the statement of a general truth or fact or custom, in which the idea of time is lost sight of. Dreimal drei ist neun. Gott ist die Liebe (B.). Borgen macht Sorgen (Prov.).

3. The **historical** present is used in vivid narrative for a past tense. Das zu Linz gegebene Beispiel findet allgemeine Nachahmung; man verflucht das Andenken des Verräters; alle Arme'en fallen von ihm ab (Sch.).

4. For the English perfect German (also French) uses the present when the action or state continues in the present time, but there is generally an adverb denoting duration of time qualifying it. Ex.: Nun bin ich sieben Tage hier (G.). Zwei Tage gehen wir schon hier herum (id.). Ich bin allhier erst kurze Zeit (F. 1868).

> This use is by no means new in German or unknown in English, *e.g.*, "I forget why." "The world by what I learn is no stranger to your generosity" (Goldsmith, quoted by Mätzner). It is closely related to the present sub 2 and 3, and generally translated by "have been" + present participle.

5. **The future present,** that is, the present with the force of the future, is much more frequent in German than in English. Ex.: Nein, nein, ich gehe nach der Stadt zurück (F. 820). Wer weiß, wer morgen über uns befiehlt (Sch.).

> It is a very old use of the present, from a time when the periphrastic future was not yet developed.

6. The English periphrastic present in "I am writing," "I do write" rarely has corresponding German phrases. For instance, thun is dialectic and archaic. Und thu' nicht mehr in Worten framen (F. 385). A large number of present participles are looked upon as adjectives and stand in the predicate after sein, but they do not form a tense (see **273**, 1). There is a difference between the simple present and sein + pres. part. The former, if it occur at all, denotes an *act* of the subject, the latter denotes a *quality* of the same or of another subject. Ex.: Man nimmt teil an etwas, one takes part in something. Jemand ist teilnehmend, one is sympathetic. Die Farbe schreit is hardly used, but die Farbe ist eine schreiende, the color is a loud one. Die Aussicht reizt einen, immer höher zu steigen, the prospect entices one to climb higher and higher, but die Aussicht ist reizend, the prospect is charming. Compare the Eng. "charming," "promising," etc.

275. The Preterit.

1. It is strictly the "historical" tense, used in narration, when one event is related in some connection with another event, as following it or preceding it. Ex.: Cäsar kam, sah und siegte. Er ward geboren, er lebte, nahm ein Weib und starb (Gellert).

> In the story of the creation in Genesis only the pret. is used until

chapter 2, verse 4, when the account is summed up Also ist Himmel und Erde geworden, which has the perfect as it should have. See **276**.

2. It represents a past action as lasting, customary; also as contemporaneous with another action. Gestern kam der Medicus hier aus der Stadt hinaus zum Amtmann (connect „hinaus" with „zum," not with „aus der Stadt") und fand mich auf der Erde unter Lottens Kindern, wie einige auf mir herumkrabbelten, andere mich neckten (G.). Kühn war das Wort, weil es die That nicht war (Sch.).

Compound Tenses.

276. The Perfect.

It is used to denote a past event as a separate act or independent fact. The act is completed, but the result of it is felt in the present and may continue in the present. Ex.: Ich habe genossen das irdische Glück (Sch.). Gott hat die Welt erschaffen = God is the creator of the world, but Im Anfang schuf Gott Himmel und Erde (B.). Du hast's erreicht, Octavio (Sch.). See **279**, 2.

1. In the best writers this distinction is generally observed, but not in the spoken language, in which the perfect is crowding out the preterit. As an illustration of the exact use of the tenses, particularly of the preterit and perfect, may be recommended the introduction to Schiller's Geschichte des Abfalls der vereinigten Niederlande.

277. The Pluperfect.

It denotes a past action which was completed before another past action began. Ex.: Tilly hatte kaum seinen Rückmarsch angetreten, als der König sein Lager zu Schwedt aufhob und gegen Frankfurt an der Oder rückte (Sch.).

278. The Future.

1. It denotes an action yet to take place. Ex.: Was wird aus dem Kindlein werden? (B.). Der Kaiser wird morgen abreisen.

2. It denotes probability and should then not be translated by an English future as a rule. Ex.: Der Hund wird sechs Jahre alt sein (= ist wohl or wahrscheinlich), the dog may be or is prob-

ably, six years old. Wer flopft? Es wird ein Bettler sein, it is probably a beggar.

3. In familiar language it stands for the imperative implying confident expectation of the result. Du wirst hier bleiben, You shall stay here. Du wirst dich hüten, Take good care not to do it.

For the present with the force of the future, see **274, 5**.

279. The Future Perfect.

1. It is the perfect transferred to the future. Vergebens werdet ihr für euren Feldherrn euch geopfert haben (Sch.). More frequently than the future, the future perfect denotes probability: Wo wird er die Nacht zugebracht haben? (Le.), Where can he have spent the night? Es wird was andres wohl bedeutet haben (Sch.), It probably meant something else.

2. As the present can have future force, so the perfect can have future perfect force. Nicht eher denk ich dieses Blatt zu brauchen, bis eine That gethan ist, die unwiderfprechlich den Hochverrat bezeugt (Sch.).

3. In M. H. G., the future perfect is unknown and its force is expressed by *ge* prefixed to the present, and by the perfect.

a. Guard against confounding the modal auxiliaries in German with the Eng. future. Approach to a future might be felt in wollen and sollen, *e. g.*, Was wollen sie denn herausverhören, wenn einer unschuldig ist? (G.). Der Reichstag zu Augsburg soll hoffentlich unsere Proje'kte zur Reife bringen (G.). See **283, 4**.

280. The Conditionals.

They are future subjunctives corresponding to the preterit and pluperfect subjunctive as the future corresponds to the present. As in all subjunctives, the idea of tense is not emphasized. Preterit subjunctive and I. conditional, pluperfect subjunctive and II. conditional are nearly identical in force, but preterit and pluperfect deserve the preference, particularly in the passive. In dependent conditional clauses the preterit or pluperfect subjunctive only can stand. In the main sentence there is no choice between them and the conditionals. Ex.: Ohne deinen Rat würde ich es nicht gethan haben or hätte ich es nicht gethan. Was würdest du an meiner Stelle thun? Wärest du hier gewesen, mein Bruder wäre nicht gestorben (B.).

281. The conditionals should be substituted for the subjunctive of the preterit and of the pluperfect: 1. When the force of the future is to be emphasized as in: Nähme der Kranke die Medizin regelmäßig ein, so würde das Fieber von dieser Stunde an allmählich verschwinden. Sie glaubten, sie würden sich leicht als Helden darstellen (Sch.). 2. When the indicative and subjunctive forms coincide as is the case with certain persons in weak verbs: Auf einen Eid würde ich ihm nicht glauben. „Glaube" might be pret. ind. Ihr würdet dies Rätsel mir erklären, sagte sie (Sch.). „Ihr werdet" could also be indicative future.

The Tense of Indirect Speech.

282. The rule is: The indirect speech retains the tense of the direct. Ex.: Die Bäume seien gebannt, sagt er, und wer sie schädige, dem wachse seine Hand heraus zum Grabe (Sch.). Egmont beteuerte, daß das Ganze nichts als ein Tafelscherz gewesen sei. Der Knabe behauptete, er hätte es nicht gethan, wenn er nicht von seinen Gefährten dazu verleitet worden wäre. Er sagte auch, er wolle es nicht wieder thun, wenn man ihm jetzt vergebe. Der Zeuge konnte nicht schwören, daß er den Angeklagten je gesehen habe.

1. But this rule is not strictly observed. If the main clause contains, for instance, a past tense, the other clause may take a preterit for the present, a pluperfect for the perfect, or a conditional for the future: Das wären die Planeten, sagte mir der Führer, sie regierten das Geschick (Sch.). Ihr würdet dies Rätsel mir erklären, sagte sie (id.). Mir meldet (pres. for perf.) er, er läge krank (id.). If any ambiguity arises, as is not unfrequently the case, this license should not be indulged in. If the main verb is in the present, it is not well to substitute the preterit or pluperfect in the subordinate clause, because this license is due to attraction of tenses, viz., preterit in one — preterit or pluperfect in the other. Compare: Er beteuert, er sei dagegen, he asserts, that he is opposed. Er beteuert, er wäre dagegen might be construed as meaning er würde dagegen sein, which means "he would be opposed." Er beteuert, er sei dagegen gewesen, he had been

opposed; er wäre bagegen gewesen might moreover be understood as having the force of the II. Conditional.

For the mood of the indirect statement, see 285. For further remarks on the use of tenses, see 284, also the General Syntax.

283.   Origin of the Compound Tenses.

1. The compound tenses in all the living languages are products of the development of so-called *periphrastic* conjugation, which uses certain independent verbs denoting existence, possession, transition, or the beginning of an action, in connection with an infinitive, participle, or gerundive. The more the inflectional endings of the simple tenses of the earlier periods weathered, the more favorable were the chances for the growth of analytical and circumlocutory tenses. Compare the Latin *amor, amatus sum* or *fui; excusavi, excusatam, -um habeo* or *teneo* with French *je suis aimé, -ée, je fus aimé, -ée; je l'ai excusé, -ée, je l'avais excusé, -ée*. The Germanic languages have only two simple tenses. Gothic shows still a mutilated passive. But the future perfect and pluperfect active and passive sprang up within historic times from a combination of an independent verb with an infinitive or participle, which were at first felt only as predicate noun or adjective. The participle in O. H. G. could be inflected like any predicate adjective.

2. At different periods of High German there were different verbs which could be thus employed. Besides the modern auxiliaries haben, sein and werden, in O. H. G. eigan, + to own. In Gothic *haban* + inf. was made to express the future, in O. H. G. *suln* (shall) and *werdan* + pres. part.; in M. H. G. besides these, *wellen, müezen*. Ich habe den Hut abgenommen or aufgesetzt means originally I have, possess the hat in some state or position, viz., in my hand (taken off) or on my head (put on). The German order, too, shows this early construction much better than the English "I have taken off my hat." Compare the Latin *Excusatum habeas me rogo*, "Have me excused, pray," „Bitte, habe (halte) mich (für) entschuldigt." Haben could only be used with transitive verbs, but losing the distinctive meaning of possession, it could combine with verbs having an object in the G. and D. and even with no object, viz., with intransitive verbs. Haben required the past participle in O. H. G. in the A., but sein required it in the N. Sein could not, from the nature of its meaning, form the perf. or pluperf. active of any transitive verb, but only of intransitives denoting a continuance of a state (bleiben, sein) or transition into another state, where it, however, collided with werben, used in the future. But notice that the idea of transition and change is in most verbs, here in question, due to the prefix. Sein + past participle could only mean existence in a certain state, at most the beginning or ceasing of an existence.

3. As to verbs of motion, their relation to these verbs is very intimate. When it is not, haben becomes the rival of sein, as soon as the activity of motion is to be brought out and not the result. That sein could be used with a past participle of a verb of motion at all, was partly brought about by its use with a present participle and infinitive. Such forms as vermutend, vermögend, nachgebend sein, vermuten sein are remnants of the use of *sin* + pres. part. or inf. in M. H. G. We do not feel the participle or infinitive as such now. They form no tense.

4. Werben + pres. part. was in M. H. G. more common than werben + inf., but the

latter was the established future in the 16th century. From "I pass into the state of praising" to "I shall praise" is not a long step.

5. The conditionals formed with würbe sprang up in the 14th century and were settled in the 16th, according to Grimm. In M. H. G. before the 13th century "*solde*," "*wolde*" were used as in the other Germanic languages, but these lacked the umlaut, and therefore were not easily distinguishable as subjunctives.

THE MOODS.

Subjunctive.

284. The indicative is the mood of reality, the subjunctive is the mood of unreality, contingency, possibility.

1. The **imperative** subjunctive helps to fill out the imperative for the third persons sg. and pl. and the first person pl. It is a strong optative, see sub 2.

Ex.: Alles schweige, jeder neige ernsten Tönen nun sein Ohr (Song). Setze jeder wie er's treibe, sehe jeder wo er bleibe (G.). Seien Sie mir willko'mmen. Lassen wir das, let us not do this. Gehen wir diesen Paragraph(en) noch mal durch, let us go over this paragraph once more. Gehen Sie. Treten die Herren gefälligst ein (rare).

Werde and sei, seid really subjunctives, are used as imperatives in the second person. Werde munter, mein Gemüte (Hymn). Sei mir gegrüßt, mein Berg (Sch.).

2. The **optative** subjunctive expresses a wish or request. The present subjunctive implies confidence of fulfilment. Only the third person is used.

Ex.: Dich führe durch das wildbewegte Leben ein gnädiges Geschick (Sch.). Dein Name sei vergessen (Uh.). Gott vermehre die Gabe (G.).

The preterit subjunctive implies less assurance, and, like the pluperfect subjunctive, even no expectation of realization.

Ex.: O wären wir weiter! o wär ich zu Haus (G.). O sähst du, voller Mondenschein . . . (F. 386). Wäre er nur noch am Leben! (Implying „er ist aber tot"). Frommer Stab, o hätt' ich nimmer mit dem Schwerte dich vertauscht (Sch.). See also F. 392–7.

3. The **potential** subjunctive expresses an opinion as such, a possibility, a mild assertion of an undoubted fact (*diplomatic subj.*); it stands in questions, direct and indirect; in exclama-

tions. The preterit and I. conditional are the potential subjunctives of the present; the pluperfect and II. conditional, of the past.

Ex.: Ich reime, dächt' ich, doch noch so ziemlich zusammen, was zusammen gehört (Le.). Das ginge noch, "that might do yet" (id.). Wer wüßte das nicht? Everybody knows that. Hätte ich doch nimmermehr gedacht, daß er so groß werden würde (Le.). Wie ließe sich alles schreiben! (G.) (Implying „es ist unmöglich"). Fast hätte ich das Beste vergessen (id.). Beinahe wäre ich gegen einen Baum gerannt. Du hättest das gewußt? (Implying „ich glaube es nicht). Nicht, daß ich wüßte, not as far as I know.

See also the modal auxiliaries, **267**.

4. The **concessive** subjunctive denotes an admission, yielding, and supposition. Generally only in the third person of the present and perfect. It borders closely upon the optative and conditional.

Ex.: Es koste was es wolle (Le.). Es sei, "(it is) granted." Geselle, du seist ein guter oder schlimmer, leg' dich aufs Ohr (Uh.). See mögen, **267**, 3.

5. The **unreal** subjunctive stands in conditional sentences both in the premise and the conclusion, *i. e.* in the dependent clause and in the main clause, when the premise is not true. The preterit and pluperfect stand in the premise; the preterit, pluperfect, and the two conditionals in the conclusion. The preterit has present and future force, the pluperfect has future force only.

Ex.: Es ließe sich alles trefflich schlichten, könnte man die Sachen zweimal verrichten (G.). Ich wäre nichts, wenn ich bliebe was ich bin (id.). Wenn wir Geld bei uns gehabt hätten, so würden wir den Armen was gegeben haben.

The premise omitted or represented by an adverb, etc.: Ich thäte das nicht an Deiner Stelle = wenn ich an Deiner Stelle wäre. Wir wären des Todes. Ohne Alpenstock wäre der Wanderer in die Tiefe hinabgefallen.

The conclusion omitted: Ja wenn wir nicht wären, sagte die Laterne zum Mond. Da ging sie aus (Folk-lore).

285. The subjunctive is the mood of the indirect statement, in which the speaker expresses the ideas of another in his own words without sharing the responsibility for, and belief in, the statement. For examples see **282**.

The third sentence shows that unreal conditional clauses are not affected when part of an indirect statement. The fourth, also the last of **328**, show how other clauses are affected.

Imperative.

286. It expresses a command and occurs only in the 2. p. sg. and pl. For the 1. and 3. p. pl., see **284**, 1. Eile mit Weile, Make haste slowly. Lehre du mich meine Leute kennen (Sch.). Bindet ihn (id.). Wartet ihr, indem wir voran laufen.

1. The pronoun is quite optional; only when there is a contrast, as in the last sentence (ihr — wir), it should stand. In the subjunctive it always stands.

The imperative is only used in the present and has future force, but by a license also a perfect imperative occurs: Besen! Besen! Seib's gewesen! says the apprentice when he wants the brooms to cease being watercarriers (G.).

287. Other verbal forms that take imperative force and a very strong one, are:

1. The infinitive: Maul (Mund) halten! Hold your tongue. Nicht anfassen! Do not touch.

2. The past participle: Die Trommel gerührt (G.). Frisch auf Kameraden, auf's Pferd, auf's Pferd! in das Feld, in die Freiheit gezogen (Sch.).

3. The present and future indicative: Georg, du bleibst um mich (G.). Du wirst den Apfel schießen von dem Kopf des Knaben (Sch.). See **278**, 3.

4. The modal auxiliaries denoting a necessity, duty, can express imperative force, also lassen. Du sollst nicht stehlen (B.). Kein Mensch muß müssen (Le.), no man ought to be compelled.

Since the Eng. "let" shows no inflection, notice the German forms: Laß uns gehen, to a person addressed as du; plural Laßt uns gehen. Lassen Sie uns gehen, to a person addressed as Sie.

Infinitive.

288. It is a verbal noun and the present infinitive has neither voice, tense, nor inflection. The compound infinitive arose like the compound tenses (see **283**): gelobt werden, to be praised; gelobt worden sein, to have been praised; gelobt haben, to have praised.

> 1. Notice the marked difference in meaning between the present of some of the modal auxiliaries + perfect infinitive, and the perfect or pluperfect + present infinitive. Ex.: Der Kutscher will den Gefangenen gesehen haben = claims to have seen him, but hat ihn sehen wollen = wanted to see him. Der Hausirer muß vorbeigegangen sein = must have passed by, but hat vorbeigehen müssen, was forced to pass by, etc.

289. We distinguish between the infinitive *without* zu and *with* zu.

> The former is the older construction. Being a noun, the infinitive always stood in the D. after zu in O. and M. H. G. But in early N. H. G., when it was no longer inflected, the prepositional infinitive gained ground and gave also rise to the gerundive (see **298**). Usage is in many cases still unsettled as to the use of zu. Its frequent use is the source of much bad style (see Sanders' „Hauptschwierigkeiten" . . . sub Inf.). The cases where the infinitive has taken the place of the present participle are mentioned below under each head. In the gerundive alone the participial form has taken the place of the infinitive. See **298**.

THE INFINITIVE WITHOUT ZU.

290. 1. It is dependent upon the modal auxiliaries. Der Bote will es aus aller Leute Mund erfahren haben. Man soll den Tag nicht vor dem Abend loben (Prov.). Also upon thun in quaint and dialect style, *e. g.*, Da thäten sie sich trennen (Uh.). See the speeches of Marthe and Margarete in F., I. Upon haben in the phrase gut haben. Du hast gut reden, it is easy enough for you to talk. Er thut nichts als . . . , he does nothing but . . .

2. In certain phrases dependent upon some verbs of motion; also upon helfen, heißen (command), lassen, lehren, lernen, machen, nennen. The verbs of motion are: spazieren reiten, fahren, gehen; schlafen gehen, sich schlafen legen, etc. Heiß' mich nicht reden,

heiß' mich schweigen; denn mein Geheimnis ist mir Pflicht (G.). Lehre mich thun nach deinem Wohlgefallen (B.). See Schiller's Tell, 1549.

3. Dependent upon certain verbs of rest: bleiben (most frequently), liegen, stehen (rarely); and upon verbs of perceiving: finden, fühlen (rarely), hören, sehen; also haben. Stecken bleiben, to stick fast (intr.). Schlafen liegen. Wir fanden den Leichnam im Walde liegen. Wir sahen den Führer über dem Abgrunde schweben. Der Tyroler hat gewöhnlich Federn am Hute stecken, der Engländer Bänder herunterhangen. Ich hab' es öfters rühmen hören, ein Komödia'nt könnt' einen Pfarrer lehren (F. 526–7).

a. Sein is still so used in dialect. Er ist fischen, jagen, he has gone afishing, ahunting; er ist fischen gewesen, he has been afishing. With all the verbs sub 3 and several sub 2 the present participle was once the rule in older German. Compare the participle in the predicate, 294, 2.

b. After fühlen, hören, lassen, sehen the infinitive has either passive or active force, and often an ambiguity arises which should be avoided by a different construction. Wir haben es sagen hören, We have heard it said. Die Dogge läßt sich nicht necken, The bulldog will not be teased. Wir hören den Knaben rufen, calling and called (generally the first). Der Lohnkutscher ließ uns nicht fahren, the hackman did not let us go, did not allow us to drive, did not have us driven. Der Meister ließ die Tochter nicht malen, did not allow her to paint and did not have her portrait painted.

4. As subject or predicate with sein and heißen, to be, to amount to: Noch ei'nmal ein Wunder hoffen hieße Gott versuchen (Sch.). Ein Vergnügen erwarten ist auch ein Vergnügen (Le.).

The Infinitive with zu.

291. 1. It expresses the purpose of an action and in general the indirect object; also necessity and possibility after neuter verbs, *e. g.*, sein, bleiben, stehen, when it has passive force. Die Sache ist nicht zu ändern. Es bleibt noch viel zu thun. Das steht noch zu überlegen. Da treibt's ihn, den köstlichen Preis zu erwerben (Sch.).

This is the old and proper use of the infinitive, originally a noun in the D. governed by zu. In N. H. G. um was added to express purpose, but it was really superfluous, though common in the spoken language. Um die Strömung abzuleiten gruben sie ein frisches Bette (Platen). Wir leben nicht um ju effen, fonbern wir effen um ju leben. The force of ju was much weakened when um could thus be added. Besides um, anſtatt and ohne can precede ju : anſtatt weg ju laufen, kam der Bär näher heran. Ohne ſich umzuſehen, lief der Dieb davon. But „um" should never be used except to express purpose. It is used too frequently. See sub 4.

2. It stands as direct object of verbs, often preceded by, or in apposition to, a pronoun or pronominal adverb + preposition. Ex.: Fang an ju hacken und ju graben (F. 2355). Niemand ſäume ju geben. Ich denke nicht daran, dir das ju gewähren.

In older periods of the language there was no ju in this case.

3. It stands as subject, in the spoken language, more frequently than without ju; there is no choice. Gefährlich iſt's den Leu ju wecken (Sch.). Eine ſchöne Menſchenſeele finden iſt Gewinn (He.).

4. As adjunct of nouns and adjectives, the latter often being qualified by ju and genug. „Die Kunſt ſich beliebt ju machen." Ju ſtolz, Dank einzuernten, wo ich ihn nicht ſäete (Le.). Du wäreſt blind genug, das nicht einzuſehn? . . . Bereit, dir zur Geſellſchaft hier ju bleiben (F. 1431).

After adjectives „um ju" is now far more common than ju alone. Ich bin ju alt, um nur ju ſpielen, ju jung, um ohne Wunſch ju ſein (F. 1546–7). Quite rare is als ju + infinitive.

5. For the independent use of infinitive, see imperative, **287**, 1. With or without ju in elliptical expressions: Was thun, ſpricht Zeus (Sch.). Was, am Rand des Grabs ju lügen! (F. 2961).

ACCUSATIVE WITH THE INFINITIVE.

292. In this construction the logical subject of the infinitive stands in the accusative. The infinitive stands with or without ju. Ex.: Hier ruhet Martin Faulermann, wenn man den ruhen ſagen kann, der ſeinen Lebtag nichts gethan (Weckherlin, quoted by Blatz). Lügen, die man Lügen ju ſein weiß (Le.).

1. Accusative with infinitive was not rare in O. H. G. in the translations from Latin and Greek. It is largely due to foreign influence. In M. H. G. it is very rare. In

modern German it is discouraged by the best authorities, though Lessing uses it quite frequently.

2. The corresponding English constructions must therefore be rendered freely into German. I believe him to be my friend, Ich glaube daß er mein Freund ist or Ich halte ihn für meinen Freund. German loses thus a compact construction.

The Infinitive as a Noun.

293. Some infinitives are felt as nouns only, *e. g.*, das Leben, das Ansehen, das Leiden. The infinitive used as noun generally has the article. Das Rauchen ist hier verboten. Beim Übersetzen muß man bis an's Unübersetzliche herangehn (G.). Der Erben Weinen ist ein heimlich Lachen (Prov.).

Participles.

294. The participles are really adjectives derived from verbal stems. The present participle retains more of the verbal construction and force than the past, in which the idea of tense only appears in intransitive verbs.

The **present participle** has active force in all verbs and the noun is the subject of the action. Der lächelnde See, die aufgehende Sonne, das schlagende Wetter, "fire-damp." Both participles can be used as nouns, adjectives, and adverbs very much as in English. They stand in apposition, in the predicate and as attributes.

1. Participles in which the noun is not the subject of the action, and those in which lies passive rather than active force, are still current, but not so frequent as in early N. H. G. They are not generally countenanced, *e. g.*, bei schlafender Nacht, "at night time," "when everybody sleeps"; eine sitzende Lebensart, a sedentary habit of life; essende Waaren, eatables (better Eßwaaren); eine vorhabende Reise, an intended journey. Some of these can be defended: fahrende Habe, movables, chattels (intrans. verb); erstaunende Nachricht, astonishing news (trans. verb); eine melkende Kuh (intrans. like „milchen"); die reitende Post, postman on horseback. Poetic are der schwindelnde Fels, the giddy rock. Von des Hauses weitschauendem Giebel (Sch.).

2. In the predicate appear now only such present participles as have become regular adjectives: bedeutend, important; reizend, charming; hinreißend, ravishing; leidend, in pain, ill health; bringend, urgent. See **274, 6.**

3. In apposition: Kochend, wie aus Ofens Rachen, glühn die Lüfte (Sch.). Ich empfange knieend dies Geschenk (id.).

4. The participial clause with the present participle is only in very restricted use in German compared with English. It cannot express an action preceding or following another action, a cause, purpose, etc. It has usually the value of an adjective clause and can often be explained as in apposition. Der Arme, sich an mich wendend, sprach: Haben Sie Mitleid, mein Herr.

295. The **past participle** of a transitive verb has passive force; that of a verb which forms its compound tenses with sein has active force: der laubumkränzte Becher (Sch.); das hergeführte Volk (id.); die abgesegelten Schiffe; der durchgefallene (unsuccessful) Candidat.

1. But not all verbs that have sein in compound tenses can be thus used; the participle must denote the state produced by the action of the verb. Die gesegelten Schiffe, der gelaufene Knecht would not do. Der entlaufene Sklave means "the runaway slave." This force is clear from the origin of the compound tense with sein (see **273, 283**).

2. Seemingly a large number of past participles have active force, but they are either quite wrong or they can be explained as having had originally passive force. Thus: „Ungebetet ißt man nicht" (Gerok); „ungegessen zu Bette gehn" are as wrong as their English equivalents: One does not eat unprayed, go to bed uneaten. „Bedient" means "in service," "invested with an office," hence a "servant," Bedienter. „Verdient," one who has merits, weil er sich um etwas oder jemand verdient gemacht hat; eingebildet means conceited, taken up with one's self; ein verlogener Mensch, a man given to lying; versoffener Mensch, given to drinking, and many other compounds with ver--: verweinte Augen, eyes red with weeping.

a. That some are now felt as having active force cannot be denied, else the wrong use mentioned could not have sprung up: gottlos, pflichtvergessen, forgetful of one's duty, of God; verschlafen, "one who slept too long"; vermessen, "presumptuous"; verlegen, embarrassed; besides the above.

296. The peculiar past participles of verbs of motion, which seemingly have active force, stand in a sort of apposition or as predicates with kommen, rarely with gehen. Ex.: Kam ein Vogel geflogen (Song). Da kommt des Wegs geritten ein schmucker Edelknecht (Uh.).

1. This use is by no means modern. Kommen and gehn are felt as auxiliaries. Compare verloren gehen.

2. Special notice deserves the past participle with heißen, sein, and nennen, which has the force of an infinitive, but belongs under this head. Das heißt schlecht geworfen, That is a bad throw. Unter ehrlichen Leuten nennt man das „gelogen." Frisch gewagt ist halb gewonnen (Prov.).

297. The participle appears in an absolute construction. The logical subject is left indefinite (Lessing is very fond of this). The logical subject stands in the accusative and with a few, like ausgenommen, eingeschlossen, abgerechnet, even in the nominative. Alle waren zugegen, der Pfarrer ausgenommen. Und dieses nun auf Laokoon angewendet, so ist die Sache klar (Le.).

1. Closely related to this construction is the absolute accusative + a past participle (see **209**) and in some cases there may be doubt as to which is meant. Und sie singt hinaus in die finstere Nacht, das Auge von Weinen getrübet (Sch.).

The past participle is in elliptical construction in the imperative, see **287**, 2.

The Gerundive.

298. It stands only attributively. In the predicate the old infinitive stands, which it has supplanted. Der noch zu verkaufende Schrank, the wardrobe which is still to be sold; but der Schrank ist noch zu verkaufen, the wardrobe is still to be sold. See **289, 452.** It has always passive force.

Though the form is rather that of the gerund than of the gerundive, in construction it closely resembles the Latin gerundive. Hence the name in German.

SYNTAX OF THE ADVERB.

299. The adverb qualifies a verb, an adjective or another adverb. Ex.: Du hast mich mächtig angezogen (F. 483). Die unbegreiflich hohen Werke sind herrlich wie am ersten Tag (F. 249–50). Das ist sehr schön geschrieben.

1. The adverbs of time and place often accompany a noun with the force of an attribute: Vor Jenem droben steht gebückt, der helfen lehrt und Hilfe schickt (F. 1009-10). Georg V. (der Fünfte), einst König von Hannover, starb im Auslande.

2. The adverb stands as a predicate: Die schönen Zeiten von Aranjuez sind nun vorüber (Sch.). Die Thür ist zu (one can supply „gemacht"). Der or dem Mini'ster ist nicht wohl.

a. Do not confound gut and wohl. Except in a few cases, as in wohl thun, to do good, wohl does not qualify a transitive verb. We do not say in German wohl schreiben, wohl antworten, wohl anfangen in the sense of English "well." Er hat es wohl geschrieben means "he wrote it, indeed, (I assure you)"; or it is concessive and can mean: "to be sure he wrote it, but then —." In the last sense wohl has no stress.

3. With adjectives or participles used as nouns that are felt rather as substantives than as adjectives or as derived from a verb, the adverb changes to an adjective: ein nah Verwandter > ein naher Verwandter; ein intim Bekannter > ein intimer Bekannter. But compare Goethe's famous line: Das Ewig-Weibliche zieht uns hinan.

300. An adverb may strengthen the force of a preposition by standing before or after the preposition + case. This is always the case when the adverb is the prefix of a separable compound verb: rings um die Stadt (herum), mitten durch den Wald, in das Dorf hinein, aus dem Garten heraus. Es ritten drei Reiter zum Thore hinaus (Uh.).

1. Mark the adverbs which are only adverbs and not adjectives: wohl, fast, schon, sehr, neulich, freilich, früh (rare), spat (rare), bald, and others.

2. The uninflected comparative and superlative of adjectives serve also as adverbs. Notice the difference between auf + A. and an + D. Sie sangen auf das beste (Uh.), they sang as best they knew how. This is *absolute* superlative. Sie sangen am besten, they sang best of all, any. This is *relative* superlative.

SYNTAX OF THE PREPOSITION.

301. The prepositions express the relations of a noun to a verb or to another noun.

1. Prepositions are originally adverbs, and the distinction between prepositions, adverbs and conjunctions is only syntactical. Denn is, for instance, a conjunction = for, and an adverb = then, than; während is a conjunction = while, and a preposition = during. Prepositions could not originally "govern" cases. A certain case was called for independently of the preposition, then still an adverb. In Greek there are prepositions governing three cases, which shows how loose the connection between case and preposition was. In fact nearly all adverbs, old and new, can be traced back

to cases of nouns or pronouns. They are isolated or "petrified" cases, and as such could only stand in the loosest connection with the living cases, which they gradually began to "govern."

2. Prepositions can govern different cases in different periods of the language. The preposition has been partly the cause of the loss of case-endings. Its function becomes the more important the more uninflectional (analytical) a language becomes. It is one of the most difficult and subtle elements to master in the study of a living language. For another reason the preposition is very important, viz., the preposition + case has supplanted and is continuing to supplant the case alone, directly dependent upon a verb or noun. The two together are much more expressive and explicit than a case alone. In die Liebe des Vaters, the genitive may be subjective or objective, but there is no ambiguity about die Liebe zum Vater, des Vaters Liebe zum Sohne.

Classification and Treatment of the Prepositions According to the Cases they Govern.

302. Prepositions governing the Genitive:

Unweit, mittels, kraft und während; laut, vermöge, ungeachtet; oberhalb und unterhalb; innerhalb und außerhalb; diesseits, jenseits, halben, wegen; statt, auch längs, zufolge, trotz.

These are all cases of substantives or adjectives (participles) and their number might be easily increased, e. g., by bezüglich, with reference to; angesichts, in the face of; seitens, on the part of; inmitten, in the midst of, etc.

(The order is the one in which they are given in German grammars. The semicolon shows the ends of the lines of the doggerel.)

We comment in alphabetical order briefly upon those that seem to require comment. Often a mere translation will suffice.

1. Anstatt, an — statt, statt, + instead of. Draus (from which, from whose breast) statt der goldenen Lieber ein Blutstrahl hoch auf springt (Uh.). An Tochter statt, in daughter's stead. Statt sometimes with the dative. It also governs an infinitive like ohne, translated by "without + participle." See Infinitive, 291, 1.

2. Außerhalb + outside of; innerhalb + inside of; oberhalb, above; unterhalb, on the lower side of, below. They are all more expressive than the simple forms. They rarely govern the dative.

3. Diesseit(s), jenseit(s), this side of, on the other side, beyond. Rarely with the dative.

4. Halben, halber, halb, on account of, + in behalf of. Follows

its case. Frequent in composition: deshalb, therefore; meinethalben, on my behalf; Alters halber, on account of age. Comp. wegen and willen.

5. **Kraft**, according to, by virtue of. Kraft des Gesetzes; kraft des Amtes. Formerly only in Kraft, *e. g.*, daß stets der liebste (Sohn) ... in Kraft allein des Rings, das Haupt, der Fürst des Hauses werde (Le.). Comp. laut.

6. **Laut**, from, „nach Laut," lauts (Luther), means "according to,' "by." Laut Befehls, by command; laut des Testamentes, according to the last will and testament.

Plural nouns without articles in which the genitive could not be distinguished stand in the dative: laut Briefen, according to letters. Laut means literally according to a verbal or written statement; kraft gives a moral reason.

7. **Mittels**, mittelst (most common), vermittelst, by means of, with. Mittelst eines Hammers, eines Bohrers. It is more expressive than mit or durch. Rarely with the dative.

8. **Ob**, rare and archaic. With genitive if causal (on account of); with dative if local (above), and temporal (during). Da weinten zusammen die Grenadier' wohl ob der kläglichen Kunde (Heine). Ob bem Wald; nid bem Wald (Sch., *Tell*); ob bem Altare (id.).

9. **Trotz**, with genitive and dative, in defiance of, in spite of; in the sense of "in rivalry with," "as well as," always with the dative. Trotz des heftigen Regens fuhren wir ab. Die Sängerin singt trotz einer Nachtigall, as well as a nightingale. Comp. the forms zu or zum Trotze preceded by a dative: Mir zum Trotze fuhr er fort zu lesen, in defiance of me or to defy me he continued reading.

10. **Unangesehen**, setting aside, unbeschadet, without detriment to, ungeachtet, notwithstanding (very frequent). The last two also with a preceding dative; bemungeachtet is felt as an adverb. These are very modern prepositions. Unweit, unfern, not far from, occur also with dative.

11. **Vermöge**, in virtue of, through, in consequence of, by dint of. Denotes a reason springing from a quality of the subject: vermöge seiner Redlichkeit, through his honesty. We could not say kraft seiner R.; vermöge (and not kraft) großer Anstrengungen, by dint of great efforts. (Perhaps from „nach Vermögen.")

12. **Während**, during. Sometimes with the dative: währenddem, meanwhile.

13. **Wegen**, on account of, both preceding and following the noun;

also with the dative. Wegen denotes also a motive and an impediment. Seiner Größe wegen konnte das Schiff nicht durch den Kanal. Der Müller war wegen seiner Stärke berühmt. Wegen from von — wegen, still common in „von Rechts wegen," strictly, in justice.

14. Willen, generally um — willen, denotes the purpose, the advantage or interest of a person. Um meiner Ruhe willen erklären Sie sich deutlicher (Sch.). Um des Sohnes willen, um meinetwillen, for the sake of or in the interest of the son, for my sake. Wegen, halben, and willen all appear with pronouns, and are used promiscuously.

15. Zufolge, as frequently with the dative, denotes the result, "in consequence of." Zufolge des Auftrages, in consequence of the commission; den Verabredungen zufolge, in accordance with the verbal agreements.

Prepositions governing the Dative.

303. Schreib: mit, nach, nächst, nebst, samt; seit, von, zu, zuwi'der; entgegen, außer, aus — stets mit dem Dativ nieder.

1. Ab, still used in the Alemanic dialect (Baden, Switzerland) as a preposition. In business style it denotes the place at which merchandise is delivered or the time after which anything is to be had: ab Hamburg, ab Neujahr, ab = "all aboard."

2. Aus denotes the starting point of a motion, the opposite of in + accusative, = "out of," "from": Aus den Augen, aus dem Sinn, "out of sight, out of mind": aus dem Fenster sehen, to look out of the window. Origin and descent: aus alten Zeiten, from olden times; aus Hannover, from Hanover. Material: aus Lehm, of clay; aus Mehl, of meal. Motive: aus Mitleid, Haß, from pity, hatred. Origin also in aus Erfahrung, from experience; aus Versehen, by mistake. Notice the idiom: aus Köln gebürtig, a native of Cologne, born in C.

3. Außer, outside of, beside, the opposite of in + dative. Denotes also exception and "in addition to." More frequent in the figurative than in the local sense, because außerhalb is more precise. Außer dem Hause, not at home; außer Hause speisen, to dine out; außer sich sein, to be beside one's self. Nur der Vetter war außer mir da. Mark once the genitive außer Landes gehen, to go to foreign parts; also the accusative in außer allen Zweifel setzen, put beyond all doubt. (Setzen being a verb of motion.)

4. Bei. Original meaning is nearness, hence by, near, with: bei der Scheune, near (by) the barn; bei der Tante, near the aunt or at the house of

the aunt; beim Zeus, by Jove; die Schlacht bei Wörth, the battle of W.; bei Tisch sein, to be at dinner; bei Tag und bei Nacht, by day and by night; bei (einem) Namen nennen, to call by name (but Friedrich mit Namen, Frederic by name); bei (rare) neunzig Gefangenen, about ninety prisoners; bei Strafe von zehn Mark, ten marks fine. Ich habe kein Geld bei mir, I have no money about me. The accusative stands in bei Seite legen, bringen, stellen, to lay, put aside. In M. H. G. after verbs of motion regularly the accusative, but in the spoken language now discarded, though still found in the classics.

5. **Binnen**, sometimes with genitive, expresses now time only, "within": binnen drei Jahren, within three years. < be — innen.

6. **Entge'gen** denotes approach, both friendly and hostile, towards and against; stands generally after its case. Wir gingen dem Freunde entgegen; fuhren dem Winde entgegen. With verbs of motion it frequently forms separable compounds and is really more adverb than preposition.

7. **Gegenü'ber**, opposite, facing; generally after its case; rarely gegen — über. Dem Schlosse gegenüber.

8. **Gemäß**, preceding and following its case, according to, in accordance with; really an adjective. Dem Versprechen gemäß, according to the promise; gemäß dem Gesetze, according to the law. It is more definite than nach.

9. **Mit** means "in company with," "with"; denotes presence, accompanying circumstances and instrument. Arm in Arm mit dir, so fordr'e ich mein Jahrhundert in die Schranken (Sch.). Mit Freuden, gladly; eile mit Weile, hasten slowly; mit Fug und Recht, justly (emphatic); mit der Zeit pflückt man Rosen, in due time . . . ; mit Fleiß, intentionally; mit dem Pfeil, dem Bogen (Sch.). (See mittels, **302, 7**.)

10. **Nach** denotes originally a "nearness to," being an adjective (nahe); then "a coming near to," and generally corresponds to Eng. "after" in point of time, order. With verbs of motion (literal and figurative) "to" and "after." Nach etwas streben, sich sehnen, to strive after, long for; nach Mitternacht; nach dir komme ich, it is my turn after you; nach Berlin reisen. "In accordance with," not so expressive as „gemäß," in this sense often after its case. Nach den Gesetzen verdient er den Tod; dem Wortlaute nach, literally. Aim: nach etwas schlagen, schießen, to strike at, shoot at. Nach etwas schmecken, riechen, etc., something has the smell, taste of; nach etwas urteilen, to judge by; nach etwas or jemand schicken, to send for. (See zu and gemäß.)

11. **Nächst** is the superlative of **nahe** (**nach**), and denotes very close nearness to in place, order, = + "next to." **Zunächst** has no different force. Und nächst dem Leben was erflehst du dir? (G.).

12. **Nebst** denotes very loose connection and connects also things and persons not necessarily belonging together; **samt**, on the other hand, only what naturally belongs together. Auf einer Stange trägt sie einen Hut nebst einer Fahne (Sch.) (a hat *and* a banner). < nebenst < L. G. *nevens*.

13. **Samt, mit samt, zu samt,** "together with." Mich samt meinem ganzen Heere bring' ich dem Herzog (Sch.). See **nebst**. It implies a close union, which does not lie even in **mit**.

14. **Seit**, older **sint**, = + since, denotes the beginning of an action and its duration to the present moment. Seit diesem Tage schweigt mir jeder Mund (Sch.). Er ist herein seit mehreren Stunden (id.), it is several hours since he came in (into the city). Seit einigen Jahren zahlt er keine Zinsen, For several years he has paid no interest.

15. **Von**, "from," denotes the starting point of a motion or action in time and place. Its case is often followed by another preposition or by her. Von der Hand in den Mund; von Worten kam's zu Schlägen, from words they came to blows. Von Ostern bis Pfingsten ist fünfzig Tage. Origin: Walther von der Vogelweide. Fürst von Bismarck. Herr von Schulemburg. Hence **von** in the names of persons denotes nobility: Herr von So und So. Von Jugend auf; von Grund aus, thoroughly; von Osten her. Separation: frei, rein von etwas. Supplants the genitive: ein Mann von Ehre, von großen Kenntnissen; der Pöbel von Paris. Denotes the personal agent: Wallenstein wurde von Piccolomini hintergangen und von vielen Generalen im Stiche (in the lurch) gelassen. Notice: Schurke von einem Wirt (Le.). Cause: naß vom (with) Tau, vom Regen.

16. **Zu** denotes first of all the direction toward a person (but **nach** toward a thing) + "to": zu jemand gehen, kommen, sprechen, etc. Sie sang zu ihm, sie sprach zu ihm (G.). Zu sich kommen, "come to"; etwas zu sich stecken, to put something in one's pocket. (This is its only use in O. H. G. In M. H. G. its use spread.) In dialect and in poetry it stands before names of cities and towns (= at). Zu Straßburg auf der Schanz (Folk-song). Ihr seid mein Gast zu Schwyz (Sch.).

In certain very numerous set phrases and proverbs **zu** stands before names of things. Direction: von Ort zu Ort, from place to place; zu Bett(e), zur Kirche, zur Schule, zu Grunde, zu Rate gehen = "take council";

many loose compounds with fahren; zu Fall, zu Statten, zu Schaben, zu Enbe, zu Ehren kommen; zu Schanden, zu Nichte, zum Schelme werben. Place where?: „zu beiden Seiten des Rheins" (Song); zu Hause, zur Hand sein; zu Füßen liegen. Manner of motion: zu Land, zu Wasser, zu Pferd (zu Roß), zu Wagen, zu Fuß = Eng. "by" and "on." Transition or change: zum König machen, wählen, ernennen; zum Narren, zum besten haben, to make a fool of. Degree or size, numbers: zum Teil, in part; zu Hunderten, by the hundred; zu dreien waren wir im Zimmer, there were three of us in the room; zum Tode betrübt (G.), sad unto death. Combination of things: Nehmen Sie nie Pfeffer, Salz ober Senf zu (with) dem Ei? Oft hatt' er kaum Wasser zu Schwarzbrot und Wurst (Bü.). Notice the use of zu before nouns followed by hinein, heraus, etc.: zum Thore hinaus; zum Fenster heraus. Time (rare): Und kommt er nicht zu Ostern, so kommt er zu Trinita't (Folk-song). After the noun = "in the direction of," "toward": dem Dorfe zu, toward the village; nach dem Dorfe, to the village.

Prepositions governing the Accusative:

304. Bis, durch, für, gegen, ohne, sonder, um, wider.

1. **Bis**, till, until, denotes the limit in time and space. When denoting space it is followed by other prepositions, except before names of places. The nouns of time rarely have an article or pronoun. Bis Fastnacht; bis ans Ende aller Dinge; bis hierher und nicht weiter; bis an den hellen Tag; neunzig bis hundert Mark; bis Braunschweig. (Bis < *bi* + *az*, + Eng. by + at.)

2. **Durch**, + "through," denotes a passing through: durch den Wald, durchs Nadelöhr. Extent of time (the case often followed by hindurch): durch Jahrzehnte hindurch; die ganze Zeit (hin)durch. Cause and occasion, very much like aus: durch Nachlässigkeit, durch eigene Schuld. Means: durch einen Pfeil verwunden, durch einen Dienstmann besorgen, attend to through a porter. (Durch more definite than mit. See this and mittels. It denotes now no longer the personal agent.)

3. **Für**, + for, denotes advantage, interest, destination: Wer nicht für mich ist, ist wider mich (B.). Er sammelt für die Armen. Die Scheere ist kein Spielzeug für Kinder. Die Wahrheit ist vorhanden für den Weisen, die Schönheit für ein fühlend Herz (Sch.). Substitution and price: Da tritt kein anderer für ihn ein (Sch.). Mein Leben ist für Gold nicht feil (Bü.). Limitation: Ich für meine Person. Genug für dieses Mal. Ihr zeigtet einen kecken Mut . . . für eure Jahre (Sch.). Stück für Stück, point by point. In its old sense (local) only in certain phrases: Schritt für (by) Schritt, Tag für (by) Tag, Satz für (after) Satz. (See vor.)

4. **Gegen** denotes "direction toward," but with no idea of approach that lies in zu and nach. It implies either friendly or hostile feeling if persons are concerned = "towards," "against." Gegen die Wand lehnen; gegen den Strom schwimmen. Wenn ich mich gegen sie verpflichten soll, so müssen sie's auch gegen mich (Sch.). Gibt es ein Mittel gegen die Schwindsucht? Gegen Dummheit kämpfen Götter selbst vergebens. Exchange, comparison : Ich wette hundert gegen eins. Roland war ein Zwerg gegen den Riesen. Indefinite time and number: "towards." Der Kranke schlief erst gegen Morgen ein. Der Feldherr hatte gegen dreihundert tausend Soldaten. Gegen drei Uhr. Gegen once governed the dative almost exclusively and traces of it are still found in Goethe.

Gen is still preserved in „gen Himmel." Gen < *gēn* < *gein* < *gegen*, + again. See entgegen, which implies a mutual advance.

5. **Ohne**, "without," the opposite of „mit," „bei." Mit oder ohne Klausel, gilt mir gleich (Sch.), "With or without reserve, it is all the same to me." Ein Ritter ohne Furcht und Tadel. In „ohnedem" is a remnant of the D. in M. H. G.; zweifelsohne of the G. occurring after the M. H. G. adverb *āne*, from. Etwas ist nicht ohne, there is something in it (Coll.). Ohne in Composition, see **489**, 3 ; + infinitive, see **291**, 1.

6. **Sonder**, "without," is now archaic except in set phrases like „sonder Gleichen," „sonder Zweifel," "without compare," "no doubt," + Eng. asunder. Once governed the accusative and genitive.

7. **Um**, "around," "about." Und die Sonne, sie machte den weiten Ritt um die Welt (Arndt). Und um ihn die Großen der Krone (Sch.). Her or herum often follows the case: In einem Halbkreis standen um ihn her sechs oder sieben große Königsbilder (Sch.). It denotes inexact time or number: Um Mitternacht begrabt den Leib (Bü.). Um drei hundert Hörer, an audience of about three hundred. (Gegen is rather "nearly," um means more or less.) But „um dreiviertel fünf" means "at a quarter to five." "At about" would be „ungefähr um" or „um ungefähr," *e. g.*, ungefähr um 6 Uhr. It denotes further exchange, price, difference in size and measure: Aug' um Auge, Zahn um Zahn (B.). Alles ist euch feil um Geld (Sch.). Um zwei Zoll zu klein. Er hat sich um zwei Pfennige verrechnet. Loss and deprivation : um's Leben bringen, to kill ; um's Geld kommen, to lose one's money. Da war's um ihn geschehn (G.), He was done for. Wer brachte mich drum? (um deine Liebe) (F. 4496), Who robbed me of it? It denotes the object striven for: um etwas werben, spielen, fragen, bitten, streiten, beneiden, etc. The object of care, mourning, weeping : Wein' um den Bruder, doch nicht um den Geliebten weine (Sch.). Schade wär's um eure Haare (id.). Nicht um diese thut's mir leid (id.).

8. **Wiber,** "against," always in the hostile sense. Denotes resistance and contrast : Was hilft uns Wehr und Waffe wider ben? (Sch.). Es geht ihm wider die Natur, It goes against his grain. + Eng. "with" in withstand.

Prepositions governing the Dative and Accusative.

305. An, auf, hinter, in, neben, über, unter, vor, zwischen.

1. In answer to the question whither? they require the accusative. In answer to the question where? the dative. Pflanze die Bäume vor das Haus. Die Bäume stehen vor dem Hause.

2. In answer to the question how long and until when? they require the accusative. In answer to the question when? the dative: Im Jahre 1872 wurde Straßburg wieder als deutsche Universität eröffnet. Wir reisen auf vierzehn Tage ins Bad.

3. When an, auf, in, über, unter, vor denote manner and cause, then auf and über always require the accusative, but an, in, unter, vor generally the dative, in answer to the questions how and why? Wir freuen uns über (= over) and auf (= looking forward to) seine Ankunft. Auf diese Weise, but in dieser Weise. Der Bettler weinte vor Freuden über die herrliche Gabe.

The above general rules, as given in Krause's grammar, will be found of much practical value.

306. 1. **An + Dative.**

After nouns and adjectives of plenty and want : Mangel an Geld, reich an Gütern. After adjectives when the place is mentioned where the quality appears : an beiden Füßen lahm, an einem Auge blind. After verbs of rest, increase or decrease, and after those denoting an immediate contact or a perception : An der Quelle saß der Knabe (Sch.). Es fehlt an Büchern. Der Auswanderer litt am Wechselfieber. Der Zigeuner führt den Bären an einer Kette. Den Vogel erkennt man an den Federn (Prov.). It denotes an office and time of day : am Theater, an der Universität, am Amte angestellt sein, to hold an office at . . . ; am Morgen, Abend; es ist an der Zeit . . . , it is time . . . .

2. An + Accusative.

After denken, erinnern, mahnen and similar ones, and verbs of motion. Denket an den Ruhm, nicht an die Gefahr. Setzen Sie sich doch ans Fenster (near the window). Inexact number: an die drei mal hundert tausend Mann (as many as). From its English cognate "on" an differs very much in meaning. "On" generally is auf. See also **300**, 2.

3. Auf + "upon." For auf + Dative, see **305**, 1, 2, 3. It denotes rest or motion upon the surface.

Auf + Accusative.

Stands after verbs of waiting, hoping, trusting, etc., *e.g.*, auf etwas warten, hoffen, sich besinnen (recall), gefaßt sein, sich freuen (see **305**, 3), verzichten, (es) auf etwas wagen, hören. Here it stands generally for the old gen. without preposition. Ich kann mich auf die genauen Umstände nicht besinnen, I cannot recall . . . Der Hund wartet auf sein Fressen. Merke auf die Worte des Lehrers. Trotz nicht auf euer Recht (Sch.). After adjectives denoting pride, envy, anger, malice, *e. g.*, eifersüchtig, neidisch, stolz, böse, erbost : eifersüchtig auf seine Ehre (Sch.) ; stolz auf seine Unschuld; erbost auf den Gefangenen (über would mean cause). Exact time, limit, and measure ; often with „bis." Here belongs the superlative, see **300**, 2. Bis auf's Blut. Bis auf Speis' und Trank (Lc.). Es ist ein Viertel auf drei, a quarter past two. Auf die Minu'te, Seku'nde, auf Schußweite, at shooting distance. Bis auf die Neige, to the last drop. Auf sieben schon eines wieder (Le.). (Nathan had "toward" or "as a return for" his seven dead sons one child in Recha.) Auf eine Mark gehen hundert Pfennige.

4. Hinter + "behind," opposite of „vor." See **305**, 1, 2.

It denotes inferiority : Die französische Artillerie stand weit hinter der deutschen zurück (ambiguous, either stood far back of the G. or was much inferior to the G.). Notice the following idioms : sich hinter etwas machen, to go at with energy. Ich kann nicht dahinter kommen, I cannot understand it. Es hinter den Ohren haben, to be sly (coll.) ; hinter die Ohren schlagen, to give a box on the ear : sich etwas hinter die Ohren schreiben, to mark well.

5. In + in, into (A.).

The German and English prepositions are more nearly identical than any other two. See **305**, 1, 2.

Jn + **Accusative.**

Denotes direction, including transition, change, division: Wenn der Leib in Staub zerfallen, lebt der große Name noch (Sch.). Deutschland zerriß auf diesem Reichstage in zwei Religio′nen und zwei politische Partei′en (id.).

6. **Neben**, near, by the side of. See **305**, 1, 2. < *eneben*, lit. "in a line with."

7. **Über** + over, above. See **305**, 1, 2, 3.

Über + **Accusative.**

After verbs denoting rule and superiority over, *e. g.*, herrschen, siegen, verfügen (dispose); laughter, astonishment, disgust, in general an expression of an affection of the mind, *e. g.*, über etwas lachen, erstaunen, sich . . . beklagen, sich . . . entrüsten, sich ärgern. (For an older simple genit.) Karl der Große siegte über die Sachsen. Das Testament verfügt über ein großes Vermögen. Wie stutzte der Pöbel über die neuen Livre′en (G.). Die Gefangenen beklagen sich über ihre Behandlung. Über sein Benehmen habe ich mich recht geärgert. It denotes time and excess in time, number, measure: Über′s Jahr, a year hence, only in certain phrases, duration: über Nacht, die Nacht über. Den Sabbath über waren sie stille (B.). Über ein Jahr, more than a year (ambiguous, either "more than a year" or "a year hence"). Über drei tausend Kanonen. über alle Begriffe schön, beautiful beyond comprehension.

When it denotes duration or simultaneousness, or when the idea of place is still felt, then the dative follows; when it denotes the reason then the accusative follows. This is clear when the same noun stands in both cases, as in Ich bin über dem Buche eingeschlafen, means "while reading it I fell asleep." Ich bin über das Buch eingeschlafen means "it was stupid, therefore I fell asleep." Über der Beschreibung da vergeß′ ich den ganzen Krieg (Sch.). Schade, daß über dem schönen Wahn des Lebens beste Hälfte dahin geht (Sch.).

Notice von etwas and über etwas sprechen. Ich habe davon gesprochen, I have mentioned it. Ich habe darüber gesprochen, I have treated of it, spoken at length.

8. **Unter** + **under.** See **305**, 3.

In the abstract sense this rule holds good. It denotes protection, inferiority, lack in numbers (Dative, opposite of über), mingling with, contemporaneous circumstance (D.). It stands for the partitive genit. (= among). Unter dem Schutze. Der Feldwebel steht unter dem Offizier. Wer will unter die Soldaten, der . . . , he who wants to become a soldier (Folk-

song). Er ist drunter geblieben, he did not reach the number. Cambrai öffnete seinem Erzbischofe unter (amid) freudigem Zurufe die Thore wieder (Sch.), Wer unter (among) diesen (D.) reicht an unsern Friedland? (Sch.) (von diesen would be "of these"). It denotes time when none of the exacter modes of expressing time is used : Wir sind geboren unter gleichen Sternen (Sch.). Unter der Regierung der Königin Victoria = in the reign ; während implies not a single act, but a commensurate duration, = during. Der Sakrista'n schlief während der Predigt, but ging unter der Predigt hinaus. In „unterdessen," and other compounds of that class, indessen, etc., the gen. is probably adverbial and not called for by the preposition.
See zwischen.

9. **Vor** + before, in front of. See **305**, 1, 2, 3.

Vor + Dative.

Introduces the object of fear and abhorrence : Kein Eisengitter schützt vor ihrer List (Sch.). Vor gewissen Erinnerungen möcht' ich mich gern hüten (id.). Mir graut vor dir. Time before which anything is to happen or has happened : Der König ist gesonnen, vor Abend in Madrid noch einzutreffen (Sch.). Vor dreißig Jahren, thirty years ago. Vor acht Tagen, a week ago. Hindrance and cause : Die Großmutter wird vor Kummer sterben (Sch.). Den Wald vor lauter Bäumen nicht sehen (Prov.). Vor Hunger, vor Durst sterben. Preference : vor allen Dingen, above all things ; herrlich vor allen.

Vor and für are doublets and come from *fora* and *furi* respectively. In M. H. G. *für* + A. answered the question whither? *vor* + D. the question where? In N. H. G. they were confounded, even in Lessing very frequently, but in the last seventy years the present syntactical difference has prevailed. Goethe and Schiller rarely confound them.

10. **Zwischen.**

"Between" *two* objects in place, time, and in the figurative sense. Kein muß es bleiben zwischen mir und ihm (Sch.). Die Wolkensäule kam zwischen das Heer der Ägypter und das Heer Israels (B.). See **305**, 1, 2 ; also unter = among, sub 8.

SYNTAX OF THE CONJUNCTIONS.

307. The conjunctions are divided : 1. Into the coordinating, like und, denn, etc. ; 2. Into the subordinating, *e. g.*, weil, da, als, etc. They are treated in the General Syntax, where see the various clauses.

GENERAL SYNTAX.

I. THE SIMPLE SENTENCE.

308. Subject and verb make up the simple sentence. This sentence may be expanded by complements of the subject and of the verb. The subject may be either a substantive, a substantive pronoun, or other words used as substantives. The attributes of the subjects may be adjective, participle, adjective pronouns, numerals. These are adjective attributes. Substantives, substantive pronouns, and the infinitive are substantive attributes. Their relation to the subject may be that of apposition and of coordination; or they may be connected by the genitive, or by preposition + case in subordination. Preposition + case is more expressive than the genitive alone, when the subject is to be defined as to time, place, value, kind, means, purpose.

The predicate is either a simple verb or a copula + adjective or substantive or pronoun which may be again expanded like the subject. The complements of the verb are object and adverb. The object is either a noun, substantive pronoun, or other words used as nouns. It stands in the accusative, dative or genitive, or is expressed by preposition + case. The adverb qualifies the verb, adjective, and other adverb. It is either an adverb proper or preposition + case of substantive or what is used as such. It may also be a genitive or an accusative.

309. As to form the main sentences may be divided as follows :

1. **Declarative sentences,** which either affirm something of the subject or deny something with regard to it. Affirmative : Kurz ift der Schmerz und ewig ift die Freude (Sch.). Du haft Diamanten und Perlen (Heine). Negative : Das Leben ift der Güter

höchstes nicht (Sch.). Sie sollen ihn nicht haben, den freien deutschen Rhein (Beck).

1. The double negative is still frequent in the classics and colloquially, but it is not in accordance with correct usage now : Keine Luft von keiner Seite (G., classical). Man sieht, daß er an nichts keinen Anteil nimmt (F. 3489) (said by Margaret, coll.). After the comparative it also occurs in the classics : Wir müssen das Werk in diesen nächsten Tagen weiter fördern, als es in Jahren nicht gedieh (Sch.).

2. After verbs of "hindering," "forbidding," "warning," like verhüten, verhindern, warnen, verbieten, etc., the dependent clause may contain „nicht„: Nur hütet euch, daß ihr mir nichts vergießt (G.). Nimm dich in Acht, daß dich Rache nicht verderbe (Sch.).

3. When the negative does not affect the predicate, the sentence may still be affirmative. Nicht mir, den eignen Augen mögt ihr glauben (Sch.). But nicht mir stands for a whole sentence.

2. **Interrogative sentences:** Hast du das Schloß gesehen? (Uh.). Wer reitet so spät durch Nacht und Wind? (G.). Double question : War der Bettler verrückt oder war er betrunken? Glaubst du das oder nicht? Willst du immer weiter schweifen? (G.). Wer weiß das nicht?

For the potential subjunctive in questions, see **284, 3**.
For the indirect question, see **325, 2**.

3. The **exclamatory sentence** has not an independent form. Any other sentence, even a dependent clause, may become exclamatory: O, du Wald, o ihr Berge drüben wie seid ihr so jung geblieben und ich bin worden so alt! (Uh.). Das ist das Los des Schönen auf der Erde! (Sch.). Was dank' (owe) ich ihm nicht alles! (id.). Wie der Knabe gewachsen ist!

For the imperative and optative sentences, see **284, 2 ; 286**.

310. Elliptical clauses generally contain only the predicate or a part of it, including the object or adverb. Guten Morgen! Gelt! Truly! Getroffen! You have hit it! Langsam ! Schnell ! etc. It is very frequent in the imperative, see **287**.

Proverbs often omit the verb : Viel Geschrei und wenig Wolle. Kleine Kinder, kleine Sorgen; große Kinder, große Sorgen. See **309, 3**, in which the last examples are really dependent questions.

Concord of Subject and Predicate.

311. The predicate (verb) agrees with the subject in number and person.

Two or more subjects (generally connected by und) require a verb in the plural: Unter den Anwesenden wechseln Furcht und Erstaunen (Sch.). Doch an dem Herzen nagten mir der Unmut und die Streitbegier (id.).

1. If the subjects are conceived as a unit and by a license greater in German than in English, the verb may stand in the singular; also in the inverted order if the first noun is in the singular. Ex.: Was ist das für ein Mann, daß ihm Wind und Meer gehorsam ist (B.). Eh' spreche Welt und Nachwelt, etc. (Sch.). Da kommt der Müller und seine Knechte. By license: Sagen und Thun ist zweierlei (Prov.). Das Mistrauen und die Eifersucht . . . erwachte bald wieder (Sch.).

2. The plural verb stands after titles in the singular in addressing royalty and persons of high standing. In speaking of ruling princes the plural also stands. Servants also use it in speaking of their masters when these have a title. Ex.: Eure (Ew.) Majestät, Durchlaucht, Excellenz befehlen? Seine Majestät der Kaiser haben geruht, etc. Der Herr Geheime Hofrat sind nicht zu Hause. Die Herrschaft sind ausgegangen.

312. After a collective noun the verb stands more regularly in the singular than in Eng. Only when this noun or an indefinite numeral is accompanied by a genitive pl., the plural verb is the rule. In early N. H. G. this plural was very common. Die Menge floh. Alle Welt nimmt Teil (G.). Und das junge Volk der Schnitter fliegt zum Tanz (Sch.). Dort kommen ein paar aus der Küche (Sch.). Eine Menge Eier sind verdorben.

313. When the subject is a neuter pronoun, es, dies, das, etc., the neuter verb agrees with the predicate noun or substantive pronoun in number: Das waren mir selige Tage (Overbeck). Es sind die Früchte ihres Thuns (Sch.). Es zogen drei Jäger wohl auf die Birsch (Uh.). In this case es is only expletive. Wer sind diese?

314. When subjects are connected by entweder — oder, nicht nur — sondern auch, weder — noch, sowohl — als (auch), the verb has the person and number of the first subject and joins this one if the subjects are of different persons. The verb for the second subject is omitted. Entweder du gehst (or gehst du) oder ich. Teils war ich schuld, teils er. Subjects of the same person connected by the above correlatives; by oder, nebst, mit, samt have as a rule a singular verb and the verb joins the second subject. Dem Volke kann weder Feuer bei noch Wasser (Sch.), Neither fire nor water can harm those people.

315. If the subjects are of different persons, the first has the preference over the second, the second over the third. Moreover, the plural of the respective pronouns is often added. Der da und ich, wir sind aus Eger (Sch.). Du und der Vetter, (ihr) geht nach Hause.

The adjective as a predicate or attribute has been sufficiently treated under the adjective, see **210-225**.

316. The noun as a predicate agrees with the subject in case; if the subject is a person, also in number and gender, but in the latter only when there are special forms for masculine and feminine. See **167**. Ex.: Die Weltgeschichte ist das Weltgericht (Sch.). Die Not ist die Mutter der Erfindung (Prov.). Das Märchen will jetzt Erzieherin werden, zuerst wollte sie Schauspielerin werden.

1. If one person is addressed as Sie or Ihr, the substantive stands of course in the singular. „Sie sind ein großer Meister im Schießen." Poetic and emphatic are such turns as: Regierte Recht so läget ihr vor mir im Staube jetzt, denn ich bin Euer König (Sch., spoken by Maria Stuart).

317. The substantive in apposition has the same concords as the substantive in the predicate, only the rule as to case is frequently found unobserved in the best writers. Was Venus band, die Bringerin des Glücks, kann Mars, der Stern des Unglücks schnell zerreißen (Sch.). Ihr kennet ihn, den Schöpfer kühner Heere (id.).

The apposition may be emphasized by nämlich and als : Ihnen, als einem gereisten Manne, glauben wir.

II. THE COMPOUND SENTENCE.

318. The compound sentence consists of two or more clauses, which may be **coordinate** (of equal grammatical value) or **subordinate** (one dependent upon the other).

COORDINATE SENTENCES.

We may distinguish various kinds of coordinate sentences, which may or may not be connected by conjunctions.

319. Copulative Sentences. The conjunctions und, auch, desgleichen, gleichfalls, ebenfalls, and their compounds, desgleichen auch, so auch, ebenso auch; nicht nur — sondern auch; nicht allein — sondern auch ; sowohl — als (auch) ; weder — noch indicate mere parataxis. Zudem, außerdem, überdies, ja, sogar, ja sogar, vielmehr emphasize the second clauses. Partitive conjunctions are teils — teils, halb — halb, zum Teil — zum Teil. Ordinal conjunctions are erstens — zweitens, etc. ; zuerst — dann — ferner, endlich, zuletzt; bald — bald. Explanatory are nämlich, und zwar. Ex.: Die Müh' ist klein, der Spaß ist groß (F. 4049). Halb zog sie ihn, halb sank er hin (G.). Ich will weder leugnen noch beschönigen, daß ich sie beredete (id.). Nicht allein die ersten Blüten fallen ab, sondern auch die Früchte (id.).

1. Notice that the adverbial conjunctions such as bald, zuletzt, dann, weder — noch, halb, teils, etc., always cause inversion. Some admit of inversion, but do not require it, *e. g.*, auch, erstens, nämlich. The ordinal conjunctions and nämlich are frequently separated by a comma, then no inversion takes place. Erstens ist es so der Brauch, zweitens will man's selber auch (Busch).

320. Adversative Sentences. 1. One excludes the other (disjunctive-adversative) : oder, or, entweder — oder, sonst (else), andernfalls, otherwise. Ex.: Er (Wallenstein) mußte entweder gar nicht befehlen oder mit vollkommener Freiheit handeln (Sch.). One contradicts the other (contradictory-adversative): sondern, vielmehr, sondern . . . vielmehr. The first clause contains nicht, zwar, freilich, allerdings, wohl. So wagten sie sich nicht in die Nähe der Feinde, sondern kehrten unverrichteter Sache zurück (Sch.).

2. The second sentence concedes the statement of the first in part or wholly. The first may contain nicht, etc., as above; the second has aber, often in the connection aber doch, dennoch aber, aber gleichwohl; allein, übrigens; nur. Allein is stronger than aber.

Mark the contrast between aber and sondern, Eng. but. Aber concedes, sondern contradicts. Er war zwar nicht krank, aber doch nicht dazu aufgelegt. "but he did not feel like it." Er war nicht krank, sondern er war nur nicht dazu aufgelegt (he only did not feel like doing it). Viele sind berufen aber wenige sind auserwählet (B.). Den Ungeheuern, den Gigantischen hätte man ihn (Corneille) nennen sollen, aber nicht den Großen (Le.). Wasser thut's freilich nicht (It is not the water that is effective in baptism), sondern das Wort Gottes, so (which) mit und bei dem Wasser ist (Lu.).

3. The second sentence states something new or different or in contrast with the first without contradicting or excluding or limiting the same. It occurs commonly in narrative and may be called "connexive- or contrasting-adversative." Conjunctions: aber, hingegen, dagegen, übrigens, trotzdem, gleichwohl, indessen, etc. Die Beleidigung ist groß; aber größer ist seine Gnade (Le.). Es scheint ein Rätsel und doch ist es keins (G.). Es ist die schönste Hoffnung; doch ist es nur eine Hoffnung (Sch.).

321. Causal Sentences. One gives the reason or cause for the other. Conjunctions: d(a)rum, deswegen, daher, denn, nämlich, etc. The clause containing the reason generally stands second, the one beginning with „denn" always. Notice denn, "for," always calls for the normal order. Ex.: Soldaten waren teuer, denn die Menge geht nach dem Glück (Sch.). Eine Durchlauchtigkeit läßt er sich nennen; drum muß er Soldaten halten können (id.).

322. Illative Sentences. One sentence is an inference or effect of the other. Closely related to the causal. Conjunctions: ſo, a'lſo, ſomi't, folglich, mithi'n, de'mnach, etc. Meine Rechte (right hand) iſt gegen den Druck der Liebe unempfindlich . . . ſo (then) ſeid ihr Götz von Berlichingen (G.). D i e Sonnen alſo ſcheinen uns nicht mehr (Sch.).

Subordinate Sentences.

323. We shall distinguish three classes of dependent clauses, according to the logical value of the part of speech they represent:
1. **Substantive clauses**, with the value of a noun.
2. **Adjective clauses**, with the value of an adjective.
3. **Adverbial clauses**, with the value of an adverb.

Substantive Clauses.

324. The clause is subject: Das eben iſt der Fluch der böſen That, daß ſie fortwährend Böſes muß gebären (Sch.). Mich reuet, daß ich's that (id.). Predicate (N.): Die Menſchen ſind nicht immer was ſie ſcheinen (Le.). Object (A.): Glaubſt du nicht, daß eine Warnungsſtimme in Träumen vorbedeutend zu uns ſpricht? (Sch.). Was man ſchwarz auf weiß beſitzt, kann man getroſt nach Hauſe tragen (F. 1906-7). Dative: Wohl dem, der bis auf die Neige (to the very end) rein gelebt ſein Leben hat (He.). Genitive: Wes das Herz voll iſt, des geht der Mund über (B.). Apposition: Den edeln Stolz, daß du dir ſelbſt nicht genügeſt, verzeih' ich dir (G.).

325. As to their contents the substantive clauses may be grouped as follows:
1. Daß, or declarative clauses, always introduced by „daß." Schon Sokrates lehrte, daß die Seele des Menſchen unſterblich ſei, or die Lehre, daß die Seele . . ., or wir glauben, daß die Seele . . .

More examples in **324.**

2. **Clauses containing indirect questions**: *a.* Questions after the predicate always introduced by ob; in the main clause may stand as correlatives es, das, dessen, davon, etc. Er hatte nicht geschrieben, ob er gesund geblieben (Bü.). (See F. 1667-70). *b.* Questions after any other part of the sentence, introduced by an interrogative pronoun, by an interrogative adverb, simple or compounded with a preposition, viz., wer, was, wie, wo, wann, womit, woher, wohin, etc. Ex.: Fraget nicht, warum ich traure (Sch.). See F. 1971. Begreifst du, wie andächtig schwärmen viel leichter als gut handeln ist? (Le.). Noch fehlt uns Kunde, was in Unterwalden und Schwyz geschehen (Sch.). *c.* The question may be disjunctive, introduced by ob — oder; ob — oder ob; ob — ob. Ex.: Aber sag' mir, ob wir stehen oder ob wir weiter gehen (F. 3906-7). Und eh' der Tag sich neigt, muß sich's erklären, ob ich den Freund, ob ich den Vater soll entbehren (Sch.).

REMARKS.—1. The mood in 1 and 2, according to circumstances, is either the indicative or the potential subjunctive. See the examples sub 1 and in 324.

2. In „daß"-clauses the other two word-orders are also possible, but without daß: Sokrates lehrte, die Seele sei unsterblich. Es wurde behauptet, gestern habe man ihn noch auf der Straße gesehen.

3. When the subject is the same in both clauses or when the subject of the dependent clause is the object of the main clause, in short, when no ambiguity is caused, the infinitive clause can stand in place of daß + dependent order. Man hofft, das untergegangene Schiff noch zu heben. Die Polizei hat dem Kaufmanne befohlen, sein Schild höher zu hängen.

3. **Clauses with indirect speech**—after verbs of saying, asserting, knowing, thinking, wishing, demanding, commanding. They either begin with daß with dependent order or they have the order of the direct speech. The subjunctive is the reigning mood. For examples and tense, see **282**.

4. **Clauses containing direct speech, a quotation**: Das Wort ist frei, sagt der General (Sch.). Der König rief: Ist der Sänger da?

Adjective Clauses.

326. The clause is introduced by a relative pronoun or by a relative adverb. Nothing can precede the pronoun in the clause except a preposition. Unless the personal pronoun is repeated after the relative, the verb stands in the third person. Ex.: Du sprichst von Zeiten, die vergangen sind (Sch.). Die Stätte, die ein guter Mensch betrat, ist eingeweiht (G.). Der du von dem Himmel bist, süßer Friede ... (id.).

For use of the pronouns and more examples, see 255-258.

327. 1. The relative pronoun can never be omitted as in English. In several relative clauses referring to the same word, the pronoun need stand only once, if the same case is required; if a different case is necessary, the pronoun should be repeated. This is often sinned against, for instance by Schiller: Sieh da die Verse, die er schrieb und seine Glut gesteht, instead of worin er ... gesteht.

2. The relative clauses beginning with wer, was without antecedents are really identical with substantive clauses, e.g., Da seht, daß ihr tiefsinnig faßt, was in des Menschen Hirn nicht paßt. Für was drein geht und nicht drein geht, ein kräftig Wort zu Diensten steht (F. 1950-3).

3. Case-attraction between relative and antecedent is now rare. Als welcher, denoting rather a cause than a quality, is now archaic, but still quite frequent in Lessing's time. Äneas, als welcher sich an den bloßen (mere) Figuren ergötzet, = "Æneas, since he delights ..." (Le.). Von der Tragödie, als über die uns die Zeit ziemlich alles daraus (of *Aristotle's Poetics*) gönnen ... "about tragedy, in so far as time has favored us ..." (id.). „Da" in the relative clause is no longer usage. Wer da stehet, sehe zu, daß er nicht falle (B.).

328. The mood depends upon circumstances. The potential subjunctive (of the preterit and pluperfect) is frequent after a negative main clause. Es ist keine große Stadt in Deutschland, die der Onkel nicht besucht hätte (= did not visit). The subjunctive of indirect speech also stands. Die Regierung der Vereinigten Staaten beschwerte sich über die Landung sovieler Armen, welche manche europäische Regierung fortschicke.

Adverbial Clauses.

329. They are introduced by the subordinating conjunctions. The main clause often has an emphatic adverb, e. g., alfo, dann, da, dahin, jetzt, daher, darum. So does not, as a rule, stand after dependent clauses expressing time and place, and generally becomes superfluous in English after dependent clauses of manner.

330. Temporal Clauses. 1. *Contemporaneous action* implying either duration or only point of time. Conjunctions: während, indem, indes (indeffen), wie, da (all meaning "while," "as"); folange (als); fo oft (als); fo bald (als); da, wo (rare and colloquial) = when; wenn (wann is old) + "when," refers to the future; als, "when," refers always to the past with the preterit; weil, dieweil, derweil, = + "while," are archaic. Solange, fo oft, fobald are now much more common without „als."

<small>Ex.: Ach! vielleicht indem (as) wir hoffen, hat uns Unheil schon getroffen (Sch.). Nur der Starke wird das Schicksal zwingen, wenn der Schwächling unterliegt (Sch.). Und wie (as) er sitzt und wie er lauscht, teilt sich die Flut empor (G.). Als des Sanctus Worte kamen, da schellt er dreimal bei dem Namen (",Sanctus . . ." is part of the mass) (Sch.). Es irrt der Mensch, folang' er strebt (F. 317). Sobald die ersten Lerchen schwirrten (erschien) ein Mädchen schön und wunderbar (Sch.). Das Eisen muß geschmiedet werden, weil es glüht (Prov.). Will mir die Hand noch reichen, derweil ich eben lad (= while I am loading the musket) (Uh.).</small>

2. *Antecedent action, i. e.*, the action of the dependent clause precedes that of the main clause. Conjunctions: nachdem, after; da, als, wenn, after, when; seitdem, seit, seitdem daß (all mean + since); sobald (als), sowie, wie, as soon as; the adverb kaum + inverted order.

<small>Ex.: Nimmer (no more) sang ich freudige Lieder, seit ich deine Stimme bin (Sch.). Wenn (after) der Leib in Staub zerfallen, lebt der große Name noch (Sch.). Und wie er winkt mit dem Finger, auf thut sich der weite Zwinger (id.). Kaum war der Vater tot, so kommt ein jeder mit seinem Ring (Le.). (Notice the inversion.)</small>

Der König verließ Nürnberg, nachdem er es zur Fürsorge mit einer hinlänglichen Besatzung versehen hatte (Sch.).

3. *Subsequent action.* The action of the dependent clause follows. Conjunctions : Ehe, bevor, + "ere", "before"; bis, until, with or without daß.

Ex.: Nie verachte den Mann, eh' bu sein Inn'res erkannt hast (He.). Bevor wir's laffen rinnen, betet einen frommen Spruch (Sch.). Bis die Glocke sich verkühlet, lasst die strenge Arbeit ruhn (id.). Ehe wir es uns versahen (unexpectedly), brach der Wagen zusammen.

a. The main clause may be emphasized by dann, damals, dann, darauf, and so, if it follows the dependent clause.

In 2 and 3 the potential subjunctive can stand.

331. Local Clauses. They denote the place and direction of the action of the main clause. They begin with wo, wohin, woher, and the main clause may contain a corresponding da, dahin, daher, hier.

Ex.: Wo Menschenkunst nicht zureicht, hat der Himmel oft geraten (Sch.). Die Welt ist vollkommen überall, wo der Mensch nicht hinkommt mit seiner Qual (id.). Denn eben wo Begriffe fehlen, da stellt ein Wort zur rechten Zeit sich ein (F. 1995-6). Kein Wasser ist zu haben, wohin man sich auch wende.

a. The demonstratives da, dahin, daher in the local clause are now archaic. Do not confound the relative clauses and indirect questions with the local clauses which generally refer to an adverb.

The potential subjunctive may stand in them.

Clauses of Manner and Cause.

332. *Modal clauses* express an accompanying circumstance and are therefore related to contemporaneous clauses. Conjunctions: indem, daß nicht, ohne daß, without, indem nicht, statt or anstatt daß, instead of. Ex.: Der Ritter ging fort, indem er auf den Gegner einen verächtlichen Blick warf. Ich bin nie in London, daß ich nicht das Museum besuchte (subj.).

1. They may have the potential subjunctive. But these clauses occur more frequently in the form of participial and infinitive clauses with

„ohne zu," „anstatt zu" : Al-Hast, anstatt zu empfangen, mußte zahlen. Er ritt fort ohne sich umzusehen.

333. *Comparative clauses* denote manner, degree, and measure. Conjunctions: wie, als, " as," " than " with the corresponding so, also, ebenso (= so) in the main clause. After the comparative als, denn, weder, "than." Other forms: gleichwie — so; so wie — so; just as — as, so. Wie denotes rather manner and quality, als the degree and quantity. When both clauses have the same predicate, contraction is common. Then wie denotes likeness, als identity.

Ex. : Ich singe wie der Vogel singt (G.). Danket Gott so warm als ich für diesen Trunk euch danke (id.). Wie du mir („thust" understood), so ich dir (Prov.). Du bist mir nichts mehr als sein Sohn (Sch.). Der träge Gang des Krieges hat dem König ebensoviel Schaden gethan als er den Rebellen Vorteil brachte (id.). Hatte sich ein Ränzlein angemäst't als wie der Doktor Luther (F. 2129-30) (als wie is colloquial). „Wie ein Ritter," " like a knight"; „als (ein) Ritter," " as a knight." Sein Glück war größer als man berechnet hatte (Sch.). Eines Hauptes (by one head) länger denn alles Volk (B.). Weder is very rare.

1. Specially to be noticed are the clauses with als ob, alswenn, generally followed by the potential or unreal subjunctive. For wenn + dependent order occurs also the inverted without wenn. Ex.: Ihr eilet ja, als wenn ihr Flügel hättet (Le.). Suche die Wissenschaft, als würdest ewig du hier sein; Tugend, als hielte der Tod dich schon am sträubenden Haar (He.). But the indicative is possible: Und es wallet und siebet und brauset und zischt wie wenn Wasser mit Feuer sich mengt (Sch.).

2. Denn is preferable after a comparative when several „als" occur. Wie is colloquial. Es fragt sich ob Lessing größer als Dichter denn als Mensch gewesen sei. Nicht in the clause after als is no longer good usage, though common in the 17th and 18th centuries. Lessing has it very frequently. Ich lebte so eingezogen, als ich in Meißen nicht gelebt hatte (Le.).

a. Nichts weniger als means " anything but," literally " nothing less than that," generally felt by English speakers as meaning " nothing but," *e. g.*, Aber ich darf sagen, daß diese Einrichtung der Fabel nichts weniger als notwendig ist, *i. e.*, that this arrangement of the plot is anything but necessary (Le.). In „nichts als" = " nothing but," as after all negative pronouns, „niemand als du" = nobody but you, als has exclusive force, = " but."

3. Other correlatives are so einer — wie; der nämliche — wie; derselbe — wie; solch-, so + positive adjective — wie (quality) and als (degree); after

zu, allzu + positive and after ein anderer stand als + daß or wenn, als and infinitive, *e. g.*, Er denft zu edel, als daß er so etwas von uns erwarten fönnte. Er ist der nämliche wie er immer war. Eure Versöhnung war ein wenig zu schnell, als daß sie dauerhaft hätte sein sollen (G.).

Notice the potential subjunctive after „als daß."

334. Under this head comes really the *proportional clause*, which expresses the proportion of the decrease or increase of what is asserted in the main clause. The conjunctions are the following correlatives: je — desto, um so (or um desto, rarely); je — je, = the — the; je nachdem (or nachdem or wie, rarely), according as. If the main clause stand first, its correlative is dispensable.

Ex.: Je mehr der Vorrat schmolz, desto schrecklicher wuchs der Hunger (Sch.). Je länger, je lieber (Prov.). Je mehr er hat, je mehr er will. (Je) nachdem einer ringt, nachdem ihm gelingt (G.), "The success depends upon the effort."

1. Je = ever; desto, "on that account," "hence," see **442**, *a*. Notice the dependent order in the first, the inverted generally in the second.

335. *Consecutive clauses* express the result or effect of the predicate of the main clause. Conjunctions: daß (sodaß), that; in the main clause, if any correlative, so, so sehr, dergestalt, derart, solch. Ex.: So verabscheut ist die Tyrannei', daß sie kein Werkzeug findet (Sch.). Er schlug, daß laut der Wald erklang und alles Eisen in Stücken sprang (Uh.).

1 The result may also be expressed in the form of a main clause or of an infinitive clause: Doch übernähm' ich gern noch ei'nmal alle Plage, so lieb war mir das Kind (F. 3123–4). Ich bin zu alt, um nur zu spielen, zu jung um ohne Wunsch zu sein (F. 1546–7).

2. Mark the potential and unreal subjunctives of the preterit and pluperfect which may stand in these clauses: Vermeint Ihr mich so jung und schwach, daß ich mit Riesen stritte? (Uh.). Das Pferd war so lahm, daß wir schneller zu Fuß heim gekommen wären.

336. *Restrictive clauses* limit the value and scope of the statement of the predicate and border closely upon the conditional and comparative clauses. Conjunctions: nur daß, only (that), außer daß, except that, in so fern (als), wofern, in wie fern, in so or in wie weit, in as far as, in as much as. The negative force is given also by the subjunctive and the normal order with the adverb denn or by es sei denn, es wäre denn, daß, which is now more common.

Ex.: Wir waren gar nicht so übel dran, nur daß wir nichts zu trinken hatten, We were not at all so badly off, only ... In so fern nun diese Wesen Körper sind, schildert die Poesie auch Körper (Le.). Er entfernte sich niemals weit, er sagt' es ihr denn (H. and D., IV. 42–3). Ich lasse dich nicht, du segnest mich denn (unless thou bless me) (B.). Ruhig (gedenke ich mich zu verhalten); es sei denn, daß (unless) er sich an meiner Ehre oder meinen Gütern vergreife (Sch.).

1. This is a very old construction, quite common in M. H. G. The negative force lies not in denn, but in the lost *ne* + the potential or concessive subjunctive. Denn < M. H. G. *danne*, is unessential. Compare M. H. G. *den lip wil ich verliesen, si en werde min wip* = my life will I lose, (she become not my wife) unless she, etc. *Swaz lebete in dem walde ez entrünne danne balde, das was zehant tot*, = Was im Walde lebte, das war auf der Stelle tot, es sei denn daß es bald davon lief or gelaufen wäre (quoted by Paul). *Ne* disappeared as early as late M. H. G., particularly after a negative main clause. It is left in nur < *ne waere* = (es) wäre nicht daß. See Paul's M. H. G. gram., § 335–40.

337. *Causal clauses* denote the cause, reason, and means. Conjunctions: da, since, weil, because, indem = by + present participle in Eng. Correlatives, if any: da'rum, da'her, so, desbalb etc. Da'durch daß, da'mit daß express rather the instrument. Weil expresses the material cause; da the logical reason; „indem" is a weak causal and borders rather closely upon the contemporaneous „indem." Denn + normal order expresses a known or admitted reason. It is emphatic. See **321**.

Ex.: Das Schlepptau (hawser) zerriß, weil der Schleppdampfer (tug) zu schnell anzog. Mit dem besten Willen leisten wir so wenig, weil uns tausend Willen kreuzen (G.). Jeden andern zu schicken ist besser, da ich so klein bin (G.). Dir blüht gewiß das schönste Glück auf Erden, da du so fromm und heilig bist (Sch.). Richelieu wußte sich nur dadurch zu helfen, daß er den Feindseligkeiten ein schleuniges Ende machte (Sch.).

1. Nun, dieweil, allbieweil, maßen, sintemal, and others, are rare and archaic.

2. The clauses with ba'burch baß, ba'mit baß border closely upon the substantive clause. Da, says Becker, denotes the real *and* logical reason, weil the logical only when the kind of reason is not emphasized. Weil stands in a clause that answers the question as to the reason. Warum wurde Wallenstein abgesetzt? Weil man ihn für einen Verräter hielt.

338. *Final clauses* express intention and object. Conjunctions: Dami't, daß, "in order that." Auf daß, und daß are archaic. In the main clause rarely stand darum, dazu, in der Absicht, zu dem Zwecke (both followed by daß).

Ex.: Darum eben leiht er keinem, damit er stets zu geben habe (Le.). Dazu ward ihm der Verstand, daß er im innern Herzen spüret, was er erschafft mit seiner Hand (Sch.). Ehre Vater und Mutter, auf daß dir's wohl gehe und du lange lebest auf Erben (B.).

1. The reigning mood of this clause is the subjunctive. If the object is represented as reached, the indicative may also stand. Um zu + inf. forms a very common final clause ; Man lebt nicht um zu essen, sondern man ißt um zu leben.

339. *Concessive clauses* make a concession to the contradiction existing between the main clause and the result expected from it in the dependent clause. They are called also adversative causal clauses. Conjunctions: obglei'ch (ob . . . gleich), obscho'n (ob . . . schon), obwohl (ob . . . wohl), ob auch, ob zwar, wenn auch, wenn gleich, ob, all = "although." The main clause may contain de'nnoch, doch, nichtsdestoweniger, gleichwohl, but so only if it stands second.

Relative clauses with indefinite relative pronouns and adverbs, wer . . . auch (immer, nur), wie . . . auch, so . . . auch (noch); inverted clauses and those with the normal order, containing the adverbs schon, gleich, zwar, wohl, freilich, noch have also concessive force.

Ex.: Ist es gleich Nacht, so leuchtet unser Recht (Sch.). (Compare Obgleich es Nacht ist, ob es gleich Nacht ist . . .) Was Feuersmut ihm auch geraubt, ein süßer Trost ist ihm geblieben (id.). Mutig sprach er zu Reinekens besten (in favor of R.) so falsch auch dieser bekannt war (G.). Ein Gott ist, ein heiliger Wille lebt, wie auch der menschliche wanke (Sch.). Erfüll' davon dein Herz, so groß es ist (F. 3452).

146 GENERAL SYNTAX—SUBORDINATE SENTENCES. [340—

Man kommt ins Gerede, wie man sich immer stellt (G.). Dem Bösewicht wird alles schwer, er thue was er will (Hölty). Zwar weiß ich viel, doch möcht' ich alles wissen (F. 601).

1. Mark also the form of the imperative and unb + inversion: Sei noch so dumm, es gibt doch jemand(en), der dich für weise hält. Der Mensch ist frei geschaffen, ist frei, und würde er in Ketten geboren (Sch.).

2. Mood : if a fact is stated, the indicative; if a supposition, the concessive and unreal subjunctive. See examples above.

3. When certain parts of speech are common to both clauses, there may be contraction. Obwohl von hohem Stamm, liebt er das Volk (Sch.).

340. *Conditional clauses* express a supposition upon which the statement of the main clause will become a fact. If the supposition is real, the conditional clause has the indicative; if only fancied or merely possible, the potential subjunctive; if it implies that the contrary of the supposition is about to happen or has happened, then it has the unreal subjunctive of the imperfect or the pluperfect. Conjunctions : wenn, if; falls, im Falle daß, in case that; wenn anders, if . . . at all; also wofern, sofern (such often difficult to distinguish from a concessive clause); wo, so (rare). The main clause may have da, dann, in dem Falle, and if it stand second, generally begins with so.

Ex.: Wenn sich die Völker selbst befrein, da kann die Wohlfahrt nicht gedeihn (Sch.). Wenn du als Mann die Wissenschaft vermehrst, so kann dein Sohn zu höh'rem Ziel gelangen (F. 1063). Wer miede nicht, wenn er's umgehen kann, das Äußerste (Sch.). So du kämpfest ritterlich, freut dein alter Vater sich (Stolberg).

1. Other forms of the conditional clause are the inverted order, the imperative, and the normal order with benn + subjunctive (= if . . . not, unless; see 336, 1). Sei im Besitze und du wohnst im Recht (Sch.), Possession is nine points of the law. Dem lieben Gotte weich' nicht aus, find'st du ihn auf dem Weg (Sch.).

2. Wofern nicht, außer wenn, es sei denn daß, if not, unless, denote an exception to a statement true in general. Der Wolf ist harmlos, außer wenn er Hunger hat. See 336, 1.

3. Sometimes the preterit ind. is substituted for the unreal subjunctive in the dependent or in the main clause or in both. Its force is

assurance, certainty. Traf ein Kürbis mein Gesicht, ach, so lebt' ich sicher nicht (Gleim). Mit diesem Pfeil durchschoß ich Euch, wenn ich mein liebes Kind getroffen hätte (Sch.). O wärst du wahr gewesen und gerade, nie kam es dahin, alles stünde anders (Sch.).

4. Contracted and abbreviated forms: Entworfen bloß ist's ein gemeiner Frevel; vollführt ist's ein unsterblich Unternehmen (Sch.). Wenn nicht, wo nicht, wo möglich are very common. Wir versuchten ihn wo möglich zu beruhigen, wenn nicht ganz zu entfernen.

For the tenses see also 275-280.

WORD-ORDER.

341. We distinguish three principal word-orders according to the position of subject and verb:

1. **The normal,** viz., subject — verb.
2. **The inverted,** viz., verb — subject.
3. **The dependent,** viz., verb at the end.

(By "verb" we shall understand for the sake of brevity the personal part and by "predicate" the non-personal part of the verb, viz., participle and infinitive.)

342. The **normal** occurs chiefly in main sentences: Der Wind weht. It is identical with the dependent order if there is only subject and verb in the dependent clause. Die Mühle geht, weil der Wind weht.

343. The **inverted** order occurs both in main and dependent clauses: Geht die Mühle? Weht der Wind, (so) geht die Mühle. It occurs:

a. In a question.

b. In optative and imperative sentences.

c. In dependent clauses, mainly conditional and after als + subjunctive, when there is no conjunction like wenn, ob, etc.

d. If for any reason, generally a rhetorical one, any other word but the subject, or if a whole clause, head the sentence.

e. For impressiveness the verb stands first.

Examples with adjuncts (objects, adverbs, etc.) added:

a. Schreibt der Freund? Bleibt der Diener nicht lange aus? Was schreibt dir der Freund?

But when the inquiry is as to the subject the normal order stands of course. Wer schreibt einen Brief? Was ist der langen Rede kurzer Sinn? (Sch.).

b. Möge nie der Tag erscheinen, wenn des rauhen Krieges Horden dieses stille Thal durchtoben (Sch.). For more examples, see **284**, 1, 2.

But the inverted order is not required: Die Zahl der Tropfen, die er hegt, sei euren Tagen zugelegt! (F. 989–990).

c. Willst du genau erfahren was sich ziemt, so frage nur bei edlen Frauen an (G.). Wird man wo (= irgendwo) gut aufgenommen, muß man nicht gleich wiederkommen (Wolff). (Er) Strich drauf ein Spange, Kett' und Ring', als wären's eben Pfifferling'; dankt' nicht weniger und nicht mehr, als ob's ein Korb voll Nüsse wär' (F. 2843–6).

Notice here the inversion after als alone, but dependent order after als ob. See **340**, 1; also F. 1122–25, 1962–3.

But for emphasis and to add vividness, the normal is still possible: Du stehest still, er wartet auf; du sprichst ihn an, er strebt an dir hinauf (F. 1168–9). This is mere parataxis.

d. Die Botschaft hör' ich wohl, allein mir fehlt der Glaube (F. 765). Ernst ist das Leben, heiter ist die Kunst (Sch.). Mich hat mein Herz betrogen (id.). Wo aber ein Aas ist, da versammeln sich die Adler (B.). Deines Geistes hab' ich einen Hauch verspürt (Uh.). See also F. 860–1, 1174–5, 1236. Übersehen kann Caylus dies Gemälde nicht haben (Le.). Geschrieben steht: „Im Anfang war das Wort" (F. 1224). See also **236**, 3.

1. The main clause, inserted in any statement or following it, has inversion according to this rule. Das, spricht er, ist kein Aufenthalt, was fördert himmelan (Sch.). Wie seid ihr glücklich, edler Graf, hub er voll Arglist an (id.). For emphasis the speaker can insert a clause uninverted: Denn, ich weiß es, er ist der Güter die er bereinst erbt, wert (H. and D., III. 53).

2. The coordinating conjunctions aber, allein, denn, nämlich, oder, sondern, und standing generally at the head of the sentence, any adverb with the force of an elliptical sentence (zwar, ja, etc., having generally a comma

after them) call for no inversion. After entweder there is option. Ex.: Aber die Kunst hat in den neueren Zeiten ungleich weitere Grenzen erhalten (Le.). Zwar euer Bart ist kraus, doch hebt ihr nicht die Riegel (F. 671). Fürwahr! ich bin der einzige Sohn nur (H. and D., IV. 91). Ja, mir hat es der Geist gesagt (id., IV. 95). Denn die Männer sind heftig (id., IV. 148).

3. When the dependent clause precedes, the main clause can for emphasis and very frequently colloquially have the normal order. Ex.: Hätte er die Ursachen dieses allgemeinen Aberglaubens an Shakspere's Schönheiten auch gesucht, er würde sie bald gefunden haben (Le.).

e. Hat die Königin doch nichts voraus vor dem gemeinen Bürgerweibe (Sch.). Stehen wie Felsen doch zwei Männer gegen einander! (H. and D., IV. 229). Generally contains doch.

344. The **dependent order** occurs only in dependent clauses. The clause begins with a relative or interrogative pronoun which may be preceded by a preposition; with a relative or interrog. adverb; or with a subordinating conjunction. Ex.: Wenn ich nicht Alexander wäre, möchte ich wohl Diogenes sein. Je mehr er hat, je mehr er will (Claudius). So stolz ich bin, muß ich mir selbst gestehn: dergleichen hab' ich nie gesehn (G.). Wie solche tiefgeprägte Bilder doch zu Zeiten in uns schlafen können, bis ein Wort, ein Laut sie weckt (Le.). See also F. 2015–18, 2062.

345. The dependent order does not occur in main clauses, but it is not the only order of the dependent clause.

1. The verb precedes two infinitives. One may be the past participle of a modal auxiliary. Ex.: Kann ich vergessen, wie's hätte kommen können? (Sch.). Daß ein Mensch doch einen Menschen so verlegen soll machen können! (Le.).

a. But in this case and in other compound tenses the "verb" (*i. e.*, the personal part) may also stand between the participle and the other auxiliary or the infinitive, *e. g.*, weil der Kaufmann das Haus soll gekauft haben or gekauft soll haben (in poetry). Gekauft haben soll is the common order.

2. The normal order may stand:

    1. In dependent clauses containing indirect speech. Er

glaubt, Shakspere habe Brutus zum Helden des Stückes machen wollen (Le.).

2. In a second or third dependent clause. See **358**.

3. In certain clauses with negative force containing an enclitic „denn": es sei denn daß + dependent order. See **336**.

4. In substantive clauses: Gott weiß, ich bin nicht schuld (Le.). This is mere parataxis without conjunction.

346. The auxiliaries haben and sein are also frequently dropped in dependent clauses to avoid an accumulation of verbal forms, both in prose and poetry. Lessing, Goethe, and Klopstock, especially the first, drop the auxiliary very freely and skillfully.

Ex.: Wie unbegreiflich ich von ihm beleidigt worden (supply bin here or before beleidigt) und noch werde (Le.). Möglich, daß der Vater die Tyranne'i des e i n e n Rings nicht länger in seinem Hause (supply hat) dulden wollen (id.).

347. The dependent order in main clauses is archaic and poetic. Ex.: Siegfried den Hammer wohl schwingen kunnt (dialect for konnte) (Uh.). Urahne, Großmutter, Mutter und Kind in dumpfer Stube beisammen sind (Schwab).

348. 1. The inverted order in the conditional clause and in a main clause for the sake of impressiveness has sprung from the order of the question. Compare, for instance: 1. Ist der Freund treu? (question). 2. Ist der Freund treu? (question). Gut, so wird er mir beistehen. 3. Ist der Freund treu (conditional clause), so wird er mir beistehen. 4. Ist mir der Freund doch treu geblieben! (impressive inversion).

2. The main clause has inversion when the dependent clause precedes, because it generally begins with an adverb like so, dann, etc. Gehst du nicht, so thust du Unrecht. Without so, the inversion really ceases. Hence we say, the normal order may still stand for emphasis. But so, etc., were so frequent that inversion became the rule. Inversion is therefore limited originally to the question and to the choice of placing the emphatic part of the sentence where it will be most prominent.

349. 1. The dependent order was in O. H. G. by no means limited to the dependent clause. Toward the 10th century it begins to become rarer in the main clause. In early M. H. G. it became limited to the dependent clause, so that now we may justly call it the "*dependent-clause order.*"

2. The verb at the end is, no doubt, a great blemish of German style—second only to the separation of the little prefix of separable compound verbs, which may turn up after many intervening parts at the close of the sentence. According to Delbrück, the dependent order—subject, object, verb—was the primitive one, still in force in Latin.

General Rules for the Order of other Parts of the Sentence besides Subject and Verb.

Position of the Predicate.

350. The predicate, be it an adjective, a substantive, participle, infinitive, or separable prefix of a compound verb or the first element of a loosely compounded verb, stands at the end of a main clause in a simple tense. The adjuncts of the predicate, such as objects, adverbs, stand between verb and predicate.

Ex.: Der Senne muß scheiden, der Sommer ist hin (Sch.). Ihr seid ein Meister (id.). Er hat verlor'ne Worte nur gesprochen (id.). Kein Schild fing diesen Mordstreich auf (id.). Straflose Frechheit spricht den Sitten Hohn (id.). Gestern fand ein Wagner=Conce'rt statt.

In the dependent clause only the verb changes position, subject and predicate remain as in the main clause, and the adjuncts stand between them. For instance: Glaubt das nicht! Ihr werdet dieses Kampfes Ende nimmer erblicken (Sch.), becomes Glaubt nicht, daß ihr dieses Kampfes Ende je erblicken werdet.

351. In the compound tense the separable prefix immediately precedes the participle, be it in a main or in a dependent clause. Dreißig Jahre haben wir zusammen ausgelebt und ausgehalten (Sch.). Die Cholera will (is about to) ü'berhand nehmen. See **137**.

Order of Objects and Cases.

352. *a.* Case of a person before a case of the thing. Aber auch noch dann . . . fuhr der Kaiser fort, den Ständen den Frieden zu zeigen (Sch.).

b. Case of a pronoun before a noun. Man bestimmte sie (them) dem allgemeinen Unwillen zum Opfer (Sch.).

c. The dative stands before the accusative; if both are persons, the accusative may stand before the dative. Er selbst hatte dem Dienste dieses Hauses seine ersten Feldzüge gewidmet (Sch.).

d. The accusative-object stands before remoter objects, a genitive or a preposition + case. But see also *a*. Man möchte sagen, Voltaire habe ein Gefühl von der Wichtigkeit dieser Persönlichkeit gehabt (H. Grimm). Die Schülerin schrieb einen Aufsatz über den Winter.

e. As to pronouns, sich stands generally before es, and both before every other pronoun. The personal pronoun stands before the demonstrative. The personal and sich may stand before the subject, if it be a noun, in the inverted and dependent orders. Er hat sich es angeeignet. Krummau (a proper name) nähert sich ihm (Sch.). Wer darf sich so etwas erlauben? Jenem den Weg zu dem bömischen Throne zu verschließen, ergriff man die Waffen schon unter Matthias (Sch.). Was ihm die vergrößerte Macht der Stände (estates) an Selbstthätigkeit noch übrig ließ, hielten seine Agnaten (relatives) unter einem schimpflichen Zwang (id.). Hat sich die Flotte ergeben? Hast du es ihm wieder gegeben?

1. *c* also includes the personal pronouns: Wie konnt' ich ohne Zeugen mich ihr nahn? (Sch.). The rules *a, c, d* are by no means strict.

353. For the position of the adjective, see the use of the adjective, **194, 212**. Notice that what depends upon an adjective, participle, or infinitive precedes these. Die Engländer sind ihrem Herrscherhause ergeben. Zum Sehen geboren, zum Schauen bestellt, dem Turme geschworen, gefällt mir die Welt (G.). Wir baten ihn, den Brief auf die Post zu geben. (Shakspere's Werke sind) keine Tugendlehren, in Kapitel gebracht und durch redende Exempel erläutert (Le.).

Position of Adverbs.

354. In general, adverbs stand before the words they qualify. The modal adverbs nicht, etwa, zwar, schon, wol, etc., and the adverbs of time immer, schon, jetzt, nie, nimmer stand generally immediately before the predicate or in place of it if there is none. Dies Bildniß ist bezaubernd schön (Mozart's Zauber=

flöte). Ein sehr heftiger Husten greift den Kranken stark an. Das schwere Herz wird nicht durch Worte leicht (Sch.). Schon viele Tage seh' ich es schweigend an (id.). Ich habe euch noch nie erkannt (B.). Hast du ihn noch nicht besucht? (Notice the opposite of the English order in "never yet," "not yet.")

355. An adverb of time stands before one of place, and both before one of manner. Ex.: Viele Bauern waren gestern nach der Stadt zu Markte gefahren. Wir fahren morgen *per* Eisenbahn nach Rudolstadt. Es tanzt sich auf diesem glatten Fußboden nicht sehr gut.

1. Of several adverbs of time or place the more general precede the more specific. Wir reisen morgen früh um 6 Uhr 59 Minuten ab. Der Polizist fand den Betrunkenen auf der Fahrstraße im Drecke liegen.

2. Adverbs of time precede objects when these are nouns, but pronouns precede all adverbs. Wir feiern bald den 4ten Juli, den Tag der Unabhängigkeitserklärung. Wir hoffen ihn morgen auf dem Bahnhofe zu treffen.

356. Only aber, nämlich, jedoch, and a few others, can separate subject and verb. Ex.: Der Richter aber sprach (Le.). Die Nachtigall jedoch singt wunderschön.

357. As to the position of the prepositions, they, with very few exceptions, precede the noun; when they follow the noun has been stated under Prepositions. See, for instance, **303, 7, 8, 10.**

Position of Clauses.

358. Dependent clauses have, in general, the positions of those parts of speech and of the sentence which they represent, *i. e.*, the substantive clause standing for the subject or object has the position of the subject or the object in the sentence, etc. No special rules are needed for them. When there are several dependent clauses, the last often takes for variety the normal order introduced by und.

The following examples show well-placed dependent clauses: Kein Kaiser kann, was unser ist, verschenken (Sch.). Versiegelt hab' ich's und verbrieft, daß er mein guter Engel ist (id.). Die Ehr', die ihm gebürt, geb' ich ihm gern; das Recht das er sich nimmt, verweigr' ich ihm (id.). Als ich jünger war, liebte ich nichts so sehr, als Roma'ne (novels) (G.). Richelieu wußte sich dadurch zu helfen, daß er den Feindseligkeiten zwischen beiden ein schleuniges Ende machte (Sch.). Mein guter Geist bewahrte mich davor, die Natter an den Busen mir zu legen (mir before die Natter in prose) (id.). Der Mensch begehrt, alles an sich zu reißen (G.). Wenn dann die rollenden Wagen vorbeigesaust sind und man hört sie nur noch in der Ferne, ... (for und man sie ... hört (Auerbach).

359. The rules given can hardly be abstracted from poetry. Even in prose they will be found frequently infringed. Rhythm, rhyme, and, in prose, emphasis control the order of words and allow of much choice. But students translating into German should adhere to the rules very strictly. It will be noticed that the German word-order coincides very nearly with the old English, and does not differ after all so much from the modern English word-order. The chief points of difference are the dependent order, the position of adverbs of time, which in English stand generally at the end, and the position of the adjuncts of adjectives, participles, and infinitives, which precede the latter instead of following them as in English.

1. The word-order required by certain conjunctions has been frequently mentioned in the General Syntax. See, for instance, 320.

SECOND PART.

ADVANCED GRAMMAR.

CONTAINING PHONOLOGY, HISTORICAL COMMENTARY ON
THE ACCIDENCE, HISTORY OF THE LANGUAGE,
AND WORD-FORMATION.

A. PHONOLOGY.

Historical Notes on the Orthography.

360. The letters used in Germany are the strongly modified Latin (Roman), called "Gothic," in vogue all over Europe during the later Middle Ages, when printing was invented. Germany is the only nation of the first rank which retains them, and for this reason they may be justly called "German" now. In Denmark, Sweden and Norway they are also still in use to a certain extent. Italy, France, England and Holland abandoned the ugly "Gothic" alphabet very early and returned to the Roman. The German people and the more conservative among the scholars make the retention of the "German" letters a matter of patriotism.

1. An edition of Schiller in Latin type ruined a Leipzig publisher twenty years ago. Yet in the 18th century much literature was printed in Latin type. It is an interesting fact, stated by a correspondent of the "*Evening Post*," of New York, that the first German book published in America was printed in Latin type by Benjamin Franklin. It was a sectarian hymn-book, "*Harfe Zions.*"

2. Nearly all German scientific books are printed in L. type to-day, because all scholars and civilized nations that would read such books are accustomed to this type. *Grimm* advocated it strongly and had all his books printed in it. *Koberstein's Literaturgeschichte; Bauer's, Krause's,* and *Wilmanns'* grammars are printed in it. That G. type was not banished from the schools by the new "Rules" is due to the personal prejudice of the Chancellor of the German Empire, who, not long ago, when a publisher sent to him a book in Latin type, returned it, because it was more troublesome for him to read than German type.

3. German children therefore still continue to learn to read eight alphabets and to write in four, viz., capital and small Latin script, and capital and small German script. In the Swiss schools German type and script have just been given up. The Latin type and script seem bound to prevail in Germany before very long.

361. The German alphabet represents the sounds of the language more adequately than the English does the English sounds, but that is not saying much. In no living language do the signs keep step with the sounds; they are always behind, nowhere more so than in English. But in German also are several signs for the same sound and one sign may have to stand for several sounds. For instance, ch in „ach" and „ich," n in fünf, fand, fang, denote different sounds; ß, f, ff, ß stand for the same sound; also ä (short) and e. The long vowel is indicated by doubling in Saal, Boot, Beet; by h in Wahl, Wohl, Weh, and not at all in Buch, Fuß, Hut. And yet, while German spells more phonetically than English, its standard of spelling is as uncertain as the English, if not more so.

_{1. In 1876 an orthographical conference was called at Berlin, which was to discuss certain modifications and propositions aiming at uniformity, laid before them by R. von Raumer. They met and agreed upon certain rules, which proved, however, unacceptable both to the government and the public.}

2. In 1879 and 1880 the various governments in Germany took the matter in hand and prescribed the spelling to be followed in their schools. Thus we have Prussian, Bavarian, Saxon, Austrian rules, but they vary very little. The kingdom of Würtemberg alone, with true Suabian tenacity, still clings to the old spellings. Some seven millions of children, therefore, now have to learn spelling according to these official rules. All new school-books must be spelt according to them. Influential journals and periodicals have taken up the matter. The excellent new edition of the classics now appearing in *Cotta's " Bibliothek der Weltliteratur"* is spelt accordingly. While these "Rules" leave much to be wished for, yet no one can deny that some of them are a great step in advance. They change the spelling about as much as the five rules for modified spellings of the American Spelling Reform Association would change English spelling. This grammar is spelt according to the rules. We shall not give them, since they can be so easily obtained. For title of the speller, see **37**.

A few explanatory remarks are given on certain points.

362. Umlaut signs.

Of the numerous signs in M. H. G. only two are left, viz., e after and ¨ over the vowel; e is to be discarded now entirely even with capitals, after which it was generally put. Umlaut of ă was always e, not to be confounded with ĕ, which is old e. In N. H. G. ä has been put for e in words whose connection with words containing a was transparent. Vater, pl. Väter, but Vetter; alt, älter, but Eltern; Mann, Männer, but Mensch.

_{1. Dictionaries and encyclopedias often put ä, Ä after ab, Ab, which is very annoying. Unfortunately none of the umlauts have a fixed place in the alphabet. They stand generally mixed up with a, o, u.}

2. ā was ae, ā̊, ǣ in M. H. G. ō̊ was rarely marked; ō̊ was oe, œ, ö̊ ; ü, also frequently not marked, was ů, ue, ů̊, ů̊. The stroke over ⸚ is the remnant of o over u, which stood for the diphthong uo. This became ū in N. H. G. (see **488**, 4), hence the stroke.

363. On the marks to show length.

1. M. H. G. ie > i, but the sign ie of the old diphthong remained and was put also where i was lengthened as in kil > Kiel, spil > Spiel.

2. H was used as a sign of length for several reasons. 1. It became silent as in zehn, Schmäher, sehen, gebeihen. It stands frequently now, where an old j or w was dropped, as in blühen, Ruhe, drohen, Kuh, Stroh, but it is not pronounced. The preceding vowel was long originally, or became long according to the general vowel-lengthening. See **488**,2. 2. O.H.G. *th* (= Eng. *th*) passed into *d*. This sign after the sound had changed appears still in the M. G. of the 12th and in the succeeding centuries, and stands not only for b but also for t.

3. Since the 15th century many MSS. have regularly th for t, and this th was used indiscriminately whether the vowel after or before it was long or short, when printing was invented. In the 16th and 17th centuries th was very frequent. Whether the breath-glide (aspiration) after t was then pronounced, and if so, whether it was appreciated and expressed by h, is a question. *Paul* thinks this was the case. It would then be a development parallel to the Eng. *t* in *tch* for *ch* (= tsh). Certain it is that h after t was no "*dehnungs-h*" originally. In Wirth and Thurm, still in vogue, in older thanne (= Tanne), thisch (= Tisch), garthen (= Garten), h could not be "*dehnungs-h*." The grammarians of the 17th and 18th centuries began to consider it a dehnungs-h and tried to limit its use. It has lost ground with every coming generation, and it is a pity that the official spelling does not abolish it entirely.

4. The doubling of vowels is the oldest method to show length. U, i, and the umlauts are never doubled.

364. The use of initial capitals.

This is a self-imposed task of great difficulty and „Kopfzerbrechen." In the MSS. capitals were only used for the beginning of a paragraph, sometimes of each line ; so also in the early printed books, in which the capitals were added by hand. In 1529 *Kolross* prescribed capitals for the beginning of every sentence, for proper names, for „Gott" and „Herr"

(Lord), as he says „Gott zu eeren und reverentz." Soon capitals spread over appellatives, then over neuter nouns, and then over the abstract. In the 17th century every noun and any part of speech that could possibly be construed as such got a capital. English can boast of some superfluous capitals in the names of the months, days of the week, points of the compass, adjectives derived from proper nouns, but German carries off the palm among the languages of civilized nations. The official spelling reduces capitals considerably.

365. The spelling of foreign words is in a hopeless muddle. There is no system and no rule. All that can be said is that there is a preference of one spelling over the other. The official spelling leaves much liberty.

ANALYSIS AND DESCRIPTION OF GERMAN SOUNDS.

366. In Part I. we have treated of the alphabet and the pronunciation of the letters in the traditional way. But this way is quite unscientific and is barely sufficient to start the student in reading. To describe the sounds of a language, however, is not an easy matter. If the instructor were acquainted with the Bell-Sweet system as presented in Sweet's "Handbook of Phonetics," Oxford, 1877 and in Sweet's "Sound-Notation," the matter would be comparatively easy and might be disposed of within small space. The system analyzes the vowels as well as the consonants according to the position of the organs, for nothing is more delusive than to "catch" vowels by the sound alone as is generally done. Sweet's Hdbk. gives specimens of German, French, English, Dutch, Danish, Icelandic, and Swedish, transcribed in Latin type, and if the student have a little perseverance, these transcriptions will be a great help to him in learning to pronounce any of the above languages.

The system uses none of those big Latin terms, which hide a multitude of inaccuracies and which are so much affected by philologians.

The Vowels.

367. 1. The most tangible quality of vowels is "roundness," produced by the rounding of the mouth-cavity in that region where the vowel is made. Pronounce ie of Biene, round it and you have ü of Bühne. Pronounce e of Beete, and round it and you have ö of Böte. Pronounce a of Falter, round it and you have o of Folter. In o is very little lip-rounding (labialization), but mostly cheek or inner rounding.

2. The second, but less palpable quality, of vowels is "narrowness." Its opposite is "wideness." A vowel is "narrow"

by the convexity of the tongue caused by a certain tenseness in it. It is "wide" when the tongue lies flat and relaxed. This is the difference between ī of Biene and ĭ of bin, between long ü of Mühle and short ü of Müller, between ō of Sohle and ŏ of soll, between the Eng. vowels of "mare" and "man," "sought" and "sot."

3. The third important element in producing vowels is the position of the tongue. Two positions should be distinguished, the vertical (height) and horizontal (forwardness or retraction). In each we distinguish three grades, viz., "high," "mid," and "low"; "back," "mixed," and "front." In the vowels of „liegt," „Licht," „lügt," „Lüde" the tongue is "high" and "front"; in the vowels of „Buch" and „Bucht" the tongue is "high" but "back." The table on next page shows the relation of the German vowels to each other and also to the English vowels.

Key-words for Vowels.

We give below some more key-words, some hints as to acquiring the sounds and some of the dialect-variations in pronunciation.

High Vowels.

368. 1. **u** (high-back-narrow round) is only long. Ex.: Hut, Tuch, Ruhe, Uhu. Short it is rare in S. G. Mutter, Futter. Since ū < uo, the second element still appears in S. G. as eh (in Gabe), but this pronunciation is not classical. See Hart's Goethe's prose, p. 40. Identical with Eng. *oo* in too, boot. Its length is either unmarked or indicated by h, *e.g.*, Tuch, Huhn, thun. It is never doubled.

2. *u* (high-back-wide-round) is identical with Eng. *u* in "full," but for a stronger labilization in G. Ex.: Mutter, Hunger, Spruch. It is always short. The ŭ pronounced by the extreme N. G. is rather like Eng. *u*.

TABLE OF ENGLISH AND GERMAN VOWELS.

	NARROW			WIDE			NARROW-ROUND			WIDE-ROUND		
	back	mixed	front	back	mixed	front	back	mixed	front	back	mixed	front
high	high-back	high-mixed	*i* high-front Biene E. bean	high-back	high-mixed	*i* high-front bitten E. bid	*u* high-back gut E. woo	high-mixed	*y* high-front Mühle N. G.	*u* high-back muß E. pull	high-mixed	*y* high-front Müller N. G.
mid	ɐ mid-back E. but	*eh* mid-mixed Gabe	*e* mid-front Seele E. sale	*a* (") mid-back Vater E. father	*eh* mid-mixed E. eye (eh[ih])	*e* mid-front Mensch E. men	*o* mid-back so E. so	mid-mixed	*ø* mid-front schön / Goethe S. G.	*o* mid-back Sonne N. G.	*oh* mid-mixed Fr. homme	*ø* mid-front schön / Götter N. G.
low	low-back	*æh* low-mixed E. err, bird	*æ* low-front E. air	*a* low-back Sc. father	*æh* low-mixed E. how (æh[oh])	e_1 lowered mid-front Ähre / *æ* low-front E. man	*o* low-back E. water	low-mixed	*œ* low-front Fr. *peur*	*ɔ* low-back E. not	low-mixed	low-front

3. **y** (high-front-narrow round). This differs from *u* by having the tongue-position of ī, that is, it is high-front, instead of high-back. Ex.: hüten, grüßen, Füße. Long all over Germany, but diphthongal in S. G. „Güte" = „Güete," which, like *ue* for ū, is not classical, though old. M. and S. G. rounding of ü is not so emphatic as N. G., so that ü sounds more like ī. Its length is sometimes shown by h, oftener unmarked. Ex.: Mühle, Stühle, Hüte, Tücher.

4. *y* (high-front-wide-round). This is N. G. short ü in Hütte, Flüsse, etc. S. G. short ü is only slightly rounded and rather the short of their long narrow ü, and therefore itself narrow. Extreme N. G. ü (in Bremen, Holstein, etc.) is rather "mixed" than front. The first ü (N. G., Hanover) is classical.

In the alphabet the ü-umlauts are represented by ü, üh, and y, as in Pfütze (short), Pfühl (long), Myrte, Ly'rif.

369. 1. **i** (high-front-narrow). The same all over Germany. Ex.: Sieg, mir, vier, sieh. Before final *l* and *r* it is slightly diphthongal, showing a "vanish" or "glide" before the consonant. Viel, vier are not fīl, fīr, but, marking the voice-glide by $_\wedge$, fi$_\wedge$l, fi$_\wedge$r. (See Sweet's Hdbk., p. 133.) Always long. It is represented by i, ih, ieh, but generally ie. Ex.: Mir, ihr, Bier, stiehlt.

2. *i* (high-front-wide). Peculiar to Hanover and M. G., as in bin, Wind, Kind. The strict Low Germans of Holstein, Hamburg, Bremen lower this *i* toward *e* as in Eng., making it e^1, so that their Kind sounds much like *kent*. In S. G. neither *ĭ* occurs. For it the medium long narrow i is substituted. Hence a S. G. pronunciation of Eng. little sounds like "leetle," while a N. G. has no difficulty with it. The wide *ĭ* of Hanover and M. Germany may be considered classical. Always short. It is represented by i; by ie in vierzehn, vierzig, generally also in vielleicht.

Mid Vowels.

370. 1. o (mid-back-narrow-round). The regular German ō of Sohn, Thron, Hof. ŏ is S. G., as in hoffen, Loch, roch. ō is represented by o, oh, oo. Ex.: Mond, wohnen, Boot.

2. o (mid-back-wide-round). ŏ of M. and N. G., where S. G. has the narrow ŏ. Ex.: Sonne, toll, Stock. This and ö are perhaps the most difficult vowels for Eng. speakers. Do not lower ŏ to low-back, making it like Eng. o of stock, not. Eng. o is equally hard for N. G., as they too feel that the effect upon the ear is much the same, and they do not readily appreciate the difference in articulation.

The o-umlaut has very different shades in different parts of the country. The S. G. ö, whether long or short, is narrow (more "close"). The N. G. is wide (more "open").

3. ə (mid-front-narrow round) is both long and short in S. G. Long ö in böse, lösen, Goethe; short ö in Löcher, Köcher, Stöcke. S. G. ö is identical with Fr. *eu* in *feu*.

4. ɞ (mid-front-wide-round) is long and short in N. G. Long ö in schön, Möve, Löwe; short ö in Götter, Spötter, Störche. Do not confound ö with the vowels of Eng. bust, bird. The o-umlauts are represented by ö and öh; by eu in French words: Couleu'r.

<small>Popularly speaking, S. G. ö is closer than N. G. ö. To acquire the sound it is best to start with e as in „beete" and contract the mouth corners, in which the rounding mainly consists in this vowel, and „böte" will have to result. In û the rounding is mainly in the lips (labialization).
In Berlin and M. G. there is a provincial pronunciation of ö which sounds very much like e. It is caused by imperfect rounding and is by no means to be imitated.</small>

371. 1. e (mid-front narrow) is easily produced. But guard against diphthongizing and widening it as in Eng. may, paid, pate. Ex.: Beet, weh, Thee, Reh. Pure Fr. and G. narrow ē sounds as if it were cut off short, and so it really is compared with Eng. ēi in say. Signs are eh, ee. Always long.

2. *e* (mid-front wide) is the common short *e* in Eng. and G. Ex.: Menſch, wenn, Bett(el).

ē (*e*₁) is slightly lowered toward the Eng. vowels of man, mare; for instance, Käſe, Ähre, wäre. Complete lowering to the Eng. vowel is provincial. Signs, e, ä, äh: wenden, Hände, Mähr. Distinguish therefore: Ehre — Ähre; Meer — Mähr.

3. **eh** (mid-mixed-narrow) is unaccented e and distinct from "long" and "short" e. It is more closely related to the Eng. "neutral" vowels of "cut" and "cur" than to any German vowel. Ex.: trage, glaube, Getränk, gewettet.

4. *a* (mid-back-wide). This has various sounds. In the city of Hanover *ā* is almost fully lowered to low-back. It sounds affected. The average G. *a* is almost identical with the *a* of Eng. father, only the latter, as I have frequently heard it, has the slightest trace of rounding.

The Austrian long *ā* has a very "deep" hollow sound. It is distinctly rounded and lowered, and is either low-mixed or low-front-wide-round. Signs, a, aa, ah: Tage, Saal, Wahl.

DIPHTHONGS.

372. There are three of these, in which both elements are short and by no means the same throughout Germany.

1. The first is represented by *ei* and *ai* in the alphabet. The value of the signs is the same in N. G. and is *ăe′*. Its first element is not fully retracted and is exactly identical with the first element of Eng. "long" *i*. In S. G. the second element is clearly raised and even narrowed ĭ, and is better represented by *ai*. The first element of S. G. *ai* is clearly mid-back. (See Sweet's Hdbk., p. 133.)

2. The second diphthong, spelt *au*, is composed of *a* and *o* (short wide *o*) = *ao*, certainly in S. G. In N. G. the second element is, in my opinion, mid-mixed narrow-round, *i.e.*, the *e* of Gabe rounded.

3. The third diphthong, spelt eu, äu, rarely oi, is oe' (e' = e raised towards i) in N. G. and oi in S. G., e. g., Freude, Geläute. The former is classical. Any approach of eu towards ei is provincial and not elegant.

373. General Remarks on the Vowels. There are thirteen vowels, counting either N. G. or S. G. ö and not counting ä lowered mid-front. There are no "low" vowels in G. at all as in Eng. naught, not, snare, err, bag. All Eng. long vowels tend toward diphthongization, as in say, so, saw. The German vowels are pure single sounds and seem to an Eng. ear cut off short, See, so. Fr. and G. vowels are alike in this respect. They are strictly narrow. While German has no low-back-round vowels (saw, sot), the front-rounding is very emphatic, and the back-vowels are very fully back, yielding a full sonorous tone. See Sweet, p. 132.

The Consonants.

OPEN CONSONANTS.

374. 1. **H** (throat-open-surd) is the same in Eng. and G. It has always the articulation of the following vowel, and might be called therefore a surd vowel. Ex.: hat, Hut, hier, horch.

Sign: h. A h not initial is always silent, e. g., gehen, geht, thun, Kathe'ber.

2. **R** (throat-open-sonant) is strongly "guttural," and the provincial N. G. pronunciation of r, rh, e. g., in Regen, Neger, Bär, Furche.

For the regular, classical r (divided) see **377**.

375. 1. **kh** (back-open-surd) is the surd guttural spirant after back vowels, viz., $\bar{a}$, $\breve{a}$, $\bar{u}$, $\breve{u}$, $\bar{o}$, $\breve{o}$.

Sign: ch. Ex.: Loch, Macht, wachen, Buch, Bauch. This is the Sc. ch, as in loch. After a, finally and before a consonant, it is more easily acquired than after u and before a front vowel. In S. G. dialect this is the only ch-sound, the front ch being unknown there.

TABLE OF GERMAN AND ENGLISH CONSONANTS.

	Throat.	Back.		Front.		Point.		Point-teeth.		Blade.		Blade-point.		Lip.		Lip-back.		Lip-teeth.	
	Surd.	Surd.	Sonant.	Surd.	Sonant.	Surd.	Sonant.	Surd.	Sonant.	Surd.	Sonant.	Surd.	Sonant.	Surd.	Sonant.	Surd.	Sonant.	Surd.	Sonant.
Open ..... (Spirants)..	H ६unb	kh ady	gh ©age is	jh lieg lieg	j jung	r rot M. & S. G.		th thin then	dh then	s G. was	z E. lagen N. G.	sh E. idjn	zh ©age (foreign)		bh E. Baſſer S. G.	wh	w E. which water	f fanb N. G.	v Warb E. vie
Divided....							G. l laß Halle				E. l								
Shut (Mutes, Explosive)..		E. & G. k	finb lang			E. t	E. d							q E. & G. p	m. E. & G. b				
Nasal			Gang				n fanb				E. n				m me mit				

376. In explanation of some of the terms it may be necessary to state the following. See Sweet, p. 31–35. *Throat* and *Back* are included in "guttural," but are formed by the root of the tongue and the soft palate. *Front, point, blade, back* refer to the tongue. "Front" means the front or middle of the tongue and the roof of the mouth (palatal). "Point" means the point of the tongue and the upper gums or teeth (alveolar, dental). "Point-teeth" means interdental. "Blade" is very forward "front." "Divided" means that the current of air is stopped in the middle of the passage and allowed to escape on the sides. *Surdness* (voicelessness) and *sonancy* (= voice, produced by the vibration of the vocal cords) apply to every consonant, though the liquids are not surd in German. *Shut* consonants or *stops* are so called from the entire closure of the passage. *Open* means no contact or closure, at most a narrowing of the passage. *Nasal* means closed mouth passage, but open nasal passago. h is a mere diacritic after k, g, etc.

2. **jh** (front-open-surd) is sometimes called the "palatal-guttural." It stands after the front (palatal) vowels (*i. e.*, after all vowels except a, o, u), including the diphthongs, ai ei, eu äu, and always in the suffix –chen. Ex.: Ich, euch, Bücher, möchte, feicht.

3. The sonants corresponding to *kh* and *jh* are *gh* and *j*; *gh* stands after back vowels, *j* after front vowels and initially. Ex.: Woge, Zuge; Ziege, Wiege, lügen, je, jagen, böge. But *gh* for g (back-shut-sonant) in this position, though very common, is not classical.

4. In the alphabet these four sounds are represented as follows:

kh by ch after back vowels, as above; by final g in N. G. after back vowels, not counting consonant suffixes, *e. g.*, Tag, Zug, bogst, wagt, Jagb. See chs, 383.

jh by ch after front vowels and consonants; always in –chen no matter what precede. Ex.: Licht, Furche, Storch, Mädchen, Mamachen, leuchten, euch, Molch, Milch. See chs, 383. Also by g final or at the end of a syllable in N. G. after front vowels and consonants, not counting consonant suffixes. Essig, wollig, lügst, liegt, segnen, legst. Also by initial ch in foreign words before front vowels, *e. g.*, Chemi'e, Che'rub, Chiru'rg. See also 383. Do not confound this sound with $H + j$ ($=$ y) in Eng. huge, hue.

gh by medial g after back vowels, *e. g.*, Lage, Bogen. See sub 3.

j by medial g after front vowels, liegen, Zeuge, güt'ger. But this sound of g is provincial even in N. G. and the "hard" one (= shut, stop) is preferable.

Regularly by j initial. In N. G. a strong friction (buzz) is heard as in Eng. ye, yew. Ex.: Jäger, jung. S. G. *j* is a mere *i*, je = *ie*, jung = *iung*. The latter is, no doubt, the better pronunciation. I have heard even a regular Eng. *j* (= *dzh*) in Bremen.

5. Sweet, I believe, was the first to notice a slight labial element after ch when preceded by u and au, indicated by *w*. Hence auch = *aokhw*. See 378.

377. **r** (point-open-sonant) is the classical r of M. and S. G. Eng. *r* is rather "blade" (dorsal) than "point."

Popularly speaking, Eng. *r* is "rolled," G. *r* is trilled. The effect upon the ear is very different in the two *r*'s, though their articulation is not so dissimilar. See Sweet, § 109 and p. 134.

378. **s, z, sh, zh** (blade and blade-point) form a group of "sibilants" closely related to each other and to Eng. *th, dh* (point-teeth). They are very much alike in Eng. and G., and no description is needed to acquire the German. (For the different varieties see Sievers' Phonetik, § 15, 2, and Sweet's Hdbk., p. 39.) The N. G. sounds are more forward than the S. G. and Eng. Eng. *th* is farthest forward (point-teeth), then *s*, and then *sh*, on the palate. In *th* the current of air passes over the "point" (tip of the tongue), in *s* over the "blade" which is back of the point, and in *sh* over blade and point, presenting more tongue-surface. In the G. sounds a slight labialization is noticeable, marked by Sweet *shw*. It consists in a slight contraction of the mouth corners.

1. **s** (blade-surd) is represented by various letters of the alphabet (except in N. G.), viz., by ſ, ȣ, ß, ſſ. Ex.: voll, Haus, Fluß, Waſſer.

2. **z** (blade-sonant) by medial and initial ſ, peculiar to N. G., as in leſen, raſen. Initial ſ begins surd, marked by Sweet $s_\wedge$, as in $s_\wedge ol$, but ends sonant. The standard is hardly fixed in favor of *s* or *z*. See **391,** 4.

3. **sh** (blade-point-surd) by ſch and ſ in the initial ſt, ſp of S. and M. G., as in Schlange, Schinken, waſchen, Stadt, Sprache. The first word would be = *shwlaqe*. By ch in foreign words, Champa'gner, Chika'ne. See **375,** 4. On ſt, ſp also **389,** 4.

4. **zh** (blade-point-sonant) occurs only in foreign words; by g in Charge, Gage, Page, Loge, Gensdarm. = j in Journal. In jovial j = j and frequently j in Journal = *dzh*, Eng. j. Compare Eng. azure, crosier, glacier.

379. **bh** (lip-sonant) is the S. and M. G. w, pronounced with the lips only. Blow to cool which would be surd *bh* and then intonate the breath (Sweet, p. 41). Do not confound with Eng. *w*, in which the back of the tongue is raised and the cheeks are narrowed. S. G. w is less consonantal than Eng. *w*.

380. f (lip-teeth-surd), **v** (lip-teeth-sonant). The above sounds are "labio-labial." These are labio-dental. The passage is formed by the lower lip and upper teeth.

1. **f** is represented by f, v, as in Hafer, faul, Sclave, Frevel, Nerv, Passiv, Levkoje; by ph in foreign words: Philologie. For pf see **389, 1**.

2. **v** is represented by w in N. G., like Eng. and Fr. *v* but less energetically buzzed. Ex.: Wagen, Löwe, Schwester. After ich, however, w is often made labio-labial in N. G., as well as in M. and S. G. The pronunciation of v as *bh* or *v* between vowels is hardly classical, for instance, Frevel = *frevel* or *frebhel*. By initial v in foreign words, as in Vaka'nz, Vase, Vehi'kel, nervö's.

381. German l, t, d, n differ somewhat from the Eng. The place of contact (on the palate) in the G. sounds is much more forward than in the Eng. and the "point" of the tongue is used in the former while the "blade" is used in the latter. Eng. "well" is the shibboleth of the German speaking Eng., and G. „wohl" that of the Englishman speaking German. The difference should be thoroughly appreciated by all who wish to speak "pure" German.

1. **l** (point-divided) is represented by l, as in Licht, Fall, wohl, Falter.

German ll is peculiarly hard. Practise upon Welle, Walle, Halle, Wolle. See **376**.

SHUT CONSONANTS OR STOPS.

382. Next comes a group of sounds in which there is a complete closure of the mouth-channel. When the closure is opened an explosion takes place, hence their name "*explosivœ*." "Stops" is a less pedantic name. When the closure is far back, formed by the root of the tongue and the soft palate, we get the back-stops *k, g*, called also not so well "*gut-*

tural" and "*palatal.*" When the closure is forward, formed by the point of the tongue and the teeth, gums, or palate, as the case may be, we have the point-stops *t, d*, called also "*dental*" or "*lingual,*" or "*alveolar.*" If the closure is made by the lips, we have the lip-stops or "*labials.*" The great difference between G. and Eng. stops, particularly the surd ones, lies in the more energetic closure and explosion of the G., amounting almost to an **H** (aspiration).

383. 1. **k** (back-shut-surd) is represented by k, as in Kaße, buk, Kragen; by ch: *a*, before s (in the same stem); *b*, in foreign words before back vowels. Ex.: *a.* Fuchs, sechs, Buchsbaum, wachsen; but wachsam. *b.* Chara'cter, Chaos, Cholera. But see **375**, 4; **378**, 3. Also by d, dt, with prolonged closure: Zude, zurüdtehren. By final g in S. G. and according to the standard pronunciation. See **375**, 4; **385**, 3; **20**.

This g is not strongly exploded, has no aspiration, and is called with final b and d by German phonetists "*tonlose media,*" by the people "hard" b, d. To English speakers it seems absurd to speak of a "surd" or "hard" b. We would call these sounds *p, t, k; i. e.* surd stops, unaspirated, slightly exploded.

a. Also by final g preceded by n, but only in N. G., as in lang, jung. See **386**, 1.

2. **g** (back-shut sonant) is represented by g initial and when doubled, as in gehen, sagen, ärgern, baggern, Egge. See **375**, 4.

384. 1. **t** (point-shut-surd) is represented by t, tt, as in Wette, heute, Tante, Hut; by th, as in That, Thal, formerly very common finally, as in Muth, Heirath, Heimath, which are now spelt without h. Also by d final, as in Tod, gescheid, sind, Kleid, Händ=chen. See **385**, 3. By dt only in Stadt and its derivatives, but formerly more frequent, as in todt, Brodt, gescheidt, Erndte, which are now spelt tot, Brot, etc.

2. **d** (point-shut-sonant) is represented by d initial and medial, as in danken, der, Boden, Kleider, Wirder.

385. 1. **p** (lip-shut-surd) is represented by p, pp (see **382**, but Eng. *p* before vowels is often as strongly aspirated, *e. g.*, pound, par, pat. Ex.: Pulver, Pracht, Haupt, Kappe, Wappen. Also by b final, as in Lieb, gab, lieb, hob, hobſt, web=t, lieb=t. See sub 3.

2. **b** (lip-shut-sonant) is represented by medial and initial b. For final b see sub 3. Ex.: Böſe, Bube, Ebbe, krabbeln.

3. Final b, b are therefore pronounced t, p all over Germany, and g as k according to the standard pronunciation, but not in N. G. See **383**, 1. For g after n see **383**, 1, *a*.

4. Before b, b, g, pronounced as surd stops, the liquids l, n, m are short, and not long as in English. Pronounce wild therefore nearly with the *lt* of Eng. *wilt*, und with the *nd* of *hunt*, not of *hound*, *wild*.

Nasals.

386. The nasals are also "shut" consonants, but they are not stops (with explosion). The air passes through the nose, and we distinguish them according to the place of contact.

q is the "back-nasal-sonant" common to Eng. and G., as in Eng. bring, G. bringe, ſinge.

1. **q** is represented by n before k, before g in N. G., and by medial ng. Ex.: Trank, Wink, bange, lange, Finger. Final ng is **q** according to the standard, *e. g.*, Geſang, hing. For N. G. final ng see **383**, 1. Also by n of en, in, on, an, ent final in foreign words, as in Dauphin, balancieren, Avancement, Escadron, Bonbon.

This is an unsuccessful attempt of Germans at pronouncing the French nasal vowels, which are not at all identical with **q** ; **q** does not exist in French. Though incorrect, this sound is given by the educated classes and by the stage.

387. **n** is the "point-nasal" (half-dental). For Eng. and G. *n*, see **381**. *n* is represented by n, nn as generally written, except where it becomes either guttural or labial by the proximity of guttural and labial consonants. (See **386**.) Ex.:

senden, Hand, Spinne, Bündel, manche, Tünche, wohnen, Thron, wandten = vantn.

388. m, the lip-nasal, is identical in Eng. and G. It is represented by m, mm: Mund, Stimme, warm; also by en after b and p, as in pumpen = *pumpm*, Treppen = *trepm*.

1. In untaught pronunciation not influenced by the letter, n is also pronounced as m before f, as in sanft, fünf, Hanf, Zukunft, Zunft. Over-precise speakers pronounce as two full syllables words like blei-ben, Lumpen, sin-ben, sin-gen, etc., but persons speaking naturally pronounce as stated above.

Compound Consonants.

389. These are composed of single sounds already described, but some of them seem to call for special mention. Their elements are closely joined together without any glide.

1. **pf** is composed of p and f, and is always represented by pf, as in Pfirsich, Kampf, Karpfen, Sumpf. But this pf is not pronounced except by a special effort. The current and "natural" pf is composed of a lip-teeth-stop and f. (This was first noticed by Sievers and Sweet.) The first element being formed by lower lip and teeth instead of by lower and upper lips, as in a real lip-stop. Final pf is in N. G. commonly made into f, but it is not to be imitated.

2. **ks** is composed of the surd back-shut and the surd blade-open, as in Eng. Represented by x, as in Art, Text, Nixe, Alexander; also by chs and chf, if of the same stem, as in Wachs, Ochsen. See **383**, 1.

3. **ts** is composed of the surd **t** (point-shut) and **s** the surd blade-open. Represented by z, as in Zunge, Ziel, Weizen, Warze; by tz, as in Sprützen, schwitzen, Katze; by c in foreign words before front vowels, as in Acce'nt, Civi'l, Recense'nt, Cöliba't, etc.; by t in foreign words before i, as in Patie'nt, Natio'n, etc.

4. G. ts differs from Eng. ts in cats, hats in this respect. in G **ts s** is long, in Eng. **ts t** is long. In ſt = **sht** and ſp = **shp** (see 378. 3) the first element is also short. In "natural" pronunciation final ȝ in N. G. is made into ŝ after n, rarely after r and l; so that ganȝ becomes Ganŝ, Schwanȝ > Schwanŝ. But this is not classical.

5. Though there are doubled letters, both vowels and consonants, there are no doubled sounds. Double vowels denote one long vowel, as in Saal, Staat, Moos, and double consonants are long energetic consonants, as in Wette, haſſen, Treppe, zerren, Treffer, Sonne, alle. But the consonants are not always long and short in G. in the same places where they are so in Eng. See, for instance, 385, 4. Final consonants are short in German. Compare Mann, wohl, Hut with Eng. man, well, hut The Eng. sonant stops *d*, *g*, *b* are very long and their sonancy is very emphatic. This is not so in German. Compare Ebbe — ebb, Egge — dagger, etc.

ON A STANDARD OF PRONUNCIATION.

390. While Germans have a common literary language, they have not a common spoken language. German cannot boast of such authorities in pronunciation as French has in Paris, in the French Academy and in the Théatre Français. Provincialism, so strong in German politics and other institutions, is particularly strong in pronunciation. All sections of the country readily acknowledge the "*Schriftsprache*" as the common language of the country, but in pronouncing the same they claim the utmost liberty.

1. One can hear professors of the German language at the universities speaking in the purest dialect-pronunciation; so one can, preachers in the churches and representatives in the state-legislatures and in the „Reichstag."

2. The great authors of the classical period, Lessing, Goethe, Schiller, Klopstock, etc.; pronounced the literary language with strong dialect coloring. One of Lessing's favorite phrases was: „Es kommt doch nichts babei heraus," which he is said to have pronounced „'s kömmt doch niſchtapei !raus." Goethe was called "*Gēte*" by them. Compare Goethe's defence of dialect in „Aus meinem Leben" (Hart's Goethe's Prose, p. 19–20).

3. To dialect pronunciation are mostly due such bad rhymes as : Leute : Weite; schön : gehn; früh : nie; Höh': See; ferne : Gehörne; which occur in their poems. Platen, Rückert, and Bodenstedt carefully avoid these rhymes. In families of culture in Cologne you hear *dit* and *dat* for dies and das. In Bremen are still families who take pride in having the children learn the L. G. dialect first.

4. In Hanover, both in the city and in the surrounding districts of the province, the pronunciation is generally considered classical, and yet Hanoverian has three strong provincialisms : 1, st, sp, which most Germans pronounce scht, schp ; 2, they pronounce the sonant stop g as the spirant, while it should be pronounced as a surd stop just what all Germans make of b and d; 3, in the city itself a is made almost into long ä.

391. The only institution that claims to have a standard and tries to come up to it is the stage. The best theatres of Germany and the better actors, followed by a very small number of the cultured, strive after a dialect-free pronunciation. The standard set up by them decides the disputed points as follows :

1. Initial st, sp are to be pronounced scht, schp. See **24**.

2. Final g is surd except after n (**386**, 1), but see the Preface : Berg berc, Weg wec, liegt lict.

3. Pronounce r trilled, not uvular or guttural, as in North Germany and in the larger cities.

4. North and Middle Germans pronounce initial s and s between vowels as sonants; the standard is not quite settled, but will probably come to sonant s.

5. The rounded vowel should be fully rounded. The extreme N. G. pronounces u, o, ü (short) in Hagebutte, komm', Hütte too much like Eng. but, come, hut. The extreme S. G. likes to unround ü $>$ i, ö $>$ e.

6. Tag, Zug, Weg have long vowels, = tāc, zūc, wēc. See sub 2; also **488**, 2, *b*.

7. The lip-teeth w and not the S. G. labio-labial bh has the preference.

392. 1. But it is possible to have a dialect-free pronunciation and yet have dialect-accent, *i. e.*, "intonation," "modulation of voice." Very pronounced are, *e. g.*, the "accents" of Berlin, Vienna, Bavaria (München), Saxony, which can be distinguished without much difficulty even in a good pronunciation. The stage favors the North German "accent," particularly the Hanoverian, and this is at bottom what is meant by saying the Hanoverian is the best pronunciation.

2. There is another reason, however, why the N. G. pronunciation is "purer," as it is generally called, than S. G. The Low German dialects are farther removed from the classical language than the High German. The contrast is felt more in North Germany than in South Germany. The school and the educated make a stronger effort to acquire the standard pronunciation as far as there is any. The N. G. is more influenced by, and has a higher respect for, the written language. He pronounces according to the letter before him. Compare, for instance, b and p, which the Saxon calls a "soft b" and a "hard b."

3. Another reason for the purity of N. G. lies also in the political and intellectual predominance of the Northern half of Germany for nearly two hundred years. The speakers of S. G. dialects are divided between Switzerland, Germany, and Austria. The modern theatre also developed earlier in N. Germany than in S. Germany.

4. The Swiss too can speak dialect-free German when conversing with strangers, of whom they of course see a great many. They make then a special effort to drop their dialect, which is nearly as far removed from the written language as is a Low German dialect.

5. One thing is surprising, viz., that the excellent G. school-system has not more power to spread a common spoken language. It is true, the school does modify the dialect, but when the child has left school, its language relapses, as a rule, into pure dialect.

SOME PHONETIC LAWS, LIKE ABLAUT, UMLAUT, GRIMM'S AND VERNER'S LAWS, ETC.

ABLAUT.

393. Ablaut is the gradation of vowels, both in stem and suffix, under the influence of accent. The vowels vary within certain series of related vowels called *ablaut-series*.

The ablaut of suffix-vowels, *e. g.*, of case-suffixes, is difficult to determine even for so early a period as O. H. G. or Ags. We shall speak only of the stem-vowel-ablaut.

The phenomenon of ablaut appears in all the I. E. languages and is characteristic of the Teutonic languages, only in so far as a very large system of verb-inflection has been developed. On the Greek ablaut, see Amer. Journ. of Phil. vol. I., No. 3, p. 281—, an article by Bloomfield.

394. Osthoff and Brugman have the credit of establishing as many as four grades or stages of ablaut, viz., *hochstufe*, strong and weak; *tiefstufe*, strong and weak, which may be called in Eng. *strong, medium, weak, zero*. They do not appear in every series. But the second has them all, viz., "*au*" strong; "*eu—iu*" medium; "*ŭ*" weak; "*ŭ*" zero. The first two stand under the strong accent; the third under the secondary, the last in the unaccented syllable.

Why there should be a difference of vowel under the strong accent is not clear, but the fact of two grades is undeniable.

1. For the I. E or Parent-speech-period three series have been reconstructed with tolerable certainty and there are traces of several more. But the exact quality of the vowels can hardly be determined. o of the first I. E. series was probably unrounded, and more a than o, see **459**.

1. e—o, G. T. e, i—a, appears in I. to V.
2. ă—ā, G. T. a—ô, in VI., see **459**, 4.
3. ē—ô, O. H. G. ā—uo, in G. tât, Ƿhat — tuon, þun.

We give the Germanic series in Braune's order. (See his Gothic grammar, followed also by Sievers in his Ags. and Paul in his M. H. G. grammar.)

395. * I. Ablaut-series.

	*1 strong.	2 medium.	3 weak.	4 zero.
G. T.	ai	ei	î	i
O. H. G.	ai, ei, ê	î		i, e
N. H. G.	ei (ie, i), ē	ei		i (ie), ē, ĕ.

Compare Gr. πέποιθα, πείθω, κλῖμαξ, πέπιθμεν; οἶμος, εἶμι, ἴμεναι, ἴμεν. I is the zero stage, because the first element of the diphthong, e—o, has disappeared, while the second, the consonant element of the falling diphthong, has become a vowel.

---

* The figures I., II., etc., always refer to the ablaut-series: the figures 1, 2, 3, 4 refer to the ablaut stage.

Ex.: 1, *lēren*, lehren, < *laizjan*, to teach; *léra*, Lehre, + Ags. *lǎr*, Eng. lore; Leiſten + last (Kluge); pret. sg. of strong verbs of Cl. I. 2 and 3, pres. of verbs of Cl. I. 4, Liſt, lernen, with the words of 1, from the same √lxs. x represents the vowel that is to appear according to accent and is an unknown quantity in the root. 1, zeigen, Zeigefinger; 2 and 3, zeihen; 4, gezichen, verzichten, all from a √dxc. Compare L. *dícere*. Notice the Eng. cognates show in 1, a, ō: ladder, wrote, last, lore, loaf; in 2 and 3: î, rise, smite; in 4, ĭ: risen, smitten, list.

396. II. Ablaut-series.

	1	2	3	4
G. T.	au	ĕu	û	ŭ
O. H. G.	ou, ô	iu, eo, io	û	ŭ, ŏ
N. H. G.	ō, ŏ	ie, eu	au	u, ō, ŏ

All four grades still apparent in German. ŭ bears the same relation to ĕu, au as ĭ to ĕi, ai. See above. Compare χέFω, χοFή, χυμός, χυτός.

Ex.: From the √lxk: 1, Lohe, flame. 2, Licht < *lieht*, leuchten, + light. 4, Luchs + lynx(?). From a √klū: 2, Leumund. 3, laut < *hlût* + loud; 4, Ludwig, Luther, Gr. κλυτός, L. *inclŭtus*. Again, 2, ſiech + sick, Seuche, and 4, Sucht. See the strong verbs of Cl. II. < √b'xd': 1, bot pret. of bieten. 2, bieten, Gebiet. 4, Bote, Gebot, Büttel + beadle. Eng. bid represents older *beodan* II. and *biddan* V. The corresponding Eng. vowels are very irregular.

397. III. Ablaut-series.

	1	2	3, 4
G. T.	a	ĕ, i	u before r, l, m, n
German	a, e (umlaut)	e, i	u, o.

As to 3 and 4, see 459, 3, *a*. The roots all end in r, l, m, n + cons.

Ex.: See the strong verbs of Cl. III. From the root of winden, wand, gewunden, + wind: 1, die Wand, wenden < *wandjan*, + Eng. wend, gewandt, wandern + wander, etc. 2, die Winde, Windel. < Germanic √bxrg. 1, barg pret. sg. 2, Berg, Gebirge, bergen. 3, 4, Burg, + burgh, borough, to burrow. Bürger, Bürge, borgen + borrow(?). Also + bury. Corresponding Eng. vowels in verbs before nasals are i in 2, a in 1, u in 4, *e. g.*, spin, span, spun. In nouns, etc., they are quite irregular, but generally also e or i, a, u, o.

398. IV. Ablaut-series.

	1	2	3, 4
G. T.	a, ê	ô	u
O. H. G.	a, â	ë, i	u, o
N. H. G.	ā	ē, ĕ, ie, i	ū, ŭ, ō, ŏ

The roots end in a single liquid or nasal, or these stand before the vowels. ê, â are not yet explained.

Ex.: Verbs of Cl. IV., stehlen, stahl, gestohlen. 1, Diebstahl. < √dxm. 1, zahm, zähmen + tame. 2, geziemen. 3, 4, Zunft. < √b'xr. 1, die Bahre, + bier, barrow(?), sich gebahren, die Gebärde, –bar. 2, gebären + bear, Eimer < *ein-ber*, Zuber < *zwiber* (see Kluge). 3, 4, die Bürde + burthen, die Geburt + birth, die Gebühr (?), gebührlich. Eng. cognates show generally ea, ō, *e. g.*, bear, bore.

399. V. Ablaut-series.

	1	2, 3, 4
G. T.	a, â	ê
O. H. G.	ă, ā	ē, i
N. H. G.	ā, ă	ē, ĕ, i, ie

Only two grades. The roots end in a single consonant, not a liquid or nasal.

Ex.: Verbs of Cl. V. < Germanic √gxb. 1, gab, Gabe. 2, 3, 4, geben, gegeben, du giebst, die and das Gift. Eng. vowels the same, + give, gave, gift.

400. VI. Ablaut-series.

	1	2, 3	4
G. T.	ô	a (o ?)	u
O. H. G.	uo	a, e	u
N. H. G.	ū, ŭ	a, e (umlaut)	ū, ŭ

4 Not in the past part., only in nouns. A difficult series.

Ex.: Verbs of Cl. VI. < √pxr. 1, fuhr, führen. 2, 3, fahren, die Fahrt. 4, die Furt + ford. < √mxl. 1, M. H. G. *muol* (now mahlte). 2, 3, mahlen, Mehl + meal, malmen, Malter. 4, Mühle + mill, Müller, Mull, Maulwurf + mole, by popular etymology < *moltwurf* + mould-warp.

Umlaut.

401. Umlaut is the modification of an accented vowel by an i (j) in the next syllable. See **362**.

1. By it a, o, u become sounds lying nearer to i. In other words, back and mixed vowels become more like front vowels through the influence of front vowels. The tongue-position of back and mixed vowels changes to "front," while the rest of the articulation remains the same. This "fronting" is called by the Germans "mouillierung," *i.e.*, palatalization. Sievers' theory is that the intervening consonants were first affected and then the immediately preceding vowel. Such palatalized consonants are the Fr. l and n still in "*feuille*" < *folium, Espagne* < *Hispania*.

2. To understand umlaut we must go back to a period in which i (j) was still tolerably intact as in O. H. G. But there was only one umlaut marked in that period, viz., that of ă and its sign was e just like the original e now distinguished by ˝ = ĕ. In M. H. G. the umlaut of the other vowels appears and is unfortunately very irregularly represented. Sievers supposes that the consonants were already palatalized in O. H. G. and that they imparted their change to the vowel in M. H. G. But it is also very likely that the vowels were already palatalized in O. H. G., only the alphabet was not sufficient to show the change.

Ex.: *lamp—lembir*, Lämmer; *gabi* > *gaebe* > gäbe, pret. sbj.; *gast—gasti* > *geste*, Gäſte; *ali-lantjo > *eli-lenti* > *ellende* > elend, unfortunate because in an "other country;" *scôni* > *schoene* > ſchön; *angil* > Engel; *bôsi* > böſe, etc.

402. The extent of this phenomenon varies with the period and the dialect. Certain consonants have prevented umlaut. But we cannot enter upon a further discussion. Compare gebulbig, gewaltig. By umlaut, then, a > ä, e; o (ɔ) > ö (≠); u > ü (≠); au > äu, eu, but this only seemingly in cases where au < û, since û passed into ü (iu) and this into eu, äu, according to **488**, 5.

1. While in German umlaut is still a living factor, it is dead in Eng. and has been for some 8-900 years. Eng. only has isolated forms with umlaut, *e. g.*, mouse—mice, cow—kine, etc., that belong to no system of inflection or derivation in which umlaut serves as the expression of a function or meaning. We call the above examples "irregular" plurals.

2. There is no such thing as "rückumlaut" = "umlaut reversed," as the old grammarians called it. *e.g.*, in benſen, baĝte, gebaĝt. See **454**, 3.

Interchanges of Vowels: e — i, ie; no Umlaut — Umlaut; u — o; ie — eu.

403. e — i (ie). 1, where e is original, that is G. T. and I. E. ĕ. ē passed into i before i (j) standing in the unaccented syllable, a process exactly analogous to umlaut; ĕ > i also before a nasal belonging to the same syllable, generally before nasal + cons. The physiological reason for the latter change is not clear.

Ex.: The present of Cl. III., IV., V., see also the O. H. G. paradigm. The first p. sg. *nimu* may be due to analogy, but in O. H. G. and Ags. ü > i also before u and it may therefore be a phonetic transition. ſiţen, liegen, bitten have i all through, see **457**, 1, but Seſſel < *sezzal*. Feld—Gefilde < *gifildi*. recht — richten < **rihtjon*, + L. *rectus*. Feber — Gefieber; fern — firn < firni. Verbs of III. Cl.: finden, ſchwimmen. Geben — Gift < *gifti*.

2, i is original, but passed into ë before a, e, o in the next syllable or if the word ended in a consonant. i remained before i (j) and before w.

The cases of i > ë are not numerous. It is a High German and Old Saxon peculiarity. Eng. has still i. This is still called Brechung after Grimm.

Ex.: leck — erquicken + quick, quicken; leben + live, lieben + cleave, ſchweben belong to ablauts. I. with the zero grade. Verweſen, to decompose, compare L. *vīrus*, Skr. *vish-am*. Leber + liver. Pech + Eng. pitch < L. *pic-s*. Steg < same root as ſteigen I.; Wechſel — + Lat. *vic-es*. er < *ir*, + Lat. *is*.

404. Umlaut — no umlaut.

Ex.: Verbs of VI. and VII. Cl., but in the latter mostly by analogy, e. g., *faru*, *ferst*, *fert* — fahre, fährſt, fährt. Alt — Eltern < *eltirôn*. Comp. + elders. Abel < *adal* — edel < *edili*. Comp. + Ethel. Very numerous and the umlaut often more or less hidden.

405. u — o. In the stem-syllable u is always the older and passed into o before a, e, o. It was preserved like i before i (j), w and a nasal belonging to the same syllable.

This process is also one of assimilation similar to umlaut, called "*brechung*" by the older grammarians.

Ex.: See verbs of Cl. II., III., IV. in the past part. and compare with them the pret. pl. and nouns from the same stem, e. g., Flucht, Zucht, Vernunft, Zunft. Sollte < *scolta* — Schuld; hold — Huld < *huldi*; hohl — Hülle, h < √kxl. Gold — Gulden (a coin), but golden + golden by analogy; Bote — Büttel < *butil*. The transition before nasals is quite modern and M. G. Comp. Sonne < *sunna*; Sommer < *sumer*: Sohn < *sunu*; past part. of III. Before n + cons. (not n) u remains now, gefunden, Bund, geſunken, Ankunft.

406. ie (io) — eu (iu). iu being levelled away and ie standing for both io and iu, this interchange is not common now. Both iu and io < G. T. ëu. ëu > iu before i (j) and w, but > eo before a, e, o; and later eo > io > ie, ie. The process is ë̇ > i and u > o in the same diphthong.

Ex.: Ablauts. and Cl. II., see **124**, Remark. Was da freucht und fleugt (Sch.). bieten — Beute (?), Beutel (?).

Grimm's Law or the "*shifting of mutes,*" Lautverschiebung.

407. It concerns the so-called "mutes," b, p, f; d, t, th; g, k, ch, media, tenuis, aspirata. This law was discovered by Rask, but first fully stated by Jacob Grimm. It includes two great shiftings, the first prehistoric, that is, General Teutonic or Germanic; the second, historical or German. The first is a peculiarity of the whole group and shared to very nearly the same extent by every member of the group; the second is a peculiarity of the German dialects proper, is partial both as to the number of sounds and of dialects affected. We very briefly represent the first shifting. See the author's article in the Amer. Jour. of Phil., vol. I., for a fuller account. Let y represent the sonant stops, z the surd ones and x the so-called "aspirate," which represents various sounds. The following formulas will be of use. G. is added now merely for illustration.

	Parent-speech, I. E.		G. T.		G.
I.	x	>	y	>	z
II.	y	>	z	>	x
III.	z	>	x	>	y

Notice I. E. is the oldest stage of the language reconstructed from the various I. E. dialects. You can substitute for I. E. any language but the Teutonic, provided you make allowance for any changes in that particular language, *e. g.*, d' has become f or d in Latin. By General Teutonic or Germanic is meant that stage which is reconstructed from all the Teutonic dialects. By G. we mean the written language of Germany; H. G. means South and Middle as opposed to Low German.

Substitute in each formula the labials, dentals, etc.

408. Form. I. 1. $x = d'$. I. E. d' = d + sonant aspiration (Ellis), "sonant affricate," this d' through G. T. dh (sonant spirant) > d > H. G. t, but dh remains in Go. and Scand., *e.g.*, I. E. * *d'ur-*, Gr. ϑύρα, L. *fores*, > G. T. * *dur-*, Eng. door > G. Thor — Thür, doublets.

2. $x = b'$. I. E. b' > G. T. bh, b > G. b, *e. g.*, I. E. √b'xd', ablauts. II., Gr. πυϑ- > G. T. √bxd, Eng. bid > G. bieten, bot, geboten. No German shifting of b > p therefore.

3. $x = g'^1$. I. E. g'¹ > G. T. gh, g > G. g, *e. g.*, < √g'¹u (Skr. √hû > G. T. √gu-), *gud-, Eng. God > G. Gott, "the being invoked" (see Kluge). No German shifting of g > k.

4. $x = g'^2$, the second series of gutturals, the "labialized" > G. T. g, gw (w) if medial, > G. g, or zero if medial, *e. g.*, I. E. * *ang'²*, L. *angustus* > G. T. *angu-*, Go. *aggwus* > G. enge < angi < * *angwjo*. I. E. * *g'²ostis*, L. *hostis* > G. T. *ghast*, *gast*, + Eng. guest > G. Gast.

409. Form. II. x in G., see later.

1. $y = d$. I. E. d > G. T. t, Eng. t. √dxnt, to eat, I. E. *dont-*, L. *dent-s* > G. T. *tunth-*, Eng. tooth > Zahn, < zand. Before d the vowel has disappeared by apocope. The form is participial = "the eater" (Kluge). Comp. L. *edere* > Eng. eat > G. essen.

2. $y = b$. I. E. b is very rare and examples doubtful.

3. $y = g^1, g^2$. I. E. g¹ > G. T. k = G. k. < √gxl., L. *gelare* > G. T. * *kald*, Eng. cold, cool + G. kalt, kühl, ablauts. VI. I. E. g² > G. T. kw, k = G. k, qu, *e. g.*, < √g²xm, L. *venio* (< * *gvemio*) > G. T. *quëman*, Eng. come, + G. kommen, adj. bequem. The phonetic change of y > z consists in the loss of sonancy.

410. Form. III. x = G. T. surd spirant, I. E. z = unaspirated surd stop.

1. z = I. E. t. t through the transition stage t' = t + surd aspiration > G. T. th > H. and L. G. d, *e. g.*, L. *tertius* > G. T. *thridj-*, Eng. third, > dritte.

2. z = p. I. E. p > G. T. f, bilabial, Eng. f > G. f: L. *pisc-is* > G. T. *fisk-os* > Fiſch, + Eng. fish.

3. z = k¹, k². I. E. k¹ > G. T. h, kh, > G. h, ch. Ex.: L. *pecus* > G. T. *fëhu*, Eng. fee, > Vieh. I. E. k² > G. T. hw, h, Eng. wh, > G. w, zero = silent h. L. *sequ-or* > G. T. *sëhw-an* > ſehen, + Eng. see. L. *quis, quod* > G. T. *hwër, hwat* + Eng. who, what, > G. wer, was.

Verner's Law.

411. After the first shifting and when the accent was not yet limited to the root-syllable (see **420**, 2) a new phenomenon appeared, viz., Verner's Law or the "shifting of spirants." The G. T. surd spirants th, kh, f, s became sonant spirants and later sonant stops, when the immediately preceding vowel was unaccented. This affects only form. III., but the transition of sonant spirants into sonant stops is identical with the transition of the sonant spirants which sprang < sonant affricate according to form. I. See **408**. Hence there is an interchange of the following consonants: th — dh, d which became G. t; f — bh, b; kh, khw — gh, ghw, g, w; s — z, r. See **416**.

As to accent, see **420**. Students who know Greek can generally go by the Greek accent, which is often still the I. E.

Ex.: Gr. πατήρ, G. T. *fathar* > *fadhar* (Go.) > *fádar* (Ags.) > G. Vater, M. Eng. has again dh (through Norse influence?), but L. *fráter*, G. T. *brôthar*, Eng. brother > G. Bruder according to form. III. G. T. *lithon, laith*, but pl. *lidhon-*, part. *lidhan-*, Eng. loathe, > G. leiben (litt by levelling), gelitten. L. *sequ-or*, G. T. *sëhwan, sahw, sëgwun-, sëgwan-*, O. S. *sehan, sah, sâwum, gisewan*, Eng. see, saw, seen (levelling) > G. ſehen, ſah, geſehen (levelling, h silent). G. T. *wësan, was, wërum-, wësan-* > Eng. was — were > G. war (levelling), waren, geweſen (levelling). Compare lieſen — los (for, levelling) — geforen.

412. In certain consonant groups the first shifting of Grimm's Law allows of modifications.

1. Original st, sk, sp remain, *e. g.*, L. *vestigium* + G. Steg, Steig; L. sc in *poscere* + G. T. sk, Eng. and G. sh, ſch in forſchen, waſchen (see **457**, 4). L. sp in *spicere, speculum* + G. ſpähen + espy, spy.

2. Before t every dental has become s, every labial f, every guttural kh, ch, while t remains intact, but st can become ss by assimilation. Examples are very numerous.

Du weißt < *waist* < **waid+t*; L. *cap-tus* + G. -haft (but see Kluge); L. *noct-em* + G. Nacht + night; Macht + might < $\sqrt{\mathrm{mxg'}}$, from which mag — mögen, ablauts. VI.; gewiß < **wid-to'* a past participle < $\sqrt{\mathrm{wxd}}$, + L. vid-, + to wit, wist. The differentiation into st and ss is difficult to explain. Kögel ascribed it to accent, but see Kluge, P. and B. Beiträge, vol. VIII. A different origin has the st of Reſt, Maſt (of a ship), Gerſte, and a very few others, viz., < zd. For these see Kluge. See also **454**, 3.

THE GERMAN SHIFTING.

The second or German shifting we shall treat chiefly with a view to represent Eng. and G. cognates. We shall not treat of every dialect separately. It must suffice to say that upon the extent of shifting the classification of the dialects is based. See **480**. For a full account, see Braune's article in P. and B. Beitr., vol. II. In fact, to Braune we owe the best light that has been thrown upon this difficult subject. This second shifting, though coming within the historic period of the language, had been much less understood and more misrepresented than the first shifting. The material was very different from that of the first shifting and the result had to be different, though Grimm supposed that the first stage was reached again in H. G. Nor is there room to enter into the chronology of the various steps, though it has been tolerably settled. The latest shifting, th > d, we find still going on in the 12th century, and is the most extensive of all the shiftings. Geographically the movement began in the South and the farther North it spread the less it grew and the later it occurred. See **480**. We follow the order of the formulas. Where Eng. is identical with G. T., as is generally the case, the Eng. examples will at the same time illustrate the corresponding sounds and the cognates of Eng. and G. For foreign words see **492-494**.

413. Form. I. 1. G. T. **d** > G. t. Eng. dead — G. tot ; do — thun ; bed — Bett; steady — ſtetig ; mother for M. Eng. moder — Mutter (see **411**); hoard + Hort.

a. Where Eng. d — G. b in a small number of words, there d has been restored in N. H. G. through L. or M. G. influence, M. H. G. showing t ; or the word has come from L. G. into the written language. Eng. dumb

—bumm; dam — Damm; down — Düne; "Dutch" is L. G. > Eng., while G. deutsch belongs to form. III. After l and r are some cases of d — b, *e.g.*, wild — wild; mild — mild; murder — Mord. These are due to a change of Ags. th > d. Also after n, *e. g.*, wind — winden; bind — binden. These are due to a change of O. H. G. t > d.

2. Eng. b and g = G. b and g, see **408**, *e. g.*, bold — bald; beck — Bach; gold — Gold; garden — Garten. For mb — mm, see **490,4**. But b and especially g have often disappeared in Eng. Compare hawk — Habicht ; Haupt, < *houbit*, — head ; Regen — rain; Wagen — wain. G. b — Eng. v, haben — have; lieben — love, etc.

3. G. T. **bb** > G. **pp**: Rappe < *rappo, G. T. *rabbo-*, but Rabe — raven. Knappe < *knappo, G. T. *knabbo-*, but Knabe — knave. Ebbe + ebb, is L. G.

4. G. T. **gg** > G. **ck**, but G. T. **gg** > Eng. **dzh** (-dge). *mugjô, Ags. *mycge*, Eng. midge — G. Mücke. * *hrugjo*, Ags. *hrycge*, Eng. ridge — G. Rücken. Eng. edge — Ecke, bridge — Brücke, etc. Egge, harrow, is L. G.

5. y = sonant stop has sprung either from I. E. x = sonant affricate according to form. I. or from I. E. z = surd stop > G. T. surd spirant according to form. III. and Verner's Law, in both cases through a sonant spirant. Notice "affricate" is a double consonant, "spirant" is a single one. The process of G. T. y > G. z is loss of sonancy the same as I. E. y > G. T. z. Notice that consonants were doubled, *i. e.*, lengthened before West-germanic j, w, r, l, as the examples show, see **389, 5**.

414. Form. II. G. T. z > G. x. 1. G. T. t > G. ts (z, ß) and this remains when initial, after r, l, n and when sprung from tt, but becomes z (Grimm's sign), supposed to have been a lisped s, and later s (ſ, ß), see **490, 2**.

In M. H. G. this z and s never rhyme, hence they must have been different sounds. tt > ts is much later than t > ts.

Examples exceedingly numerous: tongue — Zunge ; wart — Warze; holt — Holz; mint — Münze < L. *monēta* through * *múnita ;* * *sattjan* > Eng. set — G. setzen ; whet — wetzen; wheat — Weizen; sweat — schwitzen; water — Wasser; hate — Haß, hassen, etc. All seeming exceptions can be explained in some way or other, *e. g.*, in foreign words introduced since the shifting: tar — Teer < L. G.; temple — Tempel < L. *templum ;* tun

415] PHONOLOGY—PHONETIC LAWS—GERMAN SHIFTING. **187**

— Tonne < Keltic(?). The combination tr is an exception. Compare also ft, kht, st, **412**, 2. True — treu; bitter — bitter < G. T. *bitr-os;* winter — Winter. Hinter and unter are M. H. G. *hinder, under*, see **413**, 1, *a.* Words introduced before the shifting are Germanized, *e. g.,* plant — Pflanze < L. *planta;* tile — Ziegel < L. *tegula.*

2. G. T. **p** > G. **pf,** which remains initially, after m, and when sprung from pp, but passes into f after vowels and r, l.

Ex.: Eng. path — G. Pfad ; pea(-cock) — Pfau < L. *pavo;* plight — Pflicht; swamp — Sumpf(?); rump — Rumpf; hop, hip — hüpfen; stop — stopfen; sleep — schlafen; hope — hoffen; sharp — scharf; help — helfen.

a. Where Eng. and G. p correspond, they indicate either L. G. or other foreign words introduced since the shifting, *e. g.*, pocks — Pocken; poke — pochen < L. G. ; pain — Pein < L. *pœna;* pilgrim — Pilger < L. *peregrinus;* pulpit — Pult < L. *pulpitum.*

3. G. T. **k** > G. **kh, jh** (ch), except initial **k** and double **k**, which appears as ck. Eng. has frequently palatalized its **k** into tsh, written **ch, tch.**

Ex.: Eng. like — gleich; bleak — bleichen; knuckle — Knöchel; knee — Knie ; church — Kirche ; cook, kitchen — Koch, Küche. Westgerm. kk — Eng. k — G. ck : bake, baker — backen, Bäcker ; waken — wecken; acre — Acker; naked — nackt.

a. The links between G. T. z and G. x are probably surd stop + aspirate, surd stop + spirant, spirant, *e. g.*, k > k + H > kkh, an affricate, > kh. kkh is still S. G., tth is the Irish pronunciation of Eng. th. The processes are identical with those of I. E. z > G. T. x. But G. x is a long consonant or an affricate, while G. T. x < I. E. z is a single, weaker consonant. Compare the present wachen having a long and strong ch with Wacht; hoffen, Hanf with the initial f as in für, Feuer, vor. The latter corresponds to G. T. f, the former to G. T. p. See below.

415. Form. III. G. T. **x** > G. **y.** This shifting only took place in the dentals. G. T. th > G. d. Eng. thing — G. Ding; that — das; hearth — Herd; earth — Erde; brother — Bruder.

As to extent and time of this shifting, see p. 185. The process of the shifting of the G. T. surd spirant under the accent > G. sonant stop, final surd stop is identical with that of G. T. surd spirants unaccented > G. T. sonant spirant > G. T. sonant stop in certain positions. For this G. T. y > G. z, see **411**.

1. Eng. **h, gh, f** correspond to G. h, ch, f (v), but Eng. gh is often silent.

Ex.: Eng. floor — G. Flur; fowl — Vogel; heart — Herz; hart — Hirsch < hirz, ; might — Macht; fraught, freight — Fracht.

2. G. T. **hw**, Eng. **wh** — G. w. Ex.: Eng. which — G. welch; whelp — Welf.

3. All irregularities must be explained as before, either as due to levelling or to foreign origin. See **414**, 1. herd — Herde, L. G., but Hirte — shep-herd according to rule; throne — Thron < Gr.-L. *thronus*. The relation of Tausend to thousand is not cleared up.

Eng. f — G. ch, L. G., see **493**, 4. h before l and r has been lost in both languages. Comp. κλυτός, Ags. *hlûd* — Eng. loud, G. laut; < √krx, ablauts II. Lat. *cruor* — Ags. *hrea* — Eng. raw, G. roh.

THE INTERCHANGES RESULTING FROM THE SHIFTING OF G. T. SPIRANTS. See **411**.

416. Levelling has so largely done away with the results of Verner's law in German that what is left of them may be looked upon as isolated cases. They appear more in derivatives of the same stem than in the verb-inflection.

1. d — t most frequent: leiden — litt, gelitten; leiten; sieden — sott, gesotten. f — b: darf, dürfen, Notdurft — darben, verderben (?). h, ch — g: ziehen (h silent), Zucht — gezogen, Herzog. f — r: Verlust, + loss — verlieren (levelling), verloren + forlorn; kiesen — Kur, erkoren, + choose, chose, chosen (s is due to levelling).

417. Correspondences between Eng. and G. consonants outside of the shiftings.

1. Loss of n before spirants in G. T. and later. Before G. T. kh as in sahen (archaic for fangen) < *fanhan; dachte < *danhte, + thought, etc. Ags. — Eng. also before th and f, where G. has preserved n. Compare: tooth — Zahn; mouth — Mund; but south — Süd, of L. G. origin; soft — sanft, but sacht, of L. G. origin.

2. Eng. wr — G. r: Eng. write — reißen, ritzen; wrench — renken; wretch — Recke; wring — ringen.

3. Eng. w, r, l, m correspond to G. w, r, l, m.

4. For Eng. m — G. n, see **490**, 5. For Eng. mb — G. mm, see **490**, 4.

5. Eng. s (original s) — G. s: house — Haus; sink — finken.

a. Eng. x — G. r, ᛯs. The phonetic value of the sign is the same in both languages. The sign x, borrowed from Latin, stands for ᛯs, ks, ts. Ex.: Eng. wax — G. wachsen; fox — Fuchs; axle — Achse; box — Büchse < Gr. πυξίς; box — Buchsbaum < L. *buxus.* Eng. s—G. sch, see **490**, 1.

ACCENT.

418. We are following still the traditional method of treating of the accent, but, as a matter of fact, in speaking we never divide the word into the syllables or the sentence into the words as they are printed or written. Such a division is purely for the eye and artificial. We speak in "*breathgroups,*" as Sweet calls them. Sievers uses "*Spruchtakt,*" but "*Sprechtakt*" would be better. A breathgroup consists of a certain number of sounds that can be pronounced " in one breath," as we say. If one or two sounds have very strong stress then the number of " syllables " in the group is small, because the store of air is spent. If one syllable has only the amount of air spent upon a secondary or medium accent, then the number of syllables can be larger. Eng. and G. have a prevailingly falling rhythm, that is, the stress falls upon the initial sounds or syllable of a group. French is different. Its stress is very uniform and the predominant stress very difficult to place in the group. Excellent authorities, both French and Dutch, claim that the stress lies at the begining; other authorities, just as high, that it lies at the end of the group. The French groups are very long.

In G. and Eng. the amount of stress concentrated upon some part of the group varies, else there would be a great monotony as in French, but Fr. has a more varied intonation or " tone," which gives it an advantage over Eng. and G.

1. For very trustworthy division into breathgroups, see Sweet's transcriptions of Eng., G. and Fr. in his "Handbook." For the whole difficult subject of the synthesis of sounds, see Sweet and also Sievers' Phonetik, § 33. Notice that the principle of breathgroups is recognized when we speak of proclitics and enclitics. All syncope, elision, contraction, metre, assimilation take place according to this principle. When there are too many syllables to to be pronounced conveniently by one breath-impulse some are cut off and always according to a certain fixed rule varying with the different languages. Or if the sounds coming together in a group are very different we assimilate them to each other. This we call " ease of utterance " or " euphony."

419. We distinguish three degrees of accent or "stress," viz., *chief* (strong, primary), *medium* (secondary), and *weak,* marked respectively ´, `, ˘. Thus: A'pfel, ba'nkba˘r, Da'nk˘ba˘rkeit.

1. "Weak" also includes "unaccented," when there are not syllables enough, *e. g.*, O'bilga'rtĕ˘n, A'pfe˘lbau'm. But when the word is very long

or in a group of several words we may distinguish not merely between weak and unaccented, but the variety of stress can be further marked by figures, e. g., Bere′bſa⁔mfei῾t (Be unmarked or ⁴ ¹ ⁸ ²): Groß′herzogtum, Altertumskunde, Vierzigjähriger.

Accent in Uncompounded Words.

420. The chief accent rests in all uncompounded words on the stem-syllable (no matter if suffixes and inflectional endings follow). This syllable is always the first, e. g., Va′ter, vä′terlich, fo′lgſam, Lä′cherlichkeit, Klei′nod, ſchmei′cheln, die Hu⁔ngernden.

1. Exceptions: lebe′nbig from le′ben; words in -ei and -ier, -ieren, e. g., Malerei′, benebei′en, vermalebei′en, ſtubie′ren, Barbie′r; luthe′riſch (long e), meaning "Lutheran," pertaining to that confession, but lu′ther(i)ſch, of, pertaining to Luther; äthe′riſch; a few derivatives in -ha′ftig (see **526**, 2); wahrha′ftig, leibha′ftig, sometimes teilha′ftig; also wahrſchei′nlich, but see **422**, 2.

2. This limitation of the primary accent to the root syllable is a peculiarity of the Germanic languages. It is called the logical or "gebundene" accent. The other Indo-European languages have the "free" accent, which can fall on any syllable. The original accent must have been preserved in G. T. until after the shifting of I. E. z > G. T. x, because then the law of spirants (see **411**) went into effect.

3. The Teutonic element of Eng. has, of course, the same accent as G. and even the Norman-French element in Eng. has largely submitted to the Germanic accent, e. g., sea′son < L. *sutio′nem* ; rea′son < L. *ratio′nem* ; li′berty < L. *liberta′tem*. Compare the foreign accent in G. Saiſo′n, raiſonnie′ren, Qualitä′t. It is to be noted that the two past participles and the pret. pl. were not stem-accented, originally, standing in contrast with the pres. and pret. sg. The accented suffixes we cannot enumerate.

Accent in Compound Words.

421. In compound words the chief accent rests upon the stem-syllable of the first component part if the second part is a noun (subst. or adj.); on the stem-syllable of the second part if this is a verb or derived from a verb: Fa′hrſtra῾ße, Na′chtwä῾chter, Scho′ßhu῾nd, lie′brei῾ch, gna′de⁔nvo῾ll, Bei′trag, A′ntwort, Fü′rſprech, U′rteil, vo′rnehm, Mi′ßgunſt; but verſpre′chen, ertei′len, verne′hmen, betra′gen, vollbri′ngen, mißli′ngen, vollko′mmen.

1. This old principle should be understood even by the beginner, though to him there will seem to be many exceptions, which an advanced scholar will generally account for. A′ntworten, u′rteilen are no exceptions, because they are derived from the nouns

A'ntwort, U'rteil; nor are bas Verla'ngen, ber Befe'hl, verne'hmlich, because they are derived from the corresponding verbs. Vollko'mmen has the correct accent, because it is a past participle.

The prefixes are fully treated in the word-formation, which see.

422. The more striking exceptions are as follows :

1. A large group of words which have not become real compounds but have sprung from mere juxtaposition in orthography: Das Lebeho'ch, vivat; vielleí'cht, Viellie'bchen, Lebewo'hl, Vergi'ßmeinnicht, Hansna'rr, Hoherprie'ster, Langewei'le (but La'ngweil after the genuine compound Ku'rzweil), Jahrhu'nbert, Jahrze'hnt, dreiei'nig, Dreiei'nigfeit, aller– + –lie'bst, –e'rst, –hei'ligenfest, etc.; Dreifö'nigsfest. Their etymologies are apparent.

2. In a number of adjectives, most of them ending in –lich, and their derivatives, the chief accent has shifted from the original position to the syllable preceding the suffix: vorzü'glich, but Vo'rzug; vortre'fflich; abscheu'lich, but A'bscheu; ausbrü'cklich, but Au'sbruck; die Vortre'fflichkeit, die Ausfü'hrlichkeit, leibeí'gen. In some the accent is uncertain, but the chief accent on the first element is preferable, e. g., ha'nbgreiflich better than hanbgrei'flich; no'twendig, wa'hrscheinlich, ei'gentümlich. A distinction is sometimes made between ei'gentümlich, " belonging to," and eigentü'mlich, " peculiar to." Notice offenba'r.

3. barmhe'rzig, full of pity, Kar– (formerly Char) as in Karfrei'tag, Good-Friday, Karwo'che, Holy Week (K a r–, + *care*, sorrow, but also Ka'rwoche), Frohnlei'chnam, Corpus Christi, perhaps because the meaning of the first element is no longer clear. Südo'st, Südsüdo'st, nordwe'stlich as in English.

4. In a large number of adjectives in which the first element denotes a comparison or a high degree, *e.g.*, himmelho'ch, as high as heaven, eisfa'lt, as cold as ice, kohlschwa'rz, the accent may stand on the second element, but must remain on the first when the adj. is inflected. Steinrei'ch, " very rich," originally " rich in precious stones," stei'nreich, stony, are sometimes distinguished.

5. aller– is accented only in a'llerhand and a'llerlei, doubtful in several, as in a'llerseits. all– is generally unaccented: allei'n, allmä'hlich, allgemei'n, but also A'llmacht, A'llvater, A'lltag and its derivatives, but also alltä'glich, as sub 4.

6. un–. For this prefix it is difficult to find a general rule. The best founded and most practical is this, based upon nominal and verbal compounds: Un– compounded with nouns and adjectives not derived from

verbs attracts the chief accent; if they are derived from verbs, then the stem-syllable retains its original accent, *e, g.*, u′nfruchtbar, u′nbankbar, u′nklar, ll′nmenſch, but unglau′blich, unſä′glich, unentbe′hrlich, unvera′ntwortlich, unbegrei′flich. Notice, however, une′nblich, ungeheu′er — u′ngeheuer. See *a*.

a. With regard to adjectives there is also a feeling approaching a principle, that un should have the chief accent, when a regular adjective exists, of which the compound with un- denotes the contrary or negation; brau′chbar, u′nbrauchbar, ſi′chtbar, u′nſichtbar, etc. This feeling frequently unsettles the accent, as unverzei′hlich > u′nverzeihlich.

7. Ober- varies in accent in compounds consisting of three parts. When it belongs to the second part it has chief stress, and the third part secondary stress: O′berkiefer-verle′tzung, injury of the upper jawbone. But if the second and third form one subdivision and *ober-* denotes rank, then it has less stress than the third part and the second has chief stress: Oberſchu′lle′hrer = chief school-teacher; Ober=mu′nbſche′nk; Obergeri′chtsa′nwalt, chief attorney. But accent the first and last examples differently and they mean different persons, viz., O′berſchulle′hrer, teacher at a high-school; O′bergerichtsan′walt, attorney at a high-court of justice.

423. In compound **adverbs** the chief accent falls generally upon the second element, if they are compounded of a simple adverb and a preceding or following noun or pronoun; or if compounded of two adverbs, *e. g.*, bergau′f, ſtroma′b, jahrei′n, jahrau′s, zufo′lge, anſta′tt, hinü′ber, hervo′r, ſofo′rt, dahi′n, dahe′r, überau′s, überei′n, überhau′pt, vorha′nden, abha′nden.

1. This includes their derivatives ſofo′rtig, zufrie′ben, vorha′nben.

Exceptions are: 1, compounds which contain demonstrative and possessive pronouns, *e.g.*, be′mnach, be′rgeſtalt, mei′netwegen, etc.; a′nber- or a′nbers-, -′halb, -′wärts, -geſtern, *e. g.*, a′nberswo, a′nberſeits, o′berhalb, hei′mwärts, vo′r-wärts, vo′rgeſtern, etc.; be′nnoch, e′twa; 2, many compounds which are fused adverbial phrases and derivatives from compounds. They retain their original word accent, *e. g.*, a′ngeſichts, a′bſeits, na′chmittags, ü′bermorgen, zu′ſehends.

See the rhetorical accent, **426.**

424. For the secondary accent rules can be given only in derivatives and compound words.

1. Certain nominal suffixes have always medium stress.

a. Substantive suffixes: –at, –ut, –ob; –heit, –richt, –in, –keit, –lein, –ling, –nis, –sal, schaft, –tum, *e. g.*, Hei'ma`t, Klei'no`d, E'wigkei`t, Fi'nsterni`s, Trü'bsa`l, Kö'nigtu`m.

b. Adjective suffixes : –bar, –haft, –icht (?), –isch (?), –lich, –sam, –selig, *e. g.*, bella'gba`r, e'hrenha`ft, e'rdi`cht, he'rri`sch, la'ngsa`m, trü'bse`lig.

2. In nominal compounds the secondary stress falls upon the root-syllable of the second part, *e. g.*, Rü'dgra`t, Fa'hrwa`sser, Au'ßensei`te, Ni'chterfü`llung, U'ngere`chtigkeit, le'bensmü`de, hi'lfsbe=dü`rftig.

3. In double compounds when one or both parts are again compounded the secondary stress falls upon the first or the only stem-syllable of the second part. But care must be taken in properly separating the parts, *e. g.*, Be'tt-vo`rhang, Re`chnungs-a`blage, Go'lb-be`rgwe`rk, Pe'lz-ha`ndschu`h, Fe'ldma`rschall; but Ha'ndschu`h-ma`cher, Nu'ßbau`m-ho`lz, Schri'ftste`llerverei`n. The misplaced medium stress would give no meaning at all, *e. g.*, Nu'ß-bau`mholz, because bau'mho`lz is meaningless. In Feu'erversicherungs-gese`llschaft secondary accent on –st`ch– is only possible, if there is such a thing as Feu'er-re`ttungsgesellschaft.

4. The foreign endings, of course, also cross this accentuation, *e. g.*, Bu`chbrucke`rei', U`ntersekretaria't, i`rrlichtelie'ren.

425. Unaccented are all inflectional endings, many prefixes and suffixes. The syllables generally contain ε = eh.

426. The rhetorical accent can interfere with the placing of the various degrees of stress, as in English: das Wild nicht e'rjagen sondern ve'rjagen ; da'rbei and dabei' ; ei'nmal, einma'l. In Sch.'s Wallenstein occurs Ka'nn nicht sein, kann ni'cht sein, etc.

427. The accent in foreign words is as a rule foreign. Very few words have taken German accent when introduced since the O. H. G. period. Substantives in –ie and –ei, verbs in –ieren retain, for instance, the primary accent on these suffixes, *e.g.*, Magie', Theologie', Druckerei', studie'ren, hantie'ren.

B. HISTORICAL COMMENTARY UPON THE ACCIDENCE.

Comments on the Noun-Declension. 1. Vowel-Declension.

[*See table on next page.*]

There are two numbers, three genders. Only two cases have now endings, viz., G. sg. and D. pl., but other parts of speech still inflect for the N. and A. The number of cases was gradually reduced. In O. H. G. there is still an Instrumental.

428. 1. There were two large systems of declension according as the stem ended in a vowel or in a consonant. Vowel stems ended in o or in â. We generally count here also the *i-* and *u-*stems, but they really belong to the consonant stems, since i and u have the functions of consonants as well as of vowels. Stems in o (*jo, wo*) belong to the I. E. e — o ablaut-series and are always masculine or neuter. Stems in â (*jâ, wâ*) belong to the a — â series and are always feminine. *jo, wo, jâ, wâ* are counted as separate classes, because j and w produced some peculiar changes. *u*-stems are very rare, since they soon became i-stems, *e.g.*, *sunu*, pl. *suni*, Söhne. There is only one neuter *i*-stem in O. H. G., viz., *meri*, das Meer + L. *mare*.

2. The consonant stems end in n, r, in a dental and in a guttural. The most frequent are the *n*-stems, to which went over a great many fem. nouns from the earliest times, *e.g.*, *zunga* + L. *lingua* for *dingua*.

3. J. Grimm fancied that there was strength in the vowel-declension and so called it "strong," the consonant declension he called "weak." The names have been generally accepted and though Grimm's reasons are fanciful the terms have the advantage of brevity.

4. The stem and case endings have been very much reduced according to certain principles called the "laws of finals" and the "rules of syncope." We cannot illustrate these here, as it would presuppose a knowledge of the older dialects. There was also a great levelling of cases, *e. g.*, the N. sg. fem. (*â*-stem) took *a* from the A. sg. fem. Its own vowel had to go according to the law of finals.

O and Jo-Stems.

5. The nouns sub **46**, 1, in el, en (< em or en), and er are *o*-stems that lost the e of the plural in M. H. G., see **434**, 3. Masc. in er < *aere* < *âri* (originally *jo*-stems) and those of the form *vogel* retained their e longest. The nouns sub **46**, 2 are the original *jo*-stems, in which e is the remnant of *jo*, O. H. G. i. When this e was lost, the nouns were treated as common *o*-stems and now belong to the II. strong class sub **50**, 4. Notice that the umlaut of a *jo*-stem runs through sing. and pl.; the umlaut of

Masculine

	O-STEMS O.H.G. Short-stem	O-STEMS O.H.G. Long-stem	O-STEMS M.H.G.	Jo-STEMS O.H.G.	Jo-STEMS M.H.G.	I-STEMS M.H.G.	U-STEMS O.H.G.	Jâ-STEMS O.H.G.
Sg. N.	tac	fogal	vogel	hirti	hirte	gast	sunu	mâgin
G.	tages	fogales	vogel(e)s	hirtes	hirtes	gastes	sunes	mâginna
D.	tage	fogale	vogel(e)	hirte	hirte	gaste	sun(i)u	mâginna
A.	tac	fogal	vogel	hirti	hirte	gast	sunu	mâgine
I.	tagu	fogalu		hirt(i)u				
Pl. N., A.	tagâ	fogalâ	vogel(e)	hirte	hirte	geste	sun(i)u, -i	mâginne
G.	tago	fogalô	vogel(e)	hirt(e)o	hirte	geste	sun(e)o	mâginno
D.	tagum	fogalum	vogel(e)n	hirtim	hirten	gesten	sunum, -im	mâginnôm

Feminine

	A-STEMS O.H.G.	A-STEMS M.H.G.	I-STEMS O.H.G.	I-STEMS M.H.G.	N-STEMS O.H.G.	N-STEMS M.H.G.	T-STEMS O.H.G.
Sg. N.	gebâ	gebe	kraft	kraft	zunga	zunge	naht, through the sg., and in N. and A. pl.
G.	gebâ	gebe	krefti	krefte, kraft	zungun	zungen through all cases sg. & pl.	
D.	gebu	gebe	krefti	krefte, kraft	zungun		
A.	geba	gebe	kraft	kraft	zungun		
Pl. N., A.	gebâ	gebe	krefti	krefte	zungun		
G.	gebôno	geben	kreft(e)o	krefte	zungôno		nahto
D.	gebôm, ôn	geben	kreftim	kreften	zungôm, ôn		nahtum

Neuter

	O-STEMS M.H.G.	Pl. -IR. O.H.G.	Pl. -IR. M.H.G.	N-STEMS O.H.G.	N-STEMS M.H.G.
Sg. N., A.	wort	kalb	kalp	herza	herze
G.	wortes	kalbes	kalbes	herzin	herzen all through
D.	worte	kalbe	kalbe	herzin	
Pl. N., A.	wort	kalbir	kelbir	herzun	
G.	worte	kalbiro	kelber(e)	herzôno	
D.	worten	kalbirum	kelber(e)n	herzôm	

an *i*-stem appears now only in the plural. Käfe is treated like a *jo*-stem, < O. H. G. *châsi* < *câsius* < Latin *câseus*.

6. The feminines and neuters in -niś sub 50, 1 ended in M. H. G. in -*e* (-*nisse*), both in the sing. and pl. The ending of the sing. was lost in early N. H. G. Also the -*e* of the neuters with Ge- sub 50, 4 was lost, and they really belong to the first class, see 46, 2. Both groups are primitive *jo*-stems. The monosyllabic neuters of 50, 4 followed the masc. *o*-stems of 50, 2, and therefore cannot have umlaut. In O. and M. H. G. these neuters were either uninflected or took the -*ir*, -*er* of 56; see 431. The masculines sub 50, 2, 3 are *o*-stems, and come properly by their -*e*. See p. 195.

429. *I*-Stems.

The paradigms of "kraft" and "gast" show which cases were entitled to umlaut. The sg. of the masc. very early took its G. and D. from the *o*-stems. The feminine was made invariable in M. H. G. since the apparent cause of umlaut had disappeared and since all other feminines, strong and weak, did not vary in the root-vowel.

1. The old bulk of the third class is made up of *i*-stems. Their number has been increased by *u*-, *o*-, *jo*-, and *cons*-stems. Fuß and Zahn were originally *cons*-stems. Comp. Gr. ποδ-ός, L. *dent-is*. They appear as *u*-stems in Gothic, as *i*-stems in O. H. G. Nacht is also a *cons*-stem. Comp. L. *noct-is*. Isolated cases of its old inflection are Nachts the adverbial genitive and the dative plural in Weihnachten < *zen wîhen nahten*. In Nachtigall + nightingale appears the genitive of its *i*-stem inflection; compare also Bräutigam + bridegroom, lit. "bridesman." (See 489, 5). An isolated *u*-case is „Handen" < O. H. G. *hantum*, dative plural, in abhanden, lost; vorhanden + "on hand." „Nöten" is an isolated dative plural; the nominative plural is obsolete. Compare the Eng. umlaut in mouse, mice; louse, lice; loft, lift, Ags. lyft, but Go. luftus; cow, kine, etc. Das Floß is O. H. G. masculine *i* stem.

430. 1. A small group of fem. is interesting, because the sg. was levelled in favor of the longer umlaut-forms of the G. and D., while the pl. became weak at the same time. For instance, bie Ente, the duck, inflected M. H. G. at first *ant, ente, ente, ant;* pl. *ente, ente, enten, ente.* Then it became *ente* for the whole sg., *enten* for the pl., as it is now. Similarly M. H. G. *bluot*, now bie Blüte + blowth; *sûl*, now bie Säule, column; *vurch*, bie Furche + furrow, no umlaut in M. H. G.; *huf*, bie Hüfte, this form "huft" with excrescent t, + hip, also Eng. with umlaut, + Ags. *hype; stuot*, bie Stute, + stud. Thräne, Zähre + tear, Thür(?) + door, are originally plurals, that have become singulars. See Kluge.

a. In this way doublets could spring up, *e. g.*, M. H. G. sg. *stat, stete, stete, stat* furnished bie Statt + stead, bie Stabt, pl. Städte, city, and bie Stätte, pl. -n, place, spot—all + Eng. stead. Statt also occurs in the sense of representation "in place of," anstatt, an seiner Statt, an Kindesstatt, to adopt as one's own child. Another such is M. H. G. *fart*—modern bie Fahrt, pl. Fahrten, ride, and bie Fährte, pl. Fährten, track, scent.

2. All nouns in –heit, –keit, –schaft and a large group of others were in M. H. G. still strong (mostly i-stems), but are now weak.

3. The modern fem. nouns in –in, pl. –innen, are also strong in O. H. G. The suffix *-in* < *-njâ*. See paradigm of *mâgin*. They had the fate of all fem. nouns, viz., invariable in the sg., generally –en in the pl.

431. Plurals in –er. See paradigm, p. 195.

1. This sign started from old *os*-stems corresponding to L. *genus, generis; corpus, corporis*. It is rare in O. H. G. in the sg., where it may have been even reintroduced from the pl. In the G. and D. pl. *–o, –um* are the regular case-endings. *–ir* therefore is really stem-ending, but it was too convenient a form for the pl. to escape being used as a pl. sign. Some eight to ten nouns are thus inflected in O. H. G. In M. H. G. *–er* spread and gradually formed a pl. even of masculines.

2. The word Ei is originally a *jo*-stem. The double plurals in –e and –er have sprung up from the apparent necessity of distinguishing sg. and pl. of neuters, which according to the law of finals had to lose all endings. Some nouns took e, some er, some both. In the latter a distinction in meaning developed. See **58** and the inflection of *wort* and *kalb*, p. 195.

2. Consonant Declension.

432. The masculine and neuter *n*-stems ended once in *-on*, *-jon*, the feminines in *-ôn*, *-jôn*. They correspond to the L. *homo, hominis; fulmen, fulminis; ratio, rationis*. As to their frequency in the Teutonic languages, see **478**, 5. The Latin declension shows also in the singular, how the case-endings were added; in O. H. G. these appear still in the pl., *e. g.*, in *herzonô ô* is sign of G. pl. What was therefore the mere stem-suffix has become a means of inflection in the course of time.

1. *r*-stems are the names of relationship, Vater, etc. They with the dental stems were forced into the strong, first into the *o*-, then into the *i*-declension for lack of case-endings, which could appear only in the G. and D. pl., viz., *fatero, faterum*. Already in M. H. G. the umlaut appears in the *r*-stems.

2. Nouns like Güte, Menge, Größe end in *î* or *în* in O. H. G.: *guotî, managî, -în*. That is, they were *jâ-* and *jôn*-stems. They are all derivatives from adjectives, and those in *în* are later than those in *î*. In O. H. G. they had *î* or *în* throughout except in the G. and D. pl., which were *managîno, managîm* respectively. Therefore umlaut throughout. The *în*-forms had to coincide in time with the strong feminines in *-în(n)* at least in the sg. and therefore disappeared. They were rarely used in the pl. See paradigm of *mâgin*, p. 195.

433. 1. All feminines having now no inflection in the sg. and the old strong fem. having taken *e(n)* in the plural, it is difficult to tell the original vowel-stems from *n*-stems. It would be correct to summarize the changes that have taken place in them, thus:

All fem. nouns have become strong in the sg. and most of them by far, weak in the plural.

2. The fem. *â*-stems (see paradigm) had already two cases in *-en*, viz., G. and D. pl., the other two were like the whole sg. It is not to be wondered at, then, if N. and A. pl. also took *-en* and thus a sharp contrast was formed between the sg. with no variation and the pl. with *-en* throughout. By this levelling and by the *jôn* (*î* and *în*) stems the loss of *-en* in the sg. of *n*-stems was brought about.

434. 1. *-n* in the D. and G. sg. is still frequent in the 16th century and is preserved in certain phrases and in poetry. Schiller's Wallenstein's Lager has Kirchen, Stuben, Sonnen. Festgemauert in der Erben (Sch.). See **171**.

2. The masculines in *-e* are the bulk of old *n*-stems in M. H. G. Some nouns have become strong, *e. g.*, Aar, Hahn; others have become weak, Hirte (originally *jo*-stem), Helb (already in M. H. G.). See **61**; **518**, 1, 2.

3. As to the nouns in **46**, 1, in M. H. G. e was dropped after r and l in

the N. sg. and all through; after m and n only in the N. In modern G. no -e is the usage. See paradigm of *vogel*, p. 195.

435. 1. In O. H. G. were only four neuter *n*-stems, viz., *ôra*, Ohr; *ouga*, Auge; *herza*, Herz; *wanga*, Wange. In M. H. G. they inclined toward the strong and now the first three have joined the mixed declension; *wanga* has become weak and fem.; *namo*, der Name, was once neuter. Comp. L. *nomen, nominis*.

2. Interesting are bie Biene + bee and bie Birne + pear, in which the inflectional *n* has entered the stem. Compare the older *bie, bir*. This entering of *n* into the N. of masculines is very common and has furnished the bulk of strong nouns, 1. class sub 1 and 4, 4b, *e. g.*, Rücken, Galgen, Pfosten, Roggen, Schaben (but notice the isolated „es ist Schade," it is too bad). One can tell these by comparing them with their Eng. cognates + ridge, gallow(s), post, rye, etc., which show no *n*.

3. In der Heide < heidan + heathen; Christ + Christian < *kristen* < L. *christianus*; Rabe < *rabe* and *raben* + raven, n is lost as if it had been regarded an inflectional suffix and the nouns became weak.

4. In bie Ferse < *fersana*, Ags. *fyrsn*; Kette < *ketene, chetina* + Eng. chain through Romance < V. L. *cadína*, L. *caténa*; in bie Küche < *küchene, kuchîn* < V. L. *cucîna*, L. *coquina* + Eng. kitchen; in bie Mette < *metten, mettina* < V. L. *mattina*, L. *matutîna* (hora) + Eng. matin, the n has also been lost and the nouns became weak.

Comments on the Adjective-Declension.

436. O. H. G. paradigm of *o*-stems:

	Masc.	Fem.	Neuter.
Sg. N.	BLINT, blintêr	BLINT, blintíu, –(i)ú	BLINT, blintaz
G.	BLINTES	blintera, –u	BLINTES
D.	blintemu	blinteru, –a	blintemu
A.	blintan	BLINTA, –e	BLINT, blintaz
Instr.	BLINTU		BLINTU
Pl. N.	blinte	blinto	blintíu, –(i)ú
G.	blintero	blintero	blintero
D.	blintêm, –ên	blintêm, –ên	blintêm, –ên
A.	blinte	blinto	blintíu, –(i)ú

437. The adjective was once declined like the substantive, when both were still "nouns." In the Teutonic languages the so-called "uninflected" forms are still the noun inflection, because **blindoz* > blind(t) just as **dagoz* > tag. The *strong* declension is the pronominal inflection, which in some cases coincided with the substantive declension. These cases and the uninflected forms are put in small capitals in the paradigm.

1. The adjective pronouns led the way in this coalescence of the two inflections into the one *strong* one. *blintêr* is only S. G., the uninflected alone occurs in M. and L. G.

2. The double forms *blintûu, blintiû* are perhaps due to *jo*-stems (Paul). *blintiû* could give M. H. G. blinde. The M. H. G. forms, both strong and weak, differ very little from the O. H. G. In the neuter pl. *blindiu* lasted long.

3. In O. H. G. the vowel-stems are reduced to *o-* and *jo-*stems.
The *jo*-stems are still recognizable by the umlaut which runs throughout, *e.g.*, ſchön, böſe, träge.

4. The weak declension was exactly like the *n*-subst. declension. Now the sg. A. fem. and neuter are like the sg. N. just as in the substantives.

Comparison of Adjectives.

438. –er, –eſt represent O. H. G. *–iro, –ōro, –ist, –ōst*. The *o*-forms, are not frequent in O. H. G. *i* in *ir, ist* produced umlaut, which spread in M. H. G., so that even then the umlaut began to be looked upon as an essential part of comparison.

They were declined almost exclusively weak at first. e of *bezzere* (N. sg.) was lost just like the e of *vogele*, see p. 195.

1. It is generally stated that *–iro, –oro* come from an I. E. suffix *–jans*, but how has never been made clear. It is probable that, since *–oro* was at first attached only to *o*-stems, the *o* is secondary and due to the stem-suffix. The comparative-suffix seems to have been *–is* and to this *–t–* was added for the superlative. But *–t–* is probably identical with the ordinal-suffix.

Irregular Comparison.

439. beſſer < O. H. G. *bezziro*, Ags. *betera*, beſt < *bezzist*, Ags. *betst;* mehr < O. H. G. *mêro*, Go. *maiza*, meiſt < O. H. G. *meist*, Go. *maists;* minder < O. H. G. *minniro*, M. H. G. *minre*, mindeſt represents O. H. G. *minnist*, M. H. G. *minnest*.

1. All contain the regular suffixes. beſſer comes perhaps from a stem *b'ad. baß is the regularly developed comparative adverb. Comp. M. H. G. *min, mê*, Ags. *min, mâ*. *r* disappeared according to the law of finals. Whether mehr is related to L. *magis, major*, is doubtful. minder has excrescent b. The O. H. G. *nn* shows that L. *minu–s* is its cognate. mindeſt is a N. H. G. superlative < minder.

2. Erſt is < O. H. G. *êristo*, comparative *êriro*. Ehe is a modern formation for the positive, + Eng. ere, erst. Letzt comes from a stem *lat, from which Eng. late, later; last — latest; also + to let = "hinder." laß, tired. Letzt < *lezt, lat(i)st*, just as Eng. last < latest. See Kluge. Fürſt + first is < O. H. G. *furi* (adverb), *furiro, furisto*.

Comments on the Pronouns.

440. Personal Pronouns.

M. H. G. Common gender.

		I.	II.	III. refl.
Sg.	N.	ich	du, dû	—
	G.	mîn / (mînes, -er)	dîn / dîner	sîn / sîner
	D.	mir	dir	(im)
	A.	mich	dich	sich
Pl.	N.	wir	ir	—
	G.	unser	iuwer	(ir)
	D.	uns	iu	(in)
	A.	uns / unsich	iuch / iuwih	sich

III. person with form for each gender.

		I.	II.	III. refl.
Sg.	N.	ër	siu	ëz
	G.	sîn, ës	ir, ire	ës, sîn
	D.	im(e)	ir, iro	im(e)
	A.	in, inen O. H. G. inan	sie	ëz
Pl.	N., A.	si(e)	si(e), sî	siu
	G.	ir (O. H. G. iro)		
	D.	in (O. H. G. im)		

1. The pronouns of common gender come from various stems, which as well as the inflections are difficult to analyze. er, fie, eß come from two stems i (< *ei — oi*) and *ijâ*. For *eß* < *eʒ* + Goth. ita, see 490, 2. Compare L. *is, ea, id*.

2. The pronouns were extended by two endings, -er and -en, in N. H. G. The G. sg. meiner, etc., are no doubt due to the influence of the strong adjective declension and to unfer, euer (G. pl.). The same endings appear in berer and benen, but these are later, since both *mînes* and *mîner* appear in M. H. G. sporadically. *iuch*, originally A., spread over D. like the reflexive "sich." *sîn* crowded out *es* (G. masc.) already in O. H. G. and *es* (neuter G.) has general force, not referring to a single object. N. H. G. Jhro is probably an analogous form with "dero" before a title and not

the old fem. G. sg. or pl. *iro* as generally stated. *ir* (G. pl.) was still the rule in the 16th century and as G. sg. still in the 17th. beiner was established later than meiner and feiner, which were the rule early in the 17th century.

441. Possessive Pronouns.

a. The possessive pronouns are of the same origin as the genitives mein, bein, fein, etc., of the personal pronoun. They are most likely not derived from the latter as is generally stated, but rather the reverse. The adjective suffix *-in* < *in* seems to lie in them attached to the primitive stems *ma, *twa, *swa, which appear in all Indo-European languages. Comp. L. *meus, tuus, suus, mei, tui, sui.*

1. In O. H. G. the possessives were declined strong even when preceded by the definite article. In M. H. G. the weak declension came into use. The long forms in *-ig* sprang up late in the 16th century.

2. Jhr, her, their, however, is derived from the G. of the personal pronoun of the third person. It sprang up in the 12th century and was fully established in the 15th.

442. The Demonstrative Pronoun.

O. H. G.

	Masc.	Fem.	Neut.
Sg. N.	dê (thie), dër	diu	daz
G.	dës	dëra, -o	dës
D.	dëmu, M. H. G. dëm(e)	dëru, M. H. G. dër(e)	dëmu
A.	dën	dê, dea, dia	daz
In.	diu		diu
Pl. N., A.	dê, dea, dia	'deo, dio	dei, diu
G.		dëro	
D.		dêm	

a. Sievers assumes two I.-E. stems, *to, tjo ;* Paul only one, *to,* explaining i as due to the diphthongization of ê > ea > ia. *dê* without r is the older ; r is the same as in *wer, er,* + L. *quis, is. to* is treated as o and i stem. *dê* < *thai.* dei is probably dual like zwei. O. H. G. *daz* < G. T. *thata,* in which final t is a particle. The Instr. exists still in the isolated „bejto," + the in " the more," < *desde* < *des-diu.* des is the Gen.

443. O. H. G.

	Masc.	Fem.	Neut.
Sg. N.	dëse, dësê-r	deisu, diusiu	diz, dëzzi, diz
G.	dësses	dëscra, derra	dësses
	etc.	etc.	etc.

dese is composed like a strong adjective of de and a particle sa. In the G. sg. both elements are inflected, generally only the second. *diz* has in z the neuter pronominal suffix, but nothing else in it is explained. In M. H. G. the forms beginning with *di*- prevailed, always short. dieſ goes back to O. H. G. *diʒ*, but bieſeſ first appears as late as the 15th century. Hans Sachs still spells *diz, ditz*.

1. jen–er seems to contain the same suffix *-in* as the possessive pronouns. Its stem is limited to the Teutonic languages.
The origin of „ſelb" + self is dark.
ſolch + such is compounded of swa, so, ſo and lich, like, -lich.

2. The pronominal stem *hi*, which appears also in the Eng. pronoun he, his, him, her, is hidden in heute <· *hiudagu* (Instr.), heuer < *hiujaru*, heint (now dialectic) < M. H. G. *hînet* < *hînaht*, + to-night. It occurs also in the adverbs hin, her, + hi-ther. Compare L. *hi-c, hae-c, ho-c*.

444. Interrogative Pronouns.

O. H. G. Masc. and Fem.	Neuter	M. H. G.
N. huër	huaʒ	wĕr, waʒ
G. huës		wĕs
D. huëmu		wĕm(e)
A. huēn(an)	huaʒ	wĕn, waʒ
Instr.	huiu, hiu	wiu

a. From the stem *–ko* with k" that was labialized in Latin and the Teutonic languages. Compare L. *quis—quid, quod*, which perhaps requires another I. E. stem *ki*. A. *huenan* is only O. H. G. and the ending is taken from the adjective declension.

1. wie < O. H. G. wiu, huiu, + why, how, comes from this stem, G. T. *hwa-*, I. E. *ko-*, + Go. *hwaiwa*, Ags. *hū*. But the phonetic relation between wie, why and how is not yet cleared up.
Eng. whom is really the D. + wem, but served as D. and A. very early.

2. welch < O. H. G. *huëlih, wëlich*, + which < Ags. *hwylc*, lit. "how or what like."

3. weber + whether, now only conjunction, is still a pronoun in the 16th century. Formed, with the comparative suffix –ber < thar < tero, from *ko*– the interrogative stem. Comp. Gr. κότερος, archaic form.

445. Indefinite Pronouns.

1. jeber, jemanb, niemanb contain the prefix *io, ie,* je, + ever. io gave the original interrogative *weder* indefinite force, jeber < *iewĕder* < *iowĕder*. Like "either," it meant "one of two," "which ever you please." The end-

ing -er was confounded with the adjective-endings -er, -e, -es and the full forms jederer, jedere, jederes are preserved, though rare, down to the 17th century.

jemand is compounded of *ie—man*, niemand of *ni—ie—man*. As to b, see **491, 2**.

jeglich < *iegelih* < *io—gilîh*, "ever (the) like."

2. jedweder < *ie—dewëder*, "any one of two." It contains an element de, which is also in etlich, etwas. Its origin is unknown. kein < *dechein*. This also contains an obscure element *dech-*.

3. ander + other is a comparative like weder, < O. H. G. *andar* < *an—tero*.

Comments on the Conjugation.

446. Strong Verbs.

	O. H. G.		M. H. G.	
	Pres. ind.	*Subj.*		
Sg. 1.	nimu	nëme	nime	nëme
2.	nimis(t)	nëmes	nimest	nëmest
3.	nimit	nëme	nimet	nëme
Pl. 1.	nëmam(ês)	nëmêm(ês)	nëmen	nëmen
2.	nëmat, et	nëmêt	nemet	nëmet
3.	nëmant	nëmên	nëment	nëmen
	Pret. ind.	*Subj.*		
Sg. 1.	nam	nâmi	nam	næme
2.	nâmi	nâmîs	næme	næmest
3.	nam	nâmi	nam	næme
Pl. 1.	nâmum(ês)	nâmîm(ês)	nâmen	næmen
2.	nâmut	nâmît	nâmet	næmet
3.	nâmun	nâmîn	nâmen	næmen
	Imp.			
2. sg.	nim	*Inf.* nëman	nim	nëmen
1. pl.	nëmam(ês)	*Ger.* ze nëmanne	nëmen	ze nëmenne
2. pl.	nemat	*Pres. part.* nëmanti	nëmet	nëmende
		Past part. ginoman		genomen

447 **Weak Verbs.**

	O. H. G.		M. H. G.
Imp. 2. *sg.* neri	salbo	ner	salbe
Pret. nerita	salbôta, dûhta	nerte	salbete
Inf. neren	salbôn	nern	salben
Part. nerenti	salbônti	nernde	salbende
ginerit	gisalbôt	genert	gesalbet

a. Grimm called a verb "strong" because it would form its preterit of its own resources, without the aid of composition. We retain the terms "strong" and "weak" simply because they are generally used.

448. Tenses.

There are only two simple tenses left in the Germanic languages, viz., the present and the "preterit" which corresponds in form to the "perfect" of the other I. E. languages. What we call "the subjunctive" is in form the optative, the suffix for which was *iê—i*, in an *o*-verb of course *-oi*. Compare the Greek φέροι—Go. *nimai*.

449. Personal suffixes. There were two classes. The primary were added to the present and the subjunctive mood, the secondary to the preterit and the optative mood. The O. H. G. 1. pl. in *-mês* is quite a mystery. The 2. p. sg. present in *st*, prevailing in O. H. G., has sprung from analogy with *nimis—tu* and the pret.-present verbs, *e. g., canst.* "*bistu*" occurs in the very oldest sources.

1. The 1. p. sg. pres. is either u < o in nearly all verbs or m < *mi* in the few *mi*-verbs, *e.g., nimu* but *tuom*. Peculiar is that the 2. p. pret. subj. has entered the pret. ind. The regular ending was -t, as still found in Gothic and in the pret.-pres. verbs, *e.g.,* Go. *namt,* G. bu wilt, folt (now archaic).

An -e in the 1. and 3. p. sg. pret. and in the 2. p. sg. imper., due to analogy, sprang up in late M. H. G., spread in early N. H. G., became rare in 18th century, and is now archaic.

2. These suffixes were either attached to the bare stem as in the *mi*-verbs or by means of a connecting vowel generally called "thematic vowel," which was I. E. o—e for all strong verbs, and in O. H. G. i, ē or ô for weak verbs.

450. Imperative. The 2. p. sg. has the syncopated form of short-stemmed verbs which once ended in -e : neme > nimi > nim. In weak verbs the ending is amalgamated with the connecting vowel : *neri, salbo.* neri should become ner, but there was levelling in favor of the long-stemmed verb. The 1. p. pl. is exhortative. It is indicative.

451. INFINITIVE. This is a verbal noun ending in *-no-*. Perhaps an isolated accusative.

452. GERUNDIVE. It is confounded with the infinitive with which it has originally nothing to do. Suffix is *-nj-* ; hence the double n. It was inflected like any noun. Since in modern German it has taken a construction similar to the Gerundive of Latin grammar, we have called it "Gerundive." The form with *-d* occurs, according to Weinhold, as early as the 12th century in Alemanic. *zi tuonne* and *zi tuonde* were confounded. In the latter form lies the modern construction, as in eine zu beachtende Vorschrift.

453. PARTICIPLES. The suffix of the present participle was *-nt*, a consonant stem, but afterwards a *jo-, jâ-stem*, hence *nemanti*. For the nouns Freund, Feind, Heiland, see **505**.

1. The passive participles are two verbal adjectives formed by means of *-tó-* and *-nó-* (both accented) from the verb-stems, not from the tense-stems. They were at first not limited, *-tó-* to weak verbs and *-nó-* to the strong. Compare *miss-* (the modern prefix miß- + Eng. mis-) < *misto* < *mith—tó* the weak stem of the verb meiben, mied, gemieden, to avoid : gewiß < *gawiss* < *-witta* < *widtó*, from the stem of weiß, wissen; alt + old < al—tó- from the strong verb (Go.) *alan* + L. *alere*, to nourish. Besides in these and other isolated forms *-tó-* occurs in the past part. of the pret.-pres. verbs and in a class that had no connecting vowel, *e.g.*, gebracht, gedacht, etc., see **454**, 3. Compare Gr. *-τός*, L. *-tus*. *-no* is rare in non-Germanic languages; compare L. *dignus, plenus* + full.

2. *The prefix ge-.* It is the inseparable prefix *ge-* and belonged at first only to the participle of verbs compounded with it. But in simple verbs it could give the present the force of the future, it would emphasize the preterit or give it the force of the pluperfect and give the infinitive dependent upon a modal auxiliary the force of the perfect inf. Thus also in the participle it emphasized the completion of an act. Some participles very rarely took *ge-* in M. H. G., *e. g., komen, worden, funden, lâzen, frezzen, heizen.* „Gnade funden" is common in the Bible. The Patriarch in Lessing's *Nathan* uses it. Compare Eng. yclad, yclept.

454. **WEAK VERBS.**

1. The connecting vowels are i(j), ē, ō in O. H. G. The original type of connecting vowel is supposed to have been ojo—ejo, but the reduction to ē (Go. ai) and ō is by no means clear. The large majority have i(j) < *ejo, but a not small number both of originally strong and weak verbs have none. The preterit is formed by the suffix -ta, now -te. Its origin is by no means settled. Paul reconstructs two suffixes, viz., -dhō and -ta. The Old Saxon forms sagda, habda, libda with corresponding participles can only come from $\sqrt{dh\bar{a}}$, from which is also thun + to do. The majority of verbs take I. E. -ta,> tha > da > ta according to Verner's Law. See 411.

2. We distinguish originally three classes : 1, no connecting vowel in the preterit ; 2, connecting vowel and short stem ; 3, connecting vowel and long stem.

3. There was very early (in O. H. G.) a levelling between the 2. and 3. classes, because in short-stemmed verbs, in which no syncope could take place, j(i) caused doubling of the final consonant. This made them appear like long-stemmed ones. The first class has now been reduced to the three verbs benfen, bünfen, and bringen, see 119, 2. Compare O. H. G. denken, dâhta, gidâht ; dunken, dûhta, gidûht ; bringen, brâhta, gibrâht Long â < ā nasalized < an. brauchen, fürchten, suchen, wirken (< würken) belonged here also. Eng. buy, bought, bought; work, wrought, wrought show still their origin in the gh before t. Bringen is of course a strong verb and so are brûkan (II.), suochen (VI.) as their ablaut shows. Beginnen belonged here perhaps too, since we find still in dialect begonnte (F. 3176). That these verbs never had any connecting vowel is shown : 1, by the change of the guttural stop > guttural spirant which takes place only directly before t ; 2, by the umlaut in the pret. subj. For the M. H. G. forms are denken, dâhte—dæhte, gedâht ; dünken, dûhte—diuhte, gedûht ; bringen, brâhte—bræhte, (ge)brâht. bünfen, bünfte, gebünft begins as early as M. H. G. The present mir bäucht is a N. H. G. formation from the preterit. That fürchten once belonged here is shown by the archaic form „furchte," e. g., Der wack're Schwabe forcht' sich nit (U.). Lessing has „furchte," < O. H. G. furhten (vürhten), for(a)hta, gifor(a)ht (the a is a secondary development).

455. The verbs in **119**, 1, are the only verbs that still show the difference between the long and short-stemmed of the i(j)-class. They formed their principal parts in O. H. G.: brennen, branta, gibrennit—gibrantêr ; nennen, nanta, ginennit—ginantêr. According to syncope *brannita, *gibrannitêr had to become branta, gibrantêr. The i that produced umlaut in brennen *gibrennit* had disappeared from *brannita, gibranniter* and therefore there is no umlaut in brannte, gebrannt. The participle with umlaut was levelled away.

1. The umlaut in the modern pret. subj. is due to analogy with brächte, bürfte, etc. It is a Middle German feature. Even preterits indicative with e of rennen, brennen, nennen occur now and then in the classics. The levelling into fenben, fenbete, gefenbet; wenben, wenbete, gewenbet is not uncommon. Schiller has . . . bie Grenze, wo er bas von ben Schweben eroberte Cham berennte.

2. All other differences were levelled away, *e.g.,* M. H. G. *hœren, hôrte, gehœret—gehôrt,* becomes hören, hörte, gehört; fürchten, fürchtete, gefürchtet; sprengen, sprengte, gesprengt; füllen, füllte, gefüllt; becken, beckte, gebeckt.

3. A few isolated participles are left, such as gestalt (ungestalt), getrost (adverb), and others.

STRONG VERBS.

456. The Present.

1. The interchanges of e—i; ie—eu; no umlaut—umlaut in the present and the umlaut in the pret. subj. are accounted for in the phonology. See 403. See also under each class of verbs.

2. The first p. sg. has followed the analogy of the forms that have e and of the verbs of VI. which had of course no umlaut in 1. p. sg., *e.g.,* O. H. G. faru, ferist, ferit. The contrast is now for all classes between 2. and 3. pers. sg. with i, ä, etc.: bu fährst, er fährt, bu gibst, er gibt and all the other forms with a and e : fahren, ich fahre, wir fahren, ihr fahrt, sie fahren; geben, ich gebe, wir geben, ihr gebet, sie geben. Formerly the contrast was between the whole pres. sg. and the whole pl. for Cl. III., IV., V. See paradigm, p. 203.

457. Of the numerous formations of the present-stem the following are still to be recognized by certain peculiarities :

1. I. E. *jo—je,* L. *capio, fugio,* German bitten V. < *bidjan* < **bedjan,* according to the interchange of e—i, but the participle gebeten < *bedan-.* Exactly like this sitzen V., liegen V., but gesessen, gelegen. Also heben VI. and schwören VI., *e.g.,* schwören < *swern* < *swerien* < *swarjan, swôr, swaran-.* Hence i, or in the last two, a umlaut through the whole present. This was once a large group. Here belonged for instance the class benfen, bachte, see **454,** 3, + Go. *thankjan.*

2. The suffix -*n* (-*nw, nj*), which also entered the pret. if it was within the root. fragen < **frehnan,* Ags. *frignan,* but already weak in

O. H. G. erwähnen < an O. H. G. (gi-)wahhinnen, nn < nj. beginnen, rinnen and others have nw. Go. standan, German ſtunb, ſtanb—geſtanben; (gehen), gieng, gegangen, fangen, etc. Compare L. *tundo, tutudi.*

3. Reduplication, corresponding to Gr. τίθημι and πίπτω, is preserved in beben < bibên, to quake, and zittern, to tremble, both weak (Kluge).

4. sk, corresponding to L. -sco, in breſchen, forſchen, wünſchen, waſchen (see Kluge's Dict. for these words).

458. The Preterit.

1. *Reduplication.* There are traces of ablaut without reduplication, but generally the two occurred together. In Gothic are still verbs which have both. The reduplication consisted in the repetiton of the initial consonant + e or if beginning with a vowel by prefixing 'e, e.g., Go. *haldan, haihald* (ai = ĕ in Gothic), *aukan, aiauk*. O. H. G. has only one clear example, viz., *teta*, ich that. Compare L. *fallo—fefelli, tango—tetigi*. How the reduplicating syllable was lost, how it coalesced with the stem is not yet clear. Our VII. class includes the reduplicating verbs, that is, those still reduplicating in Gothic, though it is by no means certain that Gothic has preserved the original method of reduplication.

2. In O. H. G. the stem-vowel of the reduplicated preterit appears as ē and eo, e.g., *râtan rēt, fâhan fēng* and *fēng* (fâhan < fanhan). ē by diphthongization > ea > ia > ie; eo > io > ie, so that already in M. H. G. we have *ie* as the regular vowel of the preterit. Examples: *stôzan — steoz, stioz*, M. H. G. *stiez—gistôzan; hloufan — hleof, hliof*, M. H. G. *lief—gihloufan*, N. H. G. laufen—lief—gelaufen ; *fallan—fēl > feal > fial > fiel* (M. H. G.)—*gifallan*, N. H. G. fallen—fiel—gefallen; *heizzan—hēz, heaz, hiaz*, M. H. G. *hiez—giheizzan*, N. H. G. heißen—hieß —geheißen.

3. However the vowel appearing in the pret. may have arisen, it is not *ablaut*. It never appears in derivatives as all the ablaut vowels do. Unterſchieb is only a seeming exception, since it stands for the older „Unterſcheib," which was crowded out, because the verb went over into the I. Cl.

The Ablaut-series and the Verb-classes.

459. No one verb shows all the four stages of ablaut as they have been determined. See 394. The first five classes belong to the original I. E. e—o series, the VI. is the I. E. ă—ā, G. T. ă—ō series. To the latter series belong also the reduplicating verbs which have in the stem a + liquid + cons. (halten); ai (ei); and au, o.

In the first group ĕ corresponds to G. T. ĕ, i ; o to G. T. a in the pret sg., for in I. and II. we must count i and u as consonants. The five classes can be grouped as follows :

1. *a.* I., II.: i and u as consonants in the pres. and pret. sg.; as vowels in the pret. pl. and part., viz.,

   ĕ – i + cons. a – i + cons. i + cons.
   ĕ – u + cons. a – u + cons. u + cons.

The stem ends in i or u + cons.

b. III., IV., V. have in the present ĕ – i + liquid or nasal + cons. (III.); e + liquid or nasal (IV.), or e + cons. (V.). In the pret. sg. they have a. The stem ends in a liquid or nasal + cons. (III.); in a single liquid or nasal (IV.) ; in a single cons. not liquid or nasal (V.).

2. I., II., III. have the weakest stages of ablaut in the pret. pl. and participle; IV. in the part. only; V. in neither. IV. and V. have a long vowel in the pret. pl., that is very difficult to account for. O. H. G. ā corresponds to G. T. ē, the length of which may be due to compensation, *e.g.*, *gégbum > gēbum. See **458**, 1.

3. A third grouping is possible according to the quality of the vowel, viz., I. to V. run in a system of unrounded vowels, VI. runs in a system of rounded.

_{*a.* u (o) in II. is either consonant in the accented stage (pres. and pret. sg.) or vowel in the unaccented stage (pret. pl. and past part.). u before r, l, m, n in the unaccented stage is also due to their double nature, according to which they serve as vowels or as consonants. *Nasalis* and *Liquida sonans* (Brugman) are represented in all the Teutonic dialects by ur, ul, um, un, a characteristic of the whole group.}

4. VI. stands alone and contains rounded vowels. Its a cannot have been originally the same as the a of the other series. It was probably more o than a.

LEVELLING IN THE PRETERIT.

460. Tracing the classes from O. H. G. to N. H. G. we have to notice one great levelling in all the classes, viz., of sg. and pl. pret. This was started by VI. and VII., which had sg. and pl. alike. In IV. and V. the difference was only one of quantity. The sg. was short and the pl. was long. The sg. had to take a long vowel according to **488**, 2.

1. In Cl. II. G. T. au > ao > ô before dentals, before l, r, h, and finally

There were therefore already ŏ's in the pret. sg. The levelling was in favor of ō, but of ŏ before certain consonants (ff, ch, f, b — t). ŏ was already in the past part. < ŭ. Only I. and III. are left. But in I. î > ei according to **488, 5**. The pres. and pret. had to become alike. The principle of ablaut was thus interfered with in I., and the levelling in the pret. was in favor of the pl. and part., viz., i or ie according to the following consonants. III. is the only class in which the levelling was in favor of the pret. sg. Before nasal + cons. u stood in the pl. and part. A levelling in favor of the pl. was therefore not likely. In IV. and V., where such a levelling occurred, the pl. and part. had different vowels. Before l, r, + cons., to be sure, there was u in the pl., o in the part., but u — o stood in no ablaut-relation. But this levelling was the latest of all and we find none in S. G. dialects at the present day. In the written-language of the 16th and 17th centuries it is rather rare; in the 18th it is the rule with not a few exceptions. Werben, warb — wurde, geworben is the only verb of III. in which the pl.-vowel stands by the side of the sg. But this verb stands isolated from the rest as an auxiliary verb. The pret.-pres. verbs have not suffered levelling except sollen (see **471, 2**), but these have stood in an isolated position toward all the other strong verbs from prehistoric times.

461. We give a few examples of the classes in their earlier stages. Space will not permit to trace each verb of each class. It would be easy to show what verbs have died out, what verbs have become weak, and what weak or foreign verbs have become strong. The stock of verbs belonging to each class varies with every period; in fact, it is ever varying. Compare, *e.g.*, jag, jug, frag, frug VI. (see **129**), and the large number of doubtful ones in VIII.

462.   I. Cl. O. (M.) H. G.   î   ei, ê   i   i

grîfan	greif	grifum	-grifan
greifen	griff	griffen	gegriffen
zîhan	zêh	zigum	-zigan
zeihen	zieh	ziehen	geziehen
snîdan	sneit	snitum	-snitan
schneiden	schnitt	schnitten	geschnitten

1. The interchange of h—g, d—t according to Verner's Law, see **416**. î > ei according to **488, 5**. N. H. G. ï in the whole pret. by levelling. ei > ê before h, r, w. î represents both the medium stage G. T. ëi and the weak stage î. ï is the zero stage.

463. II. O. H. G.   iu — io   ou, ô   ŭ   ŏ

triofan	trouf	trufum	-trofan
triefen	troff	troffen	getroffen
kiosan	kôs	kurum	-koran
kiefen, küren	koś, kor	(er)koren	erkoren
siodan	sôt	sutum	-sotan
fieden	fott	fotten	gefotten
sûfan	souf	sufum	-sofan
faufen	foff	foffen	gefoffen

1. The interchange of iu — io according to **406**; iu in the pres. sg. triufu, triufist, triufit, but pl. triofamês, etc., inf. triofan. For a period this iu, having passed > û, became eu by diphthongization. These forms are now archaic, ie prevailing through the whole present, see **124**. M. H. G. io > ie. G. T. au > ou, but > ao > ô before dentals, l, r, h and finally. The interchange of s — r, d — t according to Verner's Law, but levelled, as in ſchneiden I., in favor of t, in the whole preterit. In M. H. G. kiesen, kos, korn, gekoren for a while, but later, kiefen, koś, gekoſen; kiefen, kor, gekoren; now küren, kor, gekoren. See **132**.

2. In this series all the four grades of ablaut are represented. ou strong; io, iu medium; û the weak; ŭ zero. û > au regularly. û appeared in verbs that had the accent on the suffix. Compare **457**.

464. III. Cl. O. (M.) H. G.   ē—i   ă   ŭ   ŭ—ŏ

i, a, u before nasal + cons.; e — i, u — o before r, l + cons.

swimman	swam	swummum	-swumman
ſchwimmen	ſchwamm	ſchwammen	geſchwommen
fintan	fant	funtum	-funtan
finden	fand	fanden	gefunden
hëlfan	half	hulfum	-holfan
helfen	half	halfen	geholfen

1. This is in N. H. G. the most primitive series. finden, fand, gefunden is already the G. T. series. In the second group (see **125, 2**) the secondary

transition of u > o is a M. G. feature. It takes place before nn and mm. The older transition from u > o before l, r + cons. is already O. H. G. See 405.

2. The interchange of ë — i is regular (see 403). It appears in III., IV., V. alike.

3. The double preterit subjunctive (see 125) is due to the levelling of the indicative. The subjunctive was regularly formed with the vowel of the pl. and umlaut of the same. Now when the vowel of the sg. spread over the pl. it is natural a new subjunctive should be formed also by umlaut: fänbe, bärge. Wherever the new pret. subj. in ä did not approach too closely to, or coincide with, the present ind., it prevailed as in the first division: finbe — fänbe, binbe — bänbe, gelinge — gelänge. Where such a coincidence was the case, the old subjunctive is still in use and preferable as in the third division: berge — (bärge) bürge, fterbe — ftürbe, werbe — würbe, see 126. Befehlen and empfehlen of IV. belong here since in M. H. G. they were *bevelhen, enpfelhen*, containing l + cons. ftehlen IV < steln has followed the analogy of III., 3, on account of ftähle, the regular subj. and ftehle the pres. ind. The 2. division has ö for older ü just as it has o for u : gewünne > gewönne, but the new ones in ä are quite common except of rinnen, on account of rennen.

4. ë — i is the medium stage, a the strong; the weak and zero appear as u — o.

465. IV. Cl. O. (M.) H. G. ē—i ă ā ŏ

stëlan	stal	stâlum	-stolan
ftehlen	ftahl	ftahlen	geftohlen
koman, quëman	quam	quâmum	-koman
fommen	fam	famen	gefommen

1. Here is again interchange of ë — i. ă prevailed in the pret. u > o regularly.

2. Queman > koman according to 489, 1. It is possible that "koman" is the weak grade (see 471, 2). ftechen belonged originally to V. ; it has no liquid. Before ch and ff the vowel is short, except in the pret. of course : ftëchen, ftach, geftochen.

466. V. Cl. O. H. G. ë   ă   â   e

gëban	gab	gâbum	-gëban
geben	gab	gaben	gegeben
ëzzan	ăz, az	âzum	-ëzzan
essen	aß	aßen	(ge)gessen
bitten	bat	bâtum	-bëtan
bitten	bat	baten	gebeten
wësan	was	wârum	-wësan
(sein)	war	waren	gewesen

1. In ë the three lowest grades are represented, there was no liquid or nasal to represent the 3. and 4. grades. ă is the strong stage. The origin of â is not certain. âz is perhaps from 'eaz, 'e being the reduplicating syllable. For bitten, see **457**, 1. In the part. the interchange of s — r was levelled away after the inf. as early as O. H. G.; in the pret. with the levelling of the vowels. Was is archaic in Feuchtersleben's : So (if) bir geschenkt ein Knöslein was. Interchange of ö — i as usual and quantity of ë depends upon the following consonants.

467. VI. Cl. O. H. G. a—e   uo, ô   uo, ô   a

	faran	fuor	fuorum	-faran
	fahren	fuhr	fuhren	gefahren
	heffen	huob	huobum	-haban
M. H. G.	heben	huop	huobum	-haben
	heben	hob, hub	hoben, huben	gehoben
				(er)haben

1. This series has only two grades, strong and weak-medium, see **400**. G. T. ô > uo > û. For e in heffen, heben, see **457**, 1. For a > o, see **489**, 3.

468. VII. Cl. Its verbs do not form an ablaut-series, see **458**.

469. VIII. Cl. Its verbs have mostly o for ă, â in the pret. and the majority belong to III., IV., V. Some of these were unsettled very early, *e. g.*, M. H. G. *pflegen* IV. and V. For â > o, ô, see **489**, 3.

The Preterit-Present Verbs.

470. In these the meaning admitted of the perfect being used as a present. They are a primitive class. Compare Gr. *οἶδα, ἴδμεν,* Lat. *odi, novi.* With a few irregularities they can yet be assigned to the regular ablaut-series as has been done (see **135**). Weak preterits were formed without connecting vowel. Therefore umlaut in the subj. The stem-vowel is the same for the old pret. pl., the new preterit, the participles and the infinitive. The participles (see **453**, 1) were formed either weak or strong, generally weak. Since the infinitive is a new formation as well as some of the strong participles, and since as in gan—gunnen (gönnen) the strong participle was formed before there was an infinitive, it is hardly correct to say the infinitive is used instead of the part. in modern German: eigen, O. H. G. *gawiʒʒan,* M. H. G. *gunnen, gegunnen, (er)kunnen* are strong participles. The others, bürfen, können, mögen, follen, were formed later. No doubt, participles like heiʒʒen, lâʒen, etc. (see **453**, 2), had their influence in the non-use of ge-. Eng. has formed no infinitive.

1. The inflection of the present is that of the regular strong pret. They have even one very old feature, viz., in 2. pers. sg. t is used, the secondary ending, while in all other strong verbs the optative has entered the indicative, *e. g., nâmi,* but *tarst* (+ durst) *darft, scalt* (+ thou shalt), *maht.* st in *canst, anst* is a mystery. This t still occurs in the 16th and 17th centuries, bu follt nicht stehlen (B.).

471. 1. O. H. G. weiʒ — wiʒʒum I. corresponds exactly to Gr. *οἶδα — ἴδμεν,* in ablaut and consonants.

2. scal, scalt (2. pers. sg.), sculum, scolta IV.

It is possible that sculum is older than the long vowel of IV. ("stâlum"), for it may be the weak grade of ablaut, like -boran, sûfan.

3. O. H. G.	muoʒ	muost	muoʒum	muosa and muosta
M. H. G.	muoʒ	muost	müeʒen	muose, muoste
			subj.	müese, müeste
N. H. G.	muß,	mußt,	müſſen,	mußte, müßte.

Of the double form *muose — muoste* the former is the older and regularly developed. *muose* < *môt-ta, muosta* has the suffix added once more. The umlaut that appears in M. H. G. and later in the pres. pl. and inf. is difficult to account for.

4. foll < schol < schal < scal. Why ſ < ſch? Compare O. and M. H. G. skal — sal, but always Schulb.

5. gönnen III. and taugen II. have become weak. They come respectively < *gan-gunnen*, in which g- is prefix, and < *touc-tugen*, to be fit, + Eng. do in "it will not do," "how do you *do*" (?).

6. eigen + own < *eigan* is the strong part. of a stem of which there appears only a pl. *aigum* in O. H. G. g according to Verner's Law. It belongs to the a — â ablaut-series like heiȝȝan — hēȝ — giheiȝȝan. tar — turren + dare has disappeared. Its meaning has passed into barf — bürfen.

472. 1. Notice that Eng. *must* is really a double pret.-pres. verb. must is the *weak* preterit used again as a present. wuṣte < weste, see **489**, 1. Compare Eng. to wit, wist, wot. See Skeat.

2. O. H. G. wili wilt, wili, pl. wellemês, wellet, wellent, pret. welta, inf. wellan. o appears for e already in this period (see **489**, 1). M. H. G. 2. pers. sg. is wilt, wil. N. H. G. willſt. This is really no pret.-pres. verb, but we have according to custom put it at the end of this class. It is really a mi-verb, whose ind. was lost. Compare L. *velim*.

Mi-Verbs.

473. ſein.

1. O. H. G. bim, bis(t), ist, birum, birut, sint. Subj. sî, etc. Inf. sîn, wësan V. Imp. wis, wesat, sît; pret. was; subj. wâri. In M. H. G. the pres. pl. runs: 1. p. birn, sint, sîn; 2. p. birt, sît, sint; 3. p. sint, sîn. In N. H. G. wir ſind < the 3. person; ihr ſeid < the subjunctive; ſie ſind is primitive, comp. L. *sunt, sint*.

2. Three stems have helped to form its conjugation, viz., $\sqrt{\text{es-}}$, $\sqrt{\text{b'x-}}$, L. *fui*, Gr. φύω, and the verb *wĕsan*. It would lead us too far to enter minutely upon the part each plays, but the development is not at all difficult to trace. Only r in *birum, birn* is a mystery, but it appears also in the reduplicating verbs of VII.

474. *gân, gên, gangan*, gehn, + go.

1. O. H. G. gâm, gâs, gât, gâm, gât, gânt; gêm, gês, gêt, gêt, gênt; the subj. only gê, gês, gê, etc. Imp. ganc, gât, gêt.

2. The verb gangan is of VII. The relation of â to ê is not clear. Kluge has shown that gên is compounded of ga (prefix) + √i, L. *ire*. Then gêm < ga-im, gês < ga-is, etc. See his Dict.

475. *stân, stên, stantan,* ſtɛɧn, + *stand*.

1. It inflects just like gên. standan, stuont — gistandan according to VI. A past participle gestân occurs also.

2. Both *gangan* and *stantan* show a secondary stem and a present-formation with n (see **457**, 2), which n also entered the preterit and the other forms.

476. *tuon,* tɧun, + *do*.

1. O. H. G. tuom, tuos, tuot, tuom, tuot, tuont; subj. tuo, tuos, tuo, tuom, tuot, tuon; pret. teta, tâti, teta, tâtum, tâtut, tâtum; subj. tâti, tatîs, tati. M. H. G. subjunctive with umlaut. Past part. gitân.

2. *teta* is the pure reduplicated perf. te + ta, the stem. The pl. in â is probably ablaut of the almost lost series I.-E. ê — ô, O. H. G. â — uo. Comp. Gr. ῥήγνυμι — ἔρρωγα. N. H. G. tɧät < M. H. G. *tet* is archaic and has a curious spelling as if it were subj.

C. HISTORY OF THE LANGUAGE.

477. "German" belongs to the Germanic or Teutonic group of languages, which again is a member of the Indo-European group. To the latter belong the following: the *Aryan* (Sanskrit, etc.), the *Iranic* (old Batric and Persian), *Greek*, *Latin*, *Keltic*, *Slavic*, *Armenian*, *Germanic*, and perhaps as a separate member *Albanian*. Whether the Germanic languages are more intimately related with one member than with another is considered very doubtful by most authorities, though some think Slavic and Germanic so related.

478. Characteristics of the Germanic languages:

1. Grimm's Law with Verner's Law (see **407—416**).

2. The double verb-inflection, one by ablaut, the other by composition. The suffixes *-da*, *-ta* in the weak preterit are quite peculiar. The tenses have been reduced to two. The future and the subjunctive (see **448**) are lost.

3. A certain "law of finals" showed itself in General Teutonic in the consonants, but the "law of final vowels" belongs entirely to the individual dialects. For instance: I.-E. *$b'eroit$ became G. T. *$beroi$, Go. *berai* (e written for Go. ai). N. sg. masc. o-stems: G. T. *$dagoz$, Go. *dags*, Scand. *dagr*, Ags. *däg*, O. H. G. *tac*.

N. sg. fem.: I.-E. *$gebâ$ > G. T. *gebô*, Ags. *giefu*, but by levelling of Acc. and Nom. O. H. G. *geba*.

4. The limitation of the accent to the stem-syllable was probably General Teutonic, though Verner's Law shows that the Indo-European accent was preserved until the surd spirants in the unaccented syllable became sonant. Gr. $\pi\alpha\tau\eta\rho$ shows I.-E. accent, but G. T. *fathár* > Go. *fadhar* > *fadar* > O. H. G. *fater*.

5. The spread of the n-declension, which in German is still going on. See **428**, 2. The locative case is lost.

6. The double adjective declension. The other I.-E. dialects decline adjective and substantive alike. The Germanic has, 1, a strong declension made up of substantive and pronominal case-endings; 2, a weak declension identical with the n-declension of substantives. See **437**.

Classification of the Germanic Languages.

479. The following is in our opinion the best classification.

I. EAST GERMANIC, viz., *Gothic*, the language of the Goths, who once probably occupied European Russia. The chief literary monument is part of the Bible translation made for the Westgoths by their bishop Ulfila (A. D. 310—381). The manuscript is of the sixth century.

a. In comparison with Anglo-Saxon and O. H. G. the language is "simple," but in spite of the great age of its literary monuments, it should be made the basis for the comparative study of the group only with great caution.

II. THE NORTH GERMANIC or SCANDINAVIAN LANGUAGES. Two groups: *East-Scandinavian*, viz., *Swedish* and *Danish; West-Scandinavian*, viz., *Norwegian* and *Icelandic*. Earliest literature of East-Scandinavian of the fourteenth century consisting of laws. Runes of the 5. (?) century. Rich literature of West-Scandinavian on Iceland, colonized by Norwegians, of the 12th century and earlier. The literary language of Norway, Sweden and Denmark is East-Scandinavian. Norwegian exists only in dialects. Icelandic is the official as well as the popular language of Iceland.

III. WEST GERMANIC DIALECTS. *English* was very early isolated from the rest of the group, being the language of the early colonists in England, who were mainly Frisians, viz., Angles, Saxons and Jutes. The Frisians emigrated from their old homes on the coast of the North Sea from the river Scheldt to the river Eider in Schleswig. The Jutes lived to the north of them. This settlement continued during the 5th and 6th centuries. In the 9th the Danish conquest occurred and in the 11th the great Norman conquest, which gave to English that great influx of Romance words and removed it still more from its cognate dialects on the continent. Literature beginning with the 7th century. Runes, Beowulf, Cædmon, etc.

a. The oldest dialects are, 1, Anglian, incl. Northumbrian and Mercian; 2, Saxon, the chief is West-Saxon; 3, Kentish.

480. The Continental West-Germanic dialects are divided according to Grimm's Law. The North and East-Germanic, and English only underwent the first shifting, that is, the General Germanic (Teutonic) shifting. The continental dialects shifted again, some more, some less.

Classification of the German Dialects.

1. The LOW (or NORTH) GERMAN shifted only th > d, compare Engl. "the" — Low German "de".

2. The MIDDLE GERMAN shifted much more.

3. The SOUTH GERMAN (*Oberdeutsch*) shifted most of all.

a. "*High German*" if it is to translate "*Hochdeutsch*" is ambiguous, since many still make "hochdeutsch" include "*Oberdeutsch*" and "*Mitteldeutsch.*" *Nieder* (low), *Mittel* (middle), and *Ober* (upper, south) refer to the geography of the country only.

481. I. THE LOW GERMAN DIALECTS.

1. *Frisian.* Though the literature is only of the 15th and 16th centuries, the language shows a stage at least some 300 years older. Its territory (see **484**) has been largely encroached upon by Low Saxon and Frankish. It embraces still the northern provinces of Holland (West Frisian); Oldenburg and the Hanoverian county of Ostfriesland (East Frisian); North Sleswic with the islands off the western Sleswic-Holstein coast (North Frisian). But the modern dialects of the region described are strongly influenced by Low Saxon.

2. *Low Saxon.* Earliest literature the Heliand of the 9th century. Territory very large.

Draw a line from Düsseldorf to Cassel curving slightly southward; from Cassel to Quedlinburg to Posen and to the boundary of the empire. All that is north of this, except Frisian and Slavic in East Prussia, is Low Saxon. Two thirds of its territory is colonial, however. The Slavic conquests from the 6th to the 9th centuries had their western limit in the following line : Kiel, halfway between Brunswick and Magdeburg, Naumburg, Coburg, Linz, Klagenfurt. What is east of it is colonial for the German language, either for Low, Middle, or High German. About half of Germany and three fourths of Prussia therefore are on once Slavic territory.

a. Frisian and Low Saxon together are now often called "*Plattdeutsch,*" which even in our day can boast of a poet, Klaus Groth (Holstein dialect), and of such a capital novelist as Fritz Reuter (Mecklenburg dialect) who died a few years ago.

3. *Low Frankish.* Literature : oldest the *Lex Salica*, very badly preserved, and fragments of a translation of the Psalms. Of the 12th century the "Eineide" by Veldeke, and in the 13th a very rich literature in Holland and Brabant. Territory: Holland (Dutch crowding out Frisian), the northern half of Belgium (Flemish), and the northern part of the Prussian Rhine Province. Dutch is now the only Low German literary language. Attempts are making to revive Flemish.

482. II. MIDDLE GERMAN.

For this group draw about the following line, which will separate it from the South German dialects: From Nancy (but this is French) across the frontier with a curve north of Strassburg to Rastatt in Baden, through Heilbronn to Eichstädt, then north to Eger, from there directly eastward, but Bohemia is Slavic, of course.

Beginning in the west we have then:

1. *Middle Frankish* (according to Braune). Its territory consists chiefly of the Rhine Province, whose centre is Cologne. Very little literature.

2. *South Frankish* and *Hessian*. South and west of 1, and north of South German line. The eastern limit would be a line drawn from Cassel to Heilbronn. A rich and old literature: Isidorus of the 8th century. The great gospel harmony of Otfrid of Weissenburg. The Ludwigslied and much more.

3. *East* or *High Frankish*. East of 2. Eastern limit is the S. G. line from Eichstädt to Eger and a line from Eger to Cassel. Its old literary centre was Fulda. The larger monuments are Tatian, and Williram's paraphrase of the Song of Songs, about the year 900.

The next three are almost entirely on colonized territory, viz., 4. *Thuringian*, north of 3 and south of the Low German line; 5. *Upper Saxon*. chiefly the present kingdom of Saxony; 6. *Silesian*. 5. and 6. are east of the rest, but do not extend to the boundary of the empire, since there is a long stretch still Slavic, though with German written language. Their literatures belong to the M. H. G. period.

483. III. SOUTH GERMAN.

The southern limit towards the Romance dialects would be, roughly speaking, a line drawn from the lake of Geneva eastward to Klagenfurt in Austria and beyond, then directly north through Pressburg to Brünn. The eastern boundary is the Hungarian, the northeastern the Slavic of Bohemia and Moravia.

1. *Alemanic*, divided into: *a. Alemanic* proper, covering Alsace, the larger part of Baden and Switzerland. *b. Suabian*, covering the larger part of Würtemberg and Suabian Bavaria. The eastern limit would be a line from Eichstädt to Füssen. The literary centre was St. Gallen. Abundant literature of the 8th and 9th centuries. The "Benedictiner Regel." The Paternoster and Credo of St. Gallen. Vocabularius St. Galli. Murbach Hymns. "Christ and the Samaritan woman." The extensive works of Notker.

2. *Bavarian-Austrian*, covering the larger part of Bavaria and non-Slavic Austria. The oldest of all Old H. G. is the Glossary of Kero (740); the Glossary of Hrabanus Maurus; the so-called "Exhurtatio" and the poem Muspilli, besides smaller pieces.

484. It is impossible for us to give here a description of the phonology of these dialects. Besides Grimm's Law the long vowels and the diphthongs are the chief criteria for their classification. Their territories have not remarkably changed. Note that Frisian has been driven out of Holland by Dutch and in Germany it leads a very precarious existence upon the islands off the coast of Hanover and Oldenburg, having been crowded out by "Plattdeutsch." Low German has also encroached upon Middle German territory in northeastern Germany. The only scientific description that we have of any modern dialect is that by Winteler of the Kerenzer dialect (Swiss-Alemanic).

History of German.

485. In point of time we divide the history both of the language and of the literature into three periods, viz., Old High-German till 1100; Middle High German till 1500; New High German since then, perhaps better till about 1800, because the literary language of the 18th century is already taking on an archaic character in comparison with the language of the last fifty years. See **487, 3**.

1. The literature of the O. H. G. period is entirely dialectic and clerical. We have one poem, unfortunately only fragmentary, the *Hildebrantslied*, that goes back in matter and meter to the period before the introduction of Christianity.

2. There has been much contention, whether there was a standard written language in the M. H. G. period. Lachmann and his school maintain that there was and that it died out with the decay of literature in the 14th century. But the opinion is losing ground. The reasons against are well stated in Paul's "Gab es eine mittelhochdeutsche Schriftsprache?" The literature was mainly lyrical and epic. Its climax falls in the 12th century. The chief differences between the O. and M. H. G. periods are: 1, the spread of umlaut; 2, the weathering of unaccented and inflectional vowels to mere e.

486. With the N. H. G. period begins the written language that became not suddenly, but gradually the standard literary language of Germany. In phonology it agrees with that of the East Frankish dialect, which is the M. G. dialect that is most closely related to S. G. Its territory was in

the very centre of Germany. Both this position and this relationship are two elements that help to account for its spread.

1. From this same centre started the Reformation. Luther's share in the establishment of the written language is generally not well stated and even overrated. Fourteen translations of the Bible had been published up to 1518 in H. G. alone, made from the Vulgate. The language was based upon the "*Kanzleisprache*," *i. e.*, the "official" language in which emperor and princes published decrees and laws and in which all government business was transacted.

2. There were at first several of these "Kanzleisprachen," differing more or less. We find traces of them as early as the 14th century. Those of Austria, Bohemia and Saxony were first amalgamated. It was this language that Luther used in his Bible translation, moulded by him, of course, as every man of genius will mould his mother-tongue. Luther, by birth a Middle German, had come in contact with people of all stations, speaking Low and South German. No Bible, the circumstances being the same, translated into strict South German would and could have been accepted by North Germany. Again Luther had sprung from among the people and had a most hearty appreciation of folk-lore and all that is "volkstümlich," of proverbs, saws and songs. This made him a translator for the people. The proverbs of Solomon and the psalms are without doubt the most taking portions of his translation.

487. The spirit of the Reformation was one roused from the lethargy of the preceding centuries and ready for something new. Luther's New Testament appeared in 1522, the whole Bible in 1534. Besides the Bible the catechism, hymns, sermons and the numerous polemical pamphlets were written and read in the new language. With the Reformation began also the public school ("*volksschule*") and the first grammars and "*formelbücher*" appeared, written often by the lawyers, who, of course, favored the "Kanzleisprache." But last and foremost of all the *invention of printing*, some fifty years before the Reformation, made a common language possible.

1. The clerks would write and spell as they spoke, *i.e.*, according to their own dialect. Printing brought about a certain uniformity in the orthography. It spread the language to the most different parts of the country. About the year 1600, books were already cheap in comparison to the costly manuscripts. In 1523 a Bible was printed at Bâle, which had as appendix a sort of dictionary explaining the terms unfamiliar to the Swiss.

2. The struggle of the new language was hardest in Switzerland. Both Catholic and Calvinist objected to a Lutheran language. In North Germany it was favored by the fact that the whole North became Protestant en masse. Yet hymns were printed there in Low German for a long time. In the 17th century High German preachers came to the North. But through printing the writings of one man exercise a great influence upon the speech of his readers. Printing in fact has introduced into the development of language a certain stiff, artificial element that the written, and especially the unwritten, dialects do not have. The printed language has more of a fixed, stereotyped character than dialect. But on the other hand we must remember that the letters of the alphabet are not the language. They are only contrivances that represent speech very imperfectly, contrivances invented several thousand years ago, which we try to apply now to that most subtle institution—language, that has been changing and developing ever since.

3. The language of the 19th century differs not a little from the language of the 16th. The differences in forms and functions have been treated to some extent in Part I. The 17th century is a dark gloomy page in the history of Germany and almost a blank in its literature. In the first half of the eighteenth we see the beginnings of the classical period. Until then Latin was the language of the learned, and in the 17th and 18th centuries there was a large number of foreign words both in the written and spoken languages that were never assimilated, but driven out again by a school of literary men that started a revival of the love of old German.

The following are the more important and far-reaching sound-changes in the transition from M. H. G. to N. H. G.

488. A. Vowels.

1. The further spread of umlaut by analogy (levelling).

Ex.: as a sign of the plural, see **48**; in derivatives as in: gläubig, väterlich, brüberlich, Brüberchen, Töchterlein ; in long-stemmed weak verbs as in: hören, hörte, gehört. < hœren, hôrte, gehôrit — gehôrter (see **455**, 2).

2. The lengthening of short accented stem-vowels in the open syllable, and of a and e before r, rt, rd. To this process the largest number of the present long vowels is due.

Ex.: Vogel, Hof — Hofes; gebären (< bërn), gewähren, leben, weben, sehen; Hahn — Hahnes; Thür, mir, wir, er, der (demonstrative), bar (but barfuß); Herb, werbe, wert, zart, Bart. Ur in the sense of "great" as in : Urgroßvater, otherwise short or long : Urlaub, Ursprung, but Urteil is always short. -art and -arz are unsettled still. Compare Harz, Warze.

a. The short vowel is retained before more than one consonant and in a closed syllable, except before r (rt, rd). Ex.: hoffen, voll, rennen, Hecke, wollen, fast, etc., but mir, wir, as above.

b. This point of N. H. G. phonology is by no means all cleared up. Paul is the only one that has thrown any light upon it. See P. and B. Beiträge, VII. p. 101-. When through inflectional endings the stem-vowel is now in an open, now in a closed syllable, the standard pronunciation demands levelling in favor of the long vowel of the open syllable. For instance, das Glas, Glases, Glase, Glas, Gläser, all with long stem-vowels. In N. G., however, Glas, Gras, Tag, Lob, (N. and A. sg.), are always short according to the law of short vowel in a closed syllable. N. and S. G. agree in the levelling between the sg. and pl. pret. of ablaut-series. IV. and V. in favor of the long vowel of the plural, *e. g.*, gab — gaben, sah — sahen.

c. This principle may be stated in another way : N. H. G. makes a M. H. G. accented syllable containing a short vowel long, either by lengthening the vowel or by lengthening, *i.e.*, "doubling," the consonant, particularly if that consonant be t or m, and if a single consonant is followed by er, el, en.

Ex.: Stätte, Sitte, kommen, Sommer, Wetter; in the pret. and past part. of the I. and II. ablaut-series: schnitt — geschnitten, sott — gesotten. This change began in the M. H. G. period, starting from L. G. it spread over M. and over S. G. as late as the 16th century.

3. Long accented vowels are shortened before more than one consonant.

a. This process is not far-reaching, but includes also the long vowels sub 4, that have sprung from diphthongs. It started with the M. G. dialects.

Ex.: echt L. G., see **493,** 4, < ēhaft ; bachte, brachte (see **454,** 3). Acht < ähte ; Herr, herrschen; horchen ; fing, hing, ging < fienc, hienc, gienc ; vier in the compounds vierzehn, -zig, viertel, etc., Mutter < muoter.

4. The simplification of the diphthongs ie > ī, still spelt ie; uo > ū; üe > ü long.

Examples very numerous: Blut < bluot; Mut < muot; Güte < güete; süß < sueze ; führen < vüeren ; blühen < blüejen ; lieb; tief; always in the preterit of Class VII. and in the present of Class II., viz., rief, fiel, bieten, fieben, but see 3.

a. This also is a M. G. feature that was fixed upon the "Schriftsprache," showing itself as early as the 13th century. The S. G. dialects do not know it yet (see *Hart's Goethe's Prose*, p. 40, bottom).

5. The diphthongization of the long vowels î, û, iu (whether < G. T. ëu or umlaut of û, value ü long) > ei, au, eu (äu), respectively.

Ex.: brei < *drî*, Weib < *wîp;* ei in the present of the I. Class; laut < *lût;* Haut < *hût;* Sau < *sû;* Häuſer < *hiusir* < *hûs;* Mäuſe < *miuse* < *mûs;* Treue < *triuwe;* euch < *iuch;* Leuchte < *liuhte;* er beut < *biutet*. The Eng. cognates, *e. g.*, the verbs of the I. Class write — wrote, shine — shone; loud, hide (< Ags. *hỹd*), sow, house, mouse — mice show that a similar diphthongization of long i and u has taken place. o in wrote, shone < Ags. *â* < *ai* corresponds to the old diphthong, M. H. G. ei as in schein, reiz, etc. Modern German ei therefore goes back to î in Heirat < hîrat; to ei in ſcheiden < *scheiden;* ai always goes back to ei, ai as in Mai, Kaiſer. au < û in Haus < *hûs;* but < ou in laufen < *loufen;* äu (eu) < iu < û by umlaut, in Häuſer < *hiusir* < *hûs;* but eu < iu (ëu) in Leute < *liute,* heulen < *hiulen;* and another eu < öu umlaut of ou (< au) in Freube < vröude (< *frauwida*), beugen < *bôugen* < *bougen* (< *baugjan*, ablauts. II.).

a. This is a S.G. feature, especially Bavarian, in which dialect it started about 1200. It spread over East Frankish and Upper Saxon in the 14th and 15th centuries and latest over Suabian. All the other dialects whether L., M. or S. G. do not know this change. "House" is still "*hûs*" in Bremen and in Bâle. The new diphthongs are still kept apart from the old ones in dialect, but the standard spoken language recognizes no difference.

489. The following changes do not affect very many words. They are mostly S. G. features and though quite old, the standard and the common spoken language do not agree upon all words. The former favors e and i, the latter ö and ü.

1. e, ë > ö in ergötzen (Classics still ergetzen), Hölle, Löffel, Löwe, zwölf (standard zwelf), ſchwören and a few others. Rarely e, ë > o or u after w: wollen < *wellen;* wohl < *wëla;* kommen < *quëman*. This is as old as O. H. G., however.

2. i > ü in Hülfe — Hilfe; ſprützen — ſpritzen; würbig; müßte; Sprichwort — Sprüchwort. i < ü in wirken + work and Kiſſen, but also still Küſſen + cushion.

3. â > ō, Ohnmacht, folk-etymology for Ohmacht < âmaht; wo < wâ; ohne < âne; Monat < mânôt; and Dohle < tâhele. Compare Wahn and Argwohn.

4. Both S. and M. G. is u > o, ü > ö, regularly before modern mm, nn and n + any other cons, but see 125, 1.

Ex.: Past part. and pret. subj. of Class III., 2.; Wonne < wunne; fromm < vrum; sonder < sunder; umsonst < umbesus; Sohn < sun. Compare Bronn (poetic), but Brunnen (why u is not clear); Mönch < münich

5. Before palatal g, ch e > i. By this -ig and -ich have become the only suffixes instead of O. and M. H. G. ec, ac, ech, ach, see 509.

Ex.: Fittich < fettach; Kranich < kranech, O. H. G. chranuh; fertig < vertec; Honig < honec.

490. B. Consonants.

1. The spread of sch for s before l, m, n, and w.

Ex.: Schlaf < slâf, + sleep; Schleim < slîm + slime; Schmeer < smer; schmeißen < smizen, + smite; Schnee < snê, + snow; Schnepfe < snepfe, + snipe; Schweiß < sweiz + sweat; schwimmen < swimmen, + swim. The Eng. cognates still show old s.

a. This is a S. G. feature, starting in the 15th century and extending over the M. G. and the colonized eastern L. G. dialects (Paul). In the 16th sch was substituted for s after r in a few words and later still in initial sp, st.

All these sch's are recognized by the standard pronunciation, but the S. and M. G. dialects know almost no limit in the use of sch. M. G. dialects substitute it even for ch, viz., misch for mich. See 391, 1.

b. S > sch also after r, *e.g.*, Hirsch < hirz + hart, Kirsche < kirse + cherry, herrschen < hersen. Since schp, scht are not recognized in the spelling of initial sp, st, Eng. st, sp, and G. st, sp correspond: Stadt, Statt, Stätte < stat, + stead; Spieß < spiz + spit.

c. This sch for s is not a phonetic change as is generally taken for granted. In the transition from O. > M. H. G. sc had become sch first before the front vowels, then before all the vowels and then before r. sc > sch before a palatal vowel is a phonetic transition called *palatalization* due to the following vowel and attended by loosening of the contact, and is known in Eng. and the Romance dialects as well. See Ellis' Early Eng. Pronunciation, p. 1154–. The transition-sound was no doubt the present Westphalian sjh, a double sound. At first only sc > sch in the above order, and not s > sch. The links were sk + pal. vowel > skj > sjh > sh.

d. Before vowels and r G. ſch corresponds to Eng. sh, *e. g.*, Schiff + ship; Scham + shame; ſchön + sheen; Schrot + shread, shroud; Schrein + shrine. When Eng. sc, sk corresponds to G. ſch, ſt, there is something wrong, due generally to foreign origin or influence, in one or the other. Compare Schule + school; Schaum + scum (Norse); Landſchaft + landscape (D.); Skandal + scandal (Fr.).

2. z (< z < t, see **414**, 1) > s, written ſ, s, ſſ, ß.

This is a S. G. feature, beginning with final z in the 13th century, spreading over M. G. L. G. still like Eng.; notice the cognates. Ex.: was < *waz* + what; aus < *ûz* + out; Waſſer < *wazzer* + water; Binſe < *binz*, + bentgrass. Examples very numerous.

3. ch = kh (< old ch, cch and medial h) has become jh after front-vowels and after r, l, and n. See **375**.

This transition is not shared by S. G. The Eng. cognates show k or silent gh for I.-E. k: nicht < *niht* (= nikht) + not, nought; Wicht < *wiht* + wight.

a. ch before s in the same syllable > ks, the same in Eng. as early as Anglo-Saxon.

Ex.: Fuchs < *fuhs* + fox; Buchs < *buhs-boum*, + box; ſechs < *sehs* + six; Achſe < *ahse*, + axle; Axt < *acchus* + axe (t is excrescent).

b. Medial h at the end of a syllable is silent now, ſehen, ſieh—ſt, but ch still in Geſicht; ſleucht — ſließen; hoch — höher; rauch still in Rauchwerk, furs, — rauh; ſchmähen — Schmach.

4. mb > mm, Eng. still mb: Lamm < *lamp — lambes* + lamb; Kummer < *kumber*, + to cumber.

5. m — n, Eng. still m. Beſen < *besem* + besom; Faden < *fadem* + fathom.

6. w < bh, the labio-labial bh has become labio-dental v in the standard pronunciation; it has disappeared after ou, iu (now au, eu); in a few cases aw > au; after l and r it became b, beginning in the 14th century. Eng. cognates show a vowel + some silent letter.

Ex.: neu < *niuwe*, + new; ſchauen < *schouwen* + show; grau < *grâ — grâwes*, + gray; blau < *blâ — blâwes* + blue, due to Fr. *bleu*. Gerben <

garwen, + yare; Schwalbe < *swalwe,* + swallow; Narbe, a scar < *narwe,* + narrow, lit. "contracted surface;" gelb < *gel — gelwes,* + yellow. Some cases show doublets due to levelling in favor of the uninflected form: fahl — falb < *val — valwes* + fallow; Sper-ling + sparrow — Sperber < *sparwaere* + sparrow-hawk.

491. 1. Other transitions are not general enough to deserve special mention. It is important to distinguish real phonetic transitions and differences between the two periods in the history of the language due to levelling and analogy. The latter have been frequently treated in the comments upon the various inflections. See the levelling in the declension of fem. nouns, 433; between sg. and pl. pret., 460.

2. The disappearance of sounds by contraction ought also to be considered, *e.g.,* of j for which a merely orthographical h has been substituted (see 363, 2) or of e in 3. pers. sg. pres. of strong verbs whose stem ends in t as schilt < *schiltet.* Examples of new sounds are e between î, uo, û and r as in Trauer < *trûre,* Geier < *gir*; of t(b) after final n and s as in jemand < *ieman,* eigentlich < *eigenliche,* Obst < *obez,* Art < *ackes.*

The German word-stock.

492. The following sources have furnished words and forms older than any occurring in the literatures:

1. *Runes, e.g.,* the famous inscription on the golden horn, which reads *ek hlewagastiz holtingaz horna tawidô* = I, Hlewagastiz (= lee-host ?) of Holstein, made (the) horn.

2. The words borrowed by Fins and Laplanders before the race-migrations, when the latter were in contact with the Scandinavians, the former with the Goths in the South, *e. g.,* "*kunungas,*" "king."

3. Words and proper names occurring in Latin and Greek authors, *e.g.,* the name "*Teutones*" would seem to go back to a period before Grimm's Law (see Kluge's dictionary); *glēsum* = amber, Ags. *glǣre,* + glass in all Germanic dialects; "*alces*" in Caesar = meaning "elk," O. H. G. *elch,* Ags. *eolch;* modern Eng. "elk" is reimported from Norse.

4. German has a much larger Germanic word-stock than Middle and modern English, because through the Norman conquest the Romance was engrafted upon old English and so many old English (Germanic) words died out. But compare the couplets calf — veal; deer — venison; sow, swine — pork; hunt — chase.

a. German, never having had to accept such a large foreign element, has treated foreign words very stepmotherly. English welcomes every stranger, at least our large dictionaries do, which contain as much as ten per centum of words that are no more English than they are German. A German, seeing such a dictionary with colored flags, steam-engines, animals, and what not, takes it for an encyclopedia. In German a foreign word has to undergo a long period of probation before it is accepted in the language and in the dictionary. Foreign words are collected mostly in the "*Fremdwörterbuch,*" *i. e.*, Dictionary of foreign words.

493. The first larger influx of foreign words into German came through contact with Roman civilization, *e.g.*, Straße, Pfahl, Käse, Küche, Kette, Münze, Keller, Fenster; the second through Christianization: Kirche, fastei'en, Kreuz, Engel, Priester, Pfaffe, predigen, and a great many others. These and other foreign words of the O. H. G. period were quite thoroughly Germanized. They took part in the shifting then going on and their accent was put upon the stem-syllable.

1. In later O. H. G. and in M. H. G. the chief source, from which foreign words came, were the crusades and the institution of chivalry; in later M. H. G. and early N. H. G., the revival of learning and the thirty years war, *e.g.*, Pala'st, Flinte, Tourni'er, Thron; in fact all older nouns in –ie'r and verbs in –ie'ren. Schiller's Wallenstein has many foreign words, *e.g.*, Armbrust; malebei'en; Panier, Pulver, Pult.

2. In the last 200 years Germans have taken up, as all nations have done, a large number of words from Greek, Latin and the Romance languages, words which the progress of civilization calls for. But beginning with the M. H. G. period German has not been able to change the foreign accent, *e.g.*, the verbs in –ie'ren, even when this ending is added to German words as hofieren, stolzieren, hausieren; Melobei' or –bie', Bastei', Bataillo'n, Balla'de, Ballo'n, Paste'te; the many nouns in –ie'. Compare English which changed in its middle period the accent of nearly all Norman-French words, *e.g.*, reason, season, melancholy. Later te'legraph, but German Telegra'ph.

a. There has sprung up since 1870 a tendency in high official circles to banish foreign words, but it is not likely to meet with much success. The military system uses hundreds of them still.

The Postmaster-General of the German empire objected to Telepho'n, because he could not decide upon the gender, and so „Fernsprecher" was made the official word. A letter to be called for must have on it „Postlagernd," not "poste restante" as formerly.

3. One more large source of borrowed words has to be mentioned which began as early as the 15th century, viz., Low German and Dutch (also English). All words that contain "p," for instance, must be either foreign (Pappel, Panther) or non-High-German, because there can be no p

230 HISTORY OF THE LANGUAGE. [494-

in H. G. (see **409**, 2). If the words do not come directly from Low German, they have been influenced by it and taken L. G. form.

Ex.: puffen, puſten, Pocke, Poſt, glatt, Plunder, Wappen. Words in gg, bb: Ebbe, Egge, Rogge, Flagge, Bagger, flügge.

4. Notice the many shipping terms: Flagge, Bord, Boot, Spriet, Leck, Wrack, Steven (v = w). Words in –cht for ft, e. g., ſacht, H. G. ſanft ; Schacht, H. G. Schaft; Schlucht for Schluft. The ending –chen is Low and M. German; –lein, South German. Fett for feiſt is L. G.

494. A small group of words was introduced twice, but at different periods, e. g., Pfalz (O. H. G.), Pala'ſt (M. H. G.)< *palatium*, but see Kluge's Dict. Zarge (O. H. G.), Tartſche (M. H. G.)+ Eng. target < V. L. *targia* (if this is not originally German and belongs to the next group). Melobei was really borrowed, Melodie is a later doublet after the many nouns in –ie. Fehlen + to fail, fallieren, to fail (in business) < F. *faillir*.

1. Compare Eng. frail and fragile ; quite — quiet ; exploit — explicite. Many originally German words, adopted by another language, are borrowed again in a foreign form : Wagen — Waggon + Eng. wain — wagon; Spion < ſpähen — German Späher; Bivouak < biwacht, Beiwacht; die Garbe, die Garderobe + guard, + wardrobe < warta, wartên — die Warte, der Wart + ward ; Stuck < Ital. *stucco* and this from G. Stück, O. H. G. *stucchi*.

2. Besides isolated and obscure German words a large number of foreign words are exposed to " folk-etymology," because they are not understood. These have been collected by *Andresen* in his "deutsche Volksetymologie." (See also Palmer's Folk-etymology). Hederich < L. *hederacea*, ground-ivy. Abenteuer (archaic spelling even Abendteuer), < M. H. G. *aventiure* < Rom. *aventure*.

3. Vielfraß, wolverine < Norse *fjallfress*=moutain-bear, as if it were a great eater ; Sündflut as if from Sünde and Flut, "the flood that came on account of sin," but it is from Sin — meaning "ever," "universal" as in Singrün, evergreen. Leumund as if it meant „Lügenmund" or „Leutemund," but < *hliumunt, hlium*, in which –*munt* is suffix, "hliu" < the same root as laut, loud + Gr. κλύω. See Maulwurf, **400**. Compare Eng. causeway < O. Fr. *chaucié* < L. *calciatam (viam);* country-dance < counter-dance, Fr. *contredanse*.

Hundreds of examples will be found in *Andresen* and *Palmer's* collections. The words in 494, 494, 1, have never been collected.

D. WORDFORMATION.

This chapter does not contain a complete German etymology. It aims merely at giving a brief, practical survey of the derivation of German words for students who know a little English and Latin. A knowledge of the older forms of some Germanic dialects cannot be expected from the student. For practical reasons only, the following subdivisions of the chapter are made.

495. We may distinguish four ways of forming and deriving words :

1. By ablaut without derivative suffix, see **496**, 1, 3.

2. By suffixing some element which was once perhaps an independent word.

3. By prefixing such element.

4. By composition of independent words.

496. The pronouns have roots peculiar to themselves and many adverbs are formed from the pronominal roots. Nouns (that is, substantives and adjectives) and verbs had probably the same roots, though it is customary to speak, in contrast to pronominal roots, only of verbal roots, from which nouns were formed later. We count as primitive all strong verbs and those nouns which have no apparent derivative suffix. From a $\sqrt{b\text{'xnd'}}$, in which x represents the vowel that is to appear according to the various ablaut-grades, both nouns and verbs were formed. In G. T this root would be *bænd*. It furnished *binden, band, gebunden*, das Band, der Bund, der Band, das Bund (for Bündel). Both nouns and verbs had their stem-suffixes, of course. These made them into words. Roots are to the etymologist what x, y, z are to the mathematician. They are something unreal and abstracted from the actual phenomena of languages. No one ever spoke in roots. In a word we distinguish the stem and the inflections. The stem minus the stem-suffix is the root. Of every root, noun and strong verb are not now extant, for instance, lieb, lob, but weak verbs by means of the suffix *jo—je*, were formed from the same root, I. E. $\sqrt{\text{lxub'}}$, G. T. $\sqrt{\text{lxub}}$, *e. g.*, (g)lauben, loben. x appears as *e—i* in lieb, Liebe < *lloba*, **lëub–* ; as a in (g)lauben, (er)lauben ; it disappears in lob, loben, the weakest or zero stage of ablaut. See 394.

1. Formed by ablaut alone, we consider strong verbs, nouns of the same roots and nouns from roots that may have no strong verb extant.

2. The stem-suffix may have been *o, jo, i, u, â, jâ* (fem.), etc. We are inclined to look upon the *jo*-stems as derivatives because they suffered umlaut, *e. g.*, Bürge, Geschütz. There is some reason for this because *jo, jâ, wo, wâ* are not primary stem-suffixes, but for our purposes there is no harm in confounding the primary and secondary suffixes.

3. Examples of the derivation of verbs and of substantives by ablaut alone.

I. ablaut-series: beißen, der Biß; reich, Neid. II.: schließen, das Schloß, der Schluß; triefen, der Tropf, die Traufe; das Loch, die Lücke. III.: schwimmen, der Schwamm, der Sumpf (?), die Schwemme; der Schlund, der Ring. IV.: bergen, der Berg, die Burg, der Bürge; schallen, schellen, der Schall. V.: geben, die Gabe (rather *geba*), gebe or gäbe (adj.). VI.: graben, das Grab, die Grube; ich muß, der Hahn, das Huhn.

To the G. T. â — ô series: thun, gethan, die That. See **476, 2**.

Derivation of Substantives

497. Derived by a late ablaut, also directly from a weak verb.

Ex.: Der Schund < schinden, = refuse; der Befehl < befehlen; der Handel < handeln; das Opfer < opfern; der Ärger < ärgern. Feminines in -e : die Winde + windlass < winden; die Fähre + ferry < *vern* < *faran*.

498. DERIVATION BY VOWEL-SUFFIXES:

1. e < î formed from adjectives, all feminine, e.g., Größe < groß; Höhe < hoch; Schöne < schön; Bälbe < balb (now only adverb); Güte < gut — *guotî* < *guot*. î produced umlaut.

2. e < i < *jo* Hirte < Herde.

3. ei < *ie* < Romance *ie, ia*, always with chief-stress upon it, at first only in foreign words, then spreading very rapidly in N. H. G.

It is attached most frequently to nouns and verbs ending in -el, -er, -en, so that the ending was felt to be -erei, e. g., Zauberei', Arzenei', Heuchelei, Jägerei. It denotes also a place of business: Druckerei, Bäckerei. It implies a slur, Juristerei, Kinderei.

4. ie only in foreign words. It is the later form of *ia, ie*, and the nouns were formed after *i* had become *ei*.

Ex.: Astronomie', Geʻographie', Theʻologie', etc. -ie has crowded out the older -ei, or they appear together with a difference of meaning. Melodei — Melodie, both mean "melody"; Partei = party, faction — Partie = game, match, company, excursion; Phantasei + fancy, — Phantasie + phantasy.

Derivation by Consonant Suffixes.

499. Liquids and their combinations.

l, generally el < O. H. G. *ul* (*al*), *il*. *il* produces umlaut. It is weak or unaccented. + Eng. le, + L. *-ul-us*. Majority of substantives are masculine.

Ex.: 1. l < *ul, al* : ber Stahl, bas Beil, Maul, bie Seele.

2. el (< *ul, al*): ber Wandel, Mangel, Nabel, Schnabel, Sattel, Nebel; bie Fackel, Gurgel, Wurzel, Fasel, Schaufel.

3. el < *il*. Most of them denote means and instruments like the feminines < *ul, al*.

Ex.: ber Beutel, Büttel (+ beadle), Löffel, Kegel + cudgel (?), Schlüssel, Ärmel, Zügel. These are very numerous.

4. el, + Eng. -le, sign of diminutives, < *ila, ili*. Neuter gender. A S. German favorite from old times, now le, l, see Goethe's famous Schweizerlieb.

Ex.: Bündel, Büchel, Rindel. Proper names: Friedel, Zacherl.

5. el in foreign words : bie Orgel < V. L. *organa;* Teufel < διάβολος ; bas Siegel < L. *sigillum;* ber Esel < L. *asinus;* ber Kümmel < L. *cuminum*.

500. l combined with other suffixes.

1. with s in fel (weak accent), fal (secondary accent) < *sal, is* + *al*, generally producing umlaut. Gender prevailingly neuter, but also a few fem. and very few masc.

Ex. of –fel: ber Wechsel, bas Rätsel, Überbleibsel, Häcksel.

Ex. of –fal: bas Schicksal, bas Labsal, bas Scheusal, bie Saumsal, bie Trübsal. Some have double gender.

2. -lein < *il* + *in*, secondary accent, very numerous, produces umlaut, noun always neuter. See **493**, 4. Now only in solemn diction and poetry.

Ex.: Kindlein, Lämmlein, Mägdlein, Söhnlein, etc. –elchen is rare : Büchelchen, F. 3779.

3. -ling < *ul, il* + *ing*, + Eng. -ling, weak accent, often with a depreciative force. Its second element was at first only added to nouns in -l, then –*ling* became the suffix.

Ex.: Frembling, Findling + foundling; Jüngling + youngling; Wißling, Däumling; Mietling, hireling; Säugling + suckling; Schößling, Zwilling.

a. –lingen (en is Dative pl.) forms many names of places, Hamelingen, Gravelingen.

4. ler < l + er is a quite modern suffix. For er, see **507**, 1. It started with nouns that came from verbs in –eln or nouns in –el.

Ex.: Künstler < künsteln; Schmeichler < schmeicheln; but Häusler < Haus; Tischler < Tisch. Implies a slur, *e.g.*, Rechtler < Recht. Comp. Eng. hostler < hostel.

501. em, m, am, en < em. Of these m, en are unaccented and form no syllable; –em has weak accent, am has secondary. < O. H. G. *m, um, am,* + Eng. m, om. For em > en, see **490**, 5.

Ex.: der Baum, + beam; Traum, + dream; Zaum + team; Schwarm + swarm; der Atem (Odem, the biblical form), Brodem; der Boden, der Busen, der Faden, der Besen; der Eidam, der Brosam, in which am has been restored in place of older –em. das Wittum belongs here, but tum has crept in for older "*widem,*" as shown in the verb widmen.

m is a suffix in -tum < √d'â, see **515**, 5.

502. en, n, < O. H. G. *an, in* + Eng. en, n, on, in.

Ex.: der Dorn, + thorn; Hafen, + haven; das Korn, + corn; das Zeichen, + token, der Degen, + thane. Regen, + rain; Wagen, + wain, wagon. Often lost in G., compare der Rabe, + raven; die Wolke, + welkin; Küche, + kitchen; Kette, + chain. en of inf. is lost in English. In G. en has crept into the Nominative and changed the inflection, see **435**, 2. In some cases, *e. g.*, Korn, Zorn + Ags. *torn,* n is the participial suffix –*no,* see **453**, 1.

1. The –en of the weak declension really belongs here, since it forms nouns denoting the agent, for instance, from verbs, bieten, der Bote, des Boten. But we feel it now as an inflectional ending. See **432**.

–ner is not a real suffix. Compare ler, **500**, 4. In Redner n belongs to the stem < *redina, redinôn.* In others n is added by analogy: Glöckner < Glocke; Kirchner < Kirche. Pförtner < *portenarius;* Söldner < *soldenarius,* Solb.

2. en < *in,* a now rare diminutive except in composition in –lein, –chen. Ex.: das Füllen (Folen) + filly, foal; Schwein, + swine < G. T. sû; das Küken for Küchlein + chicken < from the same stem as "cock."

503. nis, niss-, forms neuter and fem. nouns, generally abstract ones denoting existence and condition, sometimes place, + Eng. -ness.

Generally from noun and verb stems, but also from adjectives: die Wildnis < wild, Finsternis < finster. It represents now older *-niss-* and *-nuss-*, Go. *-nassus*, and generally produces umlaut. *-niss, -nuss* are compounded of *n* + *issi, issa* and *n* + *ussi*.

Ex.: das Begräbnis, Gefängnis, Vermächtnis; die Erlaubnis, Kenntnis, Betrübnis.

504. in, inn- forms fem. nouns, denoting females, from masc. < M. H. G. *in, în, inne* < O. H. G. *innâ, in,* + L. *ina* in *regina*.

Ex.: Gott, Göttin; Fuchs, Füchsin + vixen; Hannoveraner, Hannoveranerin. Very numerous. Not extant in Eng. except in vixen, Ags. *fyxen*. To be translated by "female," "she-," "lady-."

1. -in has become (e)n and is attached to surnames having the force of the more elegant Frau+surname without suffix, *e. g.*, die Müllern instead of Frau Müller, die Spannhafen instead of Frau Spannhafe.

505. -nd, end, (and, ant), really participial suffix (see **453**), + Eng. -end.

Ex.: der Freund+friend; Feind+fiend; Weigand, champion; Heiland,+ *Heliand*, Saviour; Valant, but the cognate ant is foreign and has chiefstress, *e. g.*, Musika'nt, Ministra'nt. No participial ending in der Abend, der Elefa'nt.

506. -ng, -ing, -ung, < older *ing, ung,* + Eng. *ing, ng,* weak accent.

Ex.: der Häring + herring; der Schilling + shilling; das Messing, brass, Ags. *mäsling*.

1. n is lost in König, + king; der Pfennig (< pfenninc) + penny.

2. ung forms numerous fem. nouns from verbs. Like Eng. ing they denote mostly action. The suffix is gaining ground. But Eng. nouns in ing are frequently best translated into German by an infinitive. Ex.: die Erfahrung, Bildung, Zeitung + tidings, Anfertigung + manufacture; Verdampfung, evaporation, etc. Riding + das Reiten; building, das Bauen.

3. ing and ung + er and en form many patronymics and names of places: Thüringen, Meiningen, Twistringen, Mohrungen, Hornung, Nibelungen, Merovinger, Zähringer, Lothringer. For er (see **507**, 2). –en is originally dative pl.

507. –er is of various origins.

1. It denotes the agent, < ere < ære < ári, + Eng. er, or, ary, + Lat. -arius.

It is attached to both nouns and verbs and is preceded by umlaut as a rule.

Ex.: Zauberer, Kämmerer, Schüler, Ritter, Schneider, Reiter, Tänzer. Very numerous.

a. Borrowed words not denoting the agent: Zentner, < L. *centenarius* + centenary, a hundred weight; Trichter < late L. *tractarius* (?), funnel.

2. –er denotes origin and home, attached to names of places and countries. Used as an adj. it does not vary.

It was originally a Genitive pl., but of the same origin with the preceding: Thüringer, Berliner, Wiener, Schweizer Käse.

3. –er without any particular force, and words with it are looked upon as primitive < *r*, *ur* (*ar*), *ir*, + Eng. r, er, re, + I.-E. -ro-.

Ex.: der Acker, Hammer, Sommer, Donner; die Ader, Feder, Leber, Schulter; das Futter, Leder, Wetter, Silber, Wasser.

4. –ier in foreign words, *e. g.*, der Cavalier, Barbier, is identical with er sub 1, but is of Romance form, < L. -*arius*.

For –er as a sign of pl., see **431**.

508. Suffix -ter, der.

1. < *tar*, forms names of relationship + Eng. ter, ther, < I.-E. -t-r. It is unaccented. Ex. der Vater, Bruder, die Mutter, Schwester, Tochter.

2. < *tara*, *tra*, *tira* + Eng. ter, der. Denotes Instrument. Not numerous, unaccented. + L. trum, G. τρον, τρια.

Ex.: Klafter, cord; die Leiter + ladder; das Gelächter + laughter; Laster < lahstar, lastar < lahan, to blame. In the last word -ster is secondary suffix. It appears also in ber Hamster, badger; bie Elster, magpie, which are of doubtful origin. Das Fenster < Lat. *fenestra*.

ber (ter) as comparative suffix, see **530**.

g, f, ich, ch.

g and f, Eng. g and k, it is difficult to separate from the rest of the stem. Nouns ending in them must be considered primitive.

509. -ich, sometimes spelt -ig, forms a few masc. nouns. It represents M. H. G. -*ech* and -*ich* < *uh*, *ah* and *ih* < *uk*, *ak*, *ik* + Eng. -ock, -k. See **489**, 5.

Ex.: ber Bottich (+ buttock), ber Habich(t) + hawk; Kranich + crane; Fittich, Teppich; das Reisich, Reisig, brushwood; ber Rettig (-ich) + radish < L. *radic-em*; Molch < M. H. G. *mol*, + mole, but means lizard. ber Essig (ig for ich), (+Eng. acid) < L. *acetum*, through *atecum* (?). Rabi'schen is of later importation. Der Käfig, Käfich, does not belong here, but < *kevje* (> kefge) < L. *cavea*.

1. -icht = ich+t, for which see **512**, 2, forms a number of neuter nouns denoting fullness, plenty, frequency. Late suffix of 15th century. Das Dickicht, + Eng. thicket (but -et is Romance); das Kehricht, sweepings; das Röhricht, reeds. Der Habicht (see above).

510. -chen forms the common neuter diminutives and has crowded out -lein in the spoken language. See **493**, 4.

Compounded of ich, see above, and n < *in*, *în*, see **502**, 2. Always produces umlaut. Has weak accent, + Eng. kin. Ex.: das Männchen, + manikin; Lämmchen, + lambkin; Würmchen, Mädchen, Veilchen.

d, t, z, s, sch.

511. 1. -d- + Eng. -th, < G. T. -'th-, < I. E. -'t-.

Ex.: Der Tob, + death; Mund, + mouth; das (die) Mahd, + aftermath; die Bude, + booth; die Bürde, burthen. Not numerous in German. Where Engl. forms abstract nouns in -th, from adjectives generally, G. forms the same in -e: Wärme, warmth; Treue, truth; Tiefe, depth.

2. -de < -*ida*, -*idâ*, unaccented; -od, -öde, -at, < -*ôta*, -*ôti*, -*uoti*, secondary accent, form neuter and fem. nouns.

238   WORDFORMATION—SUBSTANTIVES.   [512-

Ex.: Die Frembe, Freube, Gebärbe, Zierbe, Begierbe; das Getreibe < *getregede* < *gitragida*, what is born on the fields, crops, grain. Das Gelübbe, Gebäube, Gemälbe.

a. Das Kleinob, jewel; die Einöbe due to folk-etymology after Öbe, desert, then wilderness = solitude, lone-ness. Der Monat + month < *mânot;* die Heimat, + home, native land; der Zierat, ornamentation. But Heirat, marriage < *hî* < *hîw* + *rât*. Die Armut belongs here, its ut < *uoti*, O. H. G *armuoti*. Wermut, + Eng. wormwood, has this suffix, but its root is doubtful. For -at in foreign words, see **163**, 1.

512. -t forms numerous fem. nouns and a few masculines, + Eng. t when preceded by surd spirants, see **412**, 2, < original t.

Ex.: die Kraft + craft; die Macht + might; die Trift + drift; die Flucht + flight; der Frost + frost; der Geist + ghost; der Gast + guest; die Mast, + mast (of animals); Gift, + gift; Gruft + crypt.

1. This -t forms other nouns, but it then corresponds to Eng. d, rarely th; mostly < I.-E. -t- before the accent, with which the suffix of the weak past participle is identical (see **453**, 1): die Furt + ford; der Wart + ward; Saat, + seed; That, + deed; die Flut, + flood; die Blüte, bloth; die Stätte, Stabt, + stead; der Mut, + mood; die Wut, + wood (mad).

2. Notice the excrescent t, which the many nouns ending in a spirant + t encouraged, *e. g.*, der Saft + *sap;* die Art + axe; bas Obst < *obes;* in -schaft + -ship, -scape (?). After -ch, see **509**, 1. In foreign words, *e. g.*, der Palaſt, + palace; Papſt, + pope; Moraſt, + morass.

3. -ſt in Kunſt < können, Brunſt < brennen, Gunſt < gönnen is not clear. To call it "euphonic" does not explain. Arzt < O. H. G. arzât < late L. *archiater*, but phonetically not quite clear. Die Magb, Maib + maid < M. H. G. *maget*, *meit* has the suffix b-t, < G. T. th, derived from a masc. *magus*, "boy."

513.   s, ſ- is rare, + Eng. s, < *is-*, *es-*.

Ex.: Flachs + flax; Fuchs, + fox; Luchs + lynx (?); die Achse, + axle; die Hülſe, pod; der Krebs < *crebeze* + crayfish, due to popular etymology, as if "cray-fish"; die Bremſe, brake; die Horniſſe + hornet; die Gans + goose.

514.   ſch- is of various origins, but generally inseparable.

< isk- comes the frequent adjective suffix -ſch + Eng. ish, sh, *e.g.*, der Menſch < O. H. G. *mennisko*, an adjective; der Froſch + frog (see Kluge);

Welſch + welsh. In Hirſch + hart, ſch < s, z. In Kirſche + cherry < *ceresia* ſch < s. See 525, 4.

a. -ſche is added to surnames to denote Mrs., but is quite colloquial, bie Reinharbtſche for Frau Reinharbt, bie Lanbwehrſche for Frau Lanbwehr.

NOUNS DERIVED BY NOMINAL SUFFIXES, WHICH CAN BE TRACED TO INDEPENDENT WORDS STILL EXTANT IN THE OLDER GERMANIC DIALECTS.

For earlier periods of the language this derivation would therefore properly come under the head of wordcomposition.

515. The suffixes are: -heit, -keit, -rich, -ſchaft, -tum. They all form abstract fem. nouns, chiefly from substantives and adjectives, except those in -rich and -tum, and have secondary accent.

1. -heit + Eng. -hood, -head. < O. H. G. *heit*, Ags. *hâd*, meaning character, nature, rank. In a few nouns it means " a body of," and has collective force. Very frequent: bie Freiheit; Gottheit + godhead; Kinbheit + childhood; Menſchheit, mankind; Chriſtenheit, Christendom.

2. -keit composed of -heit and the adjective suffix -ec or ic, to which it was attached in M. H. G. First ec-heit, ic-heit (> echeit, icheit) > ekeit, ikeit > keit, keit. -keit is attached only to adj. in -bar, -er, -ig, -lich and -ſam. Very numerous.

Ex.: bie Dankbarkeit, Eitelkeit, Heiterkeit, Ewigkeit, Freundlichkeit, Einſamkeit. The derivation from adjectives in -ig is so common, that -igkeit was looked upon as the suffix and adjectives in -loſ and haft only form nouns in this way: bie Ehrloſigkeit, Straſloſigkeit, Lügenhaftigkeit, Krankhaftigkeit. In -ig-keit ig has been restored in many nouns, after it had helped form keit, *e. g.*, Süßigkeit < *süezekeit*; Ewigkeit < *êwecheit*. See 489, 5.

a. Mark the distinction sometimes made between nouns in -igkeit, -keit and -heit from the same adj. Die Kleinigkeit = trifle, bie Kleinheit = littleness; bie Reuigkeit = a piece of news; bie Reuheit = newness; bie Reinlichkeit, cleanliness; bie Reinheit, purity, clearness.

3. -rich + Eng. -ric, -ry < O. H. G. *rîch* + L. *rēx, rēgis*, forms a number of proper names. Denotes " powerful," " commanding." Ex.: Wüterich, blood-thirsty person, tyrant; Friebrich + Frederic; Heinrich + Henry; Wegerich, a plantain, lit. " ruler of the way."

a. -rich appears in the names for certain male birds. The oldest is Enterich + drake < *endrake*. This is certainly not identical with the above -*rich*; it may have been shaped after it on account of *antreche*, O. H. G. *antrahho*, which cannot go back to -*rich*-.

Gänferich + gander, Täuberich, cock-pigeon, are N. H. G. forms after Enterich, < Ganfer, Tauber < Gans, Taube. Fähnrich, ensign, < older G. *venre, faneri*, has -ich by analogy. Fähnbrich may be due to D. *vendric* (Wiegand) < Fahne, flag. By folk-etymology der Heberich, from L. *hederacea*.

-reich comes under composition.

4. -schaft + Eng. -ship, shape < O. H. G. *scaft*, meaning character, being, creature ; itself a derivative by t < G. T. √skap, from which to shape, schaffen. Forms mostly fem. abstract nouns and a few collectives.

Ex.: die Freundschaft + friendship ; Grafschaft, county ; Landschaft + Ags. *landscipe*, + Eng. landscape (*scape* due to D. and Norse influence) ; die Gesandschaft, embassy ; Priesterschaft, priesthood ; Verwandschaft, relationship ; Gesellschaft, company.

5. -tum + Eng. -dom < O. H. G. *tuom, M.* and *N. ;* Ags. *dôm M.* + Eng. doom = judgment, law, dominion, power. It forms neuter nouns from nouns, but neuters and masculines from adjectives. The nouns are abstract, but many denote domain and place.

Ex.: das Herzogtum + dukedom ; Königtum, + kingdom ; Heidentum, + heathendom ; Heiligtum, sanctuary ; der Irrtum, error, Reichtum + riches.

a. Mark a difference in meaning between nouns derived by means of heit, schaft, -tum from the same stem: die Eigenheit, stubbornness, peculiarity ; die Eigenschaft, quality; das Eigentum, property ; die Christenheit = Christendom; das Christentum = Christianity ; die Bürgerschaft, all the citizens; das Bürgertum, citizenship ; die Weisheit + wisdom ; das Weistum, statute.

DERIVATION OF NOUNS BY MEANS OF INSEPARABLE PREFIXES.

516. The composition of nouns by means of independent parts of speech, such as prepositions and adverbs, will not be treated here except the composition by means of those prefixes, such as bei, Ur, etc., which retained the strong form under the noun-accent, but wore down to a weaker form in the verb accentuation and thus became "inseparable." For the principle of accent, see **421**. Whenever the prefix of a noun is unaccented and has weak form, the noun is not old, but it is late and derived from the verb, except in one case, viz., the prefix *ge-, g-*.

This is really composition, but we treat of the subject here for convenience.

1. A b e r- has the force, 1) of ober- über, from Dutch = excessive. It is rare. Der Aberglaube, superstition, die Aberacht; "*proscriptio superior ;*" Aberwitz, conceit, presumption, imbecility, is M. H. G. *aberwitze, abewitze*, in which aber = abe, ab. O. H. G. *âwizzi*.

2) The force of again toward, against. It is depreciative: der Aberwandel, forfeit, back-sliding; Abername, nick-name; die Abersaat, second-sowing; der Aberkaiser=Gegenkaiser, rival emperor. In this sense = after and both probably < *af*, *ab* + *-ar* and *-tar* respectively.

2. After-+Eng. after: not the first, not genuine, second, retro-, false: Das Afterblatt, stipule (in botany); die Aftermuse, false muse; die Afterkritik, false, second-hand criticism; Afterwelt = Nachwelt, posterity; Aftermiete, subletting.

3. Ant- + Eng. an-, a-, am- in answer, acknowledge, am-bassador, + L. *ante-*, Gr. "ἀντί." Force: against, opposite, in return, removal.

Ex.: die Antwort,+answer; das Antlitz, face; der Antlaß, absolution; das Amt, office, court < O. H. G. *ambaht*, Go. *andbahti*, *and+bahto*, a servant, Eng. ambassador, embassy < Romance forms < Low L. *ambasta* < O. H. G. *ambaht*.

Unaccented it became ent (see **541**). Ant- has in some really old nouns given place to the ent- of verbs, *e.g.*, der Empfa'ng for older *ántvanc*.

4. Bei-, b- rare as old prefix, but common in modern compounds, consisting of preposition + noun, + Eng. by; in verbs be,+ Eng. by-, be- < *bî*,*be;* see Kluge. Perhaps related to Gr. ἀμφί, L. *ambi*.

Ex.: das Beispiel, example < *bispel;* die Beichte, confession < *bihte* < *bigihte* < *bi* + *jehen;* der Beischlaf, cohabitation; der Beisaß, + settler, unnaturalized comer; Beifuß, wormwood. The weak unaccented form be- is very common in late derivatives from verbs. In M. H. G. appear the doublets *bîtraht* — Betra'cht; *bigraft* — begráft; *biziht* — beziht.

5. Für- occurs only in one old noun, Fürsprech, mediator, attorney. In the 18th century für and vor were used indiscriminately and a great many compounds now have Vor- only. Unaccented Ver- sub 11.

6. Erz-, +Eng. arch-, means chief, original, great-< V. L. *arci-* < Gr. ἀρχί-.

Ex.: der Erzbischof+archbishop; Erzlügner, a great liar; Erznarr, arrant fool; Erzspieler, professional gambler.

7. Ge-, g-, the traces of its accent are difficult to find even in the oldest stages of the Germanic dialects, though there are some in Ags. (found by Kluge) and in Go. There are none left in German. It is always unaccented. < O. H. G. *ga, gi*. Its connection with L. *cum, con*, is generally asserted, but is difficult to prove. Has intensive, generally collective

force. Nouns of the form Ge—e, < *ga—jo* are almost all neuter and very numerous.

Ex.: ber Glaube + belief; ber Geselle; bas Glieb, bie Gebulb, bie Gnabe; bie Gefahr; bas Gebäube; Getreibe; Geschmeibe; Gewerbe; Gebirge; Gehölze. G- appears before l, r, n.

8. Mi ß- + Eng. mis-. Force: negative, false, failure. For its origin see 453, 1. In M. H. G. still an adjective, now inseparable, always accented prefix. Only one compound with its derivatives retains *misse-*, viz., Missethat + misdeed.

Ex: Very numerous: ber Mißbrauch, bie Mißernte, ber Mißklang, ber Mißmut, ber Mißgriff.

9. U r + Eng. or- only in "ordeal" and "ort," < older *us, ur*. Force: origin, great age, great-. Weak, unaccented form = er- in verbs and their derivatives. u always long except in Urteil. bas Urteil + ordeal; ber Ursprung, bie Urkunbe; ber Urlaub, ber Urgroßvater; bie Ursache; ber Urquell.

10. Un + Eng. un-, of like force, privative, + L. *in-*, Gr. *av-, a-*.

Ex.: bie Unart, ber Unbank, bie Ungunst, ber Unwille. In ungefähr un- stands for ohn-, < *ân gevœre*, but in Ohnmacht, ohn stands for Ohmacht < *âmaht*, containing the obsolete û privative.

11. Ver-, fr- always in this weak form and unaccented like Ge-. Traces of early accent upon it very rare, none now, + Eng. for-. Rare in older nouns, very common in later nouns derived from verbs, see 516, < O. H. G. *far, fir*.

Ex.: ber Verlust, bie Vernunft, Frevel + Ags. *fræfele ;* Fraß — fressen; Fracht + fraught, freight (see Kluge's Dict.).

12. Zer occurs only in nouns derived from verbs. See therefore 546. Ex.: bie Zerstreuung, Zerstörung.

a. For brittel, viertel, see 532, 2. Jungfer, maiden < *juncfrouwe*, daughter of a noble family. Junker, young nobleman + younker < *junc-herr*. Jungfrau, virgin, is a modern compound. In such words as Abler, Wimper, Nachbar, Schuster, and many others, the second elements are no longer felt; they are suffixes to all intents and purposes. See the dictionary for their derivation.

Composition of Nouns.

517. The second element is always a noun, in a few cases an adjective, but used as a noun. This noun always determines the gender and inflection of the compound. The first element always has the primary accent, the second the secondary accent. See 421; 424, 2. The first element may

be any other independent part of speech, a noun, adjective, verb, adverb, or preposition.

Noun + Noun.

518. The relation of the component parts is syntactical; the first element may stand in apposition to the second or it stands in case-relation to it.

In apposition: das Himmelreich, die Sommerzeit; many names of plants and trees, der Apfelbaum, die Heidelbeere.
In the G. relation: der Augapfel, der Königssohn, die Kuhmilch.
In the D. relation: der Schlaftrunk, das Tintenfaß, die Tanzstunde.
In the A. relation, including the objective Genitive: der Wegweiser, Herzog, Vatermörder.
In the Ablative relation of origin, material, cause: die Freudenthräne, der Westwind, die Stahlfeder.
In the Instr. relation, denoting instrument, means, connection: der Fußtritt, der Hufschlag, die Leimrute.
In the Locative relation, denoting place, association, even time: die Dachstube, das Bahnfleisch, Tagewerk, der Fußsoldat.

a. The earliest method of combining the nouns was that of attaching the second noun to the stem with its stem-suffix, that is, to the "theme." The vowels of the stem-suffixes became e in M. H. G. or were lost. A later way was that of joining the second noun to the Genitive sg. or pl. of the first noun. This way originated in the relation of noun and its dependent genitive. The sign of the G. sg. s, es was then added also to feminine nouns, which of course were not entitled to it.

1. Stem + noun. *Composition proper.*

a. With stem-suffix: der Tagedieb, der Hageborn, das Tagelied, die Badereise, der Bräutigam, die Nachtigall, die Gänseblume. See the examples with en sub 2, since en was originally stem-suffix. See **502,** 1.

b. Without stem-suffix. Very numerous: der Wilddieb, das Jagdhorn, das Weltmeer, das Gartenhaus, das Handwerk.

2. G. sg. or plural + noun. Secondary composition. Case-endings: (e)s, er, en. en and er were also encouraged by the other cases in which they stood, *e. g.*, N. and A. pl. and in the other cases of the sg. of masc. weak nouns. Indeed (e)s and (e)n were gradually looked upon as connecting elements between two nouns and crowded out many compounds of proper composition.

Ex.: das Sonntagskleid, das Wirtshaus, der Landesherr; der Häuserverkauf, die Kinderlehre, die Männerwürde; der Ehrenort, das Freudenfest, die Blumenlese, der Palmenbaum, Feigenbaum, der Eichenwald, der Hahnensporn.

3. ѕ between fem. noun + noun. This began as early as the 12th century. -ѕ is a favorite after nouns in t, particularly after the suffixes -t, -heit (keit), -schaft and -ung; and the foreign nouns in -ion and -tät.

Ex.: der Geburtstag; die Freiheitsliebe, Heimatsliebe; der Freundschaftsbote; das Hoffnungsglück (G.); der Weihnachtsmann, der Hochzeitstag; das Missionsblatt, die Universitätshalle, der Liebesbrief.

ADJECTIVE + NOUN.

519. The adjective appears without stem-suffix, but see **522**. The relation of adjective and noun is that of an attribute or of apposition.

Ex.: die Gutthat, die Weihnacht, Hochzeit; der Langbein, der Mitt(e)woch; die Mittfasten; die Jungfrau, die Gelbsucht, die Kurzweil; der Großmaul; der Bösewicht.

1. In many compounds the adjective is used as noun and is then inflected, generally in the weak G. pl.: die Blinden-, die Taubstummenanstalt, das Krankenhaus.

2. There is a small group of compounds in which the union of the elements is not intimate and the adjective is inflected, *e.g.*, die La`ngewe´ile, La`ngwei´le; Ho`herprie´ster, der Ho`heprie´ster; Geheimerrat, ein Geheimerrat (but also uninflected der, ein Geheimrat). Mi´tternacht is a secondary compound for the older *mitnaht* + midnight. For their accent, see **422**, 1.

520. 1. NUMERAL + NOUN.

Ex.: der Dreifuß, das Viereck, die Einbeere, der Zweikampf, der Zwieback, das Zwielicht + twilight, das Siebengestirn, die Erstgeburt.

2. ADVERB + NOUN.

Many of them are formed from compound verbs.

Ex.: die Wohlthat, die Herkunft, der Hingang, die Wollust, die Außenwelt, die Nichtanerkennung (= non-), die Abart, der Abgott, der Eingang.

3. PREPOSITION + NOUN.

The majority are formed from compound verbs. But not a small number are made directly of preposition + noun.

Ex.: die Anzahl, der Amboß, die Ansprache, der Aufgang, der Beiname, der Beitrag, die Durchfahrt, der Durchbruch, der Fürwitz or Vorwitz, die Gegengabe, die Hinterlist, der Inbegriff, der Mitmensch, der Nachkomme, das Nebengebäude, die Niederlage, das Obdach, der Oberkellner, die Oberhand, die Übermacht, der Umkreis, der Untersatz, die Unterwelt, die Vorwelt, der Widerwille, der Zuname, das Zwischenspiel.

4. Verb + Noun.

Very numerous. A few with the connecting vowel -e, which represents the suffix-vowel of weak verbs, older ô, ê.

Ex.: der Spürhund, der Singvogel, die Schreibfeder, das Lesebuch, der Lebemann, die Reiselust, der Leitstern. (See below.)

a. Osthoff (see his *Verbum in der Nominal Composition*) has proved that these compounds are not primitive in the I. E. languages, but that they are originally compounded of noun + noun, in which the first noun was felt to be, on account of its stem-suffix, a verb-stem, and this led to the formation of many compounds, in the Germanic, Greek, Slavic and Romance languages, by analogy. Thus Leitstern, + lode-star, does not come from leiten and Stern, though meaning „leitender Stern," but < M. H. G. *leitestern*, in which *leite* + lode is a noun = guidance, direction.

521. Compounds of more than two words. The accent deserves here special attention, see **421**; **424**, 3.

1. Three words, but only two parts: der Hei′rats̀a`ntrag, der Mi′tgliedsschei`n, die Da′mpf-schi`ffahrt, steam-navigation, but Da′mpfschif-fa`hrt, steamboat-ride; der Fe′ldzugs-pla`n, der Ha′ndwerks-bu`rsche, die Le′bensversicherungs-gese`llschaft.

2. Four words and more. These are not common, much rarer than is generally supposed. Oberpolizei′gerichtspräsibe`nt, Staa′tsschuldentilgungs-kommissio`nsbureau, office of the commission for the liquidation of state-debts; Stei′nkohlenbe`rgwerk, Generalfeldmarschall.

a. To get a quick survey of such a word, ⸗ ought to be inserted once at least in the first and second words and the last words might begin with a capital as in English.

b. The capacity of German for forming such compounds is generally exaggerated and that of English underrated. The custom of writing these long nouns as one word is very bad. We might just as well write them so in Eng., *e. g.*, *Fireinsurancecompany's-office*, and we should have the same compound. Official language, certain schools of philosophy and the newspaper are the main sources of such monstrosities. Moreover, the composition exists only for the eye. When we speak we do not divide according to words; we speak in breath-groups, see Sweet's Hdbk., p. 86-.

3. Similar to the compounds in **520**, 4, are such whole phrases as Ste′ll-dichei`n, rendez-vous; Thu′nichtgu`t, ne'erdowell; Tau′geni`chts, goodfornothing.

Derivation of Adjectives.

The comparison of adjectives, and the past participles come really under this head, but see **438** and **453**, 1.

522. Adjectives Formed by Ablaut.

These may be called primitive. See **496**. They fit into the ablaut-series just as substantives and verbs do. All have lost stem-suffixes except the *jo*-stems, still recognizable by the umlaut and generally by the final e.

Ex.: reif, steif, dick ; lieb, tief ; blind, hohl, schön, kühn, dumm. With -e : enge, zähe, müde, böse, träge.

Adjectives Derived by Suffix.

523. 1. -el, see **499**, roots generally obscure: eitel + idle; evil, übel; edel (+ Athel-, Ethel); dunkel.

2. -em, see **501**, rare. Ex.: warm + warm.

3. er < -*ar*, -*r*, rare, same as *ar* of nouns in **507**, 3. Ex.: wacker + watchful, brave ; bitter + bitter ; heiter, lauter, schwanger ; sicher < L. *securus*.

524. -en, -n, see **502**. Very frequent and of various sources, + Eng. en, n.

1. en < O. H. G. *an*, in a few words of doubtful origin.

Ex.: eben + even; klein, small + clean ; grün + green ; schön + sheen ; fern + far ; rein < √hri. It is late in albern < *alwoere*, lüstern, schüchtern, from adj. in -er, < -*ni*, -*njo*.

2. < *in, in*. Denoting material, "made of."

Ex.: golden for older gülden + golden ; wollen + woollen ; seiden, silken ; silbern + silver ; ledern + leather.

3. ern < n + er, due to the influence of er in such nouns as Silber, Leber and of er in the plural. Compare -ler, ner in nouns, see **500**, 4.

Ex.: steinern, of stone ; flächsern + flaxen ; thönern, of clay ; hölzern, wooden ; nüchtern (?), sober.

4. en < *an, in* < G. T. -*nó* in all strong past participles. Some fifty or sixty of these stand now "isolated," that is, separated from the verb still extant or the verb is obsolete. See **453**, 1.

Ex.: eigen + own VII. Cl., gediegen I. Cl. (old doublet of gedeihen), pure ; bescheiden VII. Cl. (old doublet of bescheiben I. Cl.), modest ; gelegen, convenient (verb obsolete); verlegen, embarrassed (v. obsolete); erhaben VI. Cl. (doublet of erhoben), lofty ; beritten I. Cl., mounted ; offen (?), open ; trocken +dry, < √$drūk$.

525. 1. -ig, + Eng. -y, represents now both older -ec, -ac and -ic. See **489**, 5.

The umlaut could occur only in the adjective which had -ic. It is a living suffix and new adjectives are still being formed with it from any part of speech except verbs.

Ex.: traurig, blutig, häufig, gültig, spaltig, gewaltig; late formations: heutig, hiesig, obig, bortig. For selig, see **528**, 2, *a*. Manch + many, < *manec*. Its ch for g is L. G. (?).

2. ig + lich = iglich, once very common and attached where there was no -ec, -ic. It is now rather adverbial, see **554**, 2, and rare in adjectives, *e.g.*, ewiglich, gnädiglich.

3. -icht < -eht, -oht, -ohti, is more common in adjectives than in substantives. See **509**.

a. -ig and -icht furnish doublets, sometimes with a distinction in force. icht with i must be due to -ig with i, as it is very late.

Ex.: steinicht + stony, thöricht, foolish, nebelicht, foggy, stachelicht, prickly. -icht implies only a slight resemblance: ölicht, slightly oily — ölig, oily.

4. -isch, -sch + Eng. ish < older *-isk-*, implies a bad sense in contrast with -lich, as in Eng. ish and like. See **514**.

Ex.: kindisch + childish, kindlich + childlike; bäu(e)risch + boorish, bäuerlich, rustic; denotes origin: preußisch + Prussian; bairisch + Bavarian. Corresponds to *-icus* in adjectives derived from L.: komisch, logisch, philologisch. See **514**.

5. -end in the present participle, see **453**; **505**.

6. -(e)t, the past participle, see **453**, 1.

But notice those that we no longer feel as participles: tot, laut, kalt, etc. Later formations: traut, zart.

526. Adjectives derived by the nominal suffixes -b a r, -h a f t, -l i ch and -s a m, which were once independent nouns (see **515**). For accent, see **424**, 1, *b*.

1. -b a r < M. H. G. *bære* < O. H. G. *bâri*, < the root of the verb gebären + Eng. bear. Should have become -ber, which really occurs in living dialects, but the levelling was in favor of the full form. Compare L. *-fer-*, Gr. φορός.

a. In meaning it corresponds to Eng. -able, -ible, -ful. It means: bearing, producing, capable of, and is attached only to nouns and verbs.

The only adjective to which it is attached is offenba'r, with the accent of the verbs offenba'ren, geba'hren.

Ex. very numerous: trennbar, separable; hörbar, audible; dankbar, grateful; ehrbar, honorable. Ur'bar < M. H. G. urbor, has the weak ablaut like the L. and Gr. forms given above.

2. -haft, a participle either from the root of haben + have, or L. *capere, captus* (Kluge).

a. It denotes "possessing," "similar to-," "approaching-." In meaning it corresponds frequently to Eng. -y (+ G. ig), -ful, -ly. It is attached to nouns, adjectives and verbs and is sometimes increased by -ig.

Ex. numerous: fehlerhaft + faulty; schabhaft, harmful; lebhaft + lively; spaßhaft, funny; wa'hrhaft, wahrha'ftig, truthful, true: schülerhaft + scholarlike, boyish; meisterhaft + masterly; leibhaftig, bodily, incarnate.

3. -lich < M. H. G. *lich* < O. H. G. *lich*, + Ags. *-lic* + Eng. ly, later again "like."

Originally an adjective, occuring only in compounds, but derived from the subst. Ags. *lic*, O. H. G. *lih* = body, form.

a. In both languages its earliest meaning is "like" or "similar to," then "appropriate," "adapted," finally it became very frequent and often without particular force.

b. The umlaut generally precedes -lich, but is not produced by it. It started originally in stems with i suffix and spread by analogy. This is the most frequent suffix and attached to substantives, adjectives, and verbs.

Ex. göttlich, godlike; ritterlich, chivalrous; traulich, familiar, devoted; fröhlich, merry + frolic; sterblich, mortal; beharrlich, persistent; begreiflich, comprehensible; erbaulich, edifying; glaublich, credible. For -iglich see 552, 2.

c. er in leserlich, fürchterlich, etc., is due to analogy. These lengthened forms have crowded out the proper old forms leslich, fürchtlich. In certain adjectives the ending has been mistaken for -ig, and the spelling has followed this notion. abelig, billig, unzählig have the suffix -lich, but cannot now be corrected. allmählich is the official spelling, though frequently allmählig is met with < allgemach, gentle, manageable.

4. -sam < older -*sam*, originally a pronoun (+ Eng. same), + Ags. *-sum*, + Eng. -some, + Gr. ὁμός, + L. *sim-ilis*.

It denotes originally identity, similarity, but has now no particular force, unless it be capacity, inclination.

Examples not so numerous, the suffix has lost ground.

Ex.: einfam + Eng. lonesome ; langfam, slow ; gemeinfam, common ; arbeitfam, industrious ; heilfam + wholesome ; graufam, cruel, + gruesome.

-voll, + ful, -los + less, come under composition, though in Eng. they might come under this head.

For -fach, -faltig, -fältig, see the numerals 531, 1.

Derivation of Adjectives by Prefixes.

527. The prefixes in substantives have the same force and accent when attached to adjectives, but only aber, erz-, ge-, un-, ur- form immediate compounds. Adjectives with the other prefixes are derived from substantives, verbs, etc. Ex.: a'berklug, e'rzfaul, getreu', u'nnütz, u'ralt, etc.

Composition of Adjectives.

528. The second element is always an adjective or participle. The first element may be any part of speech and stands in the same relation to the second as it does in a compound noun. Accent and form of the first element are also the same. Some old past participles without ge- are preserved in composition, e. g., trunken, backen, in wonnetrunken, intoxicated with delight ; hausbacken + homebaked, homely.

1. ADJECTIVE + ADJECTIVE.

Ex.: tollkühn, dummdreist ; dunkelblau ; hochmütig < Hochmut (see 2, b) ; blauäugig, rotbäckig.

2. SUBSTANTIVE + ADJECTIVE.

Ex.: tobkrank, *freibeweiß, *goldgelb, liebeskrank, wonnetrunken, *mausetot, *federleicht, liebevoll, gedankenreich, hoffnungslos, freudeleer, totenbleich, vorschriftsmäßig, amtswidrig, *blutjung, hulbreich, *felsenfest. In those with * the noun expresses a comparison and has often intensive force. Notice -reich, los, voll have almost become suffixes.

a. Adjectives in -felig are of double origin.

1. The real adjective felig, in the old sense of *kindly*, as in leutfelig, gottfelig.

2. felig < fal (see 500, 1) + ig : mühfelig, trübfelig, saumfelig < Mühfal, Trübfal, etc. It does not belong here at all.

b. A large class of adj. do not come under this head, e. g., hoffärtig, ehrgeizig ; many in -füchtig, as monbfüchtig, schwindfüchtig. They are derivatives of the compound nouns Hoffart (< hôchvart, ch and f assimilated), Monbfucht, Ehrgeiz.

3. Pronoun + Adjective.
Ex.: ſelbſtrebenb, ſelbſtgenügſam, ſelbſtlos, etc., only with ſelbſt-.

4. Verb + Adjective.
Ex.: wißbegierig, benkfaul; many with -wert and -würbig : bankenswert, liebenswürbig.

5. Numeral + Adjective.
Ex.: einäugig, zweieckig, zweiſchneibig, erſtgeboren, ei'ngeboren, only child.

6. Adverb + Adjective.
Ex.: hochgeprieſen, alt-, friſch-, neu-backen, wohlfeil, wohlgeboren.

7. Preposition + Adjectives.
Ex.: anheiſchig, einheimiſch, eingeboren, native, + inborn ; abholb, überflug, vo'rnehm, u'nterthan, vo'rlaut. fürlie'b does not belong here, für = as, „als", als lieb annehmen, anſehen. Compare zufrie'ben, at peace, content.

Derivation of Numerals.

529. Zwei is probably an old dual. Zween < zwêne has the distributive suffix ni, + Eng. twain, twin, + L. *bini*. With zwo fem., < older zwâ, zwo, compare M. Eng. twa, two, also feminine. The numerals, as far as 10 incl., can be easily compared with the cognates of other languages according to Grimm's and Verner's Laws. elf and zwelf contain perhaps a stem *lik*, ten, that appears in Slavic. They come from older *einlif, zuelif*. eilf is archaic. As to zwölf for zwelf, common in N. H. G., see **489**, 1.

1. The ending -zig, < *zug* + Eng. -ty, differs originally from zehn in accent, zehn < I.-E. *dĕkm, L. *decem*. See Verner's Law.

2. Hunbert, + hundred, is compounded of *hund* + *rath-;* the latter from the same stem as Rede, Go. *rathjan*, to count. *hund* alone means 100, compare L. *centum*, Gr. ἑκατόν according to Verner's Law. See further Kluge's Dict. Tauſend < older *tûsunt*, a fem. noun. It is not an I.-E. numeral like all the others. Root doubtful.

530. The suffixes for the ordinals are really the superlative suffixes -to, -sto. Only German and Icelandic use -sto. zweit- only sprang up in the 15th century. Instead of it was used, as in all Germanic dialects, anber + other, a comparative in -ter. Comp. L. *alter*. anber has not quite died out. Comp. zum erſten, zum anbern und zum britten Male, still used at auction. Ach Gott! wie doch mein erſter war, finb' ich nicht leicht auf bieſer Welt ben anbern, F. 2992–3. anberthalb=one and a half ; ſelbanber=lit. himself the second, *i.e.*, two of them, of us. britt- has the short vowel of the stem "*thriu,*" still in the neuter O. and M. H. G. *driu.* tt < dd < dj as in Go. *thridja,* Ags. *thridda,* + L. *ter-ti-us.* ber Hundertſte was in O. H. G. *zehanzogôsto, zehanzug* being the other word for 100; really "ten tens." For erſt, letzt, Fürſt, see **439**, 2.

Numeral Derivatives and Compounds.

531. From cardinals.

1. MULTIPLICATIVES:

Suffixes -fach, -fältig, *e. g.,* breifach, vierfach, vielfach. In O. H. G. -fach is only noun. -fach expresses a certain number of parts, divisions, = „Fächer." -falt,-faltig, fältig + -fold, expresses also variety besides quantity. It comes from the same stem as the verb falten + fold, and is quite old. -falt is archaic now. doppelt + double, is < French. t is "excrescent"; in compounds t does not appear: Doppelabler, Doppelgänger.

zwie- in zwiefach, zwiefältig, comes from older *zwi,* + Gr. *di-*, L. *bi-*.

2. ITERATIVES:

-mal, rare -ſtund, ei'nmal, zwei'mal, brei'mal, manchmal; einma'l, "once upon a time." -mal is the noun Mahl + meal, O. H. G. *mâl.* Notice „abermal(s)", once more, adverb „aber" = "again;" ein(mal) für allemal. „eins" + "once," is seemingly the neuter N. or Acc., but it is a Gen. < older "eines,": form which einſt with excrescent t, + once, "onst." „eins" is now rare and so is „ſtund." Uhland has „allſtu'nd" = all the time. Stund and halb are isolated now; mal is plural, being neuter (see **176**).

zwier, now rare, comes from older *zwiro, zwirôr* (r < ?)

532. From the ordinals:

1. Adverbs like erſtens, zweitens, etc., see **555**, 2.

2. FRACTIONS by -tel < Teil, Drittel, Viertel, Fünftel, one t is lost in writing, Zwanzigſtel. They are neuter, of course. „Dritteil", the full form is now archaic. „Zweitel" has not come up on account of the late origin of „zweite," „anderthalb" is used, see **530**. Notice der Zweitletzte, next to the last; der Drittletzte, third from the end.

See also syntax, **226-229**.

533. VARIATIVES are formed by -lei < M. H. G. *leie,* fem. meaning "kind," probably < Romance. The numeral preceding it is inflected like an adjective, mancherlei (G.), vielerlei; viererlei, four kinds, etc. But the compound is invariable.

Derivation and Composition of Verbs.

534. As primitive are regarded all strong verbs except preifen, schreiben, which are foreign, and a large number of weak verbs, which are either very old, such as haben, fragen, or they are those whose origin is obscure or whose stem no longer appears in other primitive parts of speech, e. g., holen, hoffen. All other weak verbs are derivatives except the originally strong that have become weak, e. g., walten, mahlen, beben (see Kl.). They are derived from other parts of speech by means of e, the connecting vowel representing older i, ô, ê, which unites the verbal inflections with the root or with those words from which the verb is derived. (This e may drop out.) The connecting vowel l or j (< jo) produced umlaut, which, since the j class was by far the largest of the three classes of weak verbs, was soon used through analogy as a common means of deriving verbs after umlaut had ceased to work. Besides the vowel e, there occur certain secondary suffixes, some of which have a peculiar force.

535. 1. Derivation with umlaut due, *a*, either to an old i or, *b*, to analogy, or, *c*, to the fact that there was an umlaut already in the noun-stem.

a. A large number from strong verbs of the II., III., IV., V., VI. ablaut-series with the strong ablaut, *i.e.*, with the vowel of the pret. sing., and from the reduplicating verbs with the vowel of the infinitive, *e.g.*, flößen < fließen, floß, geflossen < *flôzzan* < **flôtjan*, to cause to float, II.; senken < sinken, sank, gesunken, < *senken* < **sankjan*, to cause to sink, III.; zähmen + tame < *zemen* <**zamjan*, this < *zëmen*, IV., now a weak verb ziemen; legen < liegen, lag, gelegen, < **lagjan* + lay, V.; führen < fahren, fuhr, gefahren < *vüeren* < *fuorjan*, VI., to cause to go, to lead ; fällen < fallen, fiel, gefallen, < M. H. G. *fellen* < **falljan*, to cause to fall, + fell ; fürchten < Furcht ; lähmen < lahm; töten < tot ; trösten < **trôstjan* < *trost* + trust.

b. pflügen < Pflug, bräunen < braun; zähnen < Zahn; bäffen < baff! ; räumen < Raum ; öffnen < offen.

c. grünen < grün ; trüben < trübe.

Rem. 1. If the strong verb is intransitive then the derivative is transitive or causative ; if transitive, then the derivative is intensive or iterative, *e. g.*, schwemmen < schwimmen, to cause to swim; setzen < sitzen, to cause to sit ; beten, to pray, < bitten (?), to ask for. The same principle prevails in English: to fall — to fell, to lie — to lay, to drink — to drench.

Rem. 2. j (or i) has caused certain changes in the final consonants of the stems because these were doubled before the "lautverschiebung," and when doubled they shifted differently from the single consonants. For instance in wecken — wachen, becken — Dach, ď < kk < kj, but ch < k; in ätzen — essen, beizen — beißen, schnitzen — schneiden, hetzen — Haß, ž, tz < tt, tj. but ß < t. Similarly schöpfen (for schepfen) — schaffen ; henken — hangen, compare Eng. henchman ; biegen — bücken ; schmiegen — schmücken ; geschehen — schicken. Compare also Eng. drink — drench ; stink — stench.

2. Derivation by e without umlaut.

These are late or if old, absence of umlaut is due to the fact that certain vowels did not suffer umlaut in certain positions or that the connecting vowel was ê or ô.

Ex.: bahnen < Bahn, fußen < Fuß, ackern < Acker, formen < Form, altern < Alter. Older are beten <*betôn* < *beta,* prayer; faffen < *fazzôn* < *faz;* faften < fastôn < fasta; bulben < *dultên* < *dult.* Notice the difference between: bruden, to print, brüden, to press; kranken, to be ill, kränken, to grieve; walzen, to roll, technical as in a rolling-mill, wälzen, to roll, revolve; erkalten, to grow cold — erkälten, to take cold.

536. Derivation by e preceded by a suffix, but e drops out after l and r.

1. -ch e n, intensive force, rare: horchen, listen + hearken < hören + hear; schnarchen + snore < schnarren.

2. -e l n, always preceded by umlaut if attached to other verbs. It is also attached to substantives and adjectives.

It has intensive, iterative force and, from association with the noun-suffix, diminutive and hence derisive force. Numerous in N. H. G. on account of the many nouns in -el. Generally umlaut.

Ex.: betteln + beg(?) < beten, bitten, pray, ask; schmeicheln, flatter < schmeichen (rare), smooth; lächeln, smile < lachen + laugh; fränkeln, be sickly < kranken, be sick; frösteln, to feel chilly < Frost; liebeln, to dally < lieben, lieb; frömmeln, cant < fromm, pious; handeln, to trade < Hand.

537. 1. –n e n + Eng. -n, on (rare).

Ex.: bienen, from the same stem as De- in Demut; lernen < the same stem as lehren; rechnen < O. H. G. *rehhanôn,* + Ags. *recenian;* warnen, + warn, < same stem as wahren (?); verbannen, + condemn, also contains -n < M. H. G. *verdamnen,* but < L. *damnare.* Compare zeichnen < Zeichen + token, regnen < Regen + rain, in which n belongs to the noun, see **502.**

2. -e r n, + Eng. -r, has intensive, iterative, and causative force. Rarely preceded by umlaut; not unfrequent both in Eng. and German.

Ex. : glitzern + Eng. glitter, < *glitzen* < *glizen;* flimmern < flimmen; glimmern + Eng. glimmer < glimmen; stottern < L. G. stötern < stöten, + H. G.

ſtoßen, + Eng. stutter; zögern < *zogen* < ziehen; ſickern + Ags. *sicerian*, to trickle.

a. Nouns both sg. and pl., adjectives and their comparatives in –er have started many of these verbs, *e. g.*, ſäubern, erweitern, blättern, räbern, ärgern < arg; förbern, to promote, forbern, to demand.

538. **-ieren, -iren**, of Romance origin, always accented, at first only in borrowed words, and then added to German noun-stems. **-eien**, of similar origin, is rare.

Ex.: Foreign words: fallieren + fail, regieren + reign, ſtudieren + study, hantieren, trade (rather from French *hanter* than from Hand, see Kluge). Konterfeien, to paint + counterfeit; gebenedeiet, blessed. German stems: hauſieren, peddle; ſtolzieren, strut; halbieren. In Goethe's Faust: irrlichtelieren.

a. These were formed as early as M. H. G. in no small numbers, but were most numerous during the Thirty Years' War and the first half of the 18th century. Now they are excluded, except the oldest of them, from elevated style. These verbs are very numerous in the journals.

539. 1. **-ſen, -eſen,** + Eng. s, < O. H. G. -ison. Rare both in English and German.

Ex.: grinſen, + grin, < greinen,, M. H. G. *grīnen;* grauſen < O. H. G. *gruwison* < stem grû, G. grauſam, Gräuel, + gruesome. grapſen + Eng. grasp.

a. -ſen is hidden in geizen < gitsen < *gîtison* < subst. *gît.* Compare Eng. cleanse < clean. -ſen stands for -zen in gackſen < *gagzen*, muckſen < M. H. G. *muchzen*.

2. **-ſchen.** This is of double origin: 1) From -ſen, see **490, 1,** *b*: herrſchen < *hêrsen* < *hêrison* < Herr, *hêrro;* feilſchen < *veilsen* < feil.

2) From -sk, L. *sc*, + Eng. sh, forſchen < *forsken;* perhaps in haſchen < *hafskôn*, if that comes from a stem *haf-*. For more examples, see **457, 4.**

3. -zen < older *-zzen.* Has sometimes iterative and intensive force.

Ex.: buzen, ihrzen, erzen, to call thou, you, he; ächzen < ach, to groan; lechzen, to thirst, < *lechen* + leak; ſeufzen < *siufzen*, from the same root as ſaufen; ſchluchzen, to sob, M. H. G. *sluckzen* < ſchlucken.

a. -enzen in faulenzen < faul, is due to the influence of L. nouns in *-entia.*

4. **-igen.** This is a secondary suffix, starting with verbs derived from adjectives in –ig (see **525**), *e.g.*, würbigen < würbig, nötigen < nötig. It was felt to be a verbal suffix, hence: endigen < Ende, kreuzigen < Kreuz, reinigen < rein, huldigen < Huld. Quite numerous.

VERB FORMATION BY MEANS OF INSEPARABLE PREFIXES, viz.:

be–, ent–, er–, ge–, ver–, z–, zer–. Always unaccented.

540. be–, b– before l, + Eng. be–. See Bei–, **516**, 4.

1. Be- has lost nearly all local force of "by," "near," "around," which is felt still in behängen, cover by hanging, beschneiden, cut on all sides, to trim, but in these it approaches already its common force, which is intensive: bebauen, befragen, begehren, berühren, bedecken, berufen.

2. It makes intransitive verbs transitive: fallen—befallen + befall; reisen (in einem Lande) — ein Land bereisen, travel all over a country; fahren auf etw., but etwas befahren. This is its most frequent use.

3. In verbs from noun-stems it denotes "provide with," "make": beschuhen, provide with shoes; bevölkern, populate; befreunden + befriend; betrüben, make sad; bestärken, confirm. Notice certain participial adjectives which have no corresponding verb, *e. g.*, beleibt, corpulent; betagt, "full in years;" belesen, well read; or they are isolated from the verb, *e.g.*, bescheiden, modest; bestallt, holding an office; beschaffen, conditioned.

4. It has privative force still in benehmen, to take away; sich begeben (with G.), to give up. Compare Eng. behead and M. H. G. *behoubeten*, for which now enthaupten. N. H G. behaupten strangely represents M. H G. *behaben* and *beheben*, for which once *behouben*, to maintain, assert.

541. ent–, emp– before f, < O. H. G. *int*–. See ant–, **516**, 3.

Its force is: 1. "Opposite," "in return;" in empfehlen, recommend; empfangen, receive; entgelten, pay back, restore; see sub. 2.

2. Contrary, "against," privative, "away from:" entgelten, suffer for; entsagen, renounce; entbinden, deliver; entstehen, to lack (but see below); entdecken, entlaufen. From nominal stems: entgleisen, run off the track; entthronen, dethrone; entvölkern, depopulate.

3. "Transition into," inchoative "springing from," "out of :" entstehen, spring from, arise; entbrennen, to take fire, break out; entschlafen, fall asleep. A quite common force.

542. e r– < O. H. G. *ir, ar* + Eng. a–, see **516,** 9.

Force: 1. "Out from," "upward": erheben, arise; erwecken, awaken; erforschen, find out; erfinden, to invent.

2. Transition into another state, inchoative like ent–: erkalten, grow cold; erblühen, bloom; erbeben, tremble. Many from adjectives: erkranken, to fall ill; erblinden, to become blind.

3. Completion and success of the action: erjagen, erbetteln, to obtain by hunting, by begging; very frequent. Compare Eng. arise, abide.

543. g e–, g– before l, see **516,** 7, + Eng. a–.

Force: 1. "Together" only in few verbs like: gefrieren, congeal; gerinnen, curdle; gehören, to belong; geleiten, accompany; gefallen, to please.

2. Frequentative and intensive: geloben, gedenken, gebieten, and finally no force at all as in the past participle and in verbs like: gebeißen, gelüsten, genesen, genießen. Numerous past part. from nominal stems, with the force of "provided with," see **540,** 4: gestiefelt, in boots; gesinnt, disposed; gestirnt, + starry.

544. m i ß–, + Eng. mis–, as to its force, see **516,** 8; as to its origin, **453,** 1.

Ex.: mißglücken, to fail; mißhören, to misunderstand; mißgönnen, to grudge.

545. v e r–, f r–, < *ver, far, fir,* Go. fra, fr, + Eng. for–. Very frequent.

Force: 1. 'Through," "to the end," intensive, "too much:" verlieren, + lose, + forlorn; vergeben + forgive; veralten, grow antiquated; vergraben, hide by burying; verbergen, hide; verhindern, prevent; verschlafen, + sleep too long; verkommen, to deteriorate; verblühen, fade; verzagen, despair; verfluchen, curse; verlaufen, scatter; fressen, to eat (used of animals).

2. The opposite, the wrong, a mistake: verkaufen, verbieten, verführen; verlegen + mislay, but also (sub. 1) to publish (a book); verbauen, build wrongly; sich verlaufen, lose the way; sich verhören, to mishear; sich vergreifen, to get hold of the wrong thing; (sich) vergeben, to misdeal (in cards).

3. Waste and consumption of the object: verbauen, use up in building (see sub. 4); versaufen, waste in drinking; verspielen, lose, gamble away.

4. From nominal stems: "change into," "give the appearance of," "bring about a certain state of," *e. g.*, verglasen, glaze, turn into glass; vergolden, + gild; verknöchern, ossify; verzuckern, cover with sugar, turn into

sugar; verarmen, grow poor; verschlechtern, make or grow worse; verbauen (sub. 3), cover by building in front of.

a. ver- in past participles: verwandt, related, but of the regular verb = "applied;" verschämt, bashful.

546. zer- < M. H. G. zer-, ze-, O. H. G. zur, zar, zir, + Go. *tus*-, + Gr. δυς- + O. Eng. to-brecan, zerbrechen. Least frequent of these suffixes.

Its force is: "separation," "scattering," "dissolution," "to pieces": zerhauen, cut to pieces; zergliedern, dismember; zertrümmern, dash to pieces.

1. If be- and ver- precede other prefixes, separable or inseparable, the verb is always an inseparable compound. Ex.: verun'nglücken, beei'nträchtigen, benachrichtigen. These come from the compound nouns Unglück, Eintracht, Nachricht. See **547**. Notice the difference between bevo'rmunden < Vormund (insep.) and bevo'rstehen < bevor + stehen (sep.).

2. Notice such compounds as auf'erstehen, a'nerziehen, vorau'sverkündigen, in which the second prefix is inseparable. The first and second have no simple tenses in main clauses. Their past part. are auferstanden, anerzogen. The pret. of the third is kündigte voraus, but the past part. is vorausverkündigt, without ge-. See **550**.

Compound Verbs.

547. The first element is either substantive or adjective or adverb or preposition; the second is always a verb. The important questions are accent and whether the compounds are separable or inseparable, or both; whether direct or indirect.

1. Indirectly compounded are the verbs derived from compound substantives and adjectives. They are inseparable and have noun-accentuation, *i. e.*, accent on the first element.

Ex.: he'rbergen < He'rberge, inn; ra'tschlagen < Rat'schlag, council; wa'llfahrten < Wallfahrt, pilgrimage; frühstücken < Frühstück; argwöhnen < Argwohn, suspicion; bewillkommen < Willkommen.

2. That these are not genuine compound verbs their inflection shows. The seemingly strong verbs, as in ra'tschlagen, heiraten, etc., are not inflected strong, but weak: ratschlagte, geratschlagt; heiratete, geheiratet. Note also: handhabte, gehandhabt, not handhatte, ha'ndhabt or handgehabt.

3. Under this head come also: 1. Verbs of which the compound substantive or adjective is no longer common, *e. g.*, wetterleuchten < *weterlich*; rechtfertigen < *rechtverteg*; bra'ndschatzen < Brandschatz. 2. A few verbs which

seem due to analogy with the above and formed by mere juxtaposition of adjective or substantive and verb, *e. g.*, lie'bkosen, willfahren (accent doubtful), frohlo'cken, lie'bäugeln, wei'ssagen (as if it were from weise and sagen, but it comes from the noun *wizzago*, prophet). Principal parts: liebkosen, liebkoste, geliebkost; frohlocken, gefrohlockt.

548. All the other compound verbs are directly compounded, separable and accented on the first part excepting certain prepositions, see **549**, which form the only genuine old compounds with accent on the stem-syllable of the verb. These and the verbs in **540-546** are the compound verbs proper with the original verb-accent.

1. SUBSTANTIVE + VERB.

The substantive is the object of the verb.

Ex.: sta'ttfinden, hau'shalten, teilnehmen, bankkagen, preisgeben.

NOTE.—But for the fact that in certain tenses they are written together and the substantive is now according to the "Rules" to be written without capital, these verbs are no more compounds than the corresponding Eng. to keep house, take place, give thanks. As late as early N. H. G. these and the following groups were not treated as compounds.

2. ADJECTIVE + VERB.

The adjective is generally factitive predicate, *e. g.*, wahrnehmen, "take notice of"; totschlagen, strike dead; freisprechen, declare not guilty; vollgiessen, -schütten, see **549, 5**.

a. A large number of compounds with substantives and adjectives occur only in certain forms, viz., in the two participles and in the infinitive used as a noun, *e. g.*, blutstillend, pflichtvergessen, stillbeglückt, das Schönschreiben, das Stillschweigen.

3. ADVERB OR PREPOSITION + VERB.

The adverb qualifies the verb expressing manner, direction, time. The preposition in this case has the force of an adverb. Exceptions below.

Ex.: hi'nschicken, he'rholen, na'chmachen, vorau'ssetzen, zusa'mmenkommen, wo'hlwollen.

549. Separable and inseparable compound verbs occur with durch, (hinter), über, um, unter, voll, wider, wieder.

a. Inseparable verbs compounded with these prepositions are transitive, and have the old accentuation of verb-compounds (see **421**). Here belong also all verbs with hinter-, wider- and a few with voll-, *e. g.*, vollbri'ngen. These verbs are nearly all old, but some new ones have been formed after them. The force of the preposition has entered into and modified the meaning of the verb, so that if the simple or separable compound verb was intransitive the inseparable compound became transitive; if transitive, the compound developed a different meaning, generally figurative, often intensive. As to haben and fein see 265.

The separable compounds have not the verb-accentuation and the force of the preposition remains literal and intact.

Very few verbs allow of both compositions.

1. burch- means + "through," "thoroughly," completion of the action, "filling with," "to the end of a fixed limit of time," bu'rchbringen, crowd through, penetrate, carry to a successful issue, *e.g.*, die Kugel ift durchgebrungen, the ball went through. Trans.: Die Kugel hat das Brett durchbru'ngen, the ball penetrated the board; „von dem Gefühle feines Nichts durchbru'ngen." In „Die K. ift durch das Brett gedrungen" there is no compound. Du'rchſchauen, look through, etwas durchschau'en, see through, understand thoroughly; durchta'nzen, to spend in dancing. bu'rchtanzen, to dance through, to pass through dancing; bu'rchſehen, to look through (a hole), hurriedly through a book; the inseparable burchfe'hen is obsolete, it would have the force of durchschau'en, to understand thoroughly.

2. hinter, + behind. Separable compounds with hinter do not really occur in good style. In hi'ntergießen, -bringen it stands for hinunter = pour down, swallow. The inseparable compounds are always figurative and transitive, its force is the opposite of straight, "deceptive": hinterge'hn, deceive; hintertreiben, to prevent, circumvent; hi'ntergehen would mean the more usual hinterhe'r or hintena'ngehen, to walk behind.

3. über = *a*) separable: over, beyond, across = hinüber; *b*) in close compounds: transfer, covering, a missing, figurative sense, extent of a certain limit of time.

a. ü'berſetzen, cross, take across (a river); ü'bergehen, go over.

b. überzie'hen, cover with; überna'chten, spend the night; überſchrei'ben, head a column or chapter; überhö'ren, not to hear; überle'gen, consider; ü'berſchlagen = u'mſchlagen, tip, turn over; but überſchla'gen, calculate (expenses); überſe'tzen, to translate; überge'hen, pass over, skip; überſe'hen, overlook.

4. um. *a.* separable = around, about, again or over, upside down, change of place, loss of something, failure.

Ex.: u'mhängen (einen Mantel), put on, (ein Bild) change the place of a picture; u'mlaufen, overthrow by running; u'mkleiden, change clothing; u'mkehren, turn back; u'mkommen (viz., um's Leben), perish, u'mbringen, take the life of; ſich u'mgehen, take a roundabout course.

b. inseparable: literally denotes the encircling of an object, figuratively it has the force of hinter, deception: uma'rmen, embrace; umschif'fen, sail around, double; umflei'ben, cover, drape; umge'hen, avoid, deceive.

5. unter, separable: under, down, among (with): u'nterhalten, hold under, down; u'nterbringen, provide for (figurative); u'ntergehen, go down, set.

Inseparable, figurative sense: unterha'lten, entertain; unterfa'gen (Dat.), forbid; sich unterste'hen, make bold; unterne'hmen, undertake; unterla'ssen, leave undone; unterlie'gen, to be overcome by.

6. voll, separable: + full, always literally with verbs denoting pouring, filling and similar ones: vo'llbringen, vo'llgießen, vo'llschütten (ein Gefäß), bring, pour a vessel full. Inseparable: "to the end," accomplishment: vollfü'hren, vollbri'ngen, execute; volle'nden, finish, compare Eng. fulfi'l; vollko'mmen (part.), perfect.

7. wiber in the sense of "against" is always inseparable and unaccented, generally figurative sense: wiberle'gen, refute; wiberstre'ben (with Dative), resist; wiberspre'chen, contradict (also Dat.); wiberste'hen, to resist.

8. wieber, separable: "again," "back": wie'berholen, fetch back; wie'bergeben, give back; wie'bersagen, say again. Very loose compounds. Inseparable: figurative sense only in wieberho'len, repeat; wiberha'llen, wiberschei'nen also wie'berscheinen, wi'eberhallen; usage is unsettled in these.

a. The difference in the spelling wiber—wieber is quite modern.

550. Separable and inseparable composition with these adverbs is quite old, but in O. H. G. probably no distinction was made in force or meaning. Even now „Die Kugel hat das Brett burchbru'ngen" and „die K. ist burch das Brett gebrungen" amount to quite the same thing. In fact separable composition is no real composition. Many still write the prefixes separately before the verb where any other adverb would stand. In M. H. G. the great majority of our modern separable compounds are not felt at all as compounds. Two things have brought about this feeling that they are such:

1. The substantives compounded with the same element as the verb, e. g., U'mgang, Du'rchfahrt, A'bbruch, have lead us to associate um and gehen, burch and fahren, ab and brechen.

2. When a meaning different from the literal or common one was developed, verb and adverb were felt as belonging together, e. g., etwas bu'rchsetzen, to carry something through, to the end; vorschlagen, to propose; nachschlagen, to look up a reference, etc.

a. Very often there is no difference in meaning, but only in construction, between the simple verb + preposition and the close compound, e. g., 1, Das Pferd ist über den Graben gesprungen, = "The horse has jumped over the ditch," and, 2, das Pferd hat den Graben übersprungen, The horse has jumped the ditch. In 2, perhaps the act of the *leap* is emphasized, it did not *swim* across; in 1, the extent of the leap. But compare also the other, not literal meaning of überspri'ngen, viz., to skip, omit, in: Der Reisende hat einen Posten übersprungen, the traveller has skipped one item. Der R. ist über den Posten gesprungen would be meaningless.

Derivation of Adverbs.

The adverbs are derived from pronominal stems and from noun-stems.

551. The two suffixes *en* and *er*, < older *an(a)*, *ar(a)*, are attached to the stems.

ADVERBS FROM PRONOMINAL STEMS.

1. From the stem of the demonstrative pronoun:

a. From the stem *ta-tha*: dar, da + there, dann + then and denn, conj. "for," this double form is M. H. G., but the difference in meaning was only established as late as the 18th century, < older *danne*, *denne*, which have not been explained yet. Dannen < *dunnana* stands only in „von bannen", hence. Desto, see **442**, *a*; dort < *darôt*; doch + though (?).

b. From the stem *hi*: her + hither; hin, away; hier + here; hinnen, in von hinnen, hence. Hinten, heute, heint, heuer, see **443**, 2.

2. From the stem of the interrogative pronoun:

wann + when, wenn, if; wor-, wo + where < *uâ*, *wâr;* von wannen + whence is rare. For wie + how + why, see **444**, 1. Waru'm < *wâr* + *umbe* or *wara* + *umbe* (?).

3. From the stem *swa-*: so + so; samt, zusammen (?), sonder, als, also, sonst < *sunst*, *sust*, *sus*. From various stems: oben, + above; unten, unter, + under; nid (rare), nieden + beneath; nun + now; außen, außer; innen, inner.

552. ADVERBS FROM NOUN-STEMS.

These adverbs are always cases of nouns, the Genitive being the most frequent. See **187**.

1. *Genitive:* abends, morgens, nachts, teils, flugs, derweil, dermaßen, nichts.
s was looked upon as an adverbial ending and added to fem. nouns and even to other cases and whole adverbial phrases, *e.g.*, -seits in many compounds: die'sseits, mei'nerseits, allerdi'ngs (really a G. pl.), vo'rmals, unterwe'gs, e'hemals, allerwe'gen. Compare Eng. needs, now-a-days, always, sometimes.

2. *Dative:* zuwei'len, mitten, halben, traun (?), morgen (sg. ?), abha'nden, vor-

ha'nben, zufolge, anstatt. Compare Eng. to-morrow, o'clock, a year < on (in) the year, a day < on (in) the day, because, asleep, whilom.

3. *Accusative:* weg (ε) + away; heim + home; mal, once; bieweil, + while; überhaupt, je, nie.

–weise following at first only after a Gen., later the uninflected noun: zwangsweise, by force, ausnahmsweise, exceptionally, stückweise, piecemeal. Compare Eng. nowise, otherwise, the while.

4. *Instrumental:* heuer, this year < *hiujaru*; heute, to-day < *hiutagu*; heint < *hînaht* (a Dat.?). See **443**, 2.

553. Derivation by suffix: –lings and –wärts.

1. –lings comes from the G. of nouns in –ling and is a late formation: rücklings, backward; blindlings, blindly. Compare Eng. sideling, headlong.

2. –wärts + ward is really the G. of an adjective *wert, wart*. It is very common after prepositions: heimwärts, homeward; waldwärts, towards the forest; abwärts, downward, aside; vorwärts + forward.

ADVERBS FROM ADJECTIVES.

554. Almost all adjectives can be used as adverbs.

Adverbs with a suffix:

1. –*e*, this is now rare but once very frequent < older –*o*, which was probably the A. sg. fem.: gern(e), fern(e), balbe in Goethe's „Warte nur, balbe Ruhest du auch."

a. Remark here the doublets fast — fest, schon — schön, fruh (rare), — früh, spat (rare), — spät. Those without umlaut are the regularly formed adverbs from jo-stems. Those with umlaut are adjectives used as adverbs. In träge, böse, etc., e does not go back to –o, but O. H. G. i < jo, since they are adjectives (*jo*-stems) used as adverbs and not transformed into adverbs.

2. –lich + –ly, is really no adverbial suffix, but the adjective suffix to which the adverbial e (< o) was added, –*liche, –liho:* treulich — treu + truly, faithfully; wahrlich — wahr, gütlich — gut, freilich, to be sure, — frei; bitterlich — adjective bitter.

a. The corresponding adjective in –lich is perhaps no longer in use. Compare freilich, to be sure — frei + free.

b. –lich has also been added to other stems: einschließlich, hoffentlich, wissentlich.

555. Adverbs, cases of adjectives.

Genitive: 1. rechts, links, eilends, vergebens, stets + steadily.

2. -ens from superlatives and ordinals: erstens, höchstens, meistens, drittens. -ens contains the inflection -en of the adjective.

  a. Genitive with excrescent t. Such are felt as superlatives: jüngst, längst, nebst; einst (?), but in O.H.G. are doublets *einêst* and *einês*. Compare Eng. once < *ânes* and dial. "onst"; also amidst, amongst, dial. "acrost." Pure Gen. in Eng. else < elles, unawares, etc.

  Rem. The above explanation is rejected by *Lexer* in *Grimm's* Dict.

3. *Dative.* It is hidden in zwar < *zewâre*, lit. "for true," to be sure. Einzeln, singly < *einzel* by suffix -il from *ein(az)* < *ein;* adj. einzeln-er. In adverbial phrases: am leichtesten, am schönsten. In M. H. G. this Dative was very frequent, *e.g.,* in -*lichen,* -*lingen,* etc.

4. *Accusative,* also in the comparative and superlative degrees: wenig, viel, genug, mehr, meist, besser, höchst, möglichst. In adverbial phrases: insbesondere, fürwahr, auf's reinste, schönste. See **300, 2.**

  a. Note also those preceded by prepositions: zuletzt, +at last, neben (< eneben), zugleich, at the same time, fürba'ß or fü'rbaß, farther.

PREPOSITIONS and CONJUNCTIONS have the same origin as the adverbs, being originally adverbs.

Three classes of words may be comprised under the head of PARTICLES.

Prepositions.

556. 1. As old and simple prepositions may be regarded: ab, an, auf, aus, bei, vor and für (doublets), durch, gegen (+ again), in, mit, ob, zu, um (< *umbe*).

2. Derived by suffixes: -er, -der, -ter, mostly from pronominal stems and from the older forms *ar, dar, tar,* which are probably all three comparative suffixes: über, unter, hinter, wieder, außer. See **551, 3.**

3. A number of nouns and adjectives in the various cases: kraft, unweit, während, mittels (mittelst), statt, längs, trotz, halben, wegen, willen, nächst, nebst, laut, nach, zwischen.

  a. The number of prepositions governing the Gen. is really difficult to state, because, like many of the above and many others, they are really nouns with a G. dependent upon them, viz., zweds, behufs, betreffs, seitens, etc.

557. Compound Prepositions are generally adverbs, but the following may be classed here:

1. Preposition (or adverb) + preposition or adverb: binnen < bi + innen, bis < bi + az (az + Eng. at), neben < en + eben, zuwider; entge′gen < en + gegen (t excrescent,) etc.

2. Noun + noun, or prep. + noun, or pronoun + noun: zufolge, several in –halb and –seit: außerhalb, jenseit, anstatt.

Conjunctions.

558. 1. From pronominal stems: For da, denn, so, wenn, wie, and others, see among adverbs, **551**. Aber, auch, und, oder, sondern, weder, show suffixes.

2. From nouns and adjectives: falls, gleich, ungeachtet, weil, während, and others.

3. Compounds: adverb and preposition: bevor, sobald, mithin, somit, daher, darum, and others.

4. Preposition or adverb + pronoun or adjective: indem, seitdem, sobaß, als baß, allein, entweder < ein– de– weder, one of two; nichtsdestoweniger, nevertheless.

Interjections.

559. Interjections proper.

1. Joy is expressed by: ah, o, hei, juchhe, heisa, hurrah. Surprise: ei, potz, ha. Pain by: oh, wehe, au, ach, hu. Disgust: pfui, fi, bah. Doubt: hm, hem, hum. Commands to be silent are: pst, bst, sch; to stop or pay attention: brrr (to horses), heba, he, ho, holla, halloh.

2. Imitations of sounds in nature: plumps (fall), piff, paff, puff (shot), hui (whizz), bautz (fall), muh (cow), miau (cat), wau (dog), hopsa (stumble), bum — bum (drum).

3. Burdens of songs: Dudelbumbei, Juvivallera, schrum — schrum — schrum.

560. Certain regular words which have become exclamations, often oaths in much changed forms: Salt, Wetter, Donner und Blitzen, Potztausend, Heil, Bravo, O je, O jemine, Sapperment, Sakerlot, Mein Himmel, Donnerwetter noch einmal.

LIST OF ABBREVIATIONS AND SYMBOLS THAT REQUIRE EXPLANATIONS.

Ags. = Anglo-Saxon.
(B.) = Bible.
(Bo.) = Bodenstedt.
(Bü.) = Bürger.
(Ch.) = Chamisso.
D. = Dutch or Dative.
(F.) = Hart's Edition of Goethe's Faust, Part I.
Fr. = French.
(G.) = Goethe.
Go. = Gothic.
Gr. = Greek.
G. T. = General Teutonic.
(H. and D.) = Hart's edition of Goethe's *Hermann and Dorothea.*
(He.) = Herder.
H. G. = High German.
(Hu.) = A. von Humboldt.
I.-E. = Indo-European.
L. = Latin.
(Le.) = Lessing.

L. G. = Low German.
(Lu.) = Luther's works excepting his translation of the Bible.
M. G. = Middle German.
M. H. G. = Middle High German.
N. G. = North German or North Germany.
N. H. G. = New High German.
O. Fr. = Old French.
O. H. G. = Old High German.
(Prov.) = Proverb.
(R.) = Rückert.
Rules = the official rules for spelling, see **37**.
(Sch.) = Schiller.
S. G. = South German.
(Sh.) = Shakespere translated by Schlegel and Tieck.
(Uh.) = Uhland.
V. L. = Vulgar Latin.

< means "derived from," "sprung from," "taken from."
> means "passed or developed into," "taken into."
+ between a German and non-German word denotes common origin or "cognates." In other positions it means "accompanied or followed by."
* before a word means that that form of the word does not actually occur, but is conjectured or reconstructed.
: = :, or : as :, means a relation as in a mathematical proportion.
I, II, III after verbs indicates the strong verb-classes.
— between letters means "interchanges with," *e.g.*, h — ch as in hoher — hoch or e — i as in nehmen — nimmst.

SUBJECT-INDEX.

The numbers refer to the paragraphs. The umlauts have a separate place, ä after a, ö after o, ü after u.

Ablaut: nature of, 393; four grades, 394, 463, 2; 496; 497.
Ablaut series: and verb-classes, 122-129; I.-E., 394, 1; G. T., > O. H. G. > N. H. G., 395-400; 459-467; grouping of, 459.
Abstract nouns: article before, 149; no article, 145; 155, 2; plural of, 171; 62, Rem.
Accent: 417, 418; degrees of, 419; chief on stem-syllable, 420; 420, 2; 478, 4; Eng. in Norman-Fr. words, 420, 3; in compounds, 421-423; secondary, 424; rhetorical, 426; "free" in I.-E., 420, 2; in foreign words, 427, 420, 1; 424, 4; 493, 2; 63, 2; characteristic of Germanic Lang., 478, 4; = intonation, 392, 1.
Accidence: 38-138; Historical Commentary on, 428-476.
Accusative: office of, 198; after verbs, 198-206; two A. after verbs, 199; predicate in passive, 202, 2; cognate, 203; logical subject in, 205; after reflexive verbs, 206; adverbial, 207; difference between A. and G. of time, 208, 1; after adjectives, 207, 1; 183; absolute, 209; 297, 1; by attraction in the pred. after laſſen, 202, 1; after prepos., 304-306; with Inf., 292.
Adjective: decl. of, 69-72; 436; origin of strong decl., 437; comparison of, 73-76, see comparison, compar. and superlat.; 438, 439; used as nouns, 220, 221, 181; gender of same, 160, 3; 169; 162, 3; G. after, 182, 183; D. after, 194; A. after, 183; 207, 1.
Attributive use of, 211-217; only used attributively, 211; uninflected used attributively, 212; in the predicate, 218, 220; as nouns declined strong, 214; G. sg. m. and n., 216, 1; declined weak, 213; 217, 1; as nouns, 221, 1; origin of double decl., 215; unsettled usage as to strong and weak decl., 216, 221; after indef. pron., 214; 216, 4; 181; after person. pron., 216, 2; two or more adj., 212, 3; 217. In the predicate, 218, 219; only used in pred., 219; position of adjuncts of, 353; accent in certain compounds,

422, 1-7; derivation of, 522-528; used as adverb, 554.
Adjective Clauses: nature of, 323; 326-328; 339.
Adverbial Clauses: nature of, 323, 329; various kinds of, 330-340; see temporal, local, clauses of manner and cause (332-340), final (338), conditional, (340), etc.
Adverbs: origin of, 551-555; < G. of nouns, 187, 552; + prepos. supplanting the person. pron., 234; syntax of, 299, 300; after prepos. + noun, 300; adverbs which are only adverbs, 300, 1; 554, 2; adjective as, 300, 2; 554; comparison by, 223, 224; relative and absolute superl. of, 300, 2; nature of, 301, 1; interrogative, 251, 5; relative, 258, 326, 331; demonstrative, 327, 3; in local clauses, 331, a; position in a sentence, 354; order of adverbs of time, place, manner, 355; accent in compound, 423.
Adversative Sentences: coordinate, 320.
Affricate: 413, 5; 408, 1.
Alemanic: 483, 1.
Alphabet: printed and script, 1, 2; origin of the G. letters, 360; Latin letters in G., 360, 2; relation to G. sounds, 361.
Anglo-Saxon, see English.
Apposition: < G. of nouns, 181; 179, 1; 317.
Articles: inflect. of, 38; accent of, 39; contraction with prepositions, 40; spelling of, 39; 41; syntax of, 140-158; nature of 140; general cases of absence of, 141-146; before proper nouns, 147; before abstract nouns, 149; before names of materials, 150; before collective nouns, 151; repetition of, 158. See A., def. and indef.
Article, Def.: infl. of, 38; attraction to preceding words not prepositions, 41; contraction with preceding prepos., 40; relation to Eng. possessive pron., 154, 243, 3; distributive for Eng. "a," 156.
Article, Indef.: infl. of, 38; aphaeresis of, 41; after certain pronouns, 144, 252; before certain pronouns, 157.
Austrian: 483.

SUBJECT-INDEX. 267

Auxiliaries: of tense: infl. of, 110 ; use of, 265, 266 ; 283, 2 ; omission of, 346 ; in passive voice, 273.
 Modal: see pret. pres. verbs ; special uses of, 267 ; verbs of motion omitted after, 267, Rem. ; imperative force of, 287, 4 ; + perf. and pres. inf., 283, 1 ; 290 ; in future, 279, 3, *a*.

Bavarian-Austrian: 483, 2 ; 488, 5, *a*.
Bible: 486 ; 487.
Brechung: 405, Rem.

Capitals: initial, 364 ; in pronouns of address, 230 ; in article, 39.
Cardinals, see Numerals.
Cases: see individual cases, N., G., etc. ; order of cases in the sentence, 352.
Causal Sentences: coordinate, 321 ; subordinate, 337.
Comparative: see comparison ; use of, 222 ; by adverbs, 223, 224 ; conjunctions after, 333.
Comparative Clauses: 333, 1–3 ; with nicht, 333, 2.
Comparison: of adjectives, 73–76 ; 438 ; 439 ; irregular, 76, 1 ; defective and redundant, 76, 2 ; the suffixes, 73, 438 ; by adverbs, 223, 224, 222, 1 ; of two qualities of the same object, 224.
Compound words: accent of, 421–424 ; irregular accent of certain nouns, adjectives, and prefixes, 422 ; secondary accent in, 424 ; 521 ; see nouns, adj., etc.; 516 ; compared with Eng., 521, 2. *b*.
Compound tenses: 109–115 ; 283.
Concessive Clauses: 339.
Conditionals: formation of, 115, 283, 5 ; force of, 280, 281, 284, 5.
Conditional Clauses: tenses in, 280, 284, 5 ; nature of, 340 ; several forms of, 340, 1 ; word-order in, 343, *c*.
Conjugation: strong and weak, 101–103 ; 446, 476 ; weak, 117, 118, 447, 454, 455 ; strong, 120–133, 446, 456–469.
Conjunctions: classification of, 307 ; origin of, 301, 558.
 Coordinating: copulative, 319 ; adversative, 320 ; concessive, 320, 2 ; causal, 321 ; illative, 322.
 Subordinating: in temporal clauses, 330 ; in comparative clauses, 333 ; 334 ; in consecutive clauses, 335 ; in restrictive clauses, 336 ; causal, 337 ; final, 338 ; concessive, 339 ; conditional, 340.
Consecutive Clauses: 335.
Consonant-declension, see n-declension.
Consonant-stems: become *t*-stems, 54 ; 428, 2 ; 432, 1 ; 432–435.
Consonants: description of, 374–389 ; open, 374–381 ; shut, 382–385 ; nasals, 386–388‡ ; compound, 389 ; long, 389, 5 ; cons.-table, p. 167 ; see Grimm's and Verner's Laws; doubling or lengthening of, 389, 5 ; 413, 5 ; 488, 2, *c* ; 535, 1, R. 2.
Coordinate Sentences: 318 ; various kinds of, 319–322.
Copulative Sentences: 319.

Danish: 479, II.
Dative: office of, 189 ; as nearer object after intrans. and certain compound verbs, 190 ; as indirect object after trans. verbs, 191 ; ethical, 192 ; after impers. verbs, 193 ; after adj., 194 ; 190 ; supplanted by prepos. + case, 195 ; after prepos., 303, 305, 306.
Declension: of articles, 38 ; of nouns, 42–68 ; 428–435 ; of foreign nouns, 64, 62, 3 ; of proper nouns, 65–68 ; of the adjective, 69–72 ; of pronouns, 81–100.
Demonstrative Pronouns: 88–91 ; use of, 244–250 ; origin of, 442 ; supplanted by hier and ba + prepos., 251, 2.
Dependent Clauses, see Subordinate.
Dependent order of words: 341, 344 ; in main clauses, 347, 349 ; the oldest order, 349, 2.
Dialect: and written language, 390 ; in M. H. G., 485, 2 ; in N. H. G., 486, 487 ; in the pronunciation of the educated, 390 ; and the public school, 392, 5.
Diphthongs: pronunc. of, 32 ; analysis of, 372 ; become single vowels, 488, 4 · < long vowels, 488, 5.
Dutch: 481, 3 ; 493, 3.

East Frankish: 482, 3 ; 486.
Elliptical clauses and phrases: 310 ; 284, 5, Rem.; 287 ; 343, *d*, 2.
English: 479, III. ; 492, 4 ; umlaut in, 402, 2.
Euphony: 418, 1.
Exclamation: G. in, 188, 309, 3 ; order of words in, 343, *e* ; see interjections.

Final clauses: 338.
Flemish: 481, 3.
Foreign nouns: decl. of, 64 ; gender of, 163 ; verbs, 538.
Foreign words: spelling of, 365 ; accent, 427, 420, 1 ; 424, 4 ; in G. wordstock, 492–494.
Fractions: 533, 2.
Frisian: 481, 1.
Future: formation of, 114 ; force of, 278 ; imperative force of, 278, 3 ; 287, 3 ; present with future force, 274, 5 ; condit. for subj. of, 281 ; origin of, 283, 4 ; 279, 3.

Gender: of nouns and their distribution among the declensions according to, 43 ; syntax of, 159–169 ; grammatical and sex, 159, 160 ; concord of the

268 SUBJECT-INDEX.

same, 165-168; according to meaning, 160; according to endings, 161; doubtful and double, 162; change of, 161, Rem., 163; of compound nouns, 164; concord of, 165-168; between subject and predicate, 313, 316.
Genitive: office of, 180; various kinds of G., 180, 1-7; partitive G. passed into apposition, 181, 251; supplanted by prepos., 181; dependent upon adj., 82, 182; dependent upon verbs as nearer object, 184; as remoter object, 185; after impersonal verbs, 186; adverbial G. of place, time, etc., 187; supplanted by A., 207, Rem.; difference between A. and G., 208; after prepos., 302; in exclamations, 188.
German Dialects: classification of, 480-483; 484.
German Language: see *Schriftsprache*; history of, 478-494; relation to other Germanic languages, 480-486.
German Sounds: analysis of, 366-389.
Germanic Languages: relation to other I.-E. languages, 477; characteristics of, 478; classification of, 479-484.
Gerundive: 107; 289, Rem.; 298; 452.
Gothic: letters, 360; language, 479, 1.
Grimm's Law: 407-415; G. T. shifting, 407-410; G. shifting, 413-415; modifications of, 412; in dialects, 480; in derivative verbs, 535, 1, R. 2.

Hessian: 482, 2.
High German: explanation of terms, 480, 3, *a*. See South German.
Hildebrantslied: 485, 1.

Icelandic: 479, II; 229, 1; 530.
Illative Sentences: co-ordinate, 322.
Imperative: 105, 450; in strong verbs, 121; personal pron. in, 286, 1; future with imperative force, 278, 3; 287, 3; force of, 286; other verbal forms with the force of, 287; conditional and concessive force of, 339, 1; word-order in, 343, *b*.
Indefinite Pronouns: 94-100, 445; use of, 259-263.
Indirect Speech: tenses in, 282; mood in, 285; 325, 3; 328.
Indo-European: 477.
Infinitive: 106, 451; nature of, 288; 290, 3, *b*; perfect, 288, 1; imper. force of, 287, 1; without and with ʒu, 289-291; 291, 3-5; without ʒu, 289, Rem.; after certain groups of verbs, 290; with ʒu, do., 291, 1; as object and subject, 291, 2, 3; A. with, 292; as a noun, 293; governed by prepos. + ʒu, 291, 1; inf. clause, 325, 2, Rem. 3; 332, 1; 335, 1; position of two, in dependent clause, 345, 1; position of adjuncts of, 353.
Instrumental: 194.
Interjections: 559, 560.
Interrogative Pronouns: 92, 444; use of, 251-253; D. supplanted by wo(r) + prepos., 251, 2.

Interrogative Sentences: 309, 2; indirect, 325, 2; disjunctive, 325, 2, *c*; word-order, 343, *a*.
Inverted order of words: 341, 343; in inserted main clause, 343, 1; origin of, in conditional and in main clauses, 348, 1; after certain co-ordinating conjunctions, 319; in a clause instead of ob gleich, etc., 339.
I-stems: 52-55; 429.
Iteratives: 531, 2.

Jo-stems: 46, 2; 428; in adj., 437, 3; 496, 2; 522.

Kanzleisprache: 486, 487.

Labialization, 367, 1; 370, 4, Rem.
Language: written. See *Schriftsprache*.
Law of Finals: 478, 3.
Levelling: nature of, 491, 1; in the strong pret., 460; in the weak verbs, 454, 455.
Low Frankish: 481, 3.
Low German Dialects: 480, 1; 481; ≥ H. G., 493, 3; their relation to the written language, 392, 1-3; 391.
Low Saxon: 481, 2.
Luther: 486, 487.

Middle Frankish: 482, 1.
Middle German Dialects: 480, 2; 482; 488, 3, *a*; 488, 4.
Middle High German: 485, 2; transition of sounds to N. H. G., 488-491.
Mi-verbs: 136; 449, 1, 2; 473-476.
Modal Clauses: 332.
Modal Auxiliaries. See Auxiliaries.
Mood: see subj., imper.; in adjective clauses, 328.
Multiplicatives: 531, 1.

N-declension: of nouns, 47, 61, 62, 432-435; of adjectives, 69, 213, 215.
Narrowness of vowels: 367, 2.
Negatives: 309, 1; double negative, 309, 1; in comparative clauses, 333, 2.
New High German: 485, 486.
Nominative: 178, 179; absolute, 297; predicate, 179; A. for, in pred., 202, 1.
Normal order of words: 341, 342; in subordinate clauses, 345, 2; after co-ordinating conjunctions, 343, 2; when the subordinate clause precedes, 343, 3; 348, 2; 343, *c*; 358.
North German: see Low G.
Norwegian: 479, II.
Nouns: decl. of, 42-68; systems of noun-decl., 42; distribution of nouns among the three declensions according to gender, 43, 433; general rules for noun-decl., 43; strong decl. of, 44-60, 428-431; weak decl. of, 61, 62, 428, 2;

SUBJECT-INDEX. 269

432; mixed decl. of, 63, 435, 1; use of cases, see individual cases; derivation of, 496–516; composition, 517-521, gender of compound, 164; accent of, 421, 422. See Number, Proper N., Foreign N., Abstract N., Compound.
Number: Singular and plural of nouns: pl. the basis of classification of strong nouns, '44; no sign, 45, a; umlaut, 45, b; -e, 49-55; -er, 56-60, 431; (e)n, 61-63; pl. in -s, 60; irregular, 51, 172, 173; double forms, 58, 162, 4; 431, 2; of abstract nouns, 171; nouns only in pl., 174.
Sing. or pl. after nouns of quantity, etc., 175; why sing., 176; sing. where Eng. pl., 177; sing. neut. of pronouns refer to masc., fem., and plural nouns, 168, 313.
Sing. and pl. of verbs: 311; pl. after a collective noun, 312; "pl. of majesty," 311, 2.
Numerals: 77; infl. of, 78; when inflected, 226, 227; cardinals, 77-79; pl. in -e, 227; in -er, 228, 2; ordinals, 80, 211, 530, 532; infinitive, 100; derivation of, 529-533.

Old High German: 485.
Ordinals: see Numerals.
Orthography: division into syllables, 36; regulated by government, 37, 361, 2; historical notes on, 360-365; umlaut-signs, 362; on the marks to show length, 363; on use of capitals, 364; of foreign words, 365; government rules, 37.
O-stems: lose sign of the pl., 47, 51, 428.

Participial Clauses: 294, 4; 332, 1.
Participles: 102, 107, 453; use of, 294 -297; position of adjuncts of, 353.
Past part. without ge-, 108, 113, 453, 2; 470, 528; isolated, 129, Rem.; 131, Rem.; 524, 4; imper. force of, 287, 2; passive force of, 295; active force of, 295, 2; 296; dependent upon kommen, heißen, etc., 296; of verbs of motion, 296; absolute construction, 297.
Pres. part., 274,6; 283,3,4; 294,453; in compound tenses, 283,1, 2; 351.
Passive: see Voice.
Perfect: formation of, 112; force of, 276; with future perf. force, 279, 2; Eng. perf. — G. pres., 274, 4; imperative, 286, 1; infinitive, 288.
Personal Pronouns: 81, 82, 440; syntax of, 230-235; gender of, 81; use of, in address, 230-233; repetition of, 233, 2; omission of, 233, 1; supplanted by other pronouns and prepositions, 234; in the imper., 286, 1.
Phonology: 360-427; orthography, 360 -365; analysis of sounds, 366-389;

as standard of pronunc., 390-392; phonetic laws, 393-417; accent, 418-427.
Plattdeutsch: 481, 2, a; 484.
Pluperfect: formation of, 112; force of, 277; relation to Condit., 280, 281, 284, 5.
Plural: see Number.
Popular Etymology: 494, 2, 3.
Possessive Pronouns: 85-87; syntax of, 239-243; origin of, 441; compounds with, 87; used substantively, 240; repetition of, 241, 242, 2; relation to def. article, 154, 243, 3; supplanted by demonstr. pron., 242, 1; uninflected, 239, 243, 1; after G., 180, 4.
Predicate, 308; concord of subj. and pred., 311-317; number of verb after collective noun, 313; when subjects are connected by conjunctions, 311, 314; person of verb when subjects are of different persons, 315; position of, 350, 351.
Prepositions: syntax of, 301-306; nature of, 301, 1, 2; 556; classification of, according to cases, and treatment of, in alphabetical order, 302-306; governing the G., 302; governing the D., 303; governing the A., 304; governing D. and A., 305; general position of, 357.
Present: infl. of, 103; of weak verbs, 118, 447; of strong verbs, 121, 456; O. H. G., 446; of pret.-pres. verbs, 134; uses of, 274; periphrastic, 274, 6; imper. force, 287, 3; formation of present-stem, 457.
Preterit: infl. of, 103; weak, 454; strong, 458; levelling in, 460; double subj., 125, 126, 464, 3; 129; of pret.-pres. verbs, 134, 470; force of, 275; relation to condit., 280, 281, 284, 5; ind. for unreal subj., 340, 3.
Pret.-pres. verbs: 134; 135; 108, 2; 267; 470-472.
Pronouns: inflection of, 81-100, 440-445; syntax of, 230-263; concord with noun, 165-168, 235; origin of, 496; position of, in the sentence, 352, e; neut. pron. refers to masc. or fem. nouns, 168; neut. pron. one of two accusatives, 199, 1, 2. See reciprocal, possessive, etc., separately.
Pronunciation: of letters, 1-37, 366; standard of, 390-392; disputed points in standard, 391; Hanoverian and N. G., 390, 4; 392, 1-3; dialect in, 390, 1-3.
Proper Nouns: decl of, 65-68; article before, 147, 155, 1; gender of, 160, 2, with Rem.; 164.

Question: see Interrogative Sentences.

Reciprocal Pronouns: 84, 197, 206, 238.
Reduplication: nature of, 458; in VII. Cl.

270 SUBJECT-INDEX.

of verbs, 130, 131; in the present, 457, 3.
Reflexive Pronouns: 83, 237; personal for, 237, 1.
Relative Clauses: see Adjective Cl.
Relative Pronouns: 93; use of, 254-258; origin of, 254; supplanted by adverbs and conjunctions, 257, 258, 326, 327.
Restrictive Clauses: 336.
Roundness of vowels: 367, 1; in S. G., 391, 5.
Runes, 492, 2.
Rückumlaut: 402, 2; 455.

Scandinavian, 479, II.
Schriftsprache: 390; 485, 2; 486, 487.
Sentence: structure of simple, 308; constituents of, 308; arrangement of, see word-order: various kinds of main, 309; 284, 2; 286; compound, see coordinate and subordinate.
Shifting of mutes: see Grimm's Law.
Shifting of spirants: see Verner's Law.
Silesian: 482, 6.
Singular: see Number.
Slavic: 477; 481, 2, Rem.; 482, 4-6.
Sonancy: 376.
South Frankish: 482, 2.
South German Dialects: 480, 3; 483; 488, 5, *a*; 489; 490, 1, *a*; relation to the written language, 391, 392, 4.
Suabian: 483, 2.
Subject: 308; concord of, and predicate, 311-317; position of subject and verb, 341, 356.
Subjunctive: kinds of, 284; potential, 284, 3; 325, 2, Rem. 1; 325, 2; 328; in conditional clauses, 340, 448.
Subordinate Sentences: 318, 323, 324-340; word-order in, 343, *c*; 344-346; 350, Rem.; omission of auxil., 346; position of, 358.
Substantive Clauses: 323-325; nature of, 323; various kinds of, 325; normal order in, 345.
Superlative: see Comparison; use of, 222-225; never uninflected, 222; absolute and relative, 222; applied to two objects, 225; of adverbs, 300, 2.
Surdness: 376.
Swedish: 479, II.
Swiss: 483, 1, *a*.

Temporal Clauses: 330.
Tenses: simple, 101, 103, 448; use of, 274, 275, 283.
Compound: 109, 112-116, 276-281; origin of, 283; position of separable prefix, 351. See the separate tenses.
Thuringian: 482, 4.
Time: modes of expressing time, 226; G. of, 187; A. of, 208.

Umlaut: signs of, 31, 362; as a sign of the pl., 45, *b*; 48; in comparison of adj., 74; in pret. subj. of strong verbs, 121; in the pres. of strong verbs, 127, Rem.; 129, Rem.; 130, Rem.; 131, Rem.: 404; nature of, 401; in Eng., 402, 2; spread of, 488, 1; in derived verbs, 535.
Upper Saxon: 482, 5.

Variatives: 533.
Verb: principal parts of, 102; infl. of, 103; personal suffixes of, 104, 118, 121, 449; classification of, 264; irregular weak, 119, 454, 455; weak verbs are derivative, 117, 1.
Reduplicating: 130, 131, 458; non-thematic, see mi-verbs; anomalous, 134-136.
Compound: 137; D. after, 190; A. after, 198, 547-550; accent in, 421.
Reflexive, 138; 197; 206; 236, 2; 264.
Impersonal: subject of, 236, 1, 2, 5; cases after, 186, 193, 205; G. after, 184-186; D. after, 189-193; D. or A. after, 196, 200; A. after, 198; two A., 199, 201; neuter, 179; trans., 191, 264; intrans., 264.
V. of motion: comp. tense of, 265, 4; 266; 283, 3; 290, 2; past part. of, 296; see Number, Predicate, auxil.. pret. pres. verbs; person of, in relative clauses, 326; position of, 341, 350, Rem.; derivation of, 534-550.
Verner's Law: 411, 412, 416.
Voice: passive, infl. of, 116; construction in, 179, 2; 202, 2; 268-273; replaced by reflexive construction, 272; origin of, 273; in Go., 283, 1.
Vowel-declension: see Noun, strong; 428-431.
Vowels: quantity of, 33-35, 488, 2, *b*; analysis and description of, 367-373; vowel-table, p. 162; general remarks upon, 373; doubling of, 33, 363, 4: connecting v. in conjugation, 118; 449, 2; 454, 2, 3; in ablaut, 393-400; in umlaut, 401, 402, 404; interchanges of, 403-406; lengthening of, in W. H. G., 488, 2; shortening of, 488, 3; diphthongization of long v., 488, 5.
Vowel-stems: see Vowel-Declension.

Wordformation: 495-559; substantives, 495-521; pronouns, 496; adjectives, 522-533; verbs, 534-550; adverbs, prepositions, conjunctions, 551-558; interjections, 559.
Word-order: 341-359; normal, 342; inverted, 343; dependent, 344. See these separate heads; in poetry and prose, 359.
Word-stock: 492-494.

WORD-INDEX AND GERMAN-ENGLISH VOCABULARY.

The first contains a list of the German and English words, prefixes and suffixes specially treated in the grammar. Also the strong and irregular verbs with the principal parts, and the second or third pers. sing. of the pres. ind. and the imperative sing., if they are at all peculiar.

The umlauts have a separate place, ä after a, ö after o, ü after u.

The numbers refer to the paragraphs. I., II., III., etc., mean the strong verb-classes and ablaut series.

After the substantives the gender (*m., n., f.*) and the plural ending are always indicated of the strong nouns, the gender and *w.* (= weak) are given after the weak nouns. When there is no pl. sign at all, it is indicated by -. When the cognate Eng. word is rare, or when its meaning differs quite widely from the German word, it is placed after the common Eng. meaning.

The vocabulary is meant to cover all untranslated single words and illustrative sentences as far as § 147, except the foreign words 62, 3; 63, 2; 64.

If weak verbs must have the connecting vowel this is indicated by the preterit. - after a word means a prefix in composition, before a word it means a suffix.

A.

a, pronunc. of, 3; description of, 371, 4; quantity of, before r, rt, rb, 33, 488, 2; in ablauts., VI., 459, 4; in ablauts. I.-V., 459.
a, in Engl. phrase "so much a pound," 156.
Aas, *n., pl.* Äfer, carrion.
ab, from, 303, 1; 516, 1.
aber, but, 60, + word-order, 343, 2; 356; compared with sondern, 320, 2 R
Aber-, 516, 1.
abhanden, lost, 429, 1.
ab'schreiben, to copy, see schreiben.
Abt, *m.,* ⸚e, + abbot.
ach, alas, 60; 559, 1.
achten, with G., to attend to, in 82; (ach= tete).
ae, as sign of umlaut of a, 362, 2.
aeu as sign of umlaut, 362, 2.
After-, 516. 2.
-age, noun-suffix; fem. gender, 161, 2; 163, 5.
ai, pronunc. of, 32, 372, 1.
all, + all, 100; def. art. after, 144; neuter, 168; use of, 261; accent, 422, 5.
allein, *conj.,* but; + word-order, 343, *d.*
aller-, + superl., 222; accent, 422, 1, 5.

allerdings, certainly, 552, 1.
allerlie'bst, charming, very lovely, 222; 422, + Shakspere's *alderliefest.*
allerwärts } everywhere, 552, 1.
allerwegen }
allmählich, gradually, 526, 3, *c.*
als, before a predicate noun, 179; in apposition, 317, 3; before a relative pronoun, 327, 3; in temporal clauses, 330, 1; in comparative clauses, 333, 343, *c*; after comparative, 333, 2; after adjectives, nichts, anber-, 333, 2, *a*, 3; + daß, 333, 3.
alt, + old, *etym.,* 453, 1.
Alter, *n.,* -, age, old age.
am < an dem, + on the, 40.
-am, noun-suf., 501.
Amt, *n.,* ⸚er, *etym.,* 516, 3.
an, + on, 305, 3; 306, 1, 2; compared with auf, 300, 2.
an < an den, 40.
an'binden, to tie, see binden.
-and, noun-suffix, 505.
anber-, + other, 94; accent in comp., 423, 1; *etym.,* 445, 3; in comp., 530.
anberthalb = 1½, 530.
Anmut, *f., no pl.,* grace; gender, 164, *a.*
an'schreiben, to write down, charge, see schreiben.

272   WORD-INDEX AND GERMAN-ENGLISH VOCABULARY.

anstatt, +instead of, 302, 1; + zu and inf., 291, 1, R.; 332, 1.
Ant-, 516, 3.
-ant, 505.
Antwort, f., w., +answer; gender, 164, e.
Arm, m., -e, +arm.
Armut, f., no pl., poverty; gender, 164, a. -at, 511, 2, a; in neut. foreign nouns, 163, 1.
Atem, m., -s, no pl., breath, 47, 1; 501.
atmen, to breathe, 118, 1; (atmete).
au, pronunc. of, 32 ; analysis of, 372, 2; origin of, 488, 5; 490, 6.
auch, also, + eke ; in relat. clause, 93, 4; with wenn, ob, 339.
auf, + upon, 305, 3; compared with an, 300, 2; +daß, in order that. 338.
auf'erste hen, to rise again, 546, 2.
auf'richten, to erect, (-richtete).
Auge, n., -s, -n, +eye.
a-umlaut, see ä, e.
aus, + out of, 303, 2.
außer, besides, 303, 3 ; +daß, 336.
Axt, f., ⸗, +axe, 491, 2; 512, 2.
ä, pronunc. of, 31 ; 362 ; 371, 2, R. 3 ; see umlaut.
ätzen, to bait, corrode, +etch, 535, 1, R. 2.
äu, pronunc. of, 32 ; 372, 3; origin of, 488, 5.
äußer-, +outer, 76, 2.

B.

b, pronunc. of, 4; description of, 385, 2; final, 385, 3; „hartes" b, 383, 1. R.; 392, 2; Eng. correspondents of, 408, 2; 413, 2; 490, 6.
b-, see be-; 557, 1; 414, 3.
backen, buk, gebacken, + bake, VI., 129 ; (bäckst, bûte) ; in comp., 528.
Bad, n., -es, ⸗er, +bath.
Balke(n), m., -, beam, 46, 4.
Band, n., 58 ; m., 162, 4; 496.
Bande, f., w., +band (of robbers, etc.).
-bar, adj.-suffix, 526, 1; accent, 424, 1, b.
barmher'zig, merciful; accent, 422, 3.
baß, more, very, +better, 76; etym., 439.
Bauer, m., w., farmer, 62, 2 ; 63; strong, -, builder; n., -, cage.
Bau, m., -e, see also 51.
Baum, m., ⸗e, tree, +beam.
Bär, m., w., +bear.
be-, +be-, by, 108, 3 ; 540, 1; see bei.
beben, tremble, etym., 457, 3.
bedarf, see bedürfen.
bedecken, to cover, + deck.
bedient, etym., 295, 2.
bedingt, past part., conditioned, 125, 1.
bedürfen, +G., to need; for infl. see 135, 2.
befehlen, befahl, befohlen, to command, IV., 127 ; (befiehlst, befiehlt, befôhle).
Befestigung, f., w., fortification.
befleißen, befliß, beflissen, I., 122, 1; refl., to apply oneself to ; (du befleißest, bu or er befleißt).
befreunden, +befriend; (befreundete).

begeben, refl., + G., to give up, 540, 4; see geben.
beginnen, begann, begonnen, + begin, III., 125, 2 ; 454, 3 ; 457, 2 ; (begönne).
behaupten, to assert, 540, 4 ; (behauptete).
bei, + by, near, 303, 4; in comp., 516, 4.
beib-, +both, 100; use of, 228.
Bein, n., -e, leg, +bone.
beisammen, together, in the presence of.
beißen, biß, gebissen, + bite, I., 122, 1 ; (bu beißest, bu or er beißt).
beizen, + to bait, cauterize; etym., 535, 1, R. 2.
belesen, past part., well read, 540, 3.
bellen, boll, gebollen, + to bark, VIII., 133; (w. and bllst).
benehmen, take away, 540, 4; see nehmen.
bequem, convenient, comfortable, + becoming; 409, 3.
bergen, barg, geborgen, hide, III., 125, 3; 397; (birgst, birg, bärge and bürge).
beritten, past part., mounted; 524, 4.'
bersten, barst, geborsten, +burst, III., 125, 3; (bu birstest, bu or er birst, birst or berste ; börste or bärste).
Besagt(er), the afore + said 146, 1.
bescheiden, modest, past part., 524, 4.
besser, best, + better, best, 76, 1; 439 ; 300, 2.
besucht, frequented, 74.
beten, to pray; (betete).
Betrübnis, f. or n., -isse, sadness, grief.
Bett, n., -es, -en, + bed ; zu — + to — or in —.
beugen, + bow 488, 5.
bewegen, bewog, bewogen, to induce, VIII., 133 ; (bewegst, bewege).
bid, Eng., 396.
biegen, bog, gebogen, bend, II., 124, 2 ; (bu beugft, rare).
Biene, f., w., +bee, 455, 2.
bieten, bot, geboten, offer, II., 124, 2; 396; 408, 2; (er bietet and beut).
binden, band, gebunden, +bind, III., 125, 1; 496; (er bindet).
binnen, within, 303, 5; 557, 1.
Binse, f., w., +bentgrass, 490, 2.
Birne, f., w., +pear, 435, 3.
bis, till, until, prepos., 304, 1 ; conj., 330, 3; etym., 557, 1.
bitten, bat, gebeten, ask, + bid; V., 128, 2 ; 199; 233, 1; 457, 1; 466; (er bittet).
blank, shining, 74.
blasen, blies, geblasen, blow, VII., 130, 1; (bu bläsest, bu or er bläst).
blaß, pale, 74.
Blatt, n., -es, ⸗er, leaf, +blade.
blau +blue, 74.
blättern, to turn the leaves of a book.
Blei, n., no pl., lead.
bleiben, blieb, geblieben, remain, I., 122, 2 ; +inf., 290, 3.
bleichen, blich, geblichen, + bleach, I., 122, 1.
Blüte, +blowth, blossom ; etym., 430, 1.
Bote, m., w., messenger.
Boot, n., pl. Böte, +boat.
Bösewicht, m., pl. -e or -er, rascal, 57, 3 ; 59.

WORD-INDEX AND GERMAN-ENGLISH VOCABULARY. 273

Branntwein, m., -⸗, +brandy.
braten, briet, gebraten, roast, fry, VII., 130, 1; (brätſt, brät).
brauchen, need, compared with müſſen, 267, 4.
Braut, f., ⸗e, +bride.
Bräutigam, m., -e, +bridegroom, 429, 1.
brechen, brach, gebrochen, +break, IV., 127; (du brichſt, bricht).
brennen, brannte, gebrannt, +burn, 119, 1; 455; (brennte).
bringen, brachte, gebracht, +bring, 119, 1; 454, 2; (brächte).
Bronn, m., for Bronnen, Brunnen, well, spring, +bourn, 489, 4; 46, 4.
Broſam, m., -e, crumb; Broſame, f., w., 47, 1; 501.
Brot, n., -e, sometimes ⸗e, +bread.
Bruder, m., ⸗, +brother, 46, 48, 411, 415.
Brunnen, see Bronn.
Buch, n., ⸗er, +book.
Bulle, w., bull, see 162, 3.
bunt, variegated, 74, 5.
Burg, f., w., castle, 397; in comp., 164, c.
Burſch, m., -e, and w., fellow.

C.

c, pronunc. of, 5; in foreign words, 389, 3.
Caſuslehre, f., w., theory of the cases (of nouns).
causeway, causey, +Chauſſee, 494, 3.
ch, pronunc. of, 6; 375, 4; 378, 3; 383, 1; description of, 375; quantity of vowel before, 35; Eng. correspondents of, 410, 3; 414, 3; 415, 1, 3; 490, 8; ch — g, 416; ch — f, 493, 4; ch — t, 535, 1, R. 2.
ch, Ger. correspond. of, 414, 3; 535, 1, R. 2.
-chen, + -kin, 46, 1; 493, 4; 510; neuter gend., 161, 3; pronunc. of, 6; 375, 2.
-che(n), in verbs, 536, 1.
Chriſt, m., w., +Christian, 435, 3.
choose, +kieſen, 416, 1.
chſ, chs, pronunc. of, 29, 383, 1; 490, 3, a.
d, 14; 383, 1; Eng. correspondents of, 413, 4; 414, 3; d — ch, 535, 1, R. 2.

D.

b, pronunc. of, 7, 385, 3; description of, 384, 2. Eng. correspondents of, 410, 1; 413, 1, a; 415; b — t, 416.
-b, 511, 1.
ba, + there, adv.; before a prepos. beginning with a vowel, bar; in relat. clause, 258, 327, 2; in local clauses, 331, a; = because, since in causal clauses, 337; = as, when in temporal clauses, 330, 1, 2; etym., 551, 1; after demonstr. pron., 245, 3.
Dach, n., ⸗er, roof, +thatch.
bachte, see benken, also 417, 1.
Dame, f., w., lady, +dame.
damit, conj., in order that, 338.

da'mit, +baß = by+part. clause, 337
Dank, m., -es; pl. of, see 173.
barf, see dürfen.
baß, +that; see ber; peculiar use of, 168; for G., 183.
baß, +that, conj.; in substantive clauses, 325; + nicht = without + part. clause, 332; in other adverbial clauses, 335, 336, 338.
bäucht, see beucht.
-be, noun-suffix, 511, 2.
Dehnungs=b, 363, 2. 3.
bein, G. of bu, 81; possessive pronoun, 85.
beiner, G., see bein.
bemungeachtet, notwithstanding, prep., 302, 10.
benken, bachte, gebacht, +think, 119, 2; 402, 2; 454, 3; (bächte). Inf. as noun, bas Denken.
Denkmal, n., monument; for pl. see 58.
benn, +then, for, 301, 1; causal conjunction, 321, 337; after comparative, 333, 2; in restrictive clauses, 336; origin of, 551, 1.
ber, + the, def. art., 38–40; demonstr. pronoun 88, 442; lengthened forms in en, er, 244, 2; relat. pronoun, 93.
berart baß, so that, 335.
beren (G. pl.), 88, 93, 1; use of, 244, 1.
berent-, 87, 89.
bergeſtalt baß, in such a manner that, 335.
berer, see beren.
berjenige, he, that one, 91, 1; 247.
bero, 89, 442.
berſelbe, -ſelbige, the same, 91.
berweil, +while, 330.
bes, beß, beſſen, 89.
beſſent-, 89.
beſto, +the, 442, a; correlative of je, 364.
beucht < bünken, 119, 2; 454, 3.
beutſch, German (+Dutch), 413, 1, a.
Deutſchland, n., Germany.
-dge, Ger. correspondents of, 413, 4.
Dichter, m.. -, poet.
bich, +thee, Acc. of bu, q. v.
bie, +the, fem. def. art., see ber.
bies, bieſ(er), +this, 90; etym., 443; use of, 245, 246; bies und bas, jenes, 245, 2; supplanted by adverb+prepos., 246.
biewell, +while, 330; because, 337, 1.
Ding, n.. +thing; for pl. see 58.
bingen, bang or bung, gebungen, III., 125, 1.
bir, +thee, D. of bu, q. v.
boch, adv., yet, after all, +though, 343, e.
Doktor, m., -s, pl. -o'ren, 63, 2.
boppel-, +double, 531, 1.
Drangſal, f., -e, distress.
breſchen, braſch or broſch, gebroſchen, +thresh, III., 125, 3, 132; (bräſche or bröſche, briſcheſt, bu and er briſcht, briſch, also weak, breſcheſt, breſche).
bringen, brang, gebrungen, to penetrate, III., 125, 1; (bränge).
britt-, +third, 410, 1; 530.
bruden, to print } 535, 2.
brücken, to press }

bumpf, hollow (sound), + damp, musty (air), 74, 5.
bunkel, dark, compar. bunkler.
burch, + through, 304, 2; compar. with von, 269; with mittels and mit, 302, 7; separable and insep. prefix in comp. verbs, 549, 1.
Durchlaucht, f., w., Serene Highness.
bünken, bünkte, gebünkt, impers. verb, it seems, +(me) thinks, 119, 2; 454, 3.
bürfen, burfte, geburft, to be permitted; infl., 135, 2; past part., 108, 2; use of, 267, 2; etym., 416.

E.

e, pronunc. of, 8; description of, 371, 1–8; unaccented, 371, 3; 485, 2; sign of length, 33, 363, 1; sign of umlaut, 362; before r, rt, rh, 33, 488, 2; sign of plural, 47, 49, 51, 52; in cardinals, 227; in the adj.-suffixes -el, -er, -en, 71; connecting vowels in conjugation, 118; in case-suffix, 43, 46; derivative e in verbs, 535, 536; secondary before r, 491, 2; e — i, ie, 127, 128, 403; e — ö, 489, 1.
-e in imperative, 105; 118, 3.
-e in nouns < adj., 498, 1; gender of such nouns, 161, 2.
-e in jo-stems, 46, 47, 51, 437, 3; 498, 2; gender of such nouns, 161, 3.
-e in adverbs, 554, 1.
echt, genuine, etym., 488, 3, a.
Ecke, f., w., corner, + edge, 413, 4.
ebel, noble, 404, 71.
ehe, before, + ere, 76, 2, b; 439, 2; conj., 330, 3.
ei, pronunc. of, 32; analysis of, 372, 3; origin of, 488, 5.
-ei, noun-suffix, 498, 3; gender of such nouns, 161, 2.
Eibam, m., -e, son-in-law, 47, 1; 501.
-eien, verb-suffix < French verbs in -ier, 538.
eigen, +own, adj., 470; 471, 6; 524, 4.
eigentümlich, accent and meaning, 422, 2.
eilen, to hasten.
eim < einem, D. of ein, q. v., 41, 1.
Eimer, pail, etym., 398.
ein, + a, one, indef. art., 38, 41; after welch, was für, 92, 2, 3; indef. pronoun, 72, 95, 259, 200; ein par, ein wenig, a few, a little, 100.
ein, adv., + in; — und aus, + in and out; 528, 7.
einander, + one another; uninflected, 84.
eingeboren, for two meanings see 528, 5, 7.
einig-, indef. pron., some, 95; adj., + united.
einmal, + once, 39, 41.
ei'nnehmen, take possession of, see nehmen. In 85 genommen ein for eingenommen by poetic license.
Einöde, f., w., solitude, desert, 511, a.
eins + one, 531, 2; for cognate Acc., 204.

einst, + once, 531, 2; 555, 2.
ei'nstubie'ren, to study well, commit to memory.
einzeln, adv., singly, 555, 3.
eitel, vain; uninflected "nothing but," 212, 1.
-el, noun-suffix, 46, 428, 5; 499; gender of such nouns, 161, 1; 161, 3; adj.-suffix, 71, 523, 1; verb-suffix, 106.
elend, wretched; etym., 401, among Examples.
elf, + eleven, 77; 529.
Elk, + Elch, Elentier, 490, 3.
-eln, in verbs, 536; connecting vowel in —, 118, 3.
Eltern, parents, + elders, 174, 404.
-em in nouns, 501, 523, 2.
emp-< ent-, 541.
empfehlen, empfahl, empfohlen, recommend. IV., 127; 464, 3; (empföhle, du empfiehlst, empfiehl).
-en, noun-suffix, 46; 428, 5; 501; 502; indicates masc. gend., 160, 1; in the n-declension, 61, 62; in the pl. of foreign nouns, 64, 2, 3; in D. and A. of proper nouns, 66; in G. sg. of adj. for es, 72; 91, 3; 216, 1; in pronouns, 244, 2; 440, 2; in mixed declension, 63; in comp. nouns, 518, 1, 2.
Adj.-suffix, 71; 211; 524. In the past part., 107; 453; 502; 524. In the inf., 106; 451. In adverbs, 551.
-enb (nb), in the pres. part., 107; in nouns, 505; in the gerund, 107.
Ende, n., -s, -n, + end.
enge, narrow, 408, 4.
Engel, m., -, + angel.
-ens, adv.-suffix, 555, 2
ent-, 541.
Ente, duck, 430, 1.
entgegen, + against, "to meet," 303, 6; 557, 1; see gegen.
entfagen, to renounce.
entweder (— oder), + either — or, 343, d, 2; 558.
er, he, 81.
er for Herr, gentleman, Mr., 230, 9.
-er, noun-suffix, 428, 5; 65, 507; indicates masc. gend., 161, 1; 163, 3; as sign of plural, 56, 431.
Adj.-suffix, 71, 523, 8; 507, 2; in adverbs, 551; 556; compar. suffix, 79; 438; in the G. of pronouns, 82, 88, 244, 2; 440, 2; in verbs, see -ern.
er-, 542.
Erbe, double gender, 162, 3; neut. pl. Erbe is rare.
Erbe, f., w., + earth, 62, R.
-erei, noun-suffix, 497, 3, R.
erhaben, lofty, 129, R.; 524, 4.
erkalten, to grow cold } 535, 2.
erkälten, refl., to catch cold }
-erlich, adj.-suffix, 526, 3, c.
erlöschen, erlosch, erloschen, to go out (candle, fire), VIII., 133; (erlischest, du and er erlischt, erlisch).
-ern, adj.-suffix, 524, 3; adj. in —, uninflected, 211.

WORD-INDEX AND GERMAN-ENGLISH VOCABULARY. 275

-er(n), verb-suffix, 537, 2; connecting vowel in, 118, 3.
erreichen, +reach, attain.
erschallen, erscholl, erschollen, resound, VIII., 133; (es erschallt).
erschrecken, erschrak, erschrocken, to be frightened, IV., 127; (erschrickst, erschrickt); when trans. generally weak.
erst, first, +erst, 76, 2, b; 439, 2.
erwägen, erwog, erwogen, consider, VIII., 133; (erwägst).
erwähnen, to mention; etym., 457, 2.
Erz- + arch-, 516, 6.
es, + it, N. and A. sg neut., 81; peculiar uses of, 236; gender, 168; replacing cognate A., 204; 236, 6; G. of masc. and neuter, 82; 183; A. supplanted by prepos., 234, 1; indefinite subject, 236, 1, 2, 4, 5; grammatical subject and expletive = there, 236, 8; 313; position of es (A.), 352, e; es (N.) and inversion, 236, 3, a.
es sei denn, daß, unless, 339; 340, 2.
essen, aß, gegessen +eat, V., 128, 1; (du issest or ißt, er ißt, iß); pres. part., 294, 1; etym., 409, 1; 466.
Essig, vinegar, +acid, 509.
etlich-, some, 96.
etwas, something, anything, somewhat, 96; 199, 1; 260.
eu, pronunc. of, 32; analys. of, 372, 3; origin of, 488, 5; eu — ie, 406.
euch +you, D. and A. of ihr, q. v., 81; refl., 83; reciprocal, 84; 238.
euer +your, possessive pron., 85.
eurer for euer (G.), 82.
Ew. +your, 86; 311, 2.

F.

f, pronunc. of, 9; description of, 380; Eng. correspondents of, 410, 2; 414, 2; 415, 1; 493, 4; f — b, 416.
-fach, -fold, 531, 1.
Fach, n., ⸚er (and -e); compartment, pigeonhole;
Faden, m., pl. and meanings, see 48, 1.
fahen, archaic for fangen, q. v.; 417, 1; 458, 2.
fahren, fuhr, gefahren, drive, + fare, VI., 129; 400; 467; +spazieren, 290, 2; (fährst).
Fahrt, f., w., journey, ride, 430, 1, a.
fallen, fiel, gefallen, + fall, VII., 130, 1; 458, 2; (fällst).
falls, adverbial G. in comp., = case, 91, 3; conj., 340.
falsch + false, 74, 5.
fangen, fing, gefangen, to catch, VII., 130, 1; (fängst).
far +fern, 76, 2.
fassen, to seize, (du fassest or faßt), 118, 4.
fast, almost, 300, 1; 554, 1.
faulenzen, to be lazy, 539, 3, a.
Fabrie, f., w., trade, 430, 1, a.
fällen, to fell, 535, 1, a.
-fältig + -fold, 531, 1.

fechten, focht, gefochten + fight, VIII., 133; (du fichtst, ficht, also weak).
Feder, f., w., +feather, pen.
fehlen +fail, lack, 494.
Feind, m., -e, enemy, +fiend, 505; partial adj., 219.
Feld, n., -er, field.
Fels, m., w., } rock, 46, 4.
Felsen, m., -,
fest, firm, 554, 1.
Feuer, n., +fire; pl. of, 173.
Fichtelgebirge, n., a mountain range in N. E. Bavaria, < die Fichte, fir.
finden, fand, gefunden + find, III., 125, 1; 464; (findest).
Fink, m., w., +finch.
fischen +fish (bu fischest or fischt, er fischt), 118.
Finsternis, f., -nisse, darkness.
flach, shallow, level, 74, 5.
flechten, flocht, geflochten, to braid, VIII., 133; (du flichtst or flichst, er flicht, flicht or flechte).
Flexionslehre, f., w., accidence.
fliegen, flog, geflogen, + fly, II., 124, 2; (fleugst, fleug are archaic).
fliehen, floh, geflohen, + flee, II., 124, 2; 490, 3, b; (fleuchst, fleuch are archaic).
fließen, floß, geflossen, II., 124, 1 535, 1, a; (bu, er fleußt, archaic).
Floß, n., ⸚e, +raft, 54; 429, 1.
flößen +to float, trans., 535, 1, a.
Folgend(es) + the following, 140, 1.
forlorn, 416, 1.
fort +forth, on, 76, 2.
fr-, 545; see ver-.
fragen, frug, to ask, 129; 457, 2; construction after, 199.
Frau, f., w., woman, wife, Mrs.
Frauenzimmer, n., -, lady; 166.
Fräulein, n., -, young lady, Miss, 166.
frei + free.
freilich, to be sure, 300, 1; 339; 554, 2, a.
fressen, fraß, gefressen, + eat, V., see essen; 108, 3; 128, 1.
Freund, m., -e, +friend, 505.
der Friede(n), m., no pl., peace, 46, 4; 47, 2.
frieren, fror, gefroren, to freeze, II., 124, 2
froh, cheerful, 74, 5.
fromm, pious; harmless.
frug, pret. of fragen, 129, 461.
früh, early, 300, 1; 554, 1.
Frühstück, n., -e, } breakfast, 137, 1; 421, 1.
Frühstücken,
funden, past part. of finden, 453, 2.
Funke(n), m., spark; see 46, 4.
Furche, f., w., +furrow, 430, 1.
further, 76, 2.
Fuß, m., -es, ⸚e, +foot, 430, 1.
Füchsin, f., pl. -innen, +vixen, 504.
führen, to guide, 535, 1, a.
füllen, colt, +foal, 502, 2.
für + for, 76, 2, b; 304, 3; 306, 9; 516, 5.
fürbaß, onward, 76, 1.
fürchten, to fear; (fürchtete), 454, 3.
fürlieb nehmen, to put up with, 528, 7.
Fürst, m., w., prince, 76, 2, b; 439, 2.

G.

g, pronunc. of, 10; 375, 3, 4; 391, 2; in foreign words, 378, 4; 383, 1, Rem.; after n in N. G., 383, 1, a; Eng. correspondents of, 408, 3, 4; gg, 493, 4; description of, 383, 2; see ge-.
gan — gunnen > gönnen, 471, 5.
ganz, whole.
gar, adj., done; adv., even, very; + nicht, not at all.
Garberobe, f., w., + wardrobe.
gåren, gor, gegoren, to ferment, VIII., 133; (gårſt, rarely gierſt, often weak throughout).
ge-, g-, 516, 7; 543; in the past part., 107, 108; 453, 2; 528; in nouns of neuter gend., 161, 3; in p. p. of compound verbs, 546, 2.
gebären, gebar, geboren, to bring forth, +bear; IV., 127, 398; (pret. subj. gebäre, bu gebierſt, gebier).
geben, gab, gegeben, +give, V., 128, 1; (giebſt, gieb); 466; impersonal, 205; 236, 4; 399.
Geck, m., w., coxcomb.
Gedacht(er), the above mentioned, 146, 1; <gedenken, q. v.
Gedanke(n), m., + thought, see 46, 4; 47, 2.
gedenken, gedachte, gedacht, + think of, mention; see denken.
gedeihen, gedieh, gediehen, thrive, I., 122, 2.
Gedicht, n., -e, poem.
gediegen, adj., solid, pure, past part. of gedeihen, according to Verner's Law, 411; 524, 4.
Gefalle(n), m., pleasure (in), favor, see 46, 4; 47, 2.
gegen + against, 304, 4; see entgegen, zu, nach, um.
gegenüber, opposite, 303, 7.
gehen, ging, gegangen, + go, VII., 130, 1; 136, 1; 457, 2; 474; + inf., 290, 2; past part., 296; (bu gehſt, gehe).
Geiſel
Geißel } for meaning, etc., see 162, 3.
Geiſt, m., -er, + ghost; wit.
geizen, to be stingy, etym., 539.
Gelb und Gut, lit. money and property = all one's possessions.
gelegen, convenient, 524, 4.
gelingen, gelang, gelungen, to be successful (in), III., 125, 1.
gelten, galt, gegolten, to be worth, valid, III., 121, 125, 3; impersonal, 205; (gölte — gälte, bu giltſt, er gilt, imper. gelte as a rule).
Gemach, n., "er, apartment.
gemäß, according to, 303 8.
Gemüt, n., -er, soul, disposition.
gen, towards, 304, 4.
Genera'l, m., -e or -̈e, + general.
geneſen, genas, geneſen, to recover, V., 128, 1; (bu geneſeſt, er geneſt, geneſe).
genießen, genoß, genoſſen, to enjoy, II., 124, 1; (bu genießeſt or genießt).
gering, small, compar. of, 76, 1.

geſchäftig, busy.
geſchehen, geſchah, geſchehen, to happen, V., 128, 1; (es geſchieht).
Geſchlecht, n., -er, race, generation.
Geſchmeide, n., -, set of jewelry.
geſchweige, conj., = say nothing of, 233.
Geſelle, m., w., journeyman, fellow, companion.
Geſellſchaft, f., w., company, party.
Geſicht, n., see 57, 58.
Geſpenſt, n., -er, spook, ghost.
geſſen, past part. of eſſen, 128, R.
geſtalt, shaped, past part. < ſtellen, 455, 8.
geſund + sound, wholesome, 74, 5.
Getreide, n., -, grain, etym., 511.
getroſt, confident, 419; past part. < tröſten, 455, 8.
Gevatter, m., -, +god-father.
Gewand, n., -e, -̈er, garment, 58.
gewandt, active, clever, 74, 5; past part. of wenden, 455, 8.
Gewerbe, n., -, trade.
Gewimmel, n., -, swarming.
gewinnen, gewann, gewonnen, win, III., 125, 2; (gewönne — gewänne).
gh, G. correspondents of, 415, 1.
gewiß, certain, etym., 412, 2; past part., 453, 1.
gießen, goß, gegoſſen, +to pour, II., 124, 1; (geußt, geuß rare, gießeſt or gießt).
Gift, n., -e, poison, + gift; etym., 399; 403, 1; gender of, 162, 3.
Glas, n., -ſes, -̈er, +glass, 492, 3.
glauben + to believe.
Glaube(n), m., + belief, see 46, 4.
gleich + like; for ſogleich = immediately; + inverted order, 339.
-gleichen, in comp. with pron., +the like of, 87.
gleichen, glich, geglichen, to be like, I., 122, 1.
gleißen, w. v., deceive, 122, 1.
gleißen, gliß, gegliſſen, + glitter, I., 122, 1; bu gleißeſt or gleißt, er gleißt).
gleiten, glitt, geglitten, + glide, I., 122, 1; (er gleitet).
glimmen, glomm, geglommen, + to glimmer, VIII., 133.
Gnade, f., w., grace.
Gold, n., no pl., gold.
Gott, m., -es, -̈er, +God, 408, 8.
gönnen, not to grudge; etym., 471, 5.
graben, grub, gegraben, to dig, VI., 129; (bu gräbſt).
greifen, griff, gegriffen, to seize, I., 122, 1.
greinen, grien, gegrienen, + grin (generally weak, rare), I., 122, 1.
Graf, m., w., count.
Griffel, m., -, style (slate-pencil).
grinſen, + grin < greinen, 122, 1.
groß + great; compar. of, 73.
Großmutter, f., -̈, + grandmother.
grüßen + greet; (bu grüßeſt).
gut + good; compar. of, 76, 1; compared with wohl, 299, 2, a; 439.
gulden + golden, 524, 2.

WORD-INDEX AND GERMAN-ENGLISH VOCABULARY. 277

H.

h, pronunc. of, 11; description of, 374; Eng. correspondents of, 410, 3; 415, 1; silence of, 33; 363, 2; 491, 2; loss of, 415, 3; sign of length, 33, 363, 2, 3; h — ch, 73; 490, 3, b; h — g, 124, Rem., 416.

haben + have, infl. of, 110; contracted forms, 111, 1; impersonal, 205; in comp. tenses, 265; 283, 1, 2; + inf., 290, 1.

-haft, adj.-suffix, 526, 2.

Hagestolz, m., w., bachelor; pl. also -e.

halb, before cardinals, 226, 2; after ordinals, 229, 1.

-halben, for ... sake (of), comp. with pronouns, 87, 89; prep., 302, 4.

halber + half, prep., 302, 4.

halten, hielt, gehalten, + hold, VII., 130, 1; (du hältst, er hält).

Hand, f. ⸚e, + hand, 53; 429, 1.

-handen, in comp., 429, 1.

handeln, to act, trade.

handgemein (werden), to come to blows, 219.

Handschuh, m., -e, glove.

hangen, hing, gehangen, + hang (intr.), VII., 130, 1; (du hängst).

hassen + to hate, 414, 1 Ex.; du hassest or haßt.

hast + hast, see haben.

Haß, + hate, 414, 1 Ex.

hat + has, see haben.

hauen, hieb, gehauen, + hew, strike, VII., 131; (du haust).

Haufe(n), m., + heap, crowd, troop, 46, 4.

Haus, n., -es, ⸚er, + house; — und Hof, house and farm, — and home.

hauß + out here < hie + aus, 41, 1.

Häupten, D. pl., see 59.

Hebel, m., -, lever.

heben, hob (hub), gehoben, VI., 129; VIII., 132; 457, 1; 467; (höbe — hübe, du hebst).

Hehl, n. and m., no pl., concealment; in 82 he makes no secret of it ...

Heide, m., w., + heathen, 162, 3; 435, 3.

Heimsuchung, f., w., visitation.

heint + this night, 443, 2.

Heirat, f., w., marriage, 511, a.

heiser + hoarse.

heißen, hieß, geheißen, command, be called, + hight, VII., 108, 1; 131, 458, 2; intrans., 179, 1; trans. 201; + inf., 290, 2, 4; + past part., 296, 2; (du heißest or heißt, er heißt).

-heit + -head, 515, 1; indicates fem. gender, 161, 2; 431, 2.

heiter, serene, 71.

Held, m., w., hero.

helfen, half, geholfen, + help, III., 125, 3; past part. of, 108, 1; 464; + inf., 290, 2; (du hilfst, hilf).

Hemd, n., -es, -en, shirt.

her + hither, + here, 443, 2.

Herr, m., w., lord, master, Mr.; reduced to er, 230, 3; short e, 488, 3.

herrlich, splendid.

hervo'rthun, refl., to distinguish one's self; see thun.

Herz, n., + heart, infl. of, 63, 1; 435, 1.

Herzog, m., ⸚e, + duke, 416, 1.

Herzogtum, n., ⸚er, + dukedom.

hetzen, incite, hunt, 535, 1, b, R. 2.

heuer + this year, 443, 2.

heute + to-day, 443, 2.

hier + here, after pron., 245, 3; etym., 443, 2.

Himmel, m., -, heaven.

hin, thither, away, 443, 2.

hinter + behind, prep., 306, 4; in comp. verbs, 549, 2; adj., 76, 2.

Hirte, m., w., + herdsman.

his — its, 243, 2.

hoch + high, 73; 490, 3, b. Infl. hoher, hohe, hohes.

Hoffart, f., no pl., pride, 528, 2, b.

hoffen + hope.

hohl + hollow, compar. 74.

hold, gracious, compar. 74, 405.

holen, fetch, + hale, haul.

Hopfen, m., -, hops.

Hose, f., w., trousers, + hose.

hören + hear, instead of gehört, 108, 1; 113; + inf., 290, 3.

Huld, f., no pl., favor, grace, 405

Hund, m., -e, dog, + hound.

hundert, n., -e, + hundred, 226; 529, 2.

Hüfte, f., w., + hip, 430, 1; 512, 2.

Hündchen, n., -, little dog,

J.

i, pronunc. of, 12; description of, 369, 1, 2; < ie. 488, 4; < ü, 489, 2; < e, 489, 5.

ich + I, 81.

-ich, 509; indicates masc. gend., 161, 1; 489, 5.

-icht, 509, 1; 525, 3.

ie, pronunc. of, 33, 3; see i; in reduplicating verbs, Cl. VII., 458, 2; 488, 3, a.

ie — eu, 124, 406.

-ie, noun-suffix, 489, 4; 493, 2; indicates fem. gender, 161, 2.

-ieren, verbs in, 108, 4; 493, 2; 538.

-ig, + -y, adj.-suffix 525, 1-3; 489, 5; for -ich, 509; 526, 3, c.

-igen, verb-suf., 539, 4.

-igkeit, 515, 2.

-iglich, adj.-suf., 525, 2.

ihm, ihn, ihnen, see er, sie, es, pers. pron.

ihr, poss. pron., her, their, with cap. your, 85; origin of, 243, 2.

ihrer, G. of pers. and poss. pron., see sie, ihr.

Ihro, your, 86; 441, 2.

in + in, 306, 5; for in den, 40.

-in, noun-suffix, 504; fem. gender, 161, 2; 167: 430, 3.

indem, conj., while, 330, 1; 332; because, 337.

-ing, noun-suffix, 506.

inner + inner, 76, 2.

innerhalb, within, prep., 302.

278 WORD-INDEX AND GERMAN-ENGLISH VOCABULARY.

in fofern, in wiefern, + in so far as, 336.
irbifch + earthly.
irgenb, any, with pron. and adv., 260.
Irrtum, m., ⸗er, + error, 56.
-ifch + -ish, adj.-suffix, 211; 514; 525, 4.
its, 243, 2.

J.

j, pronunc. of, 13; 378, 4; description of, 375, 4; disappeared, 491, 2.
jagen, hunt, chase; strong pret., VI., 129.
Jahr, n., -e, + year; after numerals, 175.
Jäger, m., -, hunter.
je + ever; conj. 334 ; before cardinals with distributive force = "at a time"; je nachbem = "that depends"; + aye.
jeb(er), every, each, infl. of, 97; 216, 1; 445, 1; in comp., 97; pl. of, 261, 3; + either.
jebes, each, 168.
jebweber, every one, each, 97; 261, 3; 445, 2.
jeglich, every, + each, 97, 445, 1.
jemanb, some one, 97; 260; 445, 1.
jen(er), that, + yon, 90; 443, 1; G. sing. of, 216, 1; use of, 245, 246.
jug, see jagen.
jung + young.
Junge, m., w., boy; n., w., + young of animals.
Jungfer, f., w., maiden; etym., 516, 12, a.
Junker, young nobleman, + younker, 516, 12, a.
Juwel, n., -s, -en, + jewel.
jüngft, lately; etym., 555, 2.

K.

k, pronunc. of, 14, 383, 1; Eng. correspondents of, 409, 3; description of, 383, 1.
kahl, bald, + callow; compar. of, 74.
Kaiser, m., -, emperor, + Cæsar, Czar.
kalt + cold, etym., 409, 3.
kann, see können.
kannte, see kennen.
Kar-, in comp., 422, 3.
Katzenkönigin, f., pl. -innen, + queen of cats.
kaum, hardly; word-order, 330, 2.
Käse + cheese, 46, 3; etym., 428, 5.
keck, bold, + quick, 403, Ex.
keifen, kiff, gekiffen, + scold (like an old woman), I., 122, 1.
kein, no, none, 72; 95; 445, 2.
-keit, noun-suffix, 515, 2; fem. gend., 161, 2; 430, 2.
kennen, kannte, gekannt, to be acquainted with, 119, 1; 267, 1; (kennte).
Kette, f., w., + chain, 435, 4.
kiesen, see küren; bu kiesest or kiest.
Kind, n., -es, -er, child, 60.
Kindlein, n., -, little child.
Kirsche, f., w., + cherry.
klar + clear, 74.

Kleinod, n., -e, also -ien as if a foreign word; jewel, 511, a.
klieben, klob, gekloben, split, + cleave, II., 124, 2.
klimmen, klomm, geklommen, + climb, VIII., 133.
klingen, klang, geklungen, to sound, ring, III., 125, 1.
Knabe, m., w., boy, + knave, 413, 3.
knarren, creak.
kneifen, kniff, gekniffen, pinch, I., 122, 1.
kommen, kam, gekommen, + come, IV., 127; 465; 489, 1; umlaut in pres., 127, R.; + past part., 296; 409, 3.
konnte, see können.
Kopf, m., -es, ⸗e, head.
koften + cost; constr. with, 207, 1, R.; (kostest, kostet).
König, m., -e, + king.
können, konnte, gekonnt, + can, 135, 3; 108. 2; 267, 1.
Kraft, f., ⸗e, strength, + craft; prep., 302 5, 6.
Krebs, m., -e, + crayfish, 512.
kreischen, krisch, gekrischen, scream, I., 122, 1.
kreißen, see kreischen.
kriechen, kroch, gekrochen, + creep, crawl, II., 122, 2; (kreuchst, kreuch are archaic).
Kuh, f., ⸗e, + cow, kine.
kund + known, + (un)couth; constr. with 219.
kunnt for konnte, q. v.; in 347.
küren, kor, gekoren, + choose, II., 124, 2; 132; 411; 416, 1; 463; (bu kürst).
küssen, n., no pl., + kissing.

L.

l, pronunc. of, 15; description of, 381; 385, 4.
-l, see -el.
laben. lub, geladen, + load, summon, VI., 129; also weak; (bu lädst, er lädt).
lahm + lame, 74.
Land, n., + land, pl. see 58.
Landsmann, m., pl. -leute, fellow countryman, 172.
lang + long.
Langeweile, f., ennui; accent 422, 1.
laffen, ließ, gelaffen, + let, VII., 130, 1; past part. without ge-, 108, 1; constr. after, 199, 202, 1; 267, 7; + reflexive, 272; in the imper., 287, 4; + inf., 290, 2, 3, b; 266, 4; (bu läffeft or läßt, er läßt).
laß, weary, 74; 76, 2; 439, 2; + late.
lau, tepid, + luke, + lew, 74.
laufen, lief, gelaufen, run, VII., 131; 212, 1; 458, 2; (bu läufft).
laut + loud; etym., 396; 415; prep., 302, 6.
lauter, nothing but, 100.
lächeln, smile.
längft, long ago, 555, 3.
leben + live.
lebe'nbig + living; accent 420, 1.
legen + lay, 535, 1, a.
lehren, teach; instead of gelehrt, 108, 1;

constr. after, 199; in passive, 202, 2;
+ inf., 290, 2; 395.
-lei, 533.
Leib, m., -es, -er, body.
leiden, litt, gelitten, suffer, I., 122, 1; 411;
416, 1; (du leidest).
Leiden, n., -, suffering.
leider, unfortunately, 225, 2.
leihen, lieh, geliehen, + lend, I., 122, 2.
-lein, noun-suffix, 46, 1; 500, 2; neut.
gend., 161, 3; 493, 4.
Leitstern + lode-star, 520, 4, a.
-ler, noun-suffix, 500, 4; indicates masc.
gender, 161, 1.
lernen + learn; instead of gelernt, 108, 1;
for lehren, 199, 2; + inf., 290, 2; 395.
lesen, las, gelesen, read, V., 128, 1; 395;
(du liesest or liest, er liest, lies).
leserlich, legible, 526, 3, c.
let, in imperative, 287, 4.
letzt- + last, 439, 2; 76, 2; after ordinals,
532, 2.
Leumund, m., no pl., repute; etym., 396;
494, 3.
-leute, in comp., 172.
-lich + -like, + -ly, 211; 525, 4; 526, 3;
adverbial suffix, 554, 2.
Licht, n., + light, pl. see 58.
lieben + love, 496.
Liebesbrief, m., -e, + love-letter, 518, 3.
liegen, lag, gelegen, + to lie, V., 128, 2;
457, 1; II., 132; + inf., 290, 3.
-lig, 526, 3, c.
-ling + -ling, noun-suffix, 500, 3; indicates masc. gender, 161, 1.
-lingen, in names of places, 500, 3, a.
-lings, 553.
link-, left (hand), only used attributively
like adjectives in 211.
loben, praise, 496.
Lorber, m., -s, -(e)n, + laurel.
lore + Lehre, 395.
Los, n., -es, -e, + lot.
los + loose, + -less in adj., 526, R.
löschen, trans. and weak, to extinguish, un-
load; intrans., to be extinguished, see
erlöschen.
Ludwig + Louis + Chlodwic, 396.
Luther + Luther, 396.
Lust, f., -̈e, pleasure, + lusts.
lügen, log, gelogen, + lie, II., 124, 2; 132.
Lügen strafen, to give the lie, 199, 2.

M.

m, pronunc. of, 16; description of, 388;
Eng. correspondents of, 490, 4, 5.
-m, see em.
machen + make, + inf., 290, 2; 266, 4; das
(Acc.) macht = the reason is . . .
mag, see mögen.
Magd, f., -̈e, + maid-servant, 512, 3.
mager + meager, 71; no umlaut in compar.,
74.
Magister, m., -, + master (of arts).
mahlen + grind, originally of VI., see 400;
past part. gemahlen still common.

Maid + maid, 512, 3; (poetic form).
Majestät, f., w., + majesty.
mal, once, probably = einmal, 41, 1; in
comp., 531, 2.
man, one, 98.
manch + many a, 100; 262; 525, 1; + ein,
144.
Mann, m., + man; pl., 58, 59; in comp.,
172.
Marsch, m., -̈e, + march; f., w., + marsh,
162, 4.
marschieren + march, 108, 4.
Mast, m., -es, -en, + mast; f., w., fattening,
stall-feeding.
maßen, because, 337, 1.
matt, faint, + mate in check-mate; compar.,
74.
Maulwurf, m., -̈e, + mole, etym., 400;
494, 3.
Mäuslein, n., -, little + mouse.
Meer, n., -e, ocean, + mere.
mehr + more, compar. of, 76, 1; 100;
439; used in comparative, 224.
mehrer-, several, 76, 1; 100.
mehrst-, + most, 100.
meiden, mied, gemieden, avoid, I., 122, 2;
(meidest).
mein, G. of ich, see meiner; mein-, possess.
pron., 85; in mein Tag, Lebtag, 243, 1.
meiner, comparat., + more mine, 225, 2;
G. of ich, 86.
meinig-, poss. pron., + mine, 85.
meist + most, compar. of, 76, 1; 100.
Meißel, m., -, chisel.
melden, announce, (meldete).
melken, molk, gemolken, + milk, VIII., 133;
(du melkst and milkst, melke and milk).
Melodei, f., w., + melody, 493, 2.
Mensch, m., w., + man; n., see 59, 514.
messen, maß, gemessen, + measure, V., 128,
1; (du missest or mißt, er mißt).
Messer, n., -, knife; m., -, measures; see
162, 3.
Mette, f., w., + matins, 435, 4.
mich + me, Acc. of ich, 81.
minder, less, comparison of, 76, 1; 439;
used in compar., 224.
mines, in comp., 87.
mir + me, to me, D. of ich, 81.
miß- + mis-, 453, 1; 516, 8; 544.
Misse- see Miß-.
mit, with, 303, 9.
Mittagsstunde, f., w., hour of noon.
mittel- + middle, 76, 2, b.
mittelst, see mittel-, prep., 302, 7.
Mitternacht, f., -̈e, + midnight, 519, 2.
Mittwoch, m., also f., w., Wednesday,
164, d.
mm < mb, + Eng. mb, 490, 4.
Mohr, m., w., + Moor.
Mord, m., -es, pl. see 51.
morsch, rotten, 74.
mouse – mice, 429, 1.
mögen, mochte, gemocht + may, 135, 4; 108,
2; 267, 3; 412, 2; (er mag, pret. subj.
möchte).
Mund, m., -es, -e, older -̈e, + mouth.
Muskel, m., -n, also f., w., + muscle.

-mut, in comp., 164, a; +mood.
Mutter, f., ⸚, +mother; see Verner's Law, 411.
Mücke, f., w., +midge, 413, 4.
müde, tired.
müssen, mußte, gemußt, + must, 135, 6; 108, 2; 207, 3; 471, 3; (du mußt, er muß, müßte).

N.

n, pronunc. of, 17; nature of, 386, 387; final n in foreign words, 386, 1, Rem.; short before sonant stops, 385, 4; n = *ng*, *i. e.*, "guttural" nasal, 386, and see nt, ng; before labial, 388, 1; lost in Eng., 417, 1; entered the N. of nouns of the n-decl., 435, 2; loss of, 435, 3, 4; 502; 506, 1; Eng. correspondents of, 490, 5. See -en.
nach, after, 303, 10; see zu and gegen.
Nachbar, m., -s, -n, +neighbor. 63, 1.
nachdem, *conj.*, after, 336, 2; according as, 334.
Nacht, f., ⸚e, +night, 53, 2; 429, 1.
nahe +near, +nigh, 73.
Narr, m., w., +fool.
Natu'r, f., w., +nature.
nächst +next, 73; 303, 11.
-nd, part.-suffix, 505.
'ne for eine +a, 41, 1.
neben, by the side of, 306, 6; 557.
nebst, besides, together with, 303, 12; 555, 2.
needs, 552, 1.
nehmen, nahm, genommen, take, IV., 127; Wunder —, 199, 1, 2; (du nimmst, nimmt).
-ne(n), verb-suf., 537, 1; 118, 1, 2.
'nen for einen +, 41, 1
nennen, 119, 1; 455; constr. with, 201; 290, 2; 296, 2; 303, 4.
-ner, noun-suf., 502, 1; masc. gend., 161, 1.
neu + new.
ng, pronunc. of, 17, 383, 1, a; 386, 1.
nicht, nichts, + not, +naught, 99; 199, 1, 2; 309, 1; position of, 354; in compar. clauses, 333, 2; 490, 3; after verbs of hindering, 309, 2.
Nichte, f., w., +niece.
nichts weniger als, anything but . . . , 333, 2, a.
nid + beneath, 551, 3.
nieder-, *adj.*, +nether, 76, 2.
niemals, never.
niemand, no one, 97, 445, 1.
-nis + -ness, 50; indicates neuter and fem. nouns, 161, 2, 3; 428, 6; origin of, 503.
nt, pronunc. of, 17; 386, 1.
nobel +noble, 74.
noch, still; = nor with correlative weder; noch nicht, not yet, 354.
Norden, m., +North.
Noten, old D. pl., 429, 1.
nun +now; = because, 337, 1.
nur, only; +daß, 336; 336, 1.

O.

o, pronunc. of, 18; description of, 370, 1, 2; in ablauts, VI., 459, 4; < u, 405, 489, 4; < â, 489, 3.
ob, *prep.*, +above, 302, 8; *conj.*, whether, 325, 2; although, 339.
ober- in comp., chief, + upper; accent, 422, 7.
ober-, *adj.*, +upper, 76, 2.
obgleich, obschon, obwohl, although, 339.
Obiges +the above, 146, 1.
Ochs, m., w., +ox, 62, 2.
Odem, m., no *pl.*, breath, see Atem.
oe as sign of umlaut, 362, 2.
Ohnmacht, fainting, 489, 3; 516, 10.
ohne, without, 291, 1, R.; 304, 5; in comp., 489, 3; +516, 10; +daß = without +part. clause, 332.
ohnedem, without that, 304, 5.
Ohr, m., -es, -en, +ear.
on +an, 306, 2.
once +einst, 555, 2, a.
-or, noun-end., 63, 2.
Ort, m., *pl.* see 57, 58.
Osten, m., -s, no *pl.*, +east.
ou, Eng. — G. au, 488, 5.
o-umlaut, see ö.
ö, pronunc. of, 31; description of, 370, 3, 4; ö — e 489, 1; < û, 489, 4.

P.

p, pronunc. of, 19; description of, 385, 1; Eng. correspondents of, 413, 3; 414, 2, a; 493, 3.
Pala'st, m., *pl.* Paläste, 163, 1; 493, 1; 494.
Pantoffel, m., -s, -n, slipper.
pf, pronunc. of, 19; description of, 389, 1; Eng. correspondents of, 409. 2; 414, 2.
Pfalz, f., w., castle, +Palatinate.
Pfau, m., w., +peacock, 414, 2.
pfeifen, pfiff, gepfiffen, whistle, I., 122, 1.
Pferd, n., -es, -e, horse, +palfrey.
pflegen, pflog, gepflogen, carry on, VIII., 133; 469; (du pflegst, pflege) always weak = to cherish.
Pfund, n., -es, -e, +pound; after numerals, 175.
ph, pronunc. of, 19.
platt, flat, 74.
plump, awkward, +plump. 74.
preisen, pries, gepriesen, +praise, I., 122, 2; (du preisest, er preist).
Prinz, m., w., +prince (of a royal family).
probieren, try, 108, 4.
putzen, dress up, burnish, (du putzest), 118, 4.

Q.

q, pronunc, of, 20; 409, 3; as symbol, see n and 386.
quellen, quoll, gequollen, to gush forth, well

WORD-INDEX AND GERMAN-ENGLISH VOCABULARY. 281

up, (quillſt, quillt, quill; also weak quel=
leſt, quelle).
quëman, see kommen.

R.

r, pronunc. of, 21; 391, 3; description of, 374, 2; 377; < s, 411, 416.
Rabe, crow, +raven, 413, 3; 435, 3; 502.
Rab, n., -es, "er, wheel, 56.
Ranb, m., -es, "er, edge, brim.
raſch, quick, +rash, 74.
raſen, rage, 118, 4; (bu, er raſt).
Rat, m., -es, pl. see 173.
raten, riet, geraten, advise, VII., 130, 1; (bu råtſt, er råt).
Ratſchlag, ratſchlagen, advice, to advise, 137, 1.
rauch-, rauh, +rough, 490, 3, b.
råchen, råchte, geråcht or gerochen, + wreak vengeance, VIII., 133; generally weak; (bu råchſt).
Rätſel, n., -, +riddle.
recht, +right.
Recht, n., -e, + right, pl. jurisprudence; 221, 4, a.
rechnen, + reckon, 118, 2; 537, 1; (rech= nete).
reben, to speak (rebete), 118; 537, 1.
regnen+rain, 118, 2; 537, 1; (regnete).
reiben, rieb, gerieben, rub, +rive, I., 122, 2.
reich+rich.
Reich, n., -e, empire.
-reich + -rich, + ric, 515, 3, a.
Reichsfreiheit, f., w., +freedom of the empire, immediate dependence upon the empire.
Reichtum, m., "er, wealth.
reißen, riß, geriſſen, tear, I., 122, 1; (bu reißeſt or reißt, +write).
reiſen, travel, 118; (bu reiſeſt or reiſt).
reiten, ritt, geritten, +ride, I., 122, 1; +ſpa= zieren, ride for pleasure, 290; (bu reiteſt, er reitet).
rennen, rannte, gerannt, rush, +run, 119, 1.
retten, save (rettete).
-rich, + -ric, 515, 3.
riechen, roch, gerochen, smell, II., 124, 1.
ringen, rang, gerungen, wrestle, + wring, III., 125, 1; ringen, umringen, etc., are of different origin and weak, though umrun= gen, surrounded, is not uncommon.
rinnen, rann, geronnen, drip, III, 125, 2; 457, 2; ronn, rönne also occur.
Ritter, m., -, knight.
Rod, m., "e, coat.
roh+raw, 74; 415, 3.
Rohr, n., -e, reed, 55.
rot+red.
Röhre, f., w., pipe.
Röslein, n., -, little rose.
rufen, rief, gerufen, call, VII., 131; constr. after, 196; (bu rufſt, in classics sometimes ruſte).
runb+round.
Rücken, m., -, +ridge, 413, 4.

S.

ſ, S, pronunc. of, 22-24; 391, 4; description of, 378, 1, 2, 3; in G. sg. of m. and n. nouns, 42; of ſ. nouns, 66, 518, 3; in G. s. of Eng. adverbs (needs), 552, 1; in the pl., 60; 67; in composition with poss. pron., 87; in compound nouns, 518, 2, 3.
ſſ < ſt, 412, 2; ſ in Verner's Law, 411, 416; Eng. correspondents of, 414, 1; 417, 5; 490, 2.
-s, noun-suffix, 513; in adverbs, 552.
's for bas, 41; for es, q. v.
Sachſe, m., w., +Saxon.
ſacht, gently, + softly, 417, 1; mostly adverb.
Sad, m., "e, +sack.
ſagen+say.
-ſal, noun-suffix, 50, 51; 500, 1; nouns of doubtful gender, 161, 2, 3.
-ſam + -some, 526, 4.
ſamt, with, 303, 13.
Same(n), m., +seed; infl., 46, 4.
ſanft+soft, gentle, 74; 417, 1.
ſatt+satisfied (+sad), 74.
Saß, m., -es, "e, sentence.
ſaufen, ſoff, geſoffen, drink (of animals), II., 124, 1; 463; (bu ſäufſt, +sup and+sip).
ſaugen, ſog, geſogen,+suck, II., 124, 2; (bu ſaugſt, not ſäugſt < ſäugen).
Saus und Braus (uninflec.), revel and riot.
Säbel, m., -, +sabre.
Sänger, m., -, + singer.
Säule, f., w., column, 430, 1.
ſch, pronunc. of, 23; description of, 378, 3; 389, 4; Eng. correspondents of, 412, 1; 490, 1; origin of, 490, 1; 514.
-ſch, 514; see -liſch.
Schabe(n), m., harm, damage, 46, 4; 48, 1.
ſchaffen, ſchuf, geſchaffen, to create, +shape, VI., 129; (bu ſchafft, weak = work, procure).
-ſchaft + -ship, 515, 4; fem. gender, 161, 2; 430, 2.
ſchallen, ſcholl, geſchollen, to sound, generally weak, 133; (bu ſchallſt).
Schar, f., w., troop, host.
ſchauen, to look.
-ſche, suffix of surnames, 514, a.
ſcheiben, ſchieb, geſchieben, to separate, depart, I., 122, 2; VII., 131; (bu ſcheibeſt, er ſcheibet).
ſcheinen, ſchien, geſchienen, + shine, seem, I., 122, 2.
ſcheißen, ſchiß, geſchiſſen, cacare, I., 122, 1.
ſchellen, ſcholl, geſchollen, to ring (the bell), VIII., 133; (bu ſchillſt, ſchill are very rare, also weak).
ſchelten, ſchalt, geſcholten,+scold, III., 125, 3; 491, 2; (bu ſchiltſt, er ſchilt, ſchilt or ſchelte, ſchölte).
-ſchen, suf. in verbs, 530, 2.
ſcheren, ſchor, geſchoren,+shear, VIII., 133; (bu ſchierſt, ſchier, also weak.
ſcheuen, avoid; refl., to fear.
ſchieben, ſchob, geſchoben, push, + shove, II., 124, 2.

ſdier, *adj.*, brilliant, pure; *adv.*, almost, (quick, comp. bold+balt).
ſdießen, ſchoß, geſchoſſen, + shoot, II., 124, 1; (bu ſchießeſt or ſchießt).
Schild, *n.* and *m.*, +shield, see 58; 162, 4.
ſchinden, ſchund (ſchand), geſchunden, to skin, III., 125, 1; (bu ſchindeſt).
ſchlafen, ſchlief, geſchlafen, +sleep, VII., 130, 1; pres. part., 294, 1; (bu ſchläfſt).
ſchlaff, slack, 74.
ſchlagen, ſchlug, geſchlagen, strike, +slay, VI., 129; *recipr.*, =to fight; (bu ſchlägſt).
ſchlant, slender, 74.
ſchleichen, ſchlich, geſchlichen, to sneak, I., 122, 1.
ſchleifen, ſchliff, geſchliffen, to sharpen by grinding, I., 122, 1; weak = to raze.
ſchleißen, ſchliß, geſchliſſen, wear off, + slit, I., 122, 1; (bu ſchleißeſt or ſchleißt).
ſchliefen, ſchloff, geſchloffen, to slip, II., 124, 2; (bu ſchleuffſt, ſchleuf very rare).
ſchließen, ſchloß, geſchloſſen, close, conclude, II., 124, 2; (bu ſchließeſt or ſchließt, ſchleußt etc., rare).
ſchlinden, see ſchlingen.
ſchlingen, ſchlang, geſchlungen, to twine, +sling, devour, III., 125, 1.
Schluck, *m.*, -e, swallow; *pl.*, 51.
ſchlüpfen +slip < ſchliefen according to 535, 1, R. 2.
Schmach, *f.*, *no pl.*, disgrace, 490, 3, *b*.
ſchmachten, to pine (ſchmachtete).
ſchmeicheln, flatter, 536, 2, Ex.
ſchmeißen, ſchmiß, geſchmiſſen, throw, +smite, I., 122, 1; (bu ſchmeißeſt or ſchmeißt).
ſchmelzen, ſchmolz, geſchmolzen, +melt, VIII., 133; (bu ſchmilzſt or ſchmilzt, er ſchmilzt, trans. is weak).
Schmerz, *m.*, -es, -en, pain, +smart, 63.
ſchnauben, ſchnob, geſchnoben, snort, puff, +snuff, II., 124, 2, also weak; (bu ſchnaubſt).
Schneewittchen, +Snow-white (witt is L. G. for weiß).
ſchneiden, ſchnitt, geſchnitten, +cut, I., 122, 1; 416, 462; (bu ſchneibeſt).
ſchnieben, see ſchnauben.
ſchnitzen, carve, 535, 1, R. 2.
ſchon, already, 339; position of, 354; form of, 554.
ſchön, beautiful, 522.
ſchrauben, ſchrob, geſchroben, + screw, II., 124, 2; (bu ſchraubſt); also weak.
ſchrecken, ſchrak, geſchrocken, to be frightened, see erſchrecken.
Schreck(en), *m.*, fright; infl., 46, 4.
ſchreiben, ſchrieb, geſchrieben, write, I., 122, 2.
ſchreien, ſchrie, geſchrieen, cry, +scream, I., 122, 2.
ſchrelten, ſchritt, geſchritten, to stride, walk, I., 122, 1; (bu ſchreiteſt, er ſchreitet).
Schritt, *m.*, -es, -e, stride, step; after numerals, 175.
ſchroff, rugged, uncouth, 74.
ſchweigen, ſchwieg, geſchwiegen, to be silent, I., 122, 2
Schwein, *n.*, -c, pig, +sow, +swine, 502, 2.
ſchwellen, ſchwoll, geſchwollen, +swell, VIII., 133; (bu ſchwillſt, ſchwillt).
ſchwinden, ſchwand, geſchwunden, disappear, III., 125, 1; (bu ſchwindeſt, ſchwände — ſchwünde).
ſchwingen, ſchwang, geſchwungen, +swing, III., 125, 1; (ſchwänge and ſchwünge).
ſchwimmen, ſchwamm, geſchwommen, +swim, III., 125, 2; 464; (ſchwömme and ſchwämme).
ſchwören, ſchwur and ſchwor, geſchworen, +swear, VI., 129; VIII., 132; 457, 1; (bu ſchwörſt).
Se. < Seine, His, 311, 2.
See, *m.*, -s, -en, lake; *f.*, *w.*, +sea, 63.
ſehen, ſah, geſehen, +see, V., 128, 1; instead of geſehen, 108, 1; +inf., 290, 3; 410, 3; 411, Ex.; (bu ſiehſt, ſieh).
ſein, G. s. of er, es; see ſeiner.
ſein, his, its, 85; not referring to subject, 242, 1; 243, 2; referring to indefinite subj., 98; seemingly for ihr in „ſeiner Zeit," 343, 2.
ſein, to be, 110; 473, 1; in comp. tenses, 266, 283, 1-3; in passive, 273; +inf., 290, 3. *a*; +past part., 296, 2; +pres. part., 274, 6.
ſeiner, G. s. of er, es, of him, of it, 81.
ſeit+since, *prep.*, 303, 14; +since, *conj.*, 330, 2.
ſeitbem, see ſeit.
ſeitens, on the part of, *prep.*, 302.
-ſeits, in comp. with poss. pron., 87, 552.
-ſel, noun-suf., 46, 1; 500, 1; mostly neut. gend., 16, 18.
ſelb-, ſelber, +self, 91, 2; before numerals, 229, 1; 530; strengthens refl. pron., 237, 2; use of, 249.
ſelbander, two of them, of us (according to the person of the verb), 229, 1.
ſelbig-, same, 248, 2.
ſelbſt, see ſelb-.
-ſelig, adj.-suf., 528, 2, *a*.
-ſen +-se, verb-suf., 539, 1.
ſenden, ſandte, geſandt, +send, 119, 1; 455, 1; pret. subj., ſendete.
ſenken, ſenkte, geſenkt, *trans.*, +sink, 535, 1, *a*.
Seſſel, *m.*, -, (easy, large) chair.
Seuche, *f.*, *w.*, epidemic disease, 396.
sh — ſch, 490, 1, *d*.
shall+ſollen, 266, 5; in fut., 266, 6; 279, 3; 283, 4.
ſich, A. and D., sing. and pl. of refl. pron., him- and herself, themselves, 83; reciprocal pron., 84, each, one another; supplants pers. pron., 237, 1; 243, 3, R.; position of, 352, *e*.
ſie, N. and A., fem. sing., and pl. of all genders, +she, her, they, them, 81.
Sie, you in address, 230, 2; 233.
ſiech, infirm, +sickly, 396.
ſieden, ſott, geſotten, boil, +seethe, II., 124, 1; 416, 1; 463; (bu ſiebeſt); figur. weak.
ſin-, in comp., 494, 3.
ſingen, ſang, geſungen, +sing, III., 125, 1.
ſinken, ſank, geſunken, +sink, III., 125, 1.
Sinn und Verſtand = all reason, lit. sense and reason.

WORD-INDEX AND GERMAN-ENGLISH VOCABULARY. 283

finnen, fann, gefonnen, meditate, III., 125, 2; (fänne and fönne).
fint+since, *prep.*, 303, 14.
fintemal, because, 337, 1.
fiŧen, faŧ, geſeſſen,+sit, V., 128, 2; 457, 1; [bu ſiŧeſt, er fiŧt, ſiŧ(e)].
ſo+so; in main clauses preceded by depend. claus., 329; 333; 330, 3, *a*; 348, 2; in consecutive clauses, 335; in compar. clauses, 333, 3; in concessive cl., 339; relative adv., 257; =wenn, 340; +ein, 250, 2.
Sohn, *m.*, ⸚e,+son, 405.
ſolch+such, 91, 3; 443, 1; force of, 250; +ein, 91, 3; 144; 157; 333, 3.
ſofern, *conj.*, +in so far as, 340.
Soldat, *m.*, *w.*,+soldier.
ſollen, ſollte, geſollt, + shall, ought, 135, 5; 108, 2; 471, 2, 4; force of, 267, 5; 279, 3; 283, 2, 5.
ſonder, without, 304, 6; 489, 4.
ſondern, but, 320, 2, R.; word-order after, 343, *c*.
ſonſt, at other times, 320; 551, 3.
ſp, pronunc. of, 24; 378, 3; 389, 4; 391, 1; Eng. correspondents of, 412, 1.
Spaß, *m.*, -es, ⸚e, joke, fun.
ſpaßen, to joke, 118, 2; (ſpaßeſt, ſpaßte).
ſpät, *adv.*, late, 300, 1; 554. 1.
Spaten, *m.*, -, +spade.
Spaŧ, *m.*, *w.*, also -es, -e, +sparrow.
ſpazieren, walk about, with verbs of motion, 290, 2.
Spähen+spy, 494, 1.
ſpät, late, see also ſpat.
ſpeien, ſpie, geſpieen, + spit, + spew, I., 122, 2.
Speiſe, *f.*, *w.*, food.
ſpinnen, ſpann, geſponnen,+spin, III., 125, 2; (ſpänne and ſpönne).
Spion, *m.*, -e,+spy, 494, 1.
ſpleißen, ſpliß, geſpliſſen, + split, I, 122, 1; (bu ſpleißeſt or ſpleißt, er ſpleißt).
Sporn, *m.*,+spur, for infl. see 63, 1.
ſprechen, ſprach, geſprochen,+speak, IV., 127; (bu ſprichſt, ſprich; with A., to see, in § 66.
ſprießen, ſproß, geſproſſen,+sprout, II., 124, 1; (bu ſprießeſt or ſprießt, er ſprießt; old, ſpreußt, ſpreuß).
ſpringen, ſprang, geſprungen, + spring, run, III., 125, 1; (ſpränge).
Sproß, *m.*, -ſſes, -ſſe,+sprout, scion.
ſt, pronunc. of, 24; 378, 3; 389, 4; 391, 1; Eng. correspondents of, 412.
-ſt, superl. suffix, 73; 438, 1; in ordinals, 80; 530; in nouns, 512, 3.
Staat, *m.*, -es, -en,+state, government.
Stachel, *m.*, -, sting.
Stadt, *f.*, ⸚, city, 430, 1, *a*; 490, 1, *b*.
Stamm, *m.*, ⸚, +stem.
ſtarr, stiff,+staring, 74.
ſtatt+instead of, 302, 1; 490, 1, *b*.
Statt, *f.*, *no pl.*, place,+stead, see Stabt.
Stätte, *f.*, *w.*, spot, see above.
ſtechen, ſtach, geſtochen, sting, puncture, + stick, IV., 127; 457, 2; 465, 1; (bu ſtichſt, ſtich).

ſtecken+to stick (not ſtat, but weak).
ſtehen, ſtand (ſtund), geſtanden,+stand, 129; 136, 2; 457, 2; 475; (bu ſtehſt, ſtehe, ich ſtünde or ſtände).
ſtehlen, ſtahl, geſtohlen, + steal, IV., 127; 398; 465; (bu ſtiehlſt, ſtiehl or ſtehle, ſtöhle or ſtähle).
ſteigen, ſtieg, geſtiegen, to ascend, mount, I., 122, 2.
Stein, *m.*, -e,+stone.
Steinmeŧ, *m.*, *w.*, also strong, stone-cutter.
ſteinreich+stony, very rich, 422, 4.
ſterben, ſtarb, geſtorben,+to die, IV., 125, 3; (+starve, ſtirbſt, ſtürbe, rarely ſtärbe).
ſtieben, ſtob, geſtoben, fly, scatter like dust, I., 124, 2; (bu ſtiebſt, older ſteubſt).
Stift, gender and meaning see 58.
ſtinken, ſtant, geſtunten,+stink, III., 125, 1; (ſtänke, rarely ſtünke).
ſtolz, proud, 74.
ſtoßen, ſtieß, geſtoßen, push, thrust, VII., 131; 458, 2; (bu ſtößt, er ſtößt).
ſtraff, stretched, tight, 74.
Strauch, *m.*, ⸚e and ⸚er, shrub.
ſtrecken+stretch, in § 79 to die.
ſtreichen, ſtrich, geſtrichen, + strike out, + stroke, I., 122, 1.
ſtretten, ſtritt, geſtritten, contend, I., 122, 1; (bu ſtreiteſt); "strong," 428, 3.
Stube, *f.*, slitting-room (+stove).
Stuhl, *m.*, ⸚e. chair,+stool, throne.
ſtund, pret. of ſtehen, *q. v.*
-ſtund in comp., 531, 2.
Stute, mare,+stud, 430, 1.
ſtuŧen, be startled, clip, < same root as ſtoßen; see 535; bu ſtuŧeſt, 118, 2.
ſuchen + seek, 454, 3.
Sucht, *f.*, *w.*, passion, mania, 396; *orig.*, lingering disease; +sick.
-ſüchtig in comp., 528, 2, *b*.
Süden, *m.*, -s,+south.
Sündflut, *f.*, *w.*, Deluge, 494, 3.
ſüß+sweet.
ß, pronunc. of, 22, 35-

T.

t, pronunc. of, 25; see tþ; Eng. correspondents of, 408. 1; 412: 413, 1; 414, 1; description of, 384, 1; in þ, 389, 3, 4; excrescent, 87; 89; 92, 1; 491, 2; 512, 2, 3; stops into spirants before, 412; tr, 414, 1.
-t, noun-suffix, 512; fem. gend., 161, 2; 163, 5.
-t, in the participle of weak verbs, 453.
-t, 2. pers. sg. in pret.-pres. verbs, 470, 2.
Tafel, *f.*, *w.*, formal meal; bei —, at+table.
Tag, *m.*, -e,+day.
taugen, to be fit,+do, 471, 5.
Tauſend, *n.*, -e,+thousand, 226.
tch, G. correspondents of, 414, 3.
-te, suf. in ordinals, 80, 530.
-te, in pret., 117; 454, 1.
teils, in part; in comp. with poss. pron., 87.

-tel, in comp., 532, 2.
-ter, noun-suf., 508.
têta, see thát.
Teutones, 492, 3.
th, pronunc. of, 25 ; origin of, 363, 8 ; 384, 1.
thất + did, 274, 6 ; 290 ; 476, 2.
Thor, gend. and meaning, 162, 4 ; 408, 1.
Thráne, tear, 430, 1.
Thron, *m.*, -e and -en, + throne, 63, 1.
thun, that, gethan, + do, 136, 3 ; 454, 1 ; 476; as an auxil., 274, 6 ; 294, 1 ; (thâte).
Thür, *f., w.,* + door, 408, 1 ; 430, 1.
Thürchen, *n.,* -, little door.
Tier, *n.,* -e, animal (deer).
Tisch, *m.,* -e, table (+ disk, + dish).
Tochter, *f.,* ", + daughter, 46, 48, 408, 1.
Tob, *m.,* -es, *pl.* of, 173.
toll, mad, + dull, 74.
tragen, trug, getragen, carry, VI., 129 ; (bu trägst).
Trank, *m.,* "-e, + drink.
trauen (with D.), to trust.
treffen, traf, getroffen, hit, IV., 127 ; (bu trifft, triff).
treiben, trieb, getrieben, + drive, I., 122, 2.
treten, trat, getreten, + tread, step, V., 128, 1 ; (bu trittst, er tritt, tritt or trete).
triefen, troff, getroffen, + to drip, drop, II., 124, 1 ; 463 ; (bu triefst, rarely treufst).
triegen, see trügen.
trinken, trank, getrunken, + drink, III., 125, 1 ; (tränte, older trunte).
troden + dry, 524, 4.
Tropf(en) *m.,* -, + drop, 46, 4.
Tropf, *m.,* "-e, fool, *orig.* "struck with paralysis."
trot, in defiance, in spite of, 302, 9.
tröften, to comfort, 535, 1, *a* ; (tröftete).
-trunken, intoxicated, 528.
Trübfal, *f.,* -e, sorrow.
Trümmer, a pl., ruins, 59.
trügen, trog, getrogen, to cheat, II., 124, 2 ; 132 ; (bu trügst, older treugst).
Tuch, *n.,* -es, "-er, cloth, shawl, 58, 85, -tum, + -dom, 57, 4; mostly neut. gend., 161, 3 ; origin of, 501 ; 515, 5.
tz, pronunc. of, 389, 3 ; 414, 1 ; tz — h, f, 535, 1, *R.* 2 ; see z.

U.

u, pronunc. of, 26 ; description of, 368, 1, 2 ; < uo, 488, 4 ; u — o, 405 ; + *nasalis* and *liquida sonans*, 459, 3, *a.*
ue, as sign of umlaut, 362, 2.
um + zu, in order to, 291, 1, 4, R. ; 335, 1 ; 338, 1 ; 304, 7; in comp. verbs, 549, 4 ; + so, 324.
umringen, surrounded, see ringen.
un- + -un, accent, 422, 6 ; 516, 10.
unb + and, 319 ; + inversion, 339, 1.
-ung + -ing, 506, 2 ; gend., 161, 2.
uns, D. und A. of wir, + us, to us, 81 ; also refl., 83 ; and reciprocal pron., 84.
unser, G. of wir, 81.

unser, poss. pron., + our, 85.
unsrer, for unser, 82.
unter-, *adj.*, lower, + under, 76, 2.
unter, *prep.*, + under, 306, 8, 10 ; in comp. verbs, 549, 5.
Unterschied, *m.,* -es, -e, difference, 458, 3.
Unterthan, *m., w.,* subject (of a ruler), 63, 1.
Ur- + or-, 516, 9.
Urahne, great grandmother in § 143.
urbar, arable, 526, 1.
ů, pronunc. of, 31 ; sign of umlaut, 362, 2 ; 368, 4 ; description of, 367 ; 368, 3, 4 ; < üe, 488, 4 ; ü — i, 489, 2.
über + over, 306, 7; in comp. verbs, 549, 8.
ü'berfahren, to cross.
überhaupt, in general, 423 ; 552, 3.

V.

v, pronunc. of, 27 ; 380, 1, 2 ; see f ; 415, 1.
Vater, *m.,* ", + father, 46, 48, 2 ; 411 ; 478, 4.
Vaterland, *n.,* -es, -e, + fatherland.
ver- + for-, 516, 11 ; 545 ; in certain participles, 295, 2 ; 545, *R.*
verberben, verbarb, verborben, to spoil (intr.), III., 125, 3; (bu verbirbst, verbirb, verbürbe, rarely verbärbe).
Verbienst, gend. and meaning, 162, 3.
verbient, deserving, meritorious, 295, 2.
verbriessen, verbross, verbrossen, to vex, II., 124, 1 ; (bu verbriesset or verbriest, old verbreust).
vergessen, vergass, vergessen, + to forget, V., 128, 1 ; past part. in comp., 295, 2, *a* ; (bu vergissest or vergist, er vergisst, vergiss).
verhältnismässig, comparatively.
verkaufen, to sell.
verlassen, to forsake, see lassen.
verlegen, embarrassed, past part., 295, 2, *a* ; 524, 4.
verlernen, to forget how to . . ., + unlearn.
verlieren, verlor, verloren, + lose, II., 124, 2 ; 416.
vermöge, by virtue of, 302, 11.
verwirren, to confuse, strong past part., verworren = complicated, VIII., 133.
Vetter, *m., w.* or mixed decl., cousin, 63, 1.
Vieh, *n.,* -es, -e, cattle (+ fee), 410, 3.
viel, much, compar. of, 76, 1 ; 100 ; 199, 1, 2 ; 263.
vixen + Füchsin, 504.
voll- + full, 74, 549, 6.
voller + full, 219, 1.
vollkommen, perfect, 421, 1.
Volk, *n.,* "-er, people, + folk.
Vo'lksetymologie' + folk-etymology, 494, 2.
vom < von dem, from the, 40.
von, from, by, 303, 15; compar. with durch, 269 ; 304, 2 ; 306, 7, *R.* ; + selbst, of . . . self, 249, 2.
vor + before, in point of, 306, 9 ; 516, 5 ; compar. with für, 304, 3.
voraus'verkündigen, announce beforehand, 546, 2.
vorber-, the front one, 76, 2 (short o).

WORD-INDEX AND GERMAN-ENGLISH VOCABULARY. 285

Vorfahr, m., w., ancestor.
vorhabend, intended, 394, 1.
Vormund, m., -es, ⸗er, guardian.

W.

w, pronunc. of, 28; description of, 379; 380, 2; loss of, 417, 2; Eng. correspondents of, 410, 3; 415, 2; 490, 6.
wachſen, wuchs, gewachſen, grow, +wax, VI., 129; 417, 5, a; (du, er wächſt).
Wagen, m., +wagon, +wain, 494, 1; 48, 2.
Waggon, m., pl. in -s, car, 494, 1.
wain+Wagen, 494, 1.
wahr, true, 74.
Wahrheit, f., w., truth.
Wald, m., -es, ⸗er, forest, +wold.
walten, rule (waltete).
wandeln, walk, change, 118, 3.
wandern+wander, 118, 3.
wann+when; for relat. pron., 258; conj., 330, 1; etym., 551, 2.
war, pret. of ſein, q. v.; also wēsan.
ward, pret. sing. of werden, 111, 2; 460.
warum+why, +wherefore, 251, 4; 551, 2.
was, interrog. pron., 92; 444; use of, 251; +G., 251, 1; preceded by zu, mit, 251, 3; with für and ein, 144, 253; force of warum, 251, 4; relat. pron., 93; 256; 256, 2; indef. pron., 96; 204; 260.
was, archaic of wēsan, 466, 1.
waſchen, wuſch, gewaſchen, +wash, VI., 129; 412; (du wäſcheſt or waſchſt).
Waſſer, n., -, +water, 414, 1, Ex.
wägen, see wiegen.
während, during, 302, 11; conj., 330, 1.
-wärts, +-ward, 553, 2.
"weak," 428, 3.
weben, wob, gewoben, +weave, VIII., 133; (du webſt); weak = to move.
weder — noch + neither — nor; +whether, 444, 3; in compar. clauses, 333, Ex.
-wegen, on account of, in comp. with pron., 87, 89; prepos., 302, 13.
weh thun + D., to pain, see thun.
Weib, n., -es, ⸗er, +woman, +wife, 166.
weich, soft (+weak).
weichen, wich, gewichen, to yield, I., 122, 1; weak = to soften.
Weihnachten, Christmas, 429, 1.
weil, because, 337; +while, 330, 1.
-weiſe, -wise, 552, 3.
weiſen, wies, gewieſen, show, I., 122, 2.
weisſagen, prophecy, 547, 3; (p. p. geweiſſagt).
weiß, see wiſſen.
welch, interrog. pron., 92, 2; 444, 2; with ein, 144; 252; relat. pron., 93, 2; 255, 256; indef. pron., 96, 260; etym., 415, 2.
wem, D. of wer, q. v.; 92, 1.
wenden, wandte, gewandt, turn (+wend), 119, 1; 397; 453; (du wendeſt, pret. subj. wendete).
wenig, little, few; comparison regular or as in 76, 1.

wenn, conj., + when, = if in temporal cl., 330, 1; = if in concessive cl., 339; = if in condit. cl., 340; etym., 551, 2.
wer + who, interrog. pron., 92; 251; 410, 3; 444; relat. pron., 93, 3; 254; 256; indef. pron., 96; 254; 260; 339.
werben, warb, geworben, recruit, sue for, III., 125, 3; (du wirbſt, wirb, würbe or wärbe).
werden, ward or wurde, geworden, become (+worth), III., 125, 3; infl. of, 110; 111, 2; 460, 1; in passive, 273; in comp. tenses, 283, 2-5; + zu, 303, 16; (du wirſt, er wird, werde, würde).
werfen, warf, geworfen, throw, III., 125, 3; (du wirfſt, wirf, würfe or wärfe).
Werk, n., -es, -e, +work, 60.
wes, weſſen, wes, 92, 1; 256, 4.
weſen, wēsan, V., 128, 1; 411; 466.
weshalb, wherefore, 92, 1.
weſſen-, in comp., 92, 1.
Wicht, m., -e, +wight, +whit.
wider, against, 304, 8; in comp. verbs, 549, 7.
widmen, dedicate (widmete), 118, 2.
wie, +how, as, 444, 1; in tempor. clauses, 330, 1, 2; in compar. cl., 333; after comparative, 333, 2.
wieder, adv., again, in comp. verbs, 549, 8.
wiegen, wog, gewogen, +weigh, VIII., 133; (also wägen, du wiegſt).
wild+wild.
will, see wollen; 267, 6.
willen, for the sake of, in comp. with pron., 87, 89; prepos., 302, 14.
winden, wand, gewunden, +wind, III., 125, 1; (du windeſt).
wiſſen, wußte, gewußt, for infl. see 135, 1; 412, 2; 471, 1; 472, 1; compar. with kennen, können, 267, 1.
with+wider, 306, 8.
Wittum, n., -e, jointure, allowance, 501.
wo(r) + where, supplants cases of interrog. and relat. pron., 251, 2; 258; in local clauses, 331; in tempor. cl., 330, 1; in condit. cl., 340, 340, 4; origin of, 551, 2.
wofern, conj., in so far as, 336; 340; 340, 2.
wohl+well, pronunc. of, 381; 339; 489, 1; position of, 354; 299, 2, a.
wohlgeboren, (Your) Honor, lit. +well born.
wollen, wollte, gewollt, +will, be willing, for infl. see 135, 7, and 108, 2; 472, 2; special force of, 267, 6; 270, 3; 283, 5.
womöglich, if possible, 340, 4.
worden, past part. of werden, 108, 5.
Wort, n., -e and ⸗er, +word, 58.
Wunder, n., -, +wonder, see nehmen.
wurde, pret. of werden, 111, 2.
Wurm, m., ⸗er, and ⸗e, +worm.
wußte, see wiſſen.
Würde, f., w., dignity, +worth.

X.

x, pronunc. of, 29; 389, 2; 417, 5, *a*; Engl. x as symbol, 395.

Y.

y, pronunc. of, 31.

Z.

z, pronunc. of, 30; 389, 3, 4; Eng. correspondents of, 409, 1; 414, 1; 490, 2; 535, 1, *R*. 2.
zahm + tame, 74, 398.
Zahn, *m.*, ⸚e, + tooth, 409, 1; 417, 1.
zart, tender, 74.
zähmen + to tame, 535, 1, *a*.
Zähre, *f.*, *w.*, + tear, 430, 1.
zehn + ten, 77, 529.
Zeichen, *n.*, -, + token.
zeichnen, draw, delineate, 118, 1.
zeihen, zieh, geziehen, accuse, I., 122, 2; 395; 462.
-zen, verb-suf., 539, 3.
zer- + dis-, verb-pref., 546.
zerreißen, to tear to pieces, see reißen.
Zeuge, *m.*, *w.*, witness.

ziehen, zog, gezogen, draw, II., 124, 2; 416; (du zeuchst, zeuch are archaic).
-zig + -ty in numerals, 529, 1.
zittern, tremble, *etym.*, 457, 3.
zu + to, 303, 16; before inf., 291; before adj., 291, 4; 333, 3; see gegen and nach.
Zuber, tub, *etym.*, 398.
Zucker, *m.*, *no pl.*, + sugar.
zufolge, in accordance with, 302, 15.
zum < zu dem + to the. 40.
Zunft, *f.*, ⸚e, guild, 398.
Zunge, *f.*, *w.*, + tongue, 414, 1, Ex.
zur < zu der + to the, *fem.*, 40.
zurückbringen + bring back, see bringen.
zusammen, together.
zwar, to be sure, 339; 555, 3; position of, 354.
zween + twain, + two, 79; 529.
zwei + two; infl. of, 78; form and gend. of, 79; 529.
zwelf + twelve, 77; 529; 489, 1.
zwie- + two-, 520, 1.
zwier + twice, 531, 2.
zwingen, zwang, gezwungen, to force, III., 125, 1.
zwischen + between, 306, 10; compar. with unter, 306, 8; 305, 1, 2.
zwo + two, *fem.*, 79; 529.
ʒ, Grimm's sign for the sound between z and s, 414; > s, 490, 2.

APPENDIX.

I. Fuller Inflections for Part I., Section I.

II. Alphabetical List of Strong and Irregular Verbs.

DECLENSION OF NOUNS.

1. Strong Declension.

Characteristics: the G. sing. ends in –es or –s. Upon the four ways of forming the plural the division into classes is based.

2. I: Class. Characteristics: no suffix in the pl., but there may be umlaut of the stem-vowel.

   a. No umlaut.

Masc. der Hebel, *the lever*			Neut. das Wunder, *the wonder*		
Sing.	N.	der Hebel	*Sing.*	N.	das Wunder
	G.	des Hebels		G.	des Wunders
	D.	dem Hebel		D.	dem Wunder
	A.	den Hebel		A.	das Wunder
Plu.	N.	die Hebel	*Plu.*	N.	die Wunder
	G.	der Hebel		G.	der Wunder
	D.	den Hebeln		D.	den Wundern
	A.	die Hebel		A.	die Wunder

   b. With umlaut.

Masc. der Garten, *the garden*			Masc. der Bruder, *the brother*		
Sing.	N.	der Garten	*Sing.*	N.	der Bruder
	G.	des Gartens		G.	des Bruders
	D.	dem Garten		D.	dem Bruder
	A.	den Garten		A.	den Bruder
Plu.	N.	die Gärten	*Plu.*	N.	die Brüder
	G.	der Gärten		G.	der Brüder
	D.	den Gärten		D.	den Brüdern
	A.	die Gärten		A.	die Brüder

Fem. die Tochter, *the daughter*	Neut. das Kloster, *the cloister*
Sing. N. die Tochter	Sing. N. das Kloster
G. der Tochter	G. des Klosters
D. der Tochter	D. dem Kloster
A. die Tochter	A. das Kloster
Plu. N. die Töchter	Plu. N. die Klöster
G. der Töchter	G. der Klöster
D. den Töchtern	D. den Klöstern
A. die Töchter	A. die Klöster

3. II. Class. Characteristics: the plural ends in –e, but there is no umlaut of the stem-vowel.

Masc. der Pfad, *the path*	Neut. das Kreuz, *the cross*
Sing. N. der Pfad	Sing. N. das Kreuz
G. des Pfades	G. des Kreuzes
D. dem Pfade	D. dem Kreuze
A. den Pfad	A. das Kreuz
Plu. N. die Pfade	Plu. N. die Kreuze
G. der Pfade	G. der Kreuze
D. den Pfaden	D. den Kreuzen
A. die Pfade	A. die Kreuze

Neut. das Thor, *the gate*	Fem. die Finsternis, *the darkness*
Sing. N. das Thor	Sing. N. die Finsternis
G. des Thores	G. der Finsternis
D. dem Thore	D. der Finsternis
A. das Thor	A. die Finsternis
Plu. N. die Thore	Plu. N. die Finsternisse
G. der Thore	G. der Finsternisse
D. den Thoren	D. den Finsternissen
A. die Thore	A. die Finsternisse

4. III. Class. Characteristics: the plural ends in –e and the stem-vowel has the umlaut.

Masc. ber Sohn, *the son*	Fem. bie Faust, *the fist*
Sing. N. ber Sohn	Sing. N. bie Faust
G. bes Sohnes	G. ber Faust
D. bem Sohne	D. ber Faust
A. ben Sohn	A. bie Faust
Plu. N. bie Söhne	Plu. N. bie Fäuste
G. ber Söhne	G. ber Fäuste
D. ben Söhnen	D. ben Fäusten
A. bie Söhne	A. bie Fäuste
Fem. bie Stabt, *the city*	Fem. bie Kunst, *the art*
Sing. N. bie Stabt	Sing. N. bie Kunst
G. ber Stabt	G. ber Kunst
D. ber Stabt	D. ber Kunst
A. bie Stabt	A. bie Kunst
Plu. N. bie Städte	Plu. N. bie Künste
G. ber Städte	G. ber Künste
D. ben Städten	D. ben Künsten
A. bie Städte	A. bie Künste

5. IV. Class. Characteristics: the plural ends in –er and the stem-vowel has the umlaut. But nouns ending in –tum have the umlaut in this suffix, because they were originally compound nouns in which the last noun only is inflected.

Masc. ber Walb, *the forest*	Neut. bas Blatt, *the leaf*
Sing. N. ber Walb	Sing. N. bas Blatt
G. bes Walbes	G. bes Blattes
D. bem Walbe	D. bem Blatte
A. ben Walb	A. bas Blatt
Plu. N. bie Wälber	Plu. N. bie Blätter
G. ber Wälber	G. ber Blätter
D. ben Wälbern	D. ben Blättern
A. bie Wälber	A. bie Blätter

NEUT. das Herzogthum, *the duchy*

Sing. N. das Herzogtum
G. des Herzogtums
D. dem Herzogtum(e)
A. das Herzogtum
Plu. N. die Herzogtümer
G. der Herzogtümer
D. den Herzogtümern
A. die Herzogtümer

6. Weak Declension.

Characteristics: Masc. nouns have –en or –n in every case and number except in the N. sing. Fem. nouns have this ending in the plural only.

MASC. der Graf, *the count*

Sing. N. der Graf
G. des Grafen
D. dem Grafen
A. den Grafen
Plu. N. die Grafen
G. der Grafen
D. den Grafen
A. die Grafen

MASC. der Löwe, *the lion*

Sing. N. der Löwe
G. des Löwen
D. dem Löwen
A. den Löwen
Plu. N. die Löwen
G. der Löwen
D. den Löwen
A. die Löwen

MASC. der Komet', *the comet*

Sing. N. der Komet'
G. des Kome'ten
D. dem Kome'ten
A. den Kome'ten
Plu. N. die Kome'ten
G. der Kome'ten
D. den Kome'ten
A. die Kome'ten

FEM. die Legion', *the legion*

Sing. N. die Legion'
G. der Legion'
D. der Legion'
A. die Legion'
Plu. N. die Legio'nen
G. der Legio'nen
D. den Legio'nen
A. die Legio'nen

Fem. die Frau, *the woman*   Fem. die Gabel, *the fork*

Sing.	N.	die Frau	*Sing.* N.	die Gabel
	G.	der Frau	G.	der Gabel
	D.	der Frau	D.	der Gabel
	A.	die Frau	A.	die Gabel
Plu.	N.	die Frauen	*Plu.* N.	die Gabeln
	G.	der Frauen	G.	der Gabeln
	D.	den Frauen	D.	den Gabeln
	A.	die Frauen	A.	die Gabeln

7. Mixed Declension.

Characteristics: the G. sing. ends in –es or –s, the whole plural ends in –en or –n.

Masc. der Mast, *the mast (of a ship)*   Neut. das Auge, *the eye*

Sing.	N.	der Mast	*Sing.* N.	das Auge
	G.	des Mastes	G.	des Auges
	D.	dem Maste	D.	dem Auge
	A.	den Mast	A.	das Auge
Plu.	N.	die Masten	*Plu.* N.	die Augen
	G.	der Masten	G.	der Augen
	D.	den Masten	D.	den Augen
	A.	die Masten	A.	die Augen

Masc. der Doktor, *the doctor*   Masc. der Staat, *the state*

Sing.	N.	der Doktor	*Sing.* N.	der Staat
	G.	des Doktors	G.	des Staates
	D.	dem Doktor	D.	dem Staate
	A.	den Doktor	A.	den Staat
Plu.	N.	die Dokto'ren	*Plu.* N.	die Staaten
	G.	der Dokto'ren	G.	der Staaten
	D.	den Dokto'ren	D.	den Staaten
	A.	die Dokto'ren	A.	die Staaten

APPENDIX OF FORMS.

Neut. das Studium, *the study* Neut. das Mineral′, *the mineral.*

Sing.	N.	das Studium	Sing.	N.	das Mineral′
	G.	des Studiums		G.	des Minerals′
	D.	dem Studium		D.	dem Mineral′
	A.	das Studium		A.	das Mineral′
Plu.	N.	die Studien	Plu.	N.	die Minera′lien
	G.	der Studien		G.	der Minera′lien
	D.	den Studien		D.	den Minera′lien
	A.	die Studien		A.	die Minera′lien

Irregular Noun, das Herz, *the heart*

Sing.	N.	das Herz	Plu.	N.	die Herzen
	G.	des Herzens		G.	der Herzen
	D.	dem Herzen		D.	den Herzen
	A.	das Herz		A.	die Herzen

DECLENSION OF ADJECTIVES.

8. **Strong Declension,** without any limiting word like the definite article or the demonstrative pronoun.

		good father	*good mother*	*good child*
Sing.	N.	guter Vater	gute Mutter	gutes Kind
	G.	gutes Vaters	guter Mutter	gutes Kindes
	D.	gutem Vater	guter Mutter	gutem Kinde
	A.	guten Vater	gute Mutter	gutes Kind
Plu.	N.	gute Väter	gute Mütter	gute Kinder
	G.	guter Väter	guter Mütter	guter Kinder
	D.	guten Vätern	guten Müttern	guten Kindern
	A.	gute Väter	gute Mütter	gute Kinder

9. **Weak Declension,** the adjective is preceded by the definite article or a pronoun declined like it.

the green tree

Sing.	N.	der grüne Baum	*Plu.*	N.	die grünen Bäume
	G.	des grünen Baumes		G.	der grünen Bäume
	D.	dem grünen Baume		D.	den grünen Bäumen
	A.	den grünen Baum		A.	die grünen Bäume

the green meadow

Sing.	N.	die grüne Wiese	*Sing.*	N.	die grünen Wiesen
	G.	der grünen Wiese		G.	der grünen Wiesen
	D.	der grünen Wiese		D.	den grünen Wiesen
	A.	die grüne Wiese		A.	die grünen Wiesen

the green field

Sing.	N.	das grüne Feld	*Plu.*	N.	die grünen Felder
	G.	des grünen Feldes		G.	der grünen Felder
	D.	dem grünen Felde		D.	den grünen Feldern
	A.	das grüne Feld		A.	die grünen Felder

10. **Weak Declension,** the adjective is preceded by ein a, kein no, or by one of the Possessive Pronouns, mein, dein, sein, unser, euer, ihr, my, thy, his, our, your, their. This is sometimes called the 'mixed' declension.

my fine apple

Sing.	N.	mein schöner Apfel	*Plu.*	N.	meine schönen Äpfel
	G.	meines schönen Apfels		G.	meiner schönen Äpfel
	D.	meinem schönen Apfel		D.	meinen schönen Äpfeln
	A.	meinen schönen Apfel		A.	meine schönen Äpfel

my fine flower

Sing.	N.	meine schöne Blume	*Plu.*	N.	meine schönen Blumen
	G.	meiner schönen Blume		G.	meiner schönen Blumen
	D.	meiner schönen Blume		D.	meinen schönen Blumen
	A.	meine schöne Blume		A.	meine schönen Blumen

APPENDIX OF FORMS.

my fine book

Sing. N.	mein schönes Buch	Plu. N.	meine schönen Bücher
G.	meines schönen Buches	G.	meiner schönen Bücher
D.	meinem schönen Buche	D.	meinen schönen Büchern
A.	mein schönes Buch	A.	meine schönen Bücher

11. Examples of **adjectives with the suffixes** –el **and** –er. As to the dropping of –e see § 71.

our noble lord   *their lean ox*

Sing. N.	unser ebler Herr	Sing. N.	ihr magrer Ochs
G.	unsers eblen Herrn	G.	ihres magern Ochsen
D.	userm eblen Herrn	D.	ihrem magern Ochsen
A.	unsern eblen Herrn	A.	ihren magern Ochsen
Plu. N.	unsre eblen Herr(e)n	Plu. N.	ihre magern Ochsen
G.	unsrer eblen Herr(e)n	G.	ihrer magern Ochsen
D.	unsern eblen Herr(e)n	D.	ihren magern Ochsen
A.	unsere eblen Herr(e)n	A.	ihre magern Ochsen

12. Examples of the inflection of **compared adjectives**.

no dearer friend

Sing. N.	kein teurerer Freund	Plu. N.	keine teureren Freunde
G.	keines teureren Freundes	G.	keiner teureren Freunde
D.	keinem teureren Freunde	D.	keinen teureren Freunden
A.	keinen teureren Freund	A.	keine teureren Freunde

this more bitter kernel

Sing. N.	dieser bittrere Kern	Plu. N.	diese bittreren Kerne
G.	dieses bittreren Kernes	G.	dieser bittreren Kerne
D.	diesem bittreren Kerne	D.	diesen bittreren Kernen
A.	diesen bittreren Kern	A.	diese bittreren Kerne

that most serene face

Sing. N.	jenes heiterste Gesicht
G.	jenes heitersten Gesichtes
D.	jenem heitersten Gesichte
A.	jenes heiterste Gesicht

DECLENSION OF ADJECTIVES.

Plu. N. jene heitersten Gesichter
G. jener heitersten Gesichter
D. jenen heitersten Gesichtern
A. jene heitersten Gesichter

13. Examples of the inflection of the **adjective hoch**, high.

a high tower

Sing. N. ein hoher Turm
G. eines hohen Turmes
D. einem hohen Turme
A. einen hohen Turm

no higher tower

Sing. N. kein höherer Turm
G. keines höheren Turmes
D. keinem höheren Turme
A. keinen höheren Turm

the highest towers

Plu. N. die höchsten Türme
G. der höchsten Türme
D. den höchsten Türmen
A. die höchsten Türme

CONJUGATION OF THE WEAK VERB
loben, to praise.

Principal parts: loben, lobte, gelobt.

14. Active Voice.

Indicative. *Subjunctive.*

PRESENT.

Ich lobe, I praise
du lobst, thou praisest
er lobt, he praises
wir loben, we praise
ihr lobt, you praise
sie loben, they praise

Ich lobe, I may praise
du lobest, thou mayest praise
er lobe, he may praise
wir loben, we may praise
ihr lobet, you may praise
sie loben, they may praise

PRETERIT.

Ich lobte, I praised
du lobtest, thou praisedst
er lobte, he praised

Ich lobete, I might praise
du lobetest, thou mightest praise
er lobete, he might praise

wir lobten, we praised
ihr lobtet, you praised
sie lobten, they praised

wir lobeten, we might praise
ihr lobetet, you might praise
sie lobeten, they might praise

Perfect.

I have praised, etc.
Ich habe gelobt
du hast gelobt
er hat gelobt
wir haben gelobt
ihr habt gelobt
sie haben gelobt

I may have praised, etc.
Ich habe gelobt
du habest gelobt
er habe gelobt
wir haben gelobt
ihr habet gelobt
sie haben gelobt

Pluperfect.

I had praised, etc.
Ich hatte gelobt
du hattest gelobt
er hatte gelobt
wir hatten gelobt
ihr hattet gelobt
sie hatten gelobt

I might have praised, etc.
Ich hätte gelobt
du hättest gelobt
er hätte gelobt
wir hätten gelobt
ihr hättet gelobt
sie hätten gelobt

First Future.

I shall praise, etc.
Ich werde loben
du wirst loben
er wird loben
wir werden loben
ihr werdet loben
sie werden loben

I shall praise, etc.
Ich werde loben
du werdest loben
er werde loben
wir werden loben
ihr werdet loben
sie werden loben

Second Future.

I shall have praised, etc.
Ich werde gelobt haben
du wirst gelobt haben
er wird gelobt haben

I shall have praised, etc.
Ich werde gelobt haben
du werdest gelobt haben
er werde gelobt haben

wir werden gelobt haben
ihr werdet gelobt haben
sie werden gelobt haben

wir werden gelobt haben
ihr werdet gelobt haben
sie werden gelobt haben

First Conditional.
I should praise, etc.
Ich würde loben
du würdest loben
er würde loben
wir würden loben
ihr würdet loben
sie würden loben

Second Conditional.
I should have praised, etc.
Ich würde gelobt haben
du würdest gelobt haben
er würde gelobt haben
wir würden gelobt haben
ihr würdet gelobt haben
sie würden gelobt haben

Imperative.
Lobe, praise (thou)
lobe er, let him praise
loben wir, let us praise
lobt, praise (you)
loben sie, let them praise
loben Sie, praise (you)

Infinitives.
Present. Loben, to praise
Past. gelobt haben, to have praised

Participles.
Present. lobend, praising.
Past. gelobt, praised.

15. Passive Voice.

Indicative.

Subjunctive.

Present.

I am praised, etc.
Ich werde gelobt
du wirst gelobt
er wird gelobt
wir werden gelobt
ihr werdet gelobt
sie werden gelobt

I may be praised, etc.
Ich werde gelobt
du werdest gelobt
er werde gelobt
wir werden gelobt
ihr werdet gelobt
sie werden gelobt

Preterit.

I was praised, etc.
Ich wurde or ward gelobt
du wurdest or wardst gelobt
er wurde or ward gelobt
wir wurden gelobt
ihr wurdet gelobt
sie wurden gelobt

I might be praised, etc.
Ich würde gelobt
du würdest gelobt
er würde gelobt
wir würden gelobt
ihr würdet gelobt
sie würden gelobt

Perfect.

I have been praised, etc.
Ich bin gelobt worden
du bist gelobt worden
er ist gelobt worden
wir sind gelobt worden
ihr seid gelobt worden
sie sind gelobt worden

I may have been praised, etc.
Ich sei gelobt worden
du seist gelobt worden
er sei gelobt worden
wir seien gelobt worden
ihr seid gelobt worden
sie seien gelobt worden

Pluperfect.

I had been praised, etc.
Ich war gelobt worden
du warst gelobt worden
er war gelobt worden
wir waren gelobt worden
ihr waret gelobt worden
sie waren gelobt worden

I might have been praised, etc.
Ich wäre gelobt worden
du wärest gelobt worden
er wäre gelobt worden
wir wären gelobt worden
ihr wäret gelobt worden
sie wären gelobt worden.

First Future.

I shall be praised, etc.
Ich werde gelobt werden
du wirst gelobt werden
er wird gelobt werden
wir werden gelobt werden
ihr werdet gelobt werden
sie werden gelobt werden

I shall be praised, etc.
Ich werde gelobt werden
du werdest gelobt werden
er werde gelobt werden
wir werden gelobt werden
ihr werdet gelobt werden
sie werden gelobt werden

Second Future.

I shall have been praised, etc.   I shall have been praised, etc.
Ich werde gelobt worden sein   Ich werde gelobt worden sein
du wirst gelobt worden sein   du werdest gelobt worden sein
er wird gelobt worden sein   er werde gelobt worden sein
wir werden gelobt worden sein   wir werden gelobt worden sein
ihr werdet gelobt worden sein   ihr werdet gelobt worden sein
sie werden gelobt worden sein   sie werden gelobt worden sein

First Conditional.   Second Conditional.

I should be praised, etc.   I should have been praised, etc.
Ich würde gelobt werden   Ich würde gelobt worden sein
du würdest gelobt werden   du würdest gelobt worden sein
er würde gelobt werden   er würde gelobt worden sein
wir würden gelobt werden   wir würden gelobt worden sein
ihr würdet gelobt werden   ihr würdet gelobt worden sein
sie würden gelobt werden   sie würden gelobt worden sein

Imperative.

Sei or werde gelobt, be (thou) praised
er sei or werde gelobt, let him be praised
Seid or werdet gelobt, be (you) praised
sie seien or werden gelobt, let them be praised
Seien Sie or werden Sie gelobt, be (you) praised

Infinitive.

Present. gelobt werden, to be praised
Past. gelobt worden sein, to have been praised

16. Examples showing the use of the **connecting vowel e** both in **weak and strong** verbs, see § 118.

reben, redete, geredet, to speak

Pres. Ind.	Pret. Ind.
Ich rede	Ich redete
du redest	du redetest
er redet	er redete

wir reben wir rebeten
ihr rebet ihr rebetet
sie reben sie rebeten

spaßen, spaßte, gespaßt, to joke
fassen, faßte, gefaßt, to seize

PRES. IND.   PRES. IND.
Ich spaße   Ich fasse
du spaßest   du fassest
er spaßt   er faßt
wir spaßen   wir fassen
ihr spaßt   ihr faßt
sie spaßen   sie fassen

wandeln, wandelte, gewandelt, to walk
rechnen, rechnete, gerechnet, to reckon

PRES. IND.   PRES. IND.
Ich wandle   Ich rechne
du wandelst   du rechnest
er wandelt   er rechnet
wir wandeln   wir rechnen
ihr wandelt   ihr rechnet
sie wandeln   sie rechnen

meiden, mied, gemieden, to avoid
reiten, ritt, geritten, to ride (on horseback)

PRES. IND.   PRES. IND.
Ich meide   Ich reite
du meidest   du reitest
er meidet   er reitet
wir meiden   wir reiten
ihr meidet   ihr reitet
sie meiden   sie reiten

17. Examples of **strong verbs** that have the **interchange** of e and i or ie in the 2. and 3. p. sing. pres. ind., and in the 2. p. sing. of the imperative.

sterben, starb, gestorben, to die
treten, trat, getreten, to tread
lesen, las, gelesen, to read

Pres. Ind.	Pres. Ind.	Pres. Ind.
Ich sterbe	Ich trete	Ich lese
du stirbst	du trittst	du liest
er stirbt	er tritt	er liest
wir sterben	wir treten	wir lesen
ihr sterbt	ihr tretet	ihr leset
sie sterben	sie treten	sie lesen
Imper., stirb	Imper., tritt	Imper., lies

18. Example of a **separable compound verb** with the auxiliary verb sein in the compound tenses.

ausgehen, ging aus, ausgegangen, to go out.

Indicative.   *Subjunctive.*

PRESENT.

I go out, etc.   I may go out, etc.

Ich gehe aus	Ich gehe aus
du gehst aus	du gehest aus
er geht aus	er gehe aus
wir gehen aus	wir gehen aus
ihr geht aus	ihr gehet aus
sie gehen aus	sie gehen aus

PRETERIT.

I went out, etc.   I might go out, etc.

Ich ging aus	Ich ginge aus
du gingst aus	du gingest aus
er ging aus	er ginge aus
wir gingen aus	wir gingen aus
ihr gingt aus	ihr ginget aus
sie gingen aus	sie gingen aus

Perfect.

I have gone out, etc.	I may have gone out, etc.
Ich bin ausgegangen	Ich sei ausgegangen
du bist ausgegangen	du seist ausgegangen
er ist ausgegangen	er sei ausgegangen
wir sind ausgegangen	wir seien ausgegangen
ihr seid ausgegangen	ihr seiet ausgegangen
sie sind ausgegangen	sie seien ausgegangen

Pluperfect.

I had gone out, etc.	I might have gone out, etc.
Ich war ausgegangen	Ich wäre ausgegangen
du warst ausgegangen	du wärest ausgegangen
er war ausgegangen	er wäre ausgegangen
wir waren ausgegangen	wir wären ausgegangen
ihr waret ausgegangen	ihr wäret ausgegangen
sie waren ausgegangen	sie wären ausgegangen

First Future.

I shall go out, etc.	I shall go out, etc.
Ich werde ausgehen	Ich werde ausgehen
du wirst ausgehen	du werdest ausgehen
er wird ausgehen	er werde ausgehen
wir werden ausgehen	wir werden ausgehen
ihr werdet ausgehen	ihr werdet ausgehen
sie werden ausgehen	sie werden ausgehen

Second Future.

I shall have gone out, etc.	I shall have gone out, etc.
Ich werde ausgegangen sein	Ich werde ausgegangen sein
du wirst ausgegangen sein	du werdest ausgegangen sein
er wird ausgegangen sein	er werde ausgegangen sein
wir werden ausgegangen sein	wir werden ausgegangen sein
ihr werdet ausgegangen sein	ihr werdet ausgegangen sein
sie werden ausgegangen sein	sie werden ausgegangen sein

First Conditional.

I should go out, etc.

Ich würde ausgehen
du würdest ausgehen
er würde ausgehen
wir würden ausgehen
ihr würdet ausgehen
sie würden ausgehen

Imperative.

Gehe aus, go (thou) out
gehe er aus, let him go out
gehen wir aus, let us go out
gehet aus, go (you) out
gehen sie aus, let them go out
gehen Sie aus, go (you) out

Second Conditional.

I should have gone out, etc.

Ich würde ausgegangen sein
du würdest ausgegangen sein
er würde ausgegangen sein
wir würden ausgegangen sein
ihr würdet ausgegangen sein
sie würden ausgegangen sein

Infinitives.

Present. Ausgehen, to go out
Past. ausgegangen sein, to have gone out

Participles.

Present. ausgehend, going out.
Past. ausgegangen, gone out.

II. ALPHABETICAL LIST OF STRONG AND IRREGULAR VERBS

Remarks. — The principal parts are put in full-faced type. The second and third persons singular of the present indicative are given when the stem-vowel is i, ie, or an umlaut; also when the connecting vowel e is required, though not absolutely, in verbs whose stem ends in b, t, ß, ff, ſ, ſt. (See § 118.) The second person singular of the imperative is given when it has the short form without e, stem-vowel i or ie; also when the e is optional. A dash indicates weak or regular forms. Forms in parentheses are rare and archaic, for which the weak ones are in use now. Of the modal auxiliaries and wiſſen the whole present indicative singular and the first person plural are given. Compound verbs are given only when the simple verb has passed from present use, e. g., befehlen, gebären. English verbs in small caps are cognates of the German verbs, i. e., they have the same origin and meaning.

Infinitive.	2. and 3. p. s. pres. ind.	2. p. s. imp.	Pret. ind.	Pret. subj.	Past part.
Backen,[1] BAKE	bäckſt, bäckt	—	buk	büke	gebacken
Befehlen, command	befiehlſt, befiehlt	befiehl	befahl	befähle beföhle	befohlen
Befleißen, apply (refl.)	befleißeſt, befleißt	befleiß(e)	befliß	befliſſe	befliſſen
Beginnen, BEGIN	—	—	begann	begänne begönne	begonnen
Beißen, BITE	beißeſt, beißt	beiß(e)	biß	biſſe	gebiſſen
Bellen,[2] bark	billſt, billt	bill	boll	bölle	gebollen
Bergen, hide	birgſt, birgt	birg	barg	bärge bürge	geborgen
Berſten,[1] burst	birſteſt, birſt	birſt	barſt borſt	bärſte börſte	geborſten
Bewegen,[3] induce	—	—	bewog	bewöge	bewogen
Biegen, bend	(beugſt, beugt)	beug)	bog	böge	gebogen

[1] Frequently weak, except in the past part. [2] Now generally weak. [3] Weak, except in this figurative sense.

STRONG AND IRREGULAR VERBS.

Infinitive.	2. and 3. p. s. pres. ind.	2. p. s. imp.	Pret. ind.	Pret. subj.	Past part.
Bieten, offer	(beutſt, beut	beut)	bot	böte	geboten
Binden, BIND	bindeſt, bindet	—	band	bände	gebunden
Bitten, beg	bitteſt, bittet	—	bat	bäte	gebeten
Blaſen, BLOW	bläſeſt, bläſt	—	blies	blieſe	geblaſen
Bleiben, remain	—	—	blieb	bliebe	geblieben
Bleichen,[1] BLEACH	—	—	blich	bliche	geblichen
Braten,[2] roast	brätſt, brät	—	briet	briete	gebraten
Brechen, BREAK	brichſt, bricht	brich	brach	bräche	gebrochen
Brennen, BURN	—	—	brannte	brennte	gebrannt
Bringen, BRING	—	—	brachte	brächte	gebracht
Denken, THINK	—	—	dachte	dächte	gedacht
Dingen,[3] hire, bargain	—	—	(dang dung	dünge)	gedungen
Dreſchen, THRESH	driſcheſt, driſcht	driſch	draſch droſch	dräſche bröſche	gedroſchen
Dringen, urge	—	—	drang	dränge	gedrungen
Dünken, THINK	—	—	(däuchte	däuchte	gedäucht)
Dürfen, be allowed	darf, darfſt, darf, dürfen	(wanting)	durfte	dürfte	gedurft
Empfehlen, recommend	empfiehlſt, empfiehlt	empfiehl	empfahl	empfähle empföhle	empfohlen
Eſſen, eat	iſſeſt, iſt	iß	aß	äße	gegeſſen
Fahen, archaic for fangen					
Fahren, go, FARE	fährſt, fährt	fahr(e)	fuhr	führe	gefahren
Fallen, FALL	fällſt, fällt	—	fiel	fiele	gefallen
Falten,[4] FOLD	falteſt, faltet	—	—	—	gefalten
Fangen, catch	fängſt, fängt	—	fing (fieng	finge fienge)	gefangen
Fechten, FIGHT	fichteſt,[5] ficht[5]	ficht[5]	focht	föchte	gefochten
Finden, FIND	findeſt, findet	—	fand	fände	gefunden
Flechten, twine	flichſt,[5] flicht[5]	flicht[5]	flocht	flöchte	geflochten
Fliegen, FLY	(fleugſt, fleugt	fleug)	flog	flöge	geflogen
Fliehen, FLEE	(fleuchſt, fleucht	fleuch)	floh	flöhe	geflohen

[1] Weak when transitive; sometimes even when intransitive. [2] Sometimes weak, except in the past part. [3] Still frequently weak. [4] Now entirely weak, except in the past part. [5] The weak forms also occur.

STRONG AND IRREGULAR VERBS.

Infinitive.	2. and 3. p. s. pres. ind.	2. p. s. imp.	Pret. ind.	Pret. subj.	Past part.
Fließen, flow	(fleußest, fleußt)	fleuß)	floß	flösse	geflossen
Fragen, ask	frägst, frägt	—	frug	früge	gefragt[1]
Fressen, EAT (of animals)	frissest, frißt	friß	fraß	fräße	gefressen
Frieren, FREEZE	—	—	fror	fröre	gefroren
Gä(h)ren, ferment	(gierst, giert)	—	gohr[2]	göhre	gegohren[2]
Gebären, BEAR	(gebierst, gebiert)	gebier)	gebar	gebäre	geboren
Geben, GIVE	giebst, giebt gibst, gibt	gieb gib	gab	gäbe	gegeben
Gedeihen, thrive	—	—	gedieh	gediehe	gediehen
Gehen, GO	—	—	ging (gieng)	ginge gienge)	gegangen
Gelingen, succeed	—	—	gelang	gelänge	gelungen
Gelten, be worth	giltst, gilt	gilt	galt	gälte gölte	gegolten
Genesen, recover	genesest, genest	—	genas	genäse	genesen
Genießen, enjoy	(geneußest, geneußt)	geneuß)	genoß	genösse	genossen
Geschehen, happen	geschiehst, geschieht	(wanting)	geschah	geschähe	geschehen
Gewinnen, WIN	—	—	gewann	gewänne gewönne	gewonnen
Gießen, pour	(geußest, geußt)	geuß)	goß	gösse	gegossen
Gleichen,[3] resemble	—	—	glich	gliche	geglichen
Gleißen, GLITTER	gleißest, gleißt	—	(gliß	glisse	gegließen)
Gleiten,[4] GLIDE	gleitest, gleitet	—	glitt	glitte	geglitten
Glimmen, GLEAM	—	—	glomm	glömme	eglommen
Graben, dig	gräbst, gräbt	—	grub	grübe	gegraben
Greifen, GRIPE, grasp	—	—	griff	griffe	gegriffen
Haben, HAVE	hast, hat	—	hatte	hätte	gehabt
Halten, HOLD	hältst, hält	halt(e)	hielt	hielte	gehalten
Hangen, HANG	hängst, hängt[5]	—	hing hieng	hinge hienge	gehangen
Hauen, HEW	—	—	hieb	hiebe	gehauen
Heben, raise	—	—	hob hub	höbe hübe	gehob n

[1] Always weak, and the other forms are properly weak. [2] Also weak, especially in figurative sense. [3] Usually weak when transitive, *make* LIKE. [4] Weak forms sometimes occur. [5] hangst, hangt also occur. Often confounded with the weak and transitive hängen.

STRONG AND IRREGULAR VERBS.

Infinitive.	2. and 3. p. s. pres. ind.	2. p. s. imp.	Pret. ind.	Pret. subj.	Past part.
Heißen, call	heißest, heißt	—	hieß	hieße	geheißen
Helfen, HELP	hilfst, hilft	hilf	half	hälfe hülfe	geholfen
Jagen,[1] hunt	(jägst, jägt)	—	(jug	jüge)	gejagt
Keifen,[2] chide	—	—	kiff	kiffe	gekiffen
Kennen, KNOW	—	—	kannte	kennte	gekannt
Kiesen, see Küren					
Klieben, CLEAVE, split	—	—	klob	klöbe	gekloben
Klimmen,[3] CLIMB	—	—	klomm	klömme	geklommen
Klingen, sound	—	—	klang	klänge klünge	geklungen
Kneifen,[4] pinch	—	—	kniff	kniffe	gekniffen
Kneipen,[2] pinch	—	—	(knipp	knippe	gekuippen)
Kommen, COME	(kömmst, kömmt)	komm(e)	kam	käme	gekommen
Können, CAN	kann, kannst, kann, können	(wanting)	konnte	könnte	gekonnt
Kreischen,[5] scream	kreischest, kreischt	—	krisch	krische	gekrischen
Kriechen, creep	(kreuchst, kreucht)	kreuch)	kroch	kröche	gekrochen
Küren, choose	—	—	kor	köre	gekoren
Laden,[6] LOAD, invite	lädst, lädt	—	lud	lüde	geladen
Lassen, LET	lässest, läßt	laß(e)	ließ	ließe	gelassen
Laufen, run	läufst, läuft	—	lief	liefe	gelaufen
Leiden, suffer	leidest, leidet	—	litt	litte	gelitten
Leihen, LEND	—	—	lieh	liehe	geliehen
Lesen, read	liesest, liest	lies	las	läse	gelesen
Liegen, LIE	—	—	lag	läge	gelegen
Löschen,[7] go out	lischest, lischt	lisch	losch	lösche	geloschen
Lügen, tell a LIE	(leugst, leugt)	leug)	log	löge	gelogen
Mahlen,[8] grind	(mählst, mählt)	—	(muhl	mühle)	gemahlen
Meiden, shun	meidest, meidet	—	mied	miede	gemieden

[1] The strong forms, except perhaps jug, are colloquial. [2] Usually weak. [3] Weak forms sometimes occur. [4] Sometimes weak. [5] Now usually weak. [6] Also weak. Two verbs are hopelessly confounded in this one, viz., laden, LOAD, once always strong, and laden, *invite*, once always weak. [7] When transitive, *quench*, weak. [8] Usually weak, except in the past part.

STRONG AND IRREGULAR VERBS.

Infinitive.	2. and 3. p. s. pres. ind.	2. p. s. imp.	Pret. ind.	Pret. subj.	Past part.
Melken,[1] milk	(milkst, milkt)	milk	molk	mölke	gemolken
Messen, measure	missest, mißt	miß	maß	mäße	gemessen
Mißlingen, fail	—	—	mißlang	mißlänge	mißlungen
Mögen, MAY	mag, magst, mag, mögen	(wanting)	mochte	möchte	gemocht
Müssen, MUST	muß, mußt, muß, müssen	(wanting)	mußte	müßte	gemußt
Nehmen, take	nimmst, nimmt	nimm	nahm	nähme	genommen
Nennen, NAME	—	—	nannte	nennte	genannt
Pfeifen, whistle	—	—	pfiff	pfiffe	gepfiffen
Pflegen,[2] cherish	—	—	pflog (pflag)	pflöge	gepflogen
Preisen,[3] PRAISE	preisest, preist	—	pries	priese	gepriesen
Quellen,[4] gush	quillst, quillt	quill	quoll	quölle	gequollen
Rächen,[5] avenge	—	—	(roch)	röche	gerochen
Rat(h)en, advise	rät(h)st, rät(h)	—	riet(h)	riet(h)e	gerat(h)en
Reiben, rub	—	—	rieb	riebe	gerieben
Reißen, tear	reißest, reißt	reiß(e)	riß	risse	gerissen
Reiten, RIDE	reitest, reitet	—	ritt	ritte	geritten
Rennen, RUN	—	—	rannte	rennte	gerannt
Riechen, smell	(reuchst, reucht)	reuch	roch	röche	gerochen
Ringen, WRING, wrestle	—	—	rang	ränge	gerungen
Rinnen, RUN	—	—	rann	(ränne) rönne	geronnen
Rufen, call	—	—	rief	riefe	gerufen
Salzen,[6] SALT	salzest, salzt	—	—	—	gesalzen
Saufen, drink	säufst, säuft	sauf(e)	soff	söffe	gesoffen
Saugen, SUCK	—	—	sog	söge	gesogen
Schaffen,[7] create	—	—	schuf	schüfe	geschaffen
Schallen,[2] sound	—	—	scholl	schölle	geschollen
Scheiden, part	scheidest, scheidet	—	schied	schiede	geschieden
Scheinen, appear	—	—	schien	schiene	geschienen

[1] Now usually weak. [2] Also entirely weak. [3] Sometimes weak. [4] When transitive, *soak*, weak. [5] Now mostly weak. [6] Only the past part. is still strong. [7] In other senses weak.

STRONG AND IRREGULAR VERBS.

Infinitive.	2. and 3. p. s. pres. ind.	2. p. s. imp.	Pret. ind.	Pret. subj.	Past part.
Schelten, SCOLD	schilst, schilt	schilt	schalt	schälte schölte	gescholten
Scheren,[1] SHEAR	scherst, schert	scher	schor	schöre	geschoren
Schieben, SHOVE	—	—	schob	schöbe	geschoben
Schießen, SHOOT	(scheußest, scheußt	scheuß)	schoß	schösse	geschossen
Schinden, flay	schindest, schindet	—	schund[1]	schünde	geschunden
Schlafen, SLEEP	schläfst, schläft	schlaf(e)	schlief	schliefe	geschlafen
Schlagen, strike	schlägst, schlägt	—	schlug	schlüge	geschlagen
Schleichen, sneak	—	—	schlich	schliche	geschlichen
Schleifen,[2] whet	—	—	schliff	schliffe	geschliffen
Schleißen, SLIT	schleißest, schleißt	—	schliß	schlisse	geschlissen
Schliefen, slip	(schleufst, schleuft	schleuf)	schloff	schlöffe	geschloffen
Schließen, shut	(schleußest, schleußt	schleuß)	schloß	schlösse	geschlossen
Schlingen, SLING	—	—	schlang	schlänge	geschlungen
Schmeißen, SMITE	schmeißest, schmeißt	schmeiß(e)	schmiß	schmisse	geschmissen
Schmelzen,[3] MELT	schmilzest, schmilzt	schmilz	schmolz	schmölze	geschmolzen
Schnauben,[4] snort	—	—	schnob	schnöbe	geschnoben
Schneiden, cut	schneidest, schneidet	—	schnitt	schnitte	geschnitten
Schrauben,[5] screw	—	—	schrob	schröbe	geschroben
Schrecken,[3] be afraid	schrickst, schrickt	schrick	schrack	schräke	geschrocken
Schreiben, write	—	—	schrieb	schriebe	geschrieben
Schreien, cry	—	schrei(e)	schrie	schriee	geschrieen
Schreiten, stride	schreitest, schreitet	—	schritt	schritte	geschritten
Schroten,[6] rough-grind	schrotest, schrotet	—	—	—	geschroten
Schwären, suppurate	(schwierst, schwiert	schwier)	schwor	schwöre	geschworen
Schweigen,[3] be silent	—	—	schwieg	schwiege	geschwiegen
Schwellen,[3] SWELL	schwillst, schwillt	schwill	schwoll	schwölle	geschwollen
Schwimmen, SWIM	—	—	schwamm	schwämme schwömme	geschwommen
Schwinden, vanish	schwindest, schwindet	—	schwand	schwände schwünde	geschwunden

[1] Sometimes weak.   [2] Weak in other senses, *raze, drag*.   [3] Weak when transitive.
[4] Also weak; schnieben occurs instead of schnauben.   [5] Also weak.   [6] Only the past part. still strong.

STRONG AND IRREGULAR VERBS.

Infinitive.	2. and 3. p. s. pres. ind.	2. p. s. imp.	Pret. ind.	Pret. subj.	Past part.
Schwingen, SWING	—	—	schwang	schwänge schwünge	geschwungen
Schwören, swear	—	—	schwor schwur	schwöre schwüre	geschworen
Sehen, SEE	siehst, sieht	sieh(e)	sah	sähe	gesehen
Sein, be	bin, bist, ist ɔc.	sei	war	wäre	gewesen
Senden, SEND	sendest, sendet	—	sandte sendete	sendete	gesandt gesendet
Sieden,[1] SEETHE	siedest, siedet	—	sott	sötte	gesotten
Singen, SING	—	—	sang	sänge	gesungen
Sinken, SINK	—	—	sank	sänke	gesunken
Sinnen, think	—	—	sann	sänne sönne	gesonnen
Sitzen, SIT	sitzest, sitzt	—	saß	säße	gesessen
Sollen, should	soll, sollst, soll, sollen (wanting)	sollte	sollte	gesollt
Spalten,[2] split	spaltest, spaltet	—	—	—	gespalten
Speien, SPEW	—	—	spie	spiee	gespieen
Spinnen, SPIN	—	—	spann	spänne spönne	gesponnen
Spleißen, SPLIT	spleißest, spleißt	—	spliß	splisse	gesplissen
Sprechen, speak	sprichst, spricht	sprich	sprach	spräche	gesprochen
Sprießen, SPROUT	(spreußest, spreußt)	spreuß	sproß	sprösse	gesprossen
Springen, SPRING	—	—	sprang	spränge	gesprungen
Stechen, prick	stichst, sticht	stich	stach	stäche	gestochen
Stecken,[3] STICK	(stickst, stickt)	stick	stak	stäke	(gestocken)
Stehen, STAND	—	steh(e)	stand stund	stände stünde	gestanden
Stehlen, STEAL	stiehlst, stiehlt	stiehl	stahl	stähle stöhle	gestohlen
Steigen, ascend	—	—	stieg	stiege	gestiegen
Sterben, die	stirbst, stirbt	stirb	starb	stärbe stürbe	gestorben
Stieben, disperse	—	—	stob	stöbe	gestoben
Stinken, STINK	—	—	stank	stänke stünke	gestunken

[1] Also weak. [2] Only the past part. still strong. [3] Always weak when transitive; sometimes even when intransitive.

STRONG AND IRREGULAR VERBS.

Infinitive.	2. and 3. p. s. pres. ind.	2. p. s. imp.	Pret. Ind.	Pret. subj.	Past part.
Stoßen, push	stößest, stößt	stoß(e)	stieß	stieße	gestoßen
Streichen, STROKE	—	—	strich	striche	gestrichen
Streiten, strive	streitest, streitet	—	stritt	stritte	gestritten
Thun, DO	—	thu(e)	that	thäte	gethan
Tragen, carry	trägst, trägt	—	trug	trüge	getragen
Treffen, hit	triffst, trifft	triff	traf	träfe	getroffen
Treiben, DRIVE	—	—	trieb	triebe	getrieben
Treten, TREAD	trittst, tritt	tritt	trat	träte	getreten
Triefen,[1] DRIP	(treufst, treuft	treuf)	troff	tröffe	getroffen
Trinken, DRINK	—	—	trank	tränke trünke	getrunken
Trügen, deceive	(treugst, treugt	treug)	trog	tröge	getrogen
Verderben,[2] spoil	verbirbst, verbirbt	verbirb	verdarb	verbärbe verbürbe	verdorben
Verdrießen, vex	(verdreußest, verdreußt,	verdreuß)	verdroß	verdrösse	verdrossen
Vergessen, FORGET	vergissest, vergißt	vergiß	vergaß	vergässe	vergessen
Verlieren, LOSE	—	—	verlor	verlöre	verloren
Wachsen, grow	wächsest, wächst	—	wuchs	wüchse	gewachsen
Wägen,[5] WEIGH	—	—	wog	wöge	gewogen
Waschen, WASH	wäschest, wäscht	—	wusch	wüsche	gewaschen
Weben,[3] WEAVE	—	—	wob	wöbe	geweben
Weichen,[4] yield	—	—	wich	wiche	gewichen
Weisen, show	weisest, weist	—	wies	wiese	gewiesen
Wenden, turn	wendest, wendet	—	wandte wendete	wendete	gewandt gewendet
Werben, sue	wirbst, wirbt	wirb	warb	wärbe würbe	geworben
Werden, become	wirst, wird	werde	ward wurde	würde	geworden
Werfen, throw	wirfst, wirft	wirf	warf	wärfe würfe	geworfen
Wiegen,[5] WEIGH	—	—	wog	wöge	gewogen

[1] Sometimes weak. [2] Weak when transitive. [3] Also weak, especially in the sense of *move, hover.* [4] Weak in the sense of *soften.* [5] Wägen and wiegen are really identical. Wiegen, *rock*, is always weak.

STRONG AND IRREGULAR VERBS.

Infinitive.	2. and 3. p. s. pres. ind.	2. p. s. imp.	Pret. ind.	Pret. subj.	Past part.
Winden, WIND	windeſt, windet	—	wand	wände wünde	gewunden
Wiſſen, know	weiß, weißt, weiß, wiſſen	wiſſe	wußte	wüßte	gewußt
Wollen, WILL	will, willſt, will, wollen	wolle	wollte	wollte	gewollt
Zeihen, accuse	—	—	zieh	ziehe	geziehen
Ziehen, draw	(zeuchſt, zeucht	zeuch)	zog	zöge	gezogen
Zwingen, force	—	—	zwang	zwänge zwünge	gezwungen

www.ingramcontent.com/pod-product-compliance
Lightning Source LLC
Chambersburg PA
CBHW030733230426
43667CB00007B/702